Charity & Philanthropy

FOR DUMMIES®

A Wiley Brand

by Karl Muth, Michael Lindenmayer
and John Kluge

Foreword by Bill Drayton

CEO, Ashoka: Innovators for the Public

Charity & Philanthropy For Dummies®

Published by: **John Wiley & Sons, Ltd.,** The Atrium, Southern Gate, Chichester, www.wiley.com

This edition first published 2013

© 2014 John Wiley & Sons, Ltd, Chichester, West Sussex.

Registered office

John Wiley & Sons Ltd, The Atrium, Southern Gate, Chichester, West Sussex, PO19 8SQ, United Kingdom

For details of our global editorial offices, for customer services and for information about how to apply for permission to reuse the copyright material in this book please see our website at www.wiley.com.

For general information on our other products and services, please contact our Customer Care Department within the U.S. at 877-762-2974, outside the U.S. at (001) 317-572-3993, or fax 317-572-4002.

For technical support, please visit www.wiley.com/techsupport.

A catalogue record for this book is available from the British Library.

ISBN 978-1-119-94187-3 (pbk), ISBN 978-1-119-94394-5 (ebk), 978-1-119-94393-8 (ebk), ISBN 978-1-119-94395-2 (ebk)

Printed and bound in the United States of America by Bind-Rite

10 9 8 7 6 5 4 3 2 1

Contents at a Glance

Table of Contents

Part II: Knowing Where Your Money Goes: Which Sector Is For You?..71

Chapter 5: Encouraging Education around the World 73

Chapter 6: Surfing the Age Tidal Wave: Helping the Elderly 99

Part III: Delivering on Your Good Intentions: Practical Ways to Get Involved 219

Chapter 12: Donating Your Time to Help Out Others 221

Chapter 13: Making Use of Your Specific Talents 237

Foreword

*T*he Difference.

Giving is what makes humans different. When homo sapiens crossed the mouth of the Red Sea 50,000 years ago, we had learned how to cooperate in groups of up to 100, at most 150 people. Now America has over 300 million citezens, and India and China each has over 1 billion. Further, you and all of us, participate every day in the world-wide web, and organisations of all sorts in every sector buy and sell and serve globally.

The acceleration in people helping one another – one on one and globally and in all sorts of combinations in between – is the central historical force at work. This irresistible force is, moreover, now accelerating exponentially.

That is why this book is so important.

If there is one area in which we must now all excel, it is knowing how to give, how to make a difference for the good.

The highest level of giving is to help others give.

Nothing can bring better health or deeper happiness than enabling another person or group to give – especially if you help them give at a significant level of impact.

Both the great religious prophets and today's science agree on how centrally important it is to express love and respect in action at the highest possible level.

When you help others thus meet their highest potential as social beings, of course, you are at the same time helping society far more powerfully than you could in almost any other way.

That is true when you help a child become a loving, confident person who can and will bring change for the good whenever needed. It is true when you help a citizen group remove barriers that prevent others (be they women or new immigrants) from living and giving fully. It is certainly true when you find and back a society-wide pattern change social entrepreneur through the long years such deep change usually requires. (If there's a need, the first on the scene are these far-seeing system-change entrepreneurs. Two Ashoka examples: (a) increasing rural school enrollments 44 percent and cutting dropout rates in half in Bangladesh – largely by engaging students in teaching and in running profitable businesses; and (b) cutting rural electrification costs in Brazil 70-90 percent.)

For each need there are many avenues for giving. In this book Karl Muth, Michael Lindenmayer and John Kluge gives you an extraordinarily comprehensive map of your options and a wide range of excellently chosen examples in every field.

Given society's manifold needs, and given the greater satisfaction that comes from achieving greater impact, it is key to know how to contribute in the most significant way.

Today that means changemaking.

The rate of change has been escalating exponentially for at least three centuries. That is a mathematical fact.

The same is true for the number of people causing change.

It is also true (and I believe this is especially important) for the number of combinations, and combinations of combinations changemakers collaborating together,

As a result of these dramatically accelerating historical forces, society is now hurtling towards the most fundamental restructuring of how we work together ever. We are well into the tipping process.

Throughout history and pre-history society has been organised to achieve efficiency through repetition. Think the law firm or the assembly line. Think our traditional definition of educational success – mastering a body of knowledge and an associated set of rules so that one can go forth and be a baker or banker for life.

There's always been some change, at least evolutionary change. (The human skull became thinner and thinner over the last 50,000 years as we developed better social skills.) But we organised chiefly to achieve efficiency in repetition.

The world is failing fast.

In a world defined by the opposite of repetition, change, we must shift to an opposite way of educating and organising.

Success in growing up now must start with ensuring that every young person has mastered the social skills to be a contributing changemaker in an 'everyone a changemaker™' world and has practised and practised so that he or she confidently is a changemaker before 21. These core skills are empathy, teamwork, the new leadership (leading teams of teams where everyone is a changemaker), and changmaking.

In a world of escalating change, the rules cover less and less. Anyone who tries to be a good person by diligently following the rules will, as the inevitable if unintended result, hurt people and disrupt groups. They (and quite likely their group with them) will be marginalized, i.e., thrown out. That is one of the reasons why the skill of empathy is such a foundational essential now.

Knowledge is still very important; but without these social skills, it will be of little use. No one wants a hurtful, disruptive person, no matter how unintentionally so – regardless of their digital knowledge.

The old organisational model is equally obsolete. In it a few people ensure that everyone is organised for efficiency in repetition. This model is characterised by vertical control systems and by walls. These big organisations do the same thing the same way everywhere.

Such dinosaurs still roam the earth. But the half-life of the Fortune 500 biggest corporations has grown shorter in each successive five-year-period now for decades. In other words, their death rate is accelerating.

They are being replaced by fluid, often teams of teams. They must be fluid because they serve change processes, which, of course, are constantly changing – which requires a team of teams constantly to adjust its membership to fit the new needs. The new teams must be open because no group has but a tiny percentage of those working on a problem inside it.

Most important, you do not have a team unless everyone is an active, initiatory player. There will of course still be repetition (although automation, artificial intelligence and more are rapidly reducing its scope). However, the value will be in finding and recruiting those who can spot and develop change opportunities.

The Jesuits, Google and the Silicon Valley/Bangalore ecosystem are early examples.

Faced with this fundamental change in how the world works, you can make a real difference. You can help society and its members see the world's now speeding transition to its 'everyone a changemaker™' future. You can help build the new architecture. And you can help envision and build new ways of social investing that will contribute more effectively. These are all huge, truly historic opportunities.

Please give yourself permission to be a great giver for the good.

Bill Drayton
CEO, Ashoka: Innovators for the Public

Introduction

· ·

*T*he idea of philanthropy often conjures up ideas of lavish charity balls, Bill Gates writing enormous cheques, or international relief organisations such as the Red Cross. But charity and philanthropy aren't reserved for the ruling class, individual billionaires, or global organisations with billions of pounds in the bank: everyone can become a philanthropist and this no-nonsense guide to the subject shows you how. Indeed, you may already be one, donating to charities that support causes dear to your heart.

We're willing to bet that you're probably already more philanthropic than you give yourself credit for! For example, every time you volunteer at your child's school, give away your professional services, allow someone to use your home for an organisation's event, or buy something at a charity shop, you're being philanthropic. Instead of being a full-time job, for most people being a 'philanthropist' is something they are from time to time.

Philanthropy is a specific kind of thoughtful generosity that reveals itself through how you spend your time, use your talents, spread your treasure, and choose which transactions to engage in. This book helps you focus your own philanthropy to better suit your purpose, reflect your values, and create the results you want to see.

Above all, philanthropy is a wonderful way to interact with other people and with the world by using your resources to good effect.

About This Book

Our aim with this book is to address the number one complaint we hear from people who have more than they need and want to help others: 'Where do I begin?' Plenty of advice is available from lawyers and accountants, but much of it seems to generate business for them. Often, places to obtain guidance on philanthropy are themselves asking you for money. Where can you get sound advice from experts? Well, you've come to the right place! At certain times of the year you come across lots of information about charities you can give to – including plenty through your letterbox as Christmas approaches. You hear about credit cards that support charities, places to holiday that help the environment, and all sorts of things that, at least in theory, allow you to help the world while enjoying yourself. But how can you check up on them? How can you tell which is best and which ones to avoid?

This book allows you easy access to the cutting edge of philanthropy. We help you identify a good opportunity, avoid a bad one, and profit from the experiences of others. We reached out to our friends and colleagues around the world (all noted philanthropists) and asked them to share the most useful lessons they've learned. Often we illustrate and back up the points we make with their advice, stories, and histories.

We provide loads of strategies for your generosity, including volunteering time, donating cash or your expertise, or getting involved via social investing. We provide case studies from charities of all sorts of sizes to demonstrate what works and what doesn't.

For your convenience, we divide this book into several parts, each one focusing on an area of philanthropy. Part I, for instance, introduces the basic concepts and some of what's going on. Part II lets you identify areas where you may be able to help, and Part III helps you get involved in changing the world for the better.

We also provide loads of Internet resources so you can look deeper into the subjects that interest you the most. You may notice that some web addresses break across two lines of text. If you're reading this book in print and want to visit one of these web pages, simply key in the web address exactly as it's printed in the text, as though the line break doesn't exist. If you're reading this as an e-book, you've got it easy: just click the web address to go directly to the web page.

Foolish Assumptions

In writing this book, we make a few assumptions about you:

- ✔ You feel that you have more than you need (time, money, or another resource) and you want to use what you have to help others.
- ✔ You want to find ways to make sure that you know where your donations are going and whether they're effective.
- ✔ You're interested in transitioning from simply writing a cheque or volunteering for an afternoon to being more involved.
- ✔ You're excited by the chance to do your part to help others in your community and around the world.

Icons Used in This Book

To help you find certain types of information quickly, we use particular icons.

Beside this icon we relate something that makes your philanthropic experience easier or more fulfilling.

This icon indicates an important point or principle that's worth bearing in mind.

When something is dangerous – whether to you or your wallet – we use this icon to give you a heads-up.

Sometimes we include additional detail that isn't crucial to understanding a chapter's content. We indicate this interesting but not essential material with this icon. Skip these paragraphs if you're in a hurry to start giving!

This icon highlights practical, real-world suggestions for ways to get started in your philanthropic endeavours. If the specific suggestions we make aren't quite what you're looking for, you can use them as inspiration for your own approach.

We describe different kinds of charities and approaches to charity, and we use this icon to highlight real-life examples of these organisations and efforts.

Beyond the Book

In addition to the material in the print or e-book you're reading right now, this product also comes with some goodies you can access on the web. Check out the free Cheat Sheet at `http://www.dummies.com/cheatsheet/charityandphilanthropy` for information on how to find out about new philanthropic opportunities and how to select the right ways of giving for you.

Head to `http://www.dummies.com/extras/charityandphilanthropy` for an array of additional resources, including monthly budget calculator to help manage your own philanthropy.

Where to Go from Here

One of the coolest things about this book is that you can flip to any page, begin reading and find something useful. We have designed it to be a reference to dip in and out of: just take a look at the table of contents and start reading whatever interests you. No need to start at the beginning (or to read through to the end).

Of course, if you don't know where to start, Chapter 1 is always a good place. But if you want to jump right in, try out Chapter 4 on discovering your passion. If you're still on the fence and figuring out why (or whether) to give, check out Chapter 2. Wherever you go, you're bound to find interesting and inspiring information.

Most of all, enjoy this book and your increasing role of helping out other people.

Part I
Getting Started with Charity & Philanthropy

For Dummies can help you get started with lots of subjects. Visit www.dummies.com to learn more and do more with *For Dummies*.

In this Part

- ✔ Discover ways to find charities that are doing the most effective work and using your money most efficiently.

- ✔ Include new methods of philanthropy in your plan for generosity aside from writing cheques.

- ✔ Learn when it might be better to volunteer or donate your professional services to a charity rather than give your money.

- ✔ Find out what the common pitfalls are for everyday people who become philanthropists, and how to avoid them.

Chapter 1

Introducing Philanthropy: Your Passport to Helping Others

In This Chapter

▶ Discovering philanthropy and how to join in

▶ Considering different ways to help and causes to support

▶ Maintaining your enthusiasm and commitment

▶ Helping today and in the future

Congratulations! By buying this book you've taken an important step towards giving more effectively, enjoyably and strategically. In fact, you're already a philanthropist, because we're donating our proceeds from the book to charities (see the Appendix to see where these proceeds are going).

Perhaps you're unconvinced that buying this book qualifies you to be a philanthropist. After all, the word is associated with the likes of John D. Rockefeller, Andrew Carnegie, and, more recently, Bill and Melinda Gates and Jeffery Skoll (we write more about the latter in Chapter 11). Seems like a pretty exclusive – and well-heeled – club to get into. But when you consider what a philanthropist really is, you see that you can fit right in.

The word *philanthropy* simply means to love your fellow humans (it's a combination of two Greek words: *philos* (to love) and *anthrop* (humans)). Toss in the 'ist' at the end and the definition changes slightly to 'one who loves his (or her) fellow human beings'. And that's you!

Although the word is often used to mean handing over cash to others, philanthropy can be much more than that. Here are some of the things you can give:

✔ **Your time:** For example, volunteering to help at an event or at a charity's project site (check out Chapter 12 for more).

✔ **Your talents:** For example, *pro bono* use of your professional or other skills (read Chapter 13 to find out how).

✔ **Your treasure:** Which can include financial giving, but also that old car or the smartphone lying in your sock drawer (see Chapter 14).

✔ **Your money through your everyday transactions:** Such as buying a pair of glasses from an organisation that provides another pair to a person in the developing world (Chapter 15 has the details).

This chapter is an introduction to the book and to philanthropy and how you can start to make a difference today. We cover ways to give, selecting which organisations to help and focusing on immediate needs and longer-term aims. We also provide tips on keeping up your commitment.

Getting into the Spirit of Giving and Philanthropy

A core focus of this book is helping you to be more effective in your philanthropy. The fact that you're even holding it means that you're probably already interested in giving. Throughout this book, we help you understand the 'what' (see Part III) and the 'who' and 'where' (read the chapters in Part II) of giving, and because change is only possible when people take action, we focus throughout on the 'how' of giving. But in this section, we discuss the 'why' – the 'spirit' of giving – because it's a prime mover, the first cause, of all other charitable or philanthropic actions and endeavours you – or anyone else – take.

Without the spirit of giving, the 'what', 'who', 'where', and 'how' of giving simply don't exist.

Reasons for giving are as diverse as people: some give to help their local communities; others to help regions far across the world. Some give as a way of advocating for a cause, such as housing for the homeless or food for the hungry; others to support community resources, such as libraries and parks. Some give to provide necessities, such as fresh drinking water or access to healthy foods; others to make the highest cultural expressions of art, music, and architectural masterpieces accessible to all. Some give to help people reach their potential; others to ease the pain and fear of terminal illness.

People who give are young and old, rich and poor, from cities and the country; they're people of religious faith and none, from all racial and ethnic backgrounds, and of all educational levels. In fact, the only thing they all share is that they want to make a difference for the better.

You find your motivation by tapping into your own spirit of giving. Then you just need to find a way to express that motivation as you set about changing the world for the better.

Beacons of light

Each year, the Beacon Fellowship Charitable Trust (beaconfellowship.org.uk) gives an award to people (individuals, families, and small groups of individuals) who make particularly noteworthy philanthropic achievements in the UK and around the world. To demonstrate the wide spread of philanthropic champions and causes, and to inspire you, check out the following 2013 Beacon Fellows (some names you'll know and others will be new to you):

✔ **Harris Bokhari:** National advisory board member for the Prince of Wales's charity Mosaic (www.mosaicnetwork.co.uk), an organisation that sends mentors into primary and secondary schools to help young people living in disadvantaged communities (we discuss education philanthropy in detail in Chapter 5).

✔ **Richard Bradbury CBE:** Fundamental supporter of the charity Scope (www.scope.org.uk), which supports disabled people and their families (see Chapter 8 for more on helping the ill and disabled).

✔ **Angila Chada and Michael McKibbin:** Ambassadors for the Community Foundation for Northern Ireland (www.communityfoundationni.org), which supports community development to drive social change.

✔ **Sir Ronald Cohen:** Chair, Big Society Capital (www.bigsocietycapital.com); Former Chair, Social Investment Task Force; Former Chair Commission on Unclaimed Assets; Co-Founder and Former Chair, Bridges Ventures; and Co-founder and former Director, Social Financial UK.

✔ **Carol Colburn Grigor CBE:** Manages her family-founded Dunard Fund (opencharities.org/charities/295790), which makes donations for the training and performance of classical music, the education and display of visual arts, and construction of new architectural masterpieces (see Chapter 13 for more on these areas).

✔ **Stephen Dawson OBE:** Co-founder of Impetus Trust (www.impetus.org.uk), which supports charity sustainability, effectiveness, and growth through venture philanthropy (see Chapter 10 for details on this subject).

✔ **Lloyd Dorfman CBE:** Member of the National Theatre Board (www.nationaltheatre.org.uk), which is 'dedicated to the constant revitalisation of the great traditions of the British stage and to expanding the horizons of audiences and artists alike' (Chapter 13 covers the arts).

✔ **Sir Vernon Ellis:** Chairman of the National Opera Studio, President of English National Opera, Chair of the British Council, President of the Classical Opera Company, former Trustee of the Royal College of Music and RCM Fellow (for arts philanthropy, turn to Chapter 13).

✔ **Nick Ferguson CBE and Jane Ferguson:** Founders of The Kilfinan Trust (www.foundationscotland.org.uk/

(continued)

(continued)

programmes/kilfinan.aspx), which supports 'voluntary organisations and charities working in the Kilfinan area of Argyll and Bute' that seek to 'encourage young people to learn economic skills to stay in the Kilfinan area' and to 'help young families facing rural isolation'.

- **Michael Harris, Adam Pike, Sam Cohen, Alex Dwek, Alex Gardner, Paul Gorrie, Niccolo Manzoni, Jack Prevezer, Conor Quinn:** Founders of Young Philanthropy Syndicate, a new philanthropic model that 'enables young professionals to invest in niche projects, with the support of experienced philanthropists' (www.youngphilanthropy.org.uk).

- **Sir Thomas Hughes-Hallett:** Ex-Chief Executive of Marie Curie Cancer Care (www.mariecurie.org.uk), which provides end-of-life care to the terminally ill.

- **Harvey McGrath:** Chair of the education charity, The Prince's Teaching Institute (www.princes-ti.org.uk), an organisation committed to 'increasing aspiration and improving education in state-funded secondary schools' (read about education philanthropy in Chapter 5).

- **Paul Marshall:** Co-founder and trustee of international children's charity ARK (www.arkonline.org), which works for children's education, health, and protection (Chapter 5, 7, and 8 cover education, young people, and health matters, respectively).

- **Gordon Morrison:** Chairman of Sargent Cancer Care for Children (www.clicsargent.org.uk), which provides 'clinical, practical, financial, and emotional support to help children cope with cancer and get the most out of life' (see Chapter 8 for charity healthcare).

- **Michael Norton OBE:** Founder of over 40 charities including Youthbank (www.youthbank.org) and buzzbnk (www.buzzbnk.org), which help raise money for community programmes.

- **Kavita Oberoi:** Chair of the Global Girls' Fund Board (www.theglobalgirlsfund.com/en/home), which supports the efforts of Girl Guiding and Girl Scouting to change the lives of 'girls and young women around the world by equipping them with valuable skills, knowledge, and opportunities' (we discuss volunteering for these organisations in Chapter 12).

- **Nick O'Donohoe:** CEO of Big Society Capital and Board Member of the Global Impact Investing Network (www.thegiin.org), both of which are dedicated to increasing the scale and effectiveness of impact investing (something we examine in Chapter 16).

- **John Pontin OBE and Wendy Stephenson:** Founders of Converging World (www.theconvergingworld.org), which invests in renewable energy in order to create and support social and environmental projects (read Chapter 9 on becoming an eco-warrior).

- **JK Rowling OBE:** Founder of The Volant Charitable Trust (www.volanttrust.com), which funds research into the causes, treatments, and possible cures for multiple sclerosis and programmes and charities that seek to alleviate 'social deprivation, with a particular emphasis on women's and children's issues' (see Chapter 7 for children's philanthropy and Chapter 8 for more on tackling health issues).

- **John Stone:** Founder of The Stone Family Foundation (www.thesff.com), which supports 'innovative, sustainable, and entrepreneurial approaches to tackling major social issues across the UK and around the world' (see Chapter 16).

Identifying Ways to Give

Almost every culture and society has a tradition of giving and philanthropy. Nearly every mythology features, say, a destitute wanderer whose life is made better by the generosity of others. People are trained, from an early age, to have compassion for the sick and goodwill towards those less fortunate. But how you act on these feelings of love, understanding, and sympathy is what shapes your philanthropy.

This section discusses the different kinds of giving: from a distance or in person, on the spur of the moment or in a co-ordinated way, and to meet immediate needs or solve long-term problems.

We don't want to discourage or encourage any particular type of philanthropy, but to help you understand the various types of giving available. By becoming more familiar with the options, you can find the right opportunities for you. You can make a difference at every level and with every mix of activities. Head to Chapter 3 for a general rundown of ways to give and Part III for details on a variety of different strategies.

Giving remotely or in person

In the modern day, you have two primary kinds of giving:

- ✔ **Remote giving:** You send a cheque in the mail or use a credit card online. This type of giving offers you the opportunity to plan the amount you give, to research the charity involved, and so forth. A potential downside is that you may miss the personal connection, which for some people is the most rewarding part of philanthropy.

- ✔ **In-person giving:** You make a personal connection with the people you're helping, whether you're giving to a busker or a beggar, helping a stranger with a bus fare or serving lunch at a food bank. In-person giving is often based on the interpersonal rapport between donor and recipient. The downside is it may be difficult to gauge how to help or whether the help you're offering provides a path to a better future or only a better today.

Both ways are valuable illustrations of the spirit of giving and both have their place in philanthropy.

Acting spontaneously or in a co-ordinated fashion

Letting the spirit of generosity move you to give 'in the moment' can be enormously rewarding. Countless charities have been saved by the just-in-time cheque or the heroic volunteer. Nevertheless, when your sole method of giving is one in which you react to sudden calls to action, you may be missing the opportunity to maximise the impact of your donation. Also, by not being part of a co-ordinated or well-planned effort, your generosity is less likely to have a long-lasting impact.

Although giving to others is amazing and wonderful, seeing the results is even better – and these results often come from well-planned, well-timed giving. By thinking about what causes you want to support and then devising a strategy that enables you to support that cause for the long term – whether through donations, volunteering, or other ways to be involved – you increase exponentially the impact of your good works. We discuss ways to organise and plan your giving in Chapter 17.

Don't underestimate the power of the spirit of giving within you to help others and to make an enormous difference. Our goal with this book is to help you make the biggest difference you can – and to have fun in the process!

Addressing immediate needs or solving long-term problems

One question gets to the heart of the issues regarding how to best help others: do you give someone who's starving a fish for one dinner or do you teach that person to fish for all her meals into the future? Some people argue that a starving person needs immediate assistance (for example, you throw a drowning child a life preserver instead of standing on the riverbank lecturing about learning to swim). Others argue that immediate assistance meets only the immediate need: without addressing the underlying problems, your solution is temporary at best.

The fact is that the world needs both approaches: ways to address immediate needs and ways to solve long-term problems – and you can address both in a co-ordinated way. As you decide which charities or charitable organisations you want to support, consider their missions and find the ones that take the approaches you prefer.

Finding Causes and Organisations to Support

All the areas of need that exist in the world and all the organisations that address those needs can overwhelm even the most dedicated philanthropist. Read on to discover how to decide which cause(s) and organisation(s) to support.

Focusing on favourite causes

Do you want to see something change in the world? Because you're reading this book, the answer is probably yes. In fact, the chances are that you want to see multiple changes. To begin to narrow the field from all worthy causes (which is a very large field indeed) to causes you're particularly interested in, carry out the following process (and head to Chapter 4 for detailed information on how to search for and select causes):

1. **Make a list.** Whether your concern is reducing poverty, fighting hunger, providing healthcare, helping children, improving education, or any of the hundreds of other causes, identify the areas that mean the most to you.

   Mull over what inspires you and grabs your attention. Think of the park you played in as a child or the museum you enjoyed visiting. Think of the places where you saw a favourite concert or an animal you love. These evocative, exciting memories may be the very things that lead you to find a cause to support.

2. **Go through your list and narrow down your interests.** If you wrote 'healthcare', for example, try to narrow the category: are you more interested in fighting AIDS, researching cures for cancer, or making medications more widely available? If 'education' made your list, are you more concerned with access for the disadvantaged to universities in England or the availability of primary education in Kenya?

Such a list helps you focus your philanthropic efforts on areas that matter to you.

If you're still having a hard time deciding which cause to focus on – maybe your list is lengthy or every cause is near and dear to your heart – try the following:

 ✔ **Look for areas that overlap and identify any themes.** For example, if your list includes 'childhood nutrition' and 'fighting obesity' (see Chapter 8) and 'food deserts' (which we discuss in Chapter 15) –

you know that promoting access to healthy foods is important to you, even though you may not have identified it specifically. That awareness can help you begin to co-ordinate your efforts or search for organisations that address that issue.

✓ **Prioritise the list.** Arrange the items in order from most to least important to you and focus on the top one or two.

✓ **Tackle all the causes, one at a time.** If you find that narrowing down your list is impossible, give yourself permission to contribute to all the causes – one year at a time. Pick one to focus on this year, and next year (and every year after that) revisit your list to choose a different cause for the following year. After all, who says you can't do everything? You just can't (or shouldn't) do everything all at once. Head to Chapter 3 to find out why.

Choosing an organisation

After you identify your cause, you need to find an organisation that supports it. The difficulty comes when you realise that multiple organisations are probably addressing the issues you care about. Here are some general suggestions to help you choose:

✓ **Do an online search for charities that address the issues you care about.** Type your cause in your search engine and see what comes up, or better yet go to Charity Navigator (www.charitynavigator.org) or Charity Choice (www.charitychoice.co.uk), which list charities by categories and provide information about the organisations: their missions, contact information, and more.

✓ **Understand the scope of the problem relative to the scope of the organisation you're considering working with.** A local organisation, for example, may be excellent at providing for the needs of the local community but is unlikely to tackle the problem on a national or global scale.

✓ **Reach out to others who have experience with this area.** Think about where the most help is needed; whether the local health clinic needs help raising money or volunteers in the evenings; whether the local homeless kitchen needs people with specific culinary skills or a few extra people in the warehouse on Saturday to make a big difference. When you understand what kind of help is needed, you can determine whether that charity is a good fit for you.

Figure out how you can find the change already underway near you and help aim, focus, and accelerate it with your skills, time, and passion! It is easier and faster to ally yourself with a nearby project that is already picking up steam than to begin from square one! Head to Chapter 4 to discover what to look for in charities and how to determine whether the charity you're considering is reputable and makes good use of the donations it receives.

Staying Engaged and Committed

Often, raising your hand or stepping forward to help is a powerful act – the first step you take to bring about the changes you want to see in the world. But don't make it your only step; if you want your efforts to produce lasting impact, you need to follow it up with others.

This section describes what you can do to keep your momentum going – and growing. Plus, because you can become disappointed when (despite the best efforts) change comes slowly or solutions fall short, we also offer advice on how to avoid feeling discouraged and giving up.

Following-up and following-through

Everyone can fall into the trap of becoming involved in projects that 'spoke' to them in the moment but then faded from their minds over time. Whatever happened to that campaign you 'liked' on Facebook or supported with a signature last year? Did the park up the street get built? And what about the resort where you spent last winter's holiday – how's that project to fund an orphanage coming along?

Engaging with a cause involves more than writing a cheque or signing a petition. Follow-up and follow-through are extraordinarily meaningful in the area of charity and philanthropy.

Here are some suggestions to help you stay engaged and avoid the 'you mean a lot to me until I forget about you' syndrome that plagues busy people:

  ✔ **Keep a journal or notebook and write down ideas, websites, and locations relevant to your philanthropy.** Doing so creates a useful record for later research and a trove of information if you're ever trying to follow-up with people you meet, causes you hear about, or places you visit.

  ✔ **Schedule time – at least a couple of hours or an afternoon a month – to devote to your cause or charity.** Even if you only have time to check in on the status of the project or send relevant articles about the issue to friends, you're making a difference. The next section has more on how sharing information is a great way to maximise your impact.

Don't wait for a charity to get in touch with you – contact it! The organisation may offer an email list or a monthly meeting, but also reach out to the staff, mention that you have a bit of time and ask whether they can put you to use. If they're having trouble managing relationships with individuals like you, perhaps you can help them with better marketing materials, an easier-to-use website, or by making telephone calls to donors. Chapter 13 discusses how you can put your specific professional or personal talents to use in your charitable giving.

If your problem is lack of time, consider replacing an activity you'd like to do less of anyway with volunteering. Suppose that you watch 28 hours of telly per week (apparently about average) but have been telling yourself that you need to watch the goggle-box less and get out more: make a plan to reduce your TV time to 24 hours a week (still plenty of time to keep up with *Eastenders* and *Downton Abbey*) and devote the other 4 hours to volunteering at your favourite neighbourhood charity. You'll be amazed how much 'extra' time even busy people can find in their schedules when they replace undesirable activities with rewarding ones – you may well even find that you look forward to these times!

Sharing your hope, commitment, and energy with others

Sharing is a two-way street: you encourage others in what they're doing to help the world and let them encourage you. Here are some ideas:

✔ **Tap into the power of social media.** The Internet provides an excellent way to interact with the world and discover new opportunities that can use your time, talent, and treasure. Keep in mind, however, that going out into the world is far more inspiring than sitting at the computer.

✔ **Look for ways to incorporate volunteer activities into your social life.** Convert meetings with friends into projects, take walks to areas you wouldn't normally visit, and talk with neighbours you don't normally interact with.

You're likely to get great ideas just by listening to your friends, family, co-workers, and neighbours; and you can share great ideas with them!

✔ **Lead by example.** Most great philanthropists do so and educate those around them – not by preaching but by learning alongside them. When a friend phones to have tea on Saturday, saying that you're busy is easy; but explaining that you're volunteering at the community garden in your area is more informative, interesting, and engaging. Plus, you can invite the friend to join.

Consider making a plan with a friend whose interests are similar to your own. By doing so, you encourage one another and work together to find exciting, accessible, and rewarding causes. Local community organisations can often help you find a friend or mentor within the organisation, which is especially valuable on your first volunteering experience.

You inspire people to act simply by how you interact with them. Listen to what gets them excited and remain positive and encouraging. After all, motivating and inspiring the people around you is a type of philanthropy (check out Chapter 19 for ideas).

Staying positive

The amount of work needed in the world of philanthropy can be daunting and frustrating. Despite the thousands of mosquito nets given away, children still contract malaria. Despite so many inoculations, people continue to be stricken with preventable diseases. But *staying positive* is absolutely crucial, as is realising that the situation isn't a matter of 'you against the world'.

One way to avoid getting discouraged is to set realistic goals about how much progress can be made and how much you can contribute. The idea is to start small: walk before you try to run, as the saying goes. Here are some suggestions:

✔ **Set achievable goals that are easy to measure.** If you put more ambitious goals into your plan, be sure that you set realistic dates.

Achievable short-term goals help you stay positive. Just as you don't begin an exercise programme by setting out to run a marathon, don't set yourself up for not meeting your charitable or philanthropic goals.

✔ **Figure out how much time or money you can spare.** An hour or two per week is great! Find a way to stick with it and think of what you're doing as being like a coin bank – the total sum is what matters!

✔ **Don't overpromise and don't let an organisation dictate your volunteering.** Part of being a good volunteer is to be honest about what you can do for the organisation with which you're working. Part of being a good organisation is respecting volunteers' boundaries.

If you feel that you're being overworked or asked to do anything dangerous, bring the issue up immediately with a supervisor. The relationship between the volunteer and the organisation should be respectful and mutually beneficial.

Improving the World Today, Tomorrow, and into the Future

The old adage about giving a man a fish or teaching him to fish is a nice use of the fact that fish is both a verb and a noun, but does little to truly inform our philanthropy. In most situations, we want the world to be better both today and tomorrow. But how can we use our resources to make sure the world is on a path to getting better? The truth is that some split between today and tomorrow is necessary. But we must also recognise that the present is linked to the future: the child vaccinated today won't fall sick tomorrow, the person given a chance at school today will be a more productive member of our society tomorrow.

Making the world a better place today

The world changes slowly. But that doesn't mean that humans can't make speedy progress towards a better world! In other words, you can make a huge difference *today*. Really! The key is to think about your impact on the world in little bites, not big gulps. Considering how to 'save all the whales' or 'end cancer' may appear noble, but neither of those outcomes is going to occur this afternoon – or maybe even within your lifetime.

What can happen today is that you demonstrate an enormous dose of kindness to an older person you'd otherwise not meet (see Chapter 6 for helping the elderly), or act on your feelings of generosity towards a charity you've long admired, or finally cement your commitment to spend some time helping in your community's vegetable garden (check out Chapter 9).

Change doesn't happen suddenly, but you can achieve small things quickly. Don't hesitate or procrastinate! You can do something to make the world better in the time it takes you to read this chapter. Jump to Chapter 20 for some ways . . . now!

Having trouble? Here are some ideas to get you started:

✔ **Come up with an issue that you have been thinking about wanting to change, say, about once a month.** Now think about how you can change it a little bit today. For example, if passing someone begging for money in your area bothers you, talk with that person. Investigate what part of the social services safety net has failed and what can be done to address the situation. Often small adjustments yield substantial impacts.

✔ **Find out where in the world you think you can make the biggest difference.** Have a conversation with a friend or colleague about that subject today, instead of about England's football team losing again or why your favourite TV soap character was killed off.

✔ **Discover who in your community most needs a break, a smile, or a meal.** Provide some charity or comfort to that person today.

You've probably seen films in which, for comedic or dramatic effect, a single angry or unkind response sets off a chain of other angry or unkind responses, which pass from person to person to person until everyone is infected. Turn this dynamic on its head and make a point of setting off a chain reaction of kindness or generosity instead.

Being a champion for the next generation

You decide to give to charity for a whole variety of reasons. In fact, we outline them in Chapters 2 and 18 and reinforce them with the inspiring examples throughout this book. But one of the most important reasons for giving is that the effects of savvy generosity are long-lasting. They may well outlive you, and perhaps even last long enough for the enjoyment of your grandchildren!

A large part of charity and philanthropy is future-focused. People act because they want the world to be better, not just for today but for the future, too. Philanthropists' actions are based on the hopes of a better world: that children can live in safer places, have better lives, enjoy better schools, hold better jobs, and have better options. Therefore, making the world a better place now also means providing a better world for the next generations.

Here are a few areas in which you can make a lasting impact:

✔ **Building and infrastructure charities and aid organisations:** These organisations take on building projects, from supplying water to villages to repairing bridges to bringing electricity to remote villages. The impact of infrastructure on the next generation is enormous – having a weather-tight building in which to attend school and clean water to drink increases health, safety, and happiness. Head to Chapters 9 and 12 for more on these organisations.

✔ **Education and social services charities:** These organisations work on improving the accessibility and quality of education. Aside from the direct impact on a student, higher levels of education mean more innovation in society, more qualified candidates for political office, and better prospects for social mobility. We devote Chapter 5 to education charities.

✔ **Medical and health charities:** These organisations focus on health today, which has a huge impact on the next generation. More children have healthier childhoods, receive the necessary early childhood care and inoculations, and live in communities that are healthy enough to nurture them. Head to Chapter 7 for charities that focus on the issues children face and Chapter 8 for ones addressing healthcare issues.

However you decide to make an impact on the world, remember that you're contributing to the welfare of everyone. Many people may see philanthropy as putting one's name on a building or opening a university, but although grand, worthwhile projects are great, there's plenty of room for everyone to contribute – and be recognised.

The next generation, and the generation thereafter, will have to make the best of the world they inherit. Help to ensure that they're left a gift rather than a problem!

When musing on the long-term changes you want to see in the world, think about what problems your children are likely to face. If you don't have children, ask yourself 'if I were born today, what would I be likely to worry about?' to consider the problems the next generation may face. Whether it's climate change, disease, or food security, people are working to tackle these problems today and in the future – and you can join them!

Chapter 2

Working out Why and How You Want To Give

In This Chapter

▶ Identifying your motivation for giving

▶ Deciding how much you want to give

▶ Understanding what you receive in return for giving

▶ Keeping your expectations realistic

*W*ithout doubt, giving is a powerful and uplifting experience and helping other people is inspiring, energising, and exciting. Plus, the more you give, the better you feel. Some days you can do more to help those in need than others, but every single day that you give makes you a superhero (what name will you choose: Generosity Girl? Benefactor Boy?). With all the benefits on offer to you and the world, the real question isn't 'Why do you give?' but 'Why doesn't everyone?'

In this chapter, we look into what may lie behind your desire to help others, assist you in deciding what and how much to give, examine the benefits in more detail, and provide some hard-won tips on managing your expectations. We also examine one particular approach to philanthropy: giving as a family.

Understanding Your Philanthropic Motivation

The better you understand what motivates you to give, the better you're going to be at selecting the right charitable activity to make the world a better place.

Giving as a personal mission

For many people, giving starts after they face and survive a life-altering experience. Perhaps you or someone you love experiences a serious illness and you decide to fight for a cure. Maybe travel overseas exposes you to the realities of crushing poverty and you want to help the poor rise out of destitution through a social venture.

Regardless of the experience, your motivation comes from deep within. You identify with it on such a profound and personal level that an incredible energy fuels you to fight for a particular cause with all your heart and soul.

One of the most powerful examples of what can emerge from personal motivation is the Susan G. Komen for the Cure initiative (`ww5.komen.org/aboutus/globalinitiatives.html`). The largest grassroots breast cancer awareness campaign in the world, it has raised over $1.9 billion since 1982. The initiative was born from the efforts of Susan Komen's sister, who watched Susan fight and eventually succumb to breast cancer.

Building a career: The professional path

The feel-good effect, internal passion, and sense of purpose generated from your early giving experiences may motivate you to pursue it as a profession: that's wonderful. After you make the decision to take the professional plunge, however, determining what motivates you day to day is essential. For some people, it comes from working in the field; for others, outreach and marketing a good cause feeds their internal philanthropic fire.

A professional path in charity and philanthropy splits into three basic categories: fundraising, programme delivery, and administration. Each of these activities (and the routine tasks they involve) plays a crucial role in successful and sustainable charities, and each calls for different skills, experiences, and networks.

The key is to work out early on which pathway is most attractive to you:

- ✔ **Fundraising:** To fundraise successfully, you have to be comfortable asking people to part with their hard-earned cash to help others in need. You need to be a compelling storyteller, an adept relationship manager, and event organiser extraordinaire. Enjoying building networks of people to champion your cause is also a great help.

- ✔ **Programme delivery:** To be part of programme delivery, you need to possess – or acquire – the technical skills required to deliver on the mission of the charity. You can build these skills formally (through technical apprenticeships, internships, or at university) or gain them informally by volunteering in the field. Also helpful is understanding where in the big world of philanthropy you want to work and help others. Understanding this motivation helps you build a strong network in that area, which is incredibly helpful when searching for opportunities.

✔ **Administration:** Charities and organisations benefit tremendously from effective administrators. They help keep founders and field workers co-ordinated and make sure that donations are transparently collected, managed, and accounted for after distribution.

Administration is a great option if you prefer to work behind the scenes in an office environment, whether in an overseas country, or in the local park during community clean-up time.

When deciding which professional opportunities to explore, one major motivation to understand clearly is your view on money: what level of income are you happy with? Most charities and philanthropic organisations are small and have lean budgets and only a handful can afford to provide higher incomes. If you're seeking to do good and do well financially, consider the possibilities of social entrepreneurship (Chapter 10 has the details).

Making giving a way of life

The ultimate act of charity and philanthropy is to embrace it as a whole way of life, devoting all your resources – personal, professional, financial, and so on – and all your endeavours towards a philanthropic goal. This kind of single-minded devotion and pursuit can result in a worldwide movement (think Mahatma Gandhi, whose concept of non-violent civil disobedience changed India and was the model for Nelson Mandela, Martin Luther King Jr, and Aung San Suu Kyi) or a network of giving communities (such as Mother Teresa, whose work led to a large network of orphanages, hospices, and charities worldwide).

But these are just the most famous examples; many local heroes dedicate their lives to helping others as a way of life.

Determining the Extent of Your Philanthropy

Problems come in all sizes, shapes, and forms. Some demand a quick random act of kindness and others require that you call in the troops and prepare for an enduring battle. So you have to decide how high a mountain you want to climb and what you can contribute to the ascent.

Defining the scale of your giving

Whichever size challenge you decide is your calling, you need to consider three things to help understand the scale of your philanthropy:

- ✔ **The scope of your vision.** Do you want to address hunger in your neighbourhood or tackle worldwide hunger? One desire affects a hundred people and the other a billion. One can translate into volunteering at a local soup kitchen, the other to establishing an international food relief programme. Both are of equal importance and you need to choose the right fit for you.

- ✔ **Your role.** You have four major means of giving and playing your role through your:

  - Time (see Chapter 12)

  - Talent (see Chapter 13)

  - Treasure (see Chapter 14)

  - Transactions (see Chapter 15)

  You can mix and match these roles depending on where you are in life and the resources available to you. For a general discussion of these areas, go to Chapter 3.

- ✔ **The amount of time and resources you're willing to invest in your cause.** Start small, experiment and see what produces the best results. As you find charitable causes that are a good fit and show good results, you can always increase your contributions and participate in the increasing scale of the venture.

Knowing what you have to offer

Socrates said 'Know thyself' and we agree. Considering why, how, and to what extent you want to give provides you with an opportunity to be reflective, creative, and inspired. Take a snapshot of where you are today and envision where you want to be in the long run by following these steps:

1. **Set aside a block of uninterrupted quality time.**

   Unplug yourself from the phone, text messages, email, Internet, and TV. Yes, you can survive without them for a few hours. We promise it'll be worthwhile.

2. **Draw up a list of your time, talent, transactions, and treasure and brainstorm about charities that interest you.**

   Generate as many potential ways of contributing as possible.

You can do this step alone or with friends and family. Involving others helps you generate ideas and fresh takes on what you can offer charities as well as igniting potential collaborations and new avenues for giving.

3. **Explore the world of possibilities.**

   Exchange ideas with your trusted circle of friends and family. Swap names of organisations, websites, people, and articles. This step is the time to feed your mind and take a look at how you can get going.

4. **Distil the results of the brainstorming into the four main areas of time, talent, transactions, and treasure.**

   Start with figuring out how much of each you're willing to give, then figure out how to help. Are you an accountant? Have you asked if the organisation needs accountancy expertise? Are you wanting to volunteer? Do they train volunteers? Figuring out how you can fit into the organisation's needs is crucial to being an involved and effective supporter of an organisation – financially or otherwise!

5. **Link up these four areas with your list of selected charities (from step 2) that offer the most potential for you to contribute.**

   Judging potential can be challenging, but tools in this book can help. Also, third-party rating agencies like Charity Navigator offer input on charities' effectiveness and use of funds. Finally, using your instincts and asking questions can be very important: pick up the telephone!

Repeat this process as often as needed. Whether you've been a lifelong giver and you want a new perspective or you're a newbie finding your way, this discovery process helps you decide on your path forward. Plus, getting to know yourself is a lifelong journey. What you have to give – your time, talent, transactions, and treasure – evolves over time. By paying attention to these changes, you can find innovative ways to find a match between what you can offer and what the charity that inspires you needs.

We highly encourage you to carry a pocket-sized notebook and pen with you at all times. Ideas, reflections, and possibilities on how you can give present themselves at all hours of the day and night and in places you least suspect. Jot down these ideas and review them once a month. Then take the top ideas and put them into motion.

If at first you think that you're too strapped for cash or your particular skills have nothing to do with a charitable organisation, don't give up; think outside the box. With a little bit of reflection, you'll be pleasantly surprised at how big a difference you can make with your current abilities and resources.

Getting through Giving: What You Receive in Return

Give and you shall receive; that's the maxim for this book. If you find this idea off-putting (believing that the whole point is to share what you have with others without asking anything in return), think again. As we discuss in this section, when you engage increasingly in philanthropy you discover that you receive a bounty of benefits in return.

Benefitting emotionally

Giving feels good and is good for your health. In fact, the more you give, the stronger you make that part of your brain that's associated with compassion (if you need persuading, check out the nearby sidebar 'Brainy research on compassion'). In a way, you're working out a muscle: the more you exercise it, the stronger and healthier it gets.

Considering the financial benefits

Most governments encourage people to donate via tax incentives: the cash donated is deducted against your taxes.

The key is to make sure that the organisation is an officially recognised and registered charity and that it has the ability to issue you an official document acknowledging your contribution. This official receipt has to include the name, address, and, when possible, official registered charity number assigned to it by the government. (To find out more about tax benefits and charitable contributions, head to Chapter 17.)

Brainy research on compassion

Stanford University, California, has a department committed to studying the benefits of giving called the Center for Compassion and Altruism Research. Researchers are finding that people who exercise their compassion 'muscle' have improved health, lower levels of anxiety, and higher levels of overall resilience. To discover more about this study, visit ccare.stanford.edu.

Here are two other potential financial benefits to take into consideration:

✔ **Corporate matching programmes:** Often companies match their employees' contributions to a charity on a one-to-one basis, up to a specified amount; think of it as doubling your giving power (Chapter 14 has more details).

If you're running a charity or throwing a charitable event, always ask people to inquire whether their employers have such a programme.

✔ **Corporate volunteer programmes:** Many companies want their employees to be active members of the community and so they grant them a certain number of hours a year to donate to a good cause on their clock. Under this arrangement, your company is essentially paying you to help others, and it's a good deal for everyone. Make sure to ask your boss about it.

Recognising the social and personal benefits

Doing good for others offers tons of social benefits. The most basic one is that you make new friends. In fact, you meet people from all walks of life at all different stages of life, making for a colourful and fun experience.

You're also making the world a safer and better place for yourself and future generations. Clean air, drinkable water, food security, reduced violence, improved access to basic human rights . . . the list goes on. Positive differences – even small ones – combine to create a more peaceful and sustainable place for you to thrive.

Don't forget the professional halo effects of doing good. From a business perspective, doing good helps differentiate your company from your competitors. It shows that you care, a characteristic that more and more consumers are factoring into their purchase decision-making process. When you're a stand-up corporate citizen, people vote for you with their wallets. In Chapter 15, we look closely at how people use their purchasing power to make a difference in the world.

Managing Your Expectations

Normally giving is a feel-good experience, which is exceptional when the fit between you and the charity is perfect. Unfortunately (and sorry to bear bad tidings), not all donor–charity combinations are matches made in heaven. A mismatch in expectations between you and the charity leads to frustration and dampens your appetite for getting involved in philanthropy.

Crucial to avoiding this pitfall is to manage your expectations through the phases of searching, selecting, and committing to a charitable cause, as well as during subsequent changes. This section helps you navigate this process.

Keeping expectations in check during the exploration phase

Finding the right charity is a lot like dating and marriage. You start out exploring, flirting, and figuring out whether you like each other and eventually – if you have a profound chemistry – you walk down the aisle and get married. The same occurs when you consider working or volunteering for, or creating and managing, a charity (but without the endless debates about placecards and playlists).

Heed the following tips to ensure that your match ends up being happy:

- ✔ **Have an initial conversation about what you're looking for and what the charity needs.** Be upfront about what you want. If you're looking to join a charity in some capacity, you need to help the charity understand what you have to offer. Equally, be willing to ask the charity what it needs. Only after this initial exploratory conversation can you settle on a starting point together, which may alter as what you have to offer changes and the needs of the charity evolve.

- ✔ **If you're unsure, don't rush things.** For example, volunteer for a few mini-assignments (if you're running the charity, have the potential candidate work on a mini-project). If things go well, you can move towards bigger and better things together – and a more certain commitment.

Understanding what you want during the commitment phase

In charity work, some people commit to one cause completely while others prefer to play the field. But whether you're so passionate about a cause that you commit wholeheartedly or you have several irons in the fire, when you're good at what you do charities are naturally hungry for more of your time and want a long-term relationship. The key is to make sure that the potential charity understands your level of commitment. If you're pursuing several interests, for example, be clear on what you can give and where you draw the line in terms of your time, talent, and treasure.

The multi-charity focus and singular-charity focus have pros and cons:

✔ **Being involved in several charities:**

- Upside: You can deploy different skills and resources where they're best suited.

- Downside: Your efforts are diluted and making the most of your efforts is harder.

✔ **Going all in for a single charity:**

- Upside: You make full use of your intense day-in-and-day-out, focused level of commitment and generate sustained impact. You have the opportunity, with each contribution, to get better and faster at helping those in need.

- Downside: You can face burning out or being disappointed with a charity's lack of vision, management, or effectiveness. All eggs in one basket has its downsides as a strategy.

Managing expectations as things change

Transitioning arises from a game-changing event. The arrival of a child, for example, reduces how much time you have available; a financial transaction generates a windfall, which can change your giving capabilities; or a charity moving in a different direction than you anticipated may institute a change that requires a set and level of expertise that you don't possess.

Transitions are like paper cuts: tender affairs. From the charity's perspective, any loss is always felt. And any good charity or philanthropic endeavour does its best to keep you in the mix if you're a great match.

If the transition is one in which the charity's needs change so that your contribution is no longer a good fit, don't let that sour you on philanthropy. Instead see it as an opportunity to explore fresh opportunities. After all, you have a vast universe of ways of giving available. Embrace the transition as a chance to explore new ideas, people, and approaches to contributing.

If you go from unknown to celebrity or experience a fat payday from a transaction, expectations about what you can give are sure to skyrocket. You may want to leverage your newfound celebrity status or prefer to stick to giving as a private matter. You may decide to take a leading role in the giving community or not feel ready to scale-up your giving to match your new-found wealth. The important thing is to know what you envision for your giving and to send out a consistent signal to others with that message. Doing so makes transitions easier for everyone.

Bringing Families Together

Engaging in charity and philanthropy is a unique opportunity for families to share quality time together. Perhaps you can get involved with your siblings or parents or engage across the generations. Sometimes family members working together for a charity can be tricky; sometimes it's easy. This section offers some simple ideas to help make this a great experience for you.

Sharing with your immediate family

Your immediate family can act as champions, roadblocks, or passive observers of your charitable activities. We suggest you focus on activating the champions and transforming the passive members into active champions. Avoid burning up your time on the roadblocks. You have better things to do, such as building, supporting, or working at your preferred charity.

Central to enlisting the champions and transforming the passive members is to build an effective communication strategy. Think of this as combining the skills of marketing, public relations, and one-to-one communication. You want to craft a clear, concise, and compelling story. By engaging in effective story-telling, you can inspire the potential champions to deploy their time, talent, and treasure (we define these aspects in the earlier section 'Defining the scale of your giving'). You may even transform how they shop and activate their giving power through transactions.

If you're shy or reserved, check out *Communicating Effectively For Dummies* by Marty Brounstein (Wiley). This book can help you gain the necessary skills to show how your charitable cause is a win–win for everyone.

Bringing your extended family on board

You can also build support for your charitable vision with your extended family. In a world where most people live far from their relatives, sharing your philanthropic passion with more distant family members is an opportunity to work on a shared project. They may be easier to communicate with and persuade than people you don't know because a pre-existing trust factor exists between you and them.

The positive benefits of getting extended family on board include better ties and deeper friendships. You can also tap into a wider range of skills and know-how. Hopefully, they give you a 'friends and family' discount!

The family spirit: Steve and Rachel Durchslag

Even if your family has diverse interests you can still instil a spirit of giving that grows across the generations and throughout the family. A shining example is from the family that founded the Sara Lee Corporation. Steve Durchslag and his daughter Rachel share their stories.

Steve writes:

'In our Jewish tradition, giving isn't a choice; it's a requirement. *Tzdakah* is the Hebrew word for charity but has a broader meaning as well of incorporating the concepts of righteousness, justice, or fairness. My wife and I tried to transmit this value to our children by example. When our daughters were very little, we brought them with us to pack and deliver food baskets to the poor to provide them with a first-hand experience. As they got older, we involved them in the operations of our family foundation. They've both assumed leadership roles in the foundation and actively direct its philanthropic activities.

Our daughters internalised these values beyond our wildest expectations and insisted that their investments be managed with social justice objectives. Their politics, far to the left of their conservative father, have always championed the underserved.'

Rachel Durchslag writes:

'I grew up in a nice home in an upscale part of Chicago and always felt secure and cared-for financially. But my parents made sure we knew how lucky we were: there wasn't a single year during my childhood when we weren't involved in some sort of charitable activity. Volunteering with my family helped me understand from an early age the importance of giving back.

My parents also taught me the importance of contributing not only time, but money. They shared stories about the excitement they felt when they were able to donate to innovative social-justice programmes; their enthusiasm shaped my understanding of philanthropy as something that's not simply an obligation but a profound way of interacting with and changing the world. My parents' philanthropic causes are much different from mine, but what unites us isn't the specific causes we support but our embracing of philanthropy as a vehicle for connecting and healing the world.'

Reaching out to friends and associates

Don't neglect talking with your friends and associates, though you may need to refine your communication strategy compared to dealing with family members. Of course, you can keep the same level of intimate and personal element with friends and new-found acquaintances, but when you're bringing your vision to co-workers or other professional contacts, make sure that the cause has a broad appeal and is a suitable topic within the organisation.

If you feel strongly about enlisting others on a deeply personal level, consider inviting them to a fundraiser outside of the workplace. Doing so helps you respect everyone's boundaries.

Chapter 3

Figuring Out How and What You Can Give

*H*ere's the good news: you possess loads of gifts to share with people in need. The challenge, however, is that all people – even the wealthiest of the wealthy – have limitations on their resources. As a result, you need to figure out what you want to give and make some tough choices on how you want to give it.

In this chapter, we describe the four main powers of philanthropy – time, talent, transactions, and treasure. We also discuss how you can mix and match these gifts to your (chosen charities') best advantage.

Giving Your Time

Time is one of the rarest resources on the planet, because you can't make more of it no matter how hard you try. A day has only 24 hours, and so you need to use these hours wisely to make the most of your giving and make each moment matter.

Even in today's world, when everyone is rushing around at a frantic pace, you still have some time to give. The trick is to convert a few idle hours of TV-watching, texting, Internet-surfing and social-media activity into valuable give-back time. This section shows you how (turn to Chapter 12 for more advice on giving your time).

Brother, can you spare some time? Deciding how much you can give

The amount of time that you invest in something depends on your lifestyle. You may be a busy bee who needs to focus on freeing up tiny moments to devote to causes you care about, or you may already have the luxury of time and the freedom to dedicate most of it to the service of others. The chances are that you fall somewhere between these two extremes.

Wherever you fall on the spectrum, you *can* find time (or more time) to devote to charity work. You just need to know where to look. Try this simple exercise:

1. **Write down precisely how you spend your time during a typical week.**

   Be honest and detailed and include everything – work, recreation, activities, and so on, as well as all the little time-wasters that sneak into the mix, like popping to the local coffee shop for a skinny latte or plopping on the couch to watch your favourite television shows (yes, we too know the irresistible draw of *Top Gear* or *Call the Midwife* – replace with your personal weakness as appropriate!)

   If analysing your schedule a week at a time seems too daunting, tackle it day by day. Write down your daily routine for a week.

2. **Look at your week, now set out before you in black and white, and search for places that you can sweep clean of 'time drains' and replace with giving-back opportunities.**

   For example, instead of lolling about in bed for an extra hour or two at the weekends, perhaps you can loll on Sunday and use those 'found' hours on Saturday for your charity work.

After you determine how much time you have available, whether it's only a few minutes here and there or whole days, you can choose activities that let you make the most of it. The next three sections offer suggestions.

Maxing out your minutes

Even if, like most people, your schedule is filled with activities and obligations that you can't eliminate, you don't have to abandon your dream of helping others. Some very meaningful activities take only a few minutes of your time. Here are some suggestions to get you started:

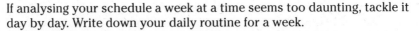

- ✔ Checking in by phone on an elderly, chronically ill, or disabled friend or family member.

- ✔ Sending an introductory email to a friend or organisation that assists in opening a helpful door. A warm introduction goes a long way in helping to facilitate networking and new possibilities.

- ✔ Writing or posting a useful or inspirational article on social media, which helps spread the word about an issue close to your heart.

Many such instances take just 10 minutes or less to accomplish. When you find yourself with a gap between commitments, max them out with acts of giving.

Becoming a weekend and weeknight warrior

Do you have the weekend and weeknights free? Of course, we know that this time is yours to unwind and spend with friends and family, but you don't need to change that; you just need to think differently about what you do to de-stress and enjoy time with loved ones. The possibilities are endless. The point is that your weekends and weeknights can be an incredible source of inspiration, new friendships, and bonding with old friends and family.

Loads of causes exist for which you can donate your time together as a family or with friends. Here are just a few examples:

- ✔ Helping reconstruct houses for the homeless

- ✔ Assisting the staff at a soup kitchen or food bank

- ✔ Offering to throw a benefit

- ✔ Lending a helping hand at a community garden

- ✔ Volunteering as a children's football team coach

- ✔ Taking a lovingly made meal round to a housebound relative

- ✔ Attending volunteer gatherings. Review the website of your charity of interest and sign up for its newsletters. These often have information about gatherings in your community.

Whether you're attending with family and/or friends or alone, these activities and others like them are great ways to give back and meet new people with shared values. And who knows, if you're single and looking to make connections you may even come across the love of your life!

Giving big time: Radical sabbaticals

Traditionally, a *sabbatical* is a year-long leave devoted to study or travel. If you have the time and resources, you can take a sabbatical to devote to a cause that's near to your heart. Taking a sabbatical is a big step, however, because you're putting your work or study aside for up to a year.

Sabbaticals provide you with the opportunity to devote all your time and energy to a cause, which makes them highly rewarding and life-affirming, but they aren't something to jump into lightly. When considering whether to bag a rad sab (!), keep these important points in mind:

- ✔ **How you plan to fund the sabbatical:** They can be self-funded or supported by sponsors. If you plan to self-fund your sabbatical, you need enough money saved to support yourself and, if the sabbatical takes you away from home, to take care of any on-going financial obligations related to your permanent residence.

  If you aren't in a position to finance a sabbatical by yourself – and many people aren't – you can contact many sources for funding. These options include scholarships, *crowdfunding* (in which you use social media to seek funding; check out Chapter 11 for more info on this strange-sounding activity), work-study abroad programmes, government grants, and part-time flexible jobs that help cover expenses during your volunteer efforts.

- ✔ **What organisation you're seeking to support:** Be sure to do your homework. You're making a significant commitment that merits careful consideration, and you need to make sure that the organisation is legitimate and trustworthy. Chapter 4 tells you how to check the credentials and trustworthiness of charitable organisations. You can also use resources such as www.charitynavigator.org for US organisations and if you are in the UK you can review www.charitycommission.gov.uk to evaluate charities you don't know much about.

  Look before you leap! Avoid scam artists. Make sure that you do a thorough appraisal and a full check on any charity or organisation before you make a financial or sabbatical-level time commitment. This check includes doing research online as well as making referral calls to people who've been on the programme before or are familiar with the organisation.

- ✔ **Preparing yourself:** If you're going into a place that faces widespread disease or conflict, or is in a remote location, make certain to educate your support network of family, friends, and professional mentors with the details of your sabbatical and provide them with a local contact point upon your arrival. Taking out comprehensive travel and medical insurance is also a wise investment.

The organisation you're working with should provide instructions and information regarding the things you need to know about the region you're travelling to and what you need to do in preparation (getting required vaccinations, securing passports and visas, and so on). It should also inform you about cultural norms and social and political issues. Other places to find updated information about travel abroad are http://www.gov.uk/foreign-travel-advice or http://travel.state.gov.

If the organisation is small, you may have to do some of this homework on your own. Larger organisations may have this information pre-packaged for you. Regardless, always make sure you do your homework and be as informed as possible so that you understand the potential benefits and risks of this commitment.

Your personal safety is important and so make sure that you think through the financial, health, and emotional commitments and risks. Understand the potential pitfalls involved and explore what you're expecting to bring to the organisation. You want your sabbatical to be an exceptional, memorable experience.

A lifetime of devotion

A few rare people are so inspired, committed, and driven to help others that they give up their whole lifetime to a cause. This approach calls for tremendous levels of persistence and perseverance, as well as many sacrifices along the way, financially and personally.

These individuals are the iconic leaders whose lives and devotion show what's possible. Here are a few of these extraordinary people:

- Paul Farmer, who's fighting diseases in the poorest places in the world.

- Alice Gugelev, who founded the Muskoka Foundation with the motto 'do good as you go', which helps travellers find opportunities to help others along the way.

- Dave and Cheryl Duffield, who founded Maddie's Fund, one of the largest initiatives to help pets find homes and avoid being killed in shelters.

This kind of devotion isn't possible for many, and millions of people make a substantial difference in the world in much smaller ways, but if you do feel called to devote your whole life to the service of others, several organisations make doing so possible, such as Doctors Without Borders/Médecins Sans Frontières (MSF) (www.doctorswithoutborders.org), Voluntary Services Overseas/Voluntary Service Organisation (www.vso.org.uk) and Volunteer Match (www.volunteermatch.org). For more information on different service organisations, visit www.volunteering.org.uk or www.do-it.org.uk.

Making Best Use of Your Talents

With the current lean days in the economy, you may be staring at your bank account and feeling limited about how much you can give. Don't worry. You can give in many ways other than simply cash. What about giving your talent, which is a highly valuable commodity? Maybe you can use it to significantly help other people realise their charitable mission.

Charities prize technical skills, not least because the market rates for such abilities are expensive. Plus, the more qualified and experienced the technical skills, the higher the premium commanded, which places hiring people with these skills out of reach of the vast majority of charities. This prohibitive cost puts charities, social ventures, and individuals at a distinct disadvantage in their efforts to deliver their programmes and grow in ways that are consistent with their missions. Your arrival and the skills you bring can be a real game-changer for them.

Charities, social ventures, and individuals in need are counting on you to help them advance their mission. The better able you are to identify, evaluate, and explain your skills, the sooner they can put you to use. In this section, we describe how to appraise your skills, communicate them to other people effectively, and discover the right fit between your abilities and the needs of a charity. You can read more about giving your talents in Chapter 13, along with some great examples of terrific talent-giving.

Taking inventory of your skills

The first step in sharing your talents is figuring out what skills you have to share. Even if your CV isn't filled with obvious attractions such as 'agricultural specialist', 'midwife' and the like, chances are that you still have skills that can benefit charitable organisations in need.

All talents and skills have their place and merit. Here are some examples of the sort of talents that you can bring:

- ✔ **Corporate skills:** Accounting, financial planning, legal, design, marketing, logistics, project management, technology, and human resources

- ✔ **Trade-related talents:** Medicine, plumbing, electrical engineering, home building, food preparation, music and video production, and farming

- ✔ **Handy-based skills:** Domestic cleaning, transportation, and building maintenance

To create a snapshot of what you have to offer, do the following:

1. **Draft a list of your skills.**

   Don't limit yourself to your current job-related skills: include every marketable skill and useful talent you have. If you're an accountant, keep a garden at home and speak French, your list is already taking shape. At the very least you can note 'accountant', 'gardener', and ' bilingual'.

2. **Rank each skill on a scale of 1 to 5, with 5 being the best score, to indicate what level of technical expertise you can offer.**

   Give yourself 4s and 5s for those skills for which you have a great deal of experience or received training. The rank for the French-speaking, gardening accountant, for example, may look like this:

   • Accountant: 5

   • Gardener: 3

   • Bilingual: 1 (her French is pretty bad!)

3. **Evaluate realistically how much time you can offer.**

   Refer to the earlier section, 'Giving Your Time' for guidance on making time for charitable endeavours.

Whether you're just starting out in your profession or are a recently retired executive at the top of your field, always be candid when creating an inventory of your talents. This helps both you and the charity find the right fit between skills and the needs of the charity.

Explaining your abilities

With the list from the preceding section in hand and an enthusiastic spring in your step, you're almost ready to share your talents with organisations that need exactly what you have to offer. Your next step though is to create a CV to give to the charity or charities that you plan to approach.

Prune your talent list to make sure that it highlights your skills in an effective way. Lead with your strongest capabilities, highlighting things at which you're highly competent. If you're great at creating databases, fixing technology systems, or performing other business tasks, certainly list them! These talents are precisely the ones that are hard to find in the not-for-profit world. But also, experience of working in a kitchen may be valuable to some organisations, and it never hurts to list these things as well.

Keep your CV short and simple. Eliminate all the 'noise' and boil down your experience and skills to one page. Well-run charities are time-strapped and they appreciate and respect your efforts to help their management team understand easily your abilities, motives, and time availability.

Problems can arise, because social ventures, charities, and individuals pursuing noble missions always need more resources than they have at hand, and their demands often exceed what you're able and willing to do. This situation can create a gap that's all too easily filled with miscommunication and potentially bad feelings. To avoid this unpleasant situation, clearly explain your skills and limitations. Doing so helps you create a mutually positive giving experience and avoid the pain that can accompany divergent visions.

Finding the right fit for your talents

Although every reputable charity and service organisation has a worthy mission, your talents and commitment are best used by an organisation that needs the things you have to offer. Finding that organisation is a two-step process:

1. **Conduct a search for opportunities that would be a good fit for your talents.**

   Online channels, corporate services, faith-based communities, and word of mouth are the main ways to find opportunities. In Chapter 13 we showcase leading examples and approaches that help you fit your skills to the right organisation.

2. **Make sure that a match exists between yourself and your charity of choice.**

   Do your homework on the charity's mission by reviewing all its online and offline information. Read articles describing the trends in the charity's field of interest and educate yourself as much as possible. In particular, try to get a clear sense of the following (by studying the organisation's literature or by asking during your interview):

   - **Organisation's current resources and current stage:** It may be a small charity just getting started that needs a helpful hand in navigating the legal and financial paperwork, or a mature charity that's launching a major capital campaign or initiative to bring its programmes to a new market.

     Being attuned to the current status of the organisation helps align your experience levels with the organisation's needs. Sometimes your skills are so newly acquired that they may not be sufficient to meet the organisation's demands. At other times, your abilities may be so advanced that their arrival overwhelms or is irrelevant to a small organisation's management.

- **Organisation's clarity of purpose and ability to deliver on its mission:** Does the organisation have a clear picture of how the world would be better if it succeeds? Do you think it can help create the world it envisions?

- **Calibre of the present team:** How open are staff members to improving the ways that they do things? Can they help you in the tasks you're going to undertake?

- **Results the charity expects from your contribution:** Are you there to make a difference for a weekend, or does the organisation expect lasting effects from your visit? How does it plan to maintain the skills or processes you bring after you leave?

If you're seeking to help an individual or informal group, be aware that formal documents and online resources describing the mission, volunteer opportunities, and so on may not be available. In that case, you can ask the person who referred you to that particular volunteer opportunity to bring you up to speed. Ask questions about past volunteer initiatives. Did they succeed? How many people were involved? What was the goal? What happened?

By understanding the needs of the organisation and its current situation, and knowing your boundaries in terms of time commitment and ability, you can find the right fit.

Egos at the door, please

Although you're a superhero for contributing your time, do leave your ego at home when you arrive on the first day of giving. Be an attentive listener and show humility, respect, and patience to help establish trust and confidence on both sides.

After making your choice and jumping on board to help the charity, you may encounter a messy situation at the organisation. If you do, avoid participating in the blame games, gossip circles, and groaning sessions – they're counterproductive and zap you of your drive to give.

Remember to be a positive, upbeat, and high-energy person with great skills, because this approach helps you to create impact, galvanise the troops, and deliver great results for the organisation.

Dealing in Transactions

Transactions, by which we mean the buying and selling of products and services, are the single most powerful tool of philanthropy available to everyone. From simple bartering to complex marketplaces, the sum of all transactions changes the condition of the entire world.

Be in no doubt: every one of your transactions makes an impact. Purchases influence the quality of air, water, and soil and affect the stability of societies, people's health, and the prospects for a sustainable planet. Yet many people are unaware of this power and how they can use commerce as a tool for philanthropy. Too many people are divorced from the production process and as a result have no idea how things are made and where things go after they're tossed in the bin.

Most consumers live in a blissful state of ignorance, except of course that ignorance is no longer so blissful: environmental degradation is on the rise, as is social unrest, and health standards are declining.

The time has come for all people to exercise their purchasing power to create a better, sustainable, and healthier life. Part of this aim is understanding how your purchases make an impact:

- ✔ Your purchases influence directly the resources used to produce goods and services.
- ✔ Cause-related marketing lets you use your cash to build awareness and produce long-term solutions (see the later section 'Examining cause-related transactions').

When you understand these two facts, you may never look at buying goods in the same way again.

Accepting that what goes in must come out

At present, the price consumers pay for most goods and services doesn't take into account the full cost of production. The costs *not* factored into the price of goods include items such as air pollution, depletion of the oceans' fish, inhumane working conditions, corruption, and weakened legal systems. But because the sticker price of a product doesn't reflect these costs, people tend not to see them.

Just because people try to skip out on paying for the full cost of production doesn't mean that they can avoid the consequences on their lives. The fact is that what goes into a product or service is exactly what comes out of it. A product whose manufacture relies on polluting technology, child labour, or toxic runoff into the oceans, for example, promotes polluting technology, child labour, and toxic runoff. The result of these *negative externalities* (the clunky term economists use for these hidden costs) is a world of unpaid-for dumping grounds and untamed cancers that riddle civilians and add risk to the free marketplace.

All humans live on one small planet, and everyone impacts, for good or ill, its future. Think carefully about what you purchase and what you do with your waste. Your choices can spur manufacturers to look for ways to become much more innovative in how they produce goods and services. As a steward of the Earth, one of your most important purposes is to leave the planet in a better place than when you arrived – a mandate that applies regardless of your creed, faith, or politics.

Empowering through transactions

Your transactions can be transformative, inspiring (or spurring) companies and manufacturers to embrace sustainable technologies and processes and fair practices. Here are a couple of ways to shop with a purpose:

✔ **Be an informed consumer:** Read the labels, company websites, news reports, and third-party reviews, and where the labels and Internet are short on information, demand more. Write to companies, government bodies, the Press, trade associations, and advocacy groups asking for more information to help you.

Companies listen. The more demand they get for this information, the more likely they are to provide it. And if you find that firms are consistently not listening, you can 'vote' for another company that *is* aligned with your values, by switching those products and services that you buy.

✔ **Buy from companies whose practices and policies reflect your values:** Nothing makes a company change faster than looking at the sales figures. When it notices that large numbers of customers are moving elsewhere or that responsible consumer choices are driving sales upward, even the most insensitive commercial executive switches direction towards the rising sales figures.

You really can influence companies with every single purchase.

Examining cause-related transactions

In addition to being a crucial agent for change in how products are produced, you can also make use of your power by purchasing goods that are linked up with a cause. *Cause-related transactions* range from products that sponsor a cure for breast cancer to broad-based initiatives such as UNICEF.

Here's how cause-related transactions work: the companies allocate part of their marketing budgets and revenues towards building awareness or making cash contributions to a cause. This arrangement gives you a chance to contribute consistently through your daily activities. We examine companies and cause-related campaigns in more detail in Chapter 15.

You hold power in your hands with each purchase, trade, and exchange, and so make sure that you use it wisely and effectively. Although you may think that your individual choice is insignificant, when you consider the combined decisions of 7 billion people, you soon see clearly that each transaction makes a huge difference.

Handing over Your Treasure

Treasure is the amount of cash that you can invest or donate to a cause, whether you have meagre means or are the lucky steward of significant wealth. Regardless of the amount you have to give, you need to take a few basic factors into consideration. We cover these aspects in this section (and we describe a few examples of excellence in giving treasure in Chapter 14).

Choosing between donations and investments

You can allocate your treasure in two basic ways – donate it or invest it in assets that generate positive social benefits.

Donating

When you donate your capital, you can make *one-off gifts* (one-time donations), *multi-year grants* (recurring transfers of money), or *grants in perpetuity* (money given by a trust or foundation essentially forever). You can tag these donations as restricted or unrestricted funds:

    ✓ **Restricted funds:** Tied to a specific programme or activity and sometimes time-bound and geographically limited. For example, specifying that your Red Cross donation is to go to help earthquake victims in India is a restricted-fund donation.

> ✔ **Unrestricted funds:** Can be deployed to the programmes and operating expenses that the management of the charity sees as most effective in fulfilling the vision of the organisation. For example, donating to the Red Cross without specifying a particular use is an unrestricted donation. Even if your original motivation to give was an earthquake in India, the donation may be used in Haiti or Mexico.

As you may expect, a conflict is at work here. Charities prefer unrestricted funding and donors prefer restricted funding. Charities want you to trust their decision-making, and they want the flexibility to react rapidly when circumstances demand. Donors want to know that their resources are going to programmes they understand and approve of.

To determine the balance between an organisation's restricted and unrestricted funding, look into how it allocates money between programmes and overheads. If the *overhead* (that is, administrative costs for items such as office expenses and executive salaries) is above 20 per cent, have a hard talk with the charity management to understand how that overhead correlates to real-world outcomes of the programmes. Then make a determination as to whether you can see a fit for your giving.

Investing positively

You can make great use of your treasure by pursuing an *impact investment approach*. In this technique, you search for and select investment opportunities that satisfy the need for a financial return while generating positive social benefits, such as eco-sustainability, fair trade, safe working conditions, and other positive effects. These investments can be in equity and debt instruments, such as stocks and bonds.

In Chapter 16, we describe the rising trend in impact investing and corporate social responsibility.

Determining how much you can give

Givers range from people with few direct means but the significant ability to raise funds from their friends, families, and community, to those who've generated or inherited multimillion pound trusts.

As a starting point the amount that you give depends on how much you have in absolute terms and how much you want (or are able) to give as a percentage of your total wealth.

You can choose from different strategies that are appropriate to your starting point and level of commitment, as we discuss in the next four sections.

When you have no means

If your bank account is hovering near zero and you live month-to-month but are still passionate about giving, you can contribute by becoming a champion advocate and fundraiser. Make use of your social capital to generate cash that you then donate or invest into a social cause of your choice.

You can choose from many tools to raise funds. We describe examples throughout this book (one, for example, is crowdfunding, which we discuss in Chapter 11). You can also gain further insight on the best practices for fundraising by reading our sister title, *Fundraising For Dummies* by John Mutz and Katherine Murray (Wiley).

When you have modest means

Into this group fall people with reasonable savings set aside for the major expenses of life and those with a healthy, reliable stream of income.

Most people in this category are *response-based* givers. For example, you receive an invitation from a friend to attend a charity event, your work has a drive for a major charity or you get solicitations in your mail. You select randomly which causes to adopt and give random sums at inconsistent intervals. Of course, this kind of donation tactic is great and does good, but it isn't a giving strategy; its random nature and inconsistent occurrence mean that your ability to make a co-ordinated, long-term impact is impeded.

One of our aims in this book is to help you shift from being a response-based giver to being a *proactive giver*. By this term we mean that you seek to donate or invest in charities or causes that generate serious results, are sustainable, and match your core values.

To shift from donating reactively to donating proactively, you identify a charity (or charities) whose mission you want to support (refer to the earlier section 'Finding the right fit for your talents' for suggestions on locating and evaluating charities). Then you determine how you can best contribute the money you've allocated for charitable giving. For example, if your charity of choice is a local food bank, you may decide to donate monthly but to increase the donation during the summer months because, while researching your choice, you discover that donations are down in the summer but the need is greater, due largely to school-aged children missing subsidised school lunches.

When you can give on a large scale

If you're fortunate enough to have significant treasure, you're in a great position to play a crucial role in helping organisations to grow or kick-starting fresh innovative charities. You may have the means to think big and also the time to nurture a social venture into maturity and scale. If so, you can make an even bigger impact.

When you can 'go all in' now

Bill Gates and Warren Buffett are leading the charge on a whole new level of giving by asking people to sign a pledge to give half of their fortune to a charitable cause instead of transferring that wealth to the next generation of family members.

Some people with lesser means are equally driven towards donating the majority of their wealth within their lifetime. These heroes include the deceased Bostonian philanthropist Tom White (the unsung hero who fuelled the early work of Paul Farmer – check out the earlier sidebar 'A lifetime of devotion' for details) and Chuck Collins, who gave away a substantial part of his inheritance in his twenties (and continues to work for economic equality).

Although a tradition of major gift-giving at the very end of people's lives has always existed (for example, the Scottish-American industrialist Andrew Carnegie at the start of the 20th century), the major development in giving today is committing to give more, earlier, and to be involved actively in pursuing solutions to the planet's problems.

Weighing the percentages of giving

You may be wondering about which is the better strategy: giving the maximum amount possible now or giving smaller but regular sums over the long haul? You need to decide what's best for yourself, but here are the pros and cons:

- ✔ **The 'giving the maximum amount now' school:** This group argues that the opportunity cost far exceeds the benefit of giving only a percentage (say, 5 per cent) of your asset base per year (an amount that leaves the bulk of the wealth untouched). In other words, the growth rate of the problems is outpacing the growth rates of the assets. Investing more resources immediately can solve the problems more quickly and free up future capital that can be used to pursue productive goals.

- ✔ **The 'give smaller but regular sums over a long period of time' school:** This group argues that spending all resources now is a high-risk proposition, because doing so eliminates your ability to generate future cash flows that may be crucial at a later stage when the root cause of a problem remains despite the best efforts and deployment of capital. These advocates believe that the slow and steady approach is the right path forward.

Whichever school you fall into and regardless of the amount, percentage, or timing of your cash giving, ask yourself what returns you're expecting and which charities are most efficient in meeting their objectives. Also, consider carefully how restricted or unrestricted you are in your contributions. The more thought, research, and prudence you put into your approach, the better able you are to identify charities that are positioned to deliver the results you want – plus the more satisfaction you feel.

Making Choices and Setting Limits: Understanding that Both Are Beneficial

If you're feeling overwhelmed by all the different ways in which you can give, don't worry. The good news is that you can mix and match. You may get satisfaction from volunteering your talent or you may find transforming the world through how you buy things more exciting. Maybe you prefer to combine approaches: volunteering your time for one cause and your money to another. Similarly, you may prefer to give a little at a time to a variety of charities or to put all your treasure behind a single cause.

Whichever path you choose, keep the following tips in mind:

- **Always pursue quality over quantity.** By focusing on a select set of causes, you increase dramatically your possibilities of making a profound and lasting impact. You become better able to direct your energies, monitor your contributions, and build enduring relationships with the individuals and organisations you help.

- **Figure out the right giving mix for you.** For example, if you're giving your time, stay mindful of your energy levels, because if you become so exhausted from over-committing, you risk doing a bad job, which hurts everyone and helps no one. You want to give your best so that everyone wins.

- **Develop the ability to say 'no'.** Being selective is powerful, although it can also feel uncomfortable. Everyone wants to say 'yes' to a worthy cause, and you have to discover how to say 'no', too. This approach is beneficial for you and the charities: you stay focused on results and the charities invest their energies finding people who are passionate about their vision.

The key to navigating this awkward situation is to accept kindly the educational materials offered by the charity – after all, seeing how people are helping to make the world a better place is always inspiring. And who knows, you may find that a particular cause becomes important to you later in life. In this way you're informed, aware, and readied to redirect your time, talent, treasure, and transactions to that fresh cause.

Chapter 4

Discovering and Implementing Your Philanthropic Passion

....

In This Chapter

▶ Bringing passion to your philanthropy

▶ Assessing the focus of your involvement

▶ Investigating charitable organisations

▶ Maximising your impact

....

*P*eople perform more successfully at activities they enjoy. The child who loves the drums but hates the piano is unlikely to become a great pianist, no matter how many lessons the parents insist on. Fortunately, philanthropy is more like a playground than an orchestra – and you get to choose what you want to do and how you want to do it. Aligning your personal passions with your philanthropic activities is important; not only do you get more satisfaction and enjoyment, but you also participate more frequently and are more effective.

This chapter focuses on aligning your interests, talents, and philanthropic energy with the causes that you're passionate about. We show you how to use your passion as you search for and choose an appropriate cause, help you decide where you can best intervene, and suggest some specific, practical ways of getting involved. Seven billion people are riding on the Earth and everyone can participate in maintaining, improving, and repairing it.

Searching for a Cause That Sparks Your Passion

You can be drawn to support causes for many reasons. Sometimes you select one consciously, your passion driving you to find out more and to get involved. Often, however, a cause discovers you, firing up your latent passion. Perhaps you're inspired to join a cause after travelling to a foreign country and experiencing something so profound that it changes how you view the world. Or maybe a family member or a close friend faced and overcame a specific challenge or disease. Perhaps you read a book or watch a television programme that compels you to reach out and lend a hand.

Whether you find a cause or a cause finds you, the key is getting involved in something that you're passionate about and discovering ways you can turn that passion into action.

Don't view philanthropy as an obligation or a bill to pay: that perspective is unlikely to turn you – or anyone – into an innovative, excited, dedicated giver! Instead, choose a direction for your philanthropy that you're passionate about so that it guides your giving and keeps you committed.

In this section, we help you discover your passion. For inspiration from some of the great philanthropists, take a look at the nearby sidebar 'Using passion to change the world'.

During your philanthropic search, take note of initiatives, foundations, and opportunities that strike you as cool, innovative, or interesting. Even if it's not precisely what you want to give to, you may be able to find a closer match later.

Using passion to change the world

Consider these famous philanthropists whose gifts helped define the 20th century's charitable momentum. They all chose areas that they were personally passionate about:

✔ **Andrew Carnegie** (1835–1919): After his formal education was cut short, he borrowed books from the personal collection of a man who made his library available every Sunday to young workers. Carnegie later funded the building of over 1,600 libraries across America to give others similar opportunities.

✔ **John D. Rockefeller** (1874–1960): Influenced by his deep religious convictions and interest in scientific and social progress, he recognised the need for research universities and contributed millions of dollars to sustain the University of Chicago for the next 100 years.

✔ **David Duffield (founder of technology company PeopleSoft) and his wife Cheryl:** After their beloved miniature schnauzer, Maddie, passed away, they began Maddie's Fund, which promotes no-kill animal shelters and has given nearly $100 million to save dogs and cats.

✔ **Sir Richard Branson (founder of the Virgin family of companies):** A serial entrepreneur himself, Sir Richard focused his philanthropy on encouraging other entrepreneurs to follow their dreams. The Branson Centre of Entrepreneurship focuses its programming on guiding and nurturing early-stage business entrepreneurs.

Beginning in Bill and Melinda's backyard

Bill and Melinda Gates's concern for the future world their children will inhabit drives the Gates Foundation's focus on healthcare, poverty, and education.

When the Gates Foundation, currently the biggest philanthropic organisation in the world, confronted the questions of early childhood education, it found that children from disadvantaged households didn't have the language and behavioural skills needed to succeed in a school setting. In Washington State, where Bill and Melinda Gates reside, tens of thousands of the children entering kindergarten every year are unprepared to begin their school experiences.

Instead of trying to fix early childhood education generally, the Gates Foundation chose Thrive By Five Washington – a public–private partnership – as its partner in the push to improve early childhood learning in the state. The programme provides parents with education on how to be better teachers to their children and offers in-home visits to provide support to at-risk families. Parents are also referred to resources for better nutrition and paediatric care.

Going with what you know: Charity begins at home

Understandably, many people look to their local area when searching for a cause to support, which is a great place to start your adventure. Plenty of ways are available to help a cause that interests you nearby, no matter where you live.

Mining your own experiences

To find your passion, you may need to look no further than your own life. Many donors begin with organisations that have touched their lives or the lives of their families. Perhaps your grandmother was treated at a particular hospital or you have fond memories of the university you attended.

If no idea strikes you immediately, the following may spark some ideas:

- ✔ **Make a list of the experiences, memories, and achievements that matter most to you and think about what made them possible.** Maybe you were able to participate in a summer learning experience because of a foundation's involvement with your school, for example.

- ✔ **Flip through your photos on Facebook or your recent diary entries.** Look for things that bothered or puzzled you. Ask yourself what you want to be different in the future. Perhaps photos of a trip abroad remind you of the level of poverty, the number of children not enrolled in school, or the lack of a recycling facility. Images of your family may make you think about the quality or type of food available to your children or the lack of activities available to your retired parents.

✔ **Ask yourself what concerns you about your town.** When you read the paper in the morning, what local stories make a particular impact? Perhaps you wonder what's going on near that road intersection across town where you feel the urge to lock your car doors.

✔ **Think ahead.** Identify which organisations, institutions, charities, and other groups you think are going to be the most important in educating, caring for, and creating opportunities in the next generation.

✔ **Remember the situations in which you helped others.** Think about how you can create such opportunities for others.

Bringing good ideas back home

Although being innovative in your giving is great, you don't need to reinvent the wheel if the charity work you want to be involved in doesn't currently exist in your area. If you see a charity you like in New York but you live in Totnes (or Tulsa or Tokyo), start researching similar, local causes. If you like how a particular volunteer organisation works somewhere else, see whether one already exists where you can put your professional skills to use. Nowadays, a Without Borders organisation exists for many, many professions – it's not just for doctors any more!

Although you may be able to duplicate one charitable model from Place A to Place B, don't assume that it will automatically work as well in the second location. If you're considering transplanting a charitable endeavour because an organisation claims its approach can be 'cloned', 'replicated', or 'scaled' between communities, remember to note the differences between the locations as well as the similarities. For instance, many success stories associated with healthcare, such as disease prevention, positive prenatal outcomes, and so on, address local problems or populations. When the programme is replicated elsewhere, its effectiveness is lost in translation.

To check out what worked (and what didn't!) in other communities, look at impact reports six months or a year after a project started, when they've had time to analyse the impact of their efforts. You can get these from the foundation or organisation – often, their websites have a 'resources' section with this information.

Opening your eyes to problems nearby

You need to decide whether to support a cause likely to make your local city/country/society better or to help a cause abroad where a few pounds can mean the difference between life and death. You may be surprised just how much help is needed in your own community. Take childhood hunger, for example.

Nearly a billion people – roughly 15 per cent of the world's population – suffer from hunger or malnutrition. Extraordinary and worrying, isn't it? About a third of children in developing countries suffer from this scourge. Issues related to food availability, food security, and malnutrition kill more people every year than AIDS and malaria combined. Nutrition is a big deal and one of the hardest health problems to solve globally.

Therefore, if your cause is children (and if so, check out Chapter 7) your initial impulse is probably to look to impoverished areas of southeast Asia or Africa, where, without doubt, the challenges are immense. But many children are hungry, homeless, underprivileged, victimised, and abandoned in Western countries, too.

In the end, the geographical area you focus on is up to you, but the sad fact is that problems are daunting in the West and in developing countries.

Gathering info about charities beyond your local area

If you can't find something within your home or family to drive your philanthropy, you may find inspiration through these organisations:

- **CharityBuzz (www.charitybuzz.com):** An online auction site offering luxury goods and dream-come-true opportunities (imagine having lunch with Paul McCartney!) to raise money for noteworthy causes.

- **CharityChoice (www.charitychoice.co.uk):** Allows British users to find a wider variety of choices through a unique search system.

- **Charity Navigator (www.charitynavigator.org):** Offers evaluations of charities, tips for donors, current information, and more. We provide additional information on this organisation in the later sidebar 'Navigating the world of charity'.

- **Funding Network (www.thefundingnetwork.org.uk):** Lets donors find a way to link up with others and multiply their effectiveness.

- **Next Billion (www.nextbillion.net):** For philanthropists, investors, business leaders, and others seeking to make sustainable change through development and enterprise.

- **Philanthropy 2173 (www.philanthropy.blogspot.de):** Read up on a decade of ideas, observations, opportunities, and more related to serving the public good.

- **Worldchanging (www.worldchanging.com):** A site devoted to improving living conditions around the world through sustainable design.

Thinking about what inspires you in other areas of your life

One method for searching for a focus for your philanthropy is to consider what inspires you elsewhere in your life – what makes you passionate, personally or professionally? Take a look at the following stories and see whether any strike a chord:

- ✔ April Artist wants to help by donating her artistic skills to a charity. She finds a local school that needs after-school art instruction, but wants to get involved with something where she can work with a larger number of people. She decides to start a YouTube channel teaching the basics of drawing and painting and, before long, has hundreds of students.

- ✔ Bryan Beekeeper loves what he does. He's interested in using his spare time on his next holiday to share his love of beekeeping with others. He's surprised to find Bees without Borders (`www.bestbees.com/2012/12/bees-without-borders`), an organisation that helps impoverished communities overseas learn about beekeeping as a micro-enterprise or microbusiness (which we define in Chapter 10) where people can make and sell honey. Before long, Bryan is emailing technical drawings of beekeeping equipment back and forth with a village thousands of miles away.

- ✔ Chandra Carpenter loves to build things in her spare time and adores the Caribbean. She gets involved with Habitat for Humanity (`www.habitat.org`) in Haiti and builds homes for people still recovering from the 2010 earthquake. Chandra's contribution is a small but invaluable part of an effort that's going to take millions of hours of labour over years.

- ✔ Don Donor doesn't have time to volunteer at the local soup kitchen, but he has some money he'd like to give to the hungry. He logs onto `www.charityportal.org.uk` and finds 20 charities working on short- and long-term solutions to the famine in Somalia, where food shortages and food price spikes have been a problem for decades.

If you're a licensed professional – from acupuncture to zoology – you may want to contact local and national professional organisations. These professional groups often keep waiting lists of people and organisations who need help but can't pay the market rate for your services. If you love your work, providing services to those who otherwise can't afford them is a great way to have a positive impact! Turn to Chapter 13 for more ideas in this area.

Some professions, such as the law and medicine, have strict ethical rules that you must follow when volunteering services. Make sure that you look into these regulations and adhere to them; otherwise, you may be risking your professional licence and your reputation, and your conduct may reflect poorly on your community of professionals. Be sure that any organisation you work with understands and respects the limits on the services you can offer.

When helping one charity isn't enough: Prioritising your efforts

No matter how much time and money you have, you're not going to solve all the problems in the world. So channel your energies into what most motivates, inspires, and animates you. If you want to feed starving children, save the whales *and* build a hospital, examine your priorities and narrow down your interests. Use the checklist in Table 4-1 to identify one or two things to support. Rate each item with a number between 1 (care the most about) and 5 (care the least about).

Table 4-1	Prioritising Your Charitable-giving Options
Charitable Focus	*Ranking (1–5)*
I want education to be more accessible and affordable in the future (Chapter 5).	
I worry about the elderly and about the world's aging population (Chapter 6).	
I want to make things better for the next generation (Chapter 7).	
I think a crisis exists in health and healthcare today (Chapter 8).	
I wonder how best to preserve, protect, and nourish the environment (Chapter 9).	

Feel free to add other categories on your own sheet – they don't have to come from chapters in this book! Keep in mind, however, that the broad areas we separate above attract individual donors in large numbers every year. Each of these categories has dozens or hundreds of areas and problems to be solved in every culture and geography. Be as broad or specific as you like, but the more specific you are in your area of interest, the more focused you can make your search for organisations to support.

TECHNICAL STUFF

Roman fever or marsh fever: Whatever you call it, it's bad

Malaria is a parasite that has two hosts: the insect and the mammal. When malaria infects a mosquito, it reproduces in the insect's gut. When an infected mosquito bites a person, tiny amounts of malaria are released into the person's bloodstream. Then the malaria reproduces again (through a different process) in the person's blood, ready to infect the next mosquito that bites that person.

The problem is that this reproduction process is harmful to the parasite's host. In people, malaria causes headaches, swelling of the brain, fevers, severe dehydration, fainting, and death. Although some treatments exist for people who are infected with malaria, they're expensive and often unavailable in rural areas.

Deciding Where to Focus Your Philanthropy

Most problems have a cause and an effect/symptom. Sometimes the best approach is to attack the origin of the problem and other times managing the effect is more important – or, indeed, all that's possible. Philanthropists and international charities address problems from both sides.

Consider the problem of famine, for example. In addition to a lack of security (war, terrorism, and so on), the *causes* of famines can include poor food production practices and inadequate access to markets. Its *effects* (or symptoms) include widespread malnutrition, disease, and displacement of populations.

To tackle the causes of famine, agricultural experts, microfinance institutions, and the World Food Programme act to put farmers back in a position to plant for the next season. To attack the effects of famine, organisations such as Doctors Without Borders (flip to Chapter 8 for more) work to alleviate the results of going without food and not having a home. Other organisations, such as the United Nations' crisis fund, address the causes and effects.

REMEMBER

As an individual donor, you can determine your *level of impact*. This doesn't mean the *amount* of impact (see the later section 'Taking Initial Steps to Maximise Your Impact' for more on that), but whereabouts in the cause-and-effect 'chain' you want to intervene: are your skills and passion best used by addressing the causes or the effects of a crisis?

This section outlines some options, using malaria – a disease that, despite co-ordinated efforts to eliminate it, kills upward of 2,000 people a day worldwide – as an example. (For details on the disease itself, head to the nearby sidebar 'Roman fever or marsh fever: Whatever you call it, it's bad'.)

Addressing the cause

Some charitable organisations make their mission to eradicate situations or factors that allow a problem to develop. If you have a leaky water pipe, for example, you don't devote all your resources to mopping up the water; you fix the pipe as well. Even better is preventing the leak in the first place. This approach is the preferred option when the causes of a problem can be prevented or addressed relatively easily and inexpensively.

For example, most experts agree that prevention of malaria is the best approach: a bed net costs far less than treating an infected person. These nets act as barriers and are cheap, costing less than £1.50 each. By preventing the disease, you relieve the infected person's pain and suffering, and eliminate the stress that having an incapacitated adult or gravely ill child can cause a family and a community. The benefits, in fact, of prevention are far-reaching:

- ✔ Children who sleep under bed nets have a significantly reduced risk of contracting malaria.
- ✔ Healthy children are more active, more likely to get educated, and more likely to become contributing members of their communities.
- ✔ Healthy parents can take better care of their children and are in a better position to provide for their families. (A sad fact is that, often, one ill parent prevents both parents from working, because the healthy parent becomes a carer to the ill one.)

So although malaria can be tackled after infection, prevention is certainly the preferred solution where possible. The same benefits that apply to bed nets can be extended to a variety of other items, from clean water to vaccinations. As you decide what level of impact you'd find more satisfying, think about what a donation achieves *and* what it prevents. Doing so allows you to maximise your philanthropic impact.

Helping to tackle the symptoms

Sometimes, prevention as we describe it in the preceding section isn't possible or has failed, because of the expense or complexity of doing so. (Prior to people figuring out that simple bed nets had a profound impact on

Starting a chapter or a brand spanking new charity

If you want to start your own charity and like the easy-to-use format of this book, check out the *Nonprofit Kit For Dummies by* Stan Hutton and Frances Phillips, which walks you through the basics of starting a charity.

Before you start up that organisation, however, consider other options. Try contacting an organisation that shares your concerns: maybe it wants to start a new chapter in your area or is looking for ideas to make improvements! Instead of starting a new charity, you can make an impact by volunteering and helping to make the existing one become more efficient.

Don't underestimate how much effort, time, and dedication you require to set up, run, and grow a new charity. Behind every organisation is someone like you, working as hard as possible to get results!

the incidence of malaria and other insect-borne diseases, for example, they tried to eliminate the microbes causing the diseases or the insects that carried them. But so far smallpox is the only infectious disease to be successfully eradicated.) Even when prevention is possible, sometimes people fall through the cracks. In these cases, attention turns to tackling the symptoms.

For example, despite the availability of preventive measures for malaria, many of the difficult circumstances that many disadvantaged populations live under can't be easily or quickly dismantled, leaving these people vulnerable. Although better policies, practices, and programmes may help future generations of children, millions are suffering right now. This urgency drives some charities, even though the type of assistance they can offer – such as establishing health clinics – doesn't solve the root cause of the problem.

Child sponsorship is another example of a successful model of philanthropy. Here, the charity filters your money to a child far away, and your money helps with costs that the child's parents or community can't cover. In most such charities, you receive letters and/or photographs from your child, as well as updates on the child's health, progress in school, and family situation, which lets the donor build a closer relationship with the recipient of the funding and the surrounding area or community (in Chapter 7, we discuss these child sponsorship charities in much more detail).

Checking Out Your Chosen Charities: Due Diligence

One of the most difficult problems facing the philanthropist is the huge number of charities and causes available – and the selection grows with each passing year. Currently, over 180,000 charities are registered in the UK and nearly 1.6 million operate in the US! Some are large, well-known charities, but most are small organisations run by a few passionate people on a small budget. With so many options, you're likely to find several that focus on the area you've selected as your cause.

Fortunately, checking out a charitable organisation is easier than ever, as is building a subsequent relationship with it. Most organisations have websites (nowadays, websites are such a priority that some organisations even have them before they're operating), and Internet-based rating sites can provide independent advice.

In this section, we explain what a charity is, go over how to evaluate the charities that you're considering, and share how to build a relationship with the charity you select.

Getting the basics on charitable organisations

Everyone knows what a charity is, right? Well, to a degree. You probably know, for example, that a charity is an organisation that accepts donations, turns them around and uses them to do good. If you want to plan your charitable endeavours with an eye to maximising their impact, however, you require a deeper understanding of how they're structured and what they can do. This awareness also helps you make more informed judgements about whether a charitable organisation is meeting its mission to your satisfaction.

For example, you need to know whether the organisation you're considering giving money to is a corporation. Harvard Corporation (the President and Fellows of Harvard University) is a corporation, as is the American Red Cross, as is Oxford University. The Boy Scouts and Girl Scouts are both corporations, as are other familiar municipal and national organisations we recognise from everyday life, from the London Underground to the various chapters of Doctors Without Borders.

In the US, charities typically start life as limited liability corporations, which then obtain charitable status with the IRS (Internal Revenue Service). This means that their primary motive for existence (unlike most corporations) is not to make a profit and that donations made to the organisation are generally tax-deductible. When the IRS recognises the organisation's charitable status, donations to the organisation (even donations made before the IRS recognised the organisation's charitable status) are tax-deductible.

In Australia and the UK, charities are corporations limited by guarantee, which means that they don't distribute their profits to shareholders. UK charities function very much like charities in the US and are assigned an HMRC (Her Majesty's Revenue and Customs) reference number.

In addition, charities are different to social ventures and social investment companies. How they're structured impacts what they're allowed to do and their tax status. Read on for the details.

Distinguishing between charities, social ventures, and social investment companies

A charity is typically a corporation limited by guarantee – or, in the US, covered by section 501(c)(3) – which subsists on a combination of its investments (often called its *endowment*), donations, and grants (which are like donations given out by organisations rather than by individuals). A corporation that's *limited by guarantee* (or, in the case of the US, is a 501(c)(3) entity) can make a profit, but it doesn't distribute that profit to shareholders. Instead, it's returned to the corporation to fund its mission.

Social ventures are corporations designed to make the world a better place. Most social ventures that manufacture or operate physical businesses tend to be corporations, while most social ventures that focus on investing money tend to be partnerships. When considering using them, the structure of the organisation is far less important than its mission and, perhaps most of all, how well it performs in achieving that mission.

Social investment companies are organisations that help you invest your money in ways that improve the world.

Both social ventures and social investment companies are usually for-profit corporations. What separates them from other for-profit companies isn't their legal status but their mission and (often) what motivates their managers. We talk more about social ventures and social investment in Chapters 10 and 16 respectively.

Organisations know that they're competing for your attention, generosity, time, and resources. If you have questions about an organisation, go ahead and ask. If you're uncomfortable with the answers you receive, consider moving on. So many worthwhile causes are out there that you don't need to feel pressured to give to an organisation you're uncomfortable with!

Accepting that tax matters

Tax law is a complex area. Donations to organisations that have obtained charitable status may be tax-deductible, but if you're not careful you may end up giving money to an organisation and not receiving a tax deduction. Here's how to avoid this scenario (if you have questions or your donations are large, be sure to consult an accountant or tax expert):

Tax deductions and politically active organisations

A fine line exists between what charities can and can't do politically. If an organisation is politically active, check with a tax professional before assuming that your financial support for the organisation is tax-deductible. If your donation is deemed to be political rather than charitable, you may lose any tax benefit you gain from making the donation and be forced to pay penalties.

Some politically active organisations have been accused of funding terrorism or other misdeeds overseas, bringing problems to their managers, employees, and donors. Particularly if you support refugee organisations, those operating in conflict zones, or charities working in the Middle East, you need to be aware of this situation. The US Department of State (www.state.gov) and the UK government (under the Home Secretary's jurisdiction, www.homeoffice.gov.uk) keep lists of proscribed groups. The EU is revising its rules on prohibited groups as this volume goes to press.

Check out Chapter 17 for more information.

✔ **In the US:** Ask whether the recipient organisation is a 501(c)(3) entity. Donations to 501(c)(3) corporations are tax-deductible.

✔ **In the UK and Europe:** Ask whether the organisation is a registered charity listed by your government and get its tax reference number. To receive tax relief, claim the tax relief on your Self Assessment tax return or at your Tax Office. (Note that submissions to the tax office in the UK eliminate the need for the old 'white form' filings by post.)

In the UK and US you can give money before it's taxed, increasing the impact of your donation. In the UK, you can give through the Payroll Giving scheme, where you donate from your gross salary before any tax has been deducted. In the US, you can donate stock that has gone up in value since you bought it (though if you sold the stock and then gave the proceeds from the sale, you typically would have to pay capital gains tax). In the UK, Gift Aid lets the charity keep any tax benefit (head to Chapter 17 for details).

Asking the right questions

Knowing a little bit about the organisation you support (or plan to support) is important. To help you understand charities in more depth, you can use the questions in the following four sections. Answering these questions helps you become a more educated participant and a stronger advocate for your organisation.

One of the best things you can do is to call the organisation and speak to someone. Be alert to the fact, however, that time spent on the phone with you is time not spent on the organisation's core mission.

Everything has a cost...

A small bookstore in Boulder, Colorado, called Left Hand Books, is run as a collective, with no owner and volunteer shopkeepers. Hence, 100 per cent of its budget goes to its mission of making progressive literature available to the public in a medium-sized American college town. But its model is inefficient. Managing volunteers is hard and incentivising them to come to work on time is extremely difficult.

Would the bookstore be a more efficient organisation if it took 5 per cent of its budget to hire a cashier instead of using volunteers? Or would this harm its '100 per cent of budget goes to mission' message? Or would hiring employees run counter, philosophically, to the purpose of the organisation? These are difficult questions, but worthwhile ones to ask.

How long has this organisation been around?

Great new organisations start all the time and you don't have to wait until one has been around for years before you support its work. But if it has been around a while, you want to pay attention to the organisation's track record: for example, how many of the staff members are volunteers and what's its annual budget?

Is this organisation registered with the government?

Some socially-minded organisations may not be registered with the government as charities. This is fine! In fact, many of these are profit-making businesses and shouldn't be registered with the government as non-profit. Trust your instincts – if an organisation has a mission that seems wholly philanthropic but isn't registered with the government, ask why.

How much of my donation goes towards the issues I care about?

One of the most common questions from volunteers and donors is 'if I give Charity X £10, how many pounds of that go directly to the mission of the charity?' This question seems simple – after all, donors have a right to feel that their donations are being used to support the organisation's mission – but the issue is more complex, because it speaks to a bigger debate: how much overhead cost is reasonable?

Elsewhere in the book, we address this issue in more detail, but here are the main arguments: some people argue that the ideal charity has no overhead costs and is '100 per cent efficient', meaning that all the donated money goes to fulfilling the mission. Others argue that reasonable administrative expenditure can help a charity function more efficiently and effectively. The nearby sidebar 'Everything has a cost. . .' contains an example.

What was last year's operating budget?

Typically (though it's not required), organisations post last year's operating budget on their websites. Sometimes an organisation posts earlier budgets or what's anticipated for the current year. If more than one year is provided, try to sort out (particularly for a young organisation) what's typical and what's an unusual expense. For a small charity, buying that laser printer or laptop can bring up the percentage of the budget allocated to 'overheads' or 'office supplies' by a few percentage points – be sensitive to the challenges of running a small organisation!

When you're looking at potential recipients for your generosity, ensure that you're comparing like for like to avoid missing out on an opportunity to help a great organisation. Remember that charities relying on items that vary a lot in price (for instance, medical supplies or air freight) or providing a service that requires expensive assets (such as a veterinary clinic or a homeless shelter) almost always have higher overhead costs than other organisations.

The line between overheads and the mission budget isn't black and white. Some organisations purposely classify things that would normally be 'overheads' into the mission budget to bring down the overheads portions of their budgets. If the percentage of your donation used for mission-related activities is important to you, spend some time to figure out how much the organisation really spends on its stated mission.

Rating and ranking charities

Humans like to rank things: favourite colours, most-hated foods, or best films of the 1990s. Well, now you can do the same with charities, and you don't need to spend loads of time looking into all the charities and putting them in order from fantastic to terrible. Non-profit-ranking organisations such as Charity Navigator (www.charitynavigator.org) and Charity Portal (www.charityportal.org.uk) do it for you, helping you to make better decisions. These can be more useful than, say, the *Guardian*'s annual list of Britain's top 1,000 charities by donations (which is helpful only if you like looking at long lists of numbers with little other information).

Such companies not only observe and rank charities, but also influence the behaviour of charitable organisations, making them take issues such as accountability, transparency, and reporting more seriously. In this sense, large charity-rating sites play a financial gatekeeper role, preventing disreputable or questionable charities from accessing large pools of donor money.

The newest rating method used by Charity Navigator includes three areas of common concern for donors:

✔ **Financial health:** This category is important to monitor over the life of the charity, not simply in the current fiscal year. Past mistakes may be indicative of management or governance problems that need to be resolved before the charity is entrusted with more funding. Look further into large present-period expenses that endanger the organisation's financial health.

✔ **Operational transparency:** Prompt, complete, and honest reporting – particularly involving large expensive projects – is central to a charity's credibility. Fortunately, over the past two decades, charities overall have vastly improved their degree of transparency. Charity annual reports in the 1980s and early 1990s were often vague, four-page affairs mailed out along with fundraising brochures. Today, most charities provide substantial information, such as project reports, audited financial statements, and discussions of recent successes and failures, which is often available online.

✔ **Accountability – reporting of individual projects or organisational results:** Reporting results doesn't mean taking photographs of smiling children near the project; it means building a set of goals against which projects undertaken in the past year (and, ideally, in future years) can be measured and improved. Charities that rate high in accountability hire independent consultants or find outside help in developing these standards in order to measure achievements (or shortcomings), report promptly the findings and make them available to donors, and ensure that no special expertise is required to dissect and digest the information.

Navigating the world of charity

Charity Navigator (CN), founded in 2001 by John Dugan, is America's largest and most influential charity-rating organisation. Its primary goal is to guide intelligent giving by providing those looking to make charitable contributions with an easy way to determine where to direct their funds. The organisation, which provides information at no cost to users and the charities it evaluates, relies heavily on voluntary user donations to make the service possible.

CN gathers its data from the annual informational reports that charities submit to the American tax authorities and from the charities' websites. The rating system currently considers 24 areas of measurement in financial health, transparency, and accountability. The ratings – from zero (Exceptionally Poor) to four (Exceptional) – show givers how efficiently a charity uses its support, how well it has sustained its programmes and services over time, and its level of commitment to good governance, best practices, and openness with information. CN assesses roughly 5,500 registered US charities, which receive approximately 50 per cent of all charitable contributions made by Americans each year, and includes charities in every category and location.

As an independent watchdog and advocate for the interests of donors, CN alerts users when a charity may be having some significant ethical challenges or other issues that diminish confidence in the charity's self-reported data. In addition, CN provides a variety of other information and resources on its website, including top ten lists, hot topics, tips, articles, and blogs.

CN is working towards adding a third dimension to its rating system to evaluate the quality of charities by reporting on the results of their work.

Taking Initial Steps to Maximise Your Impact

For most people, the decision of whether to donate is largely emotional. It involves not only how you feel about the organisation's achievements or progress in its mission, but also how you feel about yourself. Of course, sometimes your budget is tight or you move away from the area in which the organisation works. But usually, the reasons for your decision to give (or not give) are less rational, perhaps more impulsive, and even somewhat random.

Don't get us wrong: feeling emotional about making a difference in the world is a good thing. It's the source of your motivation to act and persevere when progress doesn't come as quickly as you'd like. If, however, you want to maximise the positive impact you have, you need to pair your emotional commitment with cold, hard, practical actions.

By taking the steps we outline in this section, you can expand, in all sorts of ways, the good you do – which is even *more* to feel good about.

Managing your relationship with the charity

After you donate to a charity, you form a relationship with the organisation. Some send you emails, others use the post and still others call during dinner or before the holiday season – often with the same question: 'will you please give us money again?'

As someone for whom charitable giving isn't an occasional, random event but a commitment to having a sustained impact, chances are you're looking for more from that relationship. This section outlines suggestions to help you develop a more informed relationship with your charity and make strategic adjustments that allow you to feel more satisfied in your endeavours.

Keeping track of what the charity's doing

Make sure that you know what the charity does and how it does it. Charities are supposed to behave in a predictable way with your money. If they aren't meeting your expectations – or have a sudden change in direction – check in on them. Knowing whether your expectations are being met and respected is important to your continued involvement.

Keeping track of what an organisation is doing after your initial support is rewarding and informative; it's a wonderful opportunity to stay involved or donate again. Recent news can also be a good conversation-starter, a way to tell friends and colleagues about the organisation you're now involved with (head to the later section 'Spreading the word to help your cause' for ways to get others involved).

Look on the organisation's website for current information, read the reports and newsletters that it makes available, and periodically see what charity-rating organisations say about it (refer to the earlier section 'Rating and ranking charities').

Maintaining a donation scorecard

Think of each act of philanthropy as a learning experience.

Keep a scorecard to track the money you give away, perhaps in a spreadsheet, a pack of note cards, or an old spiral-bound notebook. At the end of the year, rate how satisfied you are with your charitable choices and reflect upon the acts of giving that made you the happiest. Most likely they're not the largest in monetary value or those you deliberated over the most carefully. Ask yourself the following questions:

- ✔ What do the most satisfying donations have in common?
- ✔ Would you have rather given more money to one cause and not funded another cause at all?
- ✔ Can you perhaps make more of an impact this coming year by giving your time in place of money (or the opposite) to your favourite cause?

When you figure out which acts are most rewarding – and why – you're a step closer to unlocking your personal philanthropic passions.

Spreading the word to help your cause

When you realise that you care passionately about a particular cause, promoting it has real value. If you attract other people and convince them to take an interest, you increase the amount of thinking, action, and donating that occurs. The number of methods for spreading your enthusiasm to others equals the number of people and personalities on the planet, but here's a list with ideas to get you started:

- ✔ **Talk it up:** Instead of starting off conversations with the weather or sport, talk about the exciting things you're doing to save the world.

- ✔ **Use technology to spread the word:** Tap into the power of social networking sites such as Facebook and Twitter to connect your friends with the causes you care about. You can include links for information, send alerts to friends and followers that, say, you're heading to a fundraiser or an all-day volunteering event, and so on.

- ✔ **Become an ambassador for your charity:** Modesty and reserve are great in the right circumstances, but when you want to increase the number of people who know about and contribute to a cause, you need to toss those traits out the window. Let those around you know that you're supporting a worthwhile cause and encourage them to follow you. If you feel uncomfortable doing so, remind yourself that your tooting the charity's horn, not your own. So honk away to your heart's content!

The question isn't 'why help others discover a cause you love?' but 'why not?'.

Amplifying your giving

Check with your employer about whether it matches charitable donations. Thousands of employers match 100 per cent of employees' charitable giving and tens of thousands match a portion of their employees' charitable gifts. Ask your human resources department for a form to fill out – you need to make a copy of your receipt or invoice for your donation.

The UK's official ambassador for philanthropy

Prime Minister Gordon Brown appointed Dame Stephanie Shirley as the UK Government's Founding Ambassador for Philanthropy in 2009 (www.ambassadorsforphilanthropy.com). She writes:

'Apparently I was selected because the powers that be thought I represented a modern model of philanthropy. I hope my selection was because I'd moved from being a cheque-writing giver to someone with strategic ambitions and goals. I also had first-hand knowledge of the goodness and generosity of the British, who welcomed me as a child refugee out of Nazi Germany. I've always been thankful for being welcomed and will never forget it.

In stark contrast to the US, British philanthropists aren't known for talking publicly about their giving and yet this was the simple idea: give philanthropists a voice. If I hear how you do your strategic philanthropy, I may model it. Try it on for size. After all, every single person can become an ambassador for philanthropy.'

Employer matches are one of the best and quickest ways to increase the impact of your philanthropy. If your employer has a charitable-gift-matching programme, find out how to participate and let other employees know about it. If your employer doesn't match charitable donations, ask why. Millions of pounds of potential donations to charities are lost every year because employees don't know about these programmes or don't bother to participate.

For more on multiplying the effect of your charitable donations, head to Chapter 14.

If you're giving a large gift of stock, talk to your accountant or a solicitor familiar with HM Revenue's rules and policies (in the US, consult your tax attorney) about the tax implications. Generally, making donations from taxable accounts and ones that aren't subject to early withdrawal penalties is more advantageous and more sensible. Giving stock is one of the most powerful ways to give, but doing so carefully maximises your impact while minimising your tax burden. Chapter 17 contains more information.

Doing good and doing business at the same time

Philanthropists and social entrepreneurs are building a more efficient and sustainable society that rewards innovation while safeguarding the planet and its resources. The growth of socially- and environmentally-minded businesses creates new incentives, new markets, and new consumers, and most importantly fosters an environment in which businesses compete to give something back to society. You and your business can be part of these endeavours and reap the rewards of doing so.

The key to pairing business goals with philanthropic goals is to think in practical terms. Here's how to go about it:

1. **Find partners who can work with you to turn your dream of a better world into reality.** They need to be as passionate about your cause as you are.

2. **Think of the long-term environmental and social footprint of any enterprise you're engaged in.** Pay particular attention to things such as:

   • How your organisation's structures and incentives influence people's behaviours: for example, do your business's policies engender the kind of sustainable behaviour you want to see?

- What talents you and colleagues have available and how you can tap them to make a positive difference.

- What areas or components of your business's current investments, practices, and long-term purpose promote or can be made to promote sustainability or philanthropy.

3. **Check out new business ideas and think how they may apply to your philanthropic ideas.** Go to business-oriented websites that focus on the management, publicity, or financial challenges facing your organisation. Also consider joining local professional organisations (or global online ones!) that allow you to learn from others facing similar challenges.

Pursuing short-term profit at the expense of high social and environmental costs may be a viable strategy for, say, the next quarter, but long term a business must recognise that it, its investors, and its customers inhabit the planet and so have a responsibility to it.

Guiding family businesses toward philanthropy

Julia Hieber of the Wendel International Centre for Family Enterprise (INSEAD) guides family businesses towards sustainable solutions and philanthropic practices.

'I dream of a human- as well as an eco-friendly compromise between business and societal interests for our present and upcoming generations. Therefore, I initiated the partnership between Ashoka (www.ashoka.org and www.changemakers.org), the world's leading organisation of social entrepreneurs, and the Family Business Network (www.fbn-i.org), an international non-profit association with over 5,500 family business owners as members. The partnership was a huge success. As the demand for socially responsible business practices increased, more and more organisations

focused on linking businesses with social entrepreneurs have emerged, such as www.buildingmarkets.org, the Transformational Business Network (www.tbnetwork.org) and www.clearlysos.com.

I see my work as "pollination": connecting funders, innovators, opportunities, and organisations. My advice to budding philanthropists is to get involved in building bridges between your various networks (professional contacts, social acquaintances, university networks, and others) to promote long-lasting social change! Make sure that you admire and respect the people and organisations you work with, and that they support you in putting your vision into practice. The impact is then far beyond what an individual alone can ever achieve.'

Part II
Knowing Where Your Money Goes: Which Sector Is For You?

Top Five Things to Consider When Choosing an Area of Focus

✔ Who do you want to help most? If its children, look at education, nutrition, safety initiatives and other areas shown to make a big difference in the lives of the young. If it's the elderly, think about healthcare, social activities and opportunities for seniors to become more active and engaged in the community.

✔ How do you work? Search out where your particular approach will make the most impact. There are some areas of philanthropy that are desperate for volunteers and others that are chronically underfunded. By looking at what you can offer you can more easily choose the area where you're needed — and where you have the potential to make the biggest difference.

✔ What are the problems you want to see solved in your lifetime? What characteristics do they have? Who have you seen advocate for solutions to these problems lately? Be sure to examine the momentum already underway in this area and find organisations to support that are already in line with your philanthropic goals.

✔ Are your goals short-term or long-term? Figure out whether you're comfortable helping an organisation with very long-term goals (e.g. curing cancer) or whether you'd prefer to work on projects that you'd get to see completed (e.g. building a park for the local school). By being realistic about your needs you can be realistic about the type of philanthropy you'll find most interesting and most satisfying.

✔ Don't worry about finding a perfect fit. One of the biggest problems in the philanthropic world, and one of the prime reasons for donor dissatisfaction is concern over whether a certain opportunity is a perfect fit. Look into an organisation carefully and don't settle for 'near enough' — it's your hard-earned money at stake here. On the other hand however - don't wait forever to act! Measure up each opportunity carefully and make informed decisions that are right for you.

Go to www.dummies.com/extras/charityandphilanthropy for free online bonus content.

In this Part

✔ Locate an area where you can have a huge impact on the lives of others and understand how the charities active in that area interact with those they serve.

✔ Learn why many problems are so difficult to solve, from education to healthcare.

✔ Find out about amazing new initiatives that are helping people live longer, healthier lives from childhood into old age and how charities are supporting a transition to a world where lives are not only longer, but also better.

✔ Examine how simple ideas, like giving lessons to children over the Internet or creating places in cities for children to play safely, have enormous effects that are likely to make our planet better for decades to come.

✔ Get informed about how everything from exercise to nutrition, to reducing pollution and supporting carers can be part of this exciting new world where people live longer, healthier, happier lives.

Chapter 5

Encouraging Education Around the World

*E*ducation is the gift that really does keep on giving. It upholds the old adage that the best way to help people long term is to show them how to fish as opposed to simply giving them a single fish. When you consider your charitable giving, remember that education is one of the best returns on a charitable investment because everyone wins.

This chapter delves into the different ways you can become an active proponent of quality education for all. We examine a few areas of educational philanthropy and help you decide which type of opportunity is the right fit for your generosity. We take a look at supporting large-scale, physical institutions and small, grass-roots projects – whether through academic education, vocational training, or encouraging cultural pursuits as a passionate pastime – and becoming involved with the positive work of youth groups.

Going to the Head of the Class: Education Philanthropy

> *Education is not the filling of a pail but the lighting of a fire.*
>
> —*William Butler Yeats*

Education opens minds – and doors: that's one of ours!

Some form of public education has existed in the UK since the 7th century, in the US since the 18th century and in every nation that has enjoyed the blessings of democracy and liberty, which shows how education lifts up individuals and societies.

In this section, we look at why education is so important and suggest a few ways for you to get started in helping.

Looking at the positive effects of an educated population

If you need any persuading, here are just a few of the positive effects of education:

- **Improved economic outlook:** A direct, positive connection exists between education and economic progress for individuals and societies. In rich and poor countries, more education translates to more opportunity, more economic stability, and higher income. According to the Center for Global Development, in many poor countries, every additional year of education increases a person's income by 10 per cent, and no country since ancient Rome has achieved continuous and rapid economic growth without reaching an adult literacy rate of at least 40 per cent.

- **Improved health:** People who have more education generally enjoy better health, not only because their higher incomes provide more access to healthcare, but also because they're more likely to use health services effectively, more likely to have proper nutrition, and less likely to smoke or use alcohol to excess. In addition, educated mothers are more likely to raise healthier children.

Making higher-level education attainable, although a worthy goal, isn't necessary to see this last benefit. In developing countries, for example, people who have attained a primary (or grade school) education are half as likely to contract HIV/AIDS as those who don't attain a primary education.

- **More stable, safer societies:** Societies with higher literacy rates generally have more engaged citizens, assert more personal liberties, and better protect human rights. In addition, as education increases, criminal behaviour decreases.

Studies in the UK, US, and Sweden indicate a cause-and-effect relationship between education and crime. In all three countries, criminals tended to be less educated than the rest of the population. One interesting finding in the Swedish study, in which researchers looked at the effects of school reforms that increased mandatory education from

7 to 9 years of age, is that more education has generational effects. Not only were crime rates lower for the men directly affected by the reforms, but also they were lower for those men's sons.

Spreading education around rich and poor countries alike gives rise to challenges related to the quality of education and the lack of access to it. Fortunately, you can play your part in many different but equally rewarding ways:

✔ **Become a teacher and join a programme that provides educators to disadvantaged communities:** Teach First (www.teachfirst.org.uk) is the top organisation in this field in the UK and Teach for America is the equivalent in the US (www.teachforamerica.org). The Teach First/Teach for America model places top college graduates and professionals in low-income areas in the UK and US. Teach for All (www.teachforall.org) applies this model on a worldwide scale, placing nations' top graduates and professionals in the low-income areas of their countries. Contact any of these organisations and speak to a recruiter to find out more information.

✔ **Get involved as a volunteer in your local school:** Involved adults can lift any school system. You can volunteer in the classroom, offer after-school or in-school tutoring, and become an active participant of your local Parent Teacher Organisation.

✔ **Donate to an institution that offers educational opportunities and resources:** The later section 'Supporting Educational Establishments' has more details.

✔ **Find other organisations devoted to education and get involved:** Go to the Education section of Charity Choice (www.charitychoice.co.uk/charities/education-and-training) or the Prince's Trust (www.princeofwales.gov.uk/the-prince-of-wales/the-princes-charities). If you're especially interested in promoting education for children in impoverished parts of the world, check out Care International (www.careinternational.org.uk).

✔ **Apply your talents and work for an organisation that figures out how to get affordable learning tools and programmes to poor communities in developing economies:** One such company is Bridge International (for more details and its opportunities, see www.bridgeinternational academies.com). Head to the section 'Bridging the education gap' for details on the particular education challenges facing students in growing economies.

✔ **Apply your skills and know-how to open-source learning platforms such as Khan Academy** (www.khanacademy.org) **and edX** (www.edx.org)**:** Take a look at the later section 'Providing free education to anyone anywhere: Open-source learning'.

Girl power: Educating women

As important as education is for all people, it has particular importance for girls and women in impoverished countries due to the *multiplier effect* (that is, an investment in educating girls and women yields benefits far in excess of the original investment). Consider these facts:

✔ A woman with six or more years of education is more likely to seek prenatal and postnatal care, reducing the risk of infant and maternal mortality.

✔ Educated mothers are 50 per cent more likely to have their children immunised against preventable diseases than mothers who received no schooling. They're also more likely to have fewer children and provide better education and healthcare for those children.

✔ Countries with more gender equality are more likely to enjoy higher economic growth, and educated women are more likely to participate in the formal labour market and have higher incomes than their uneducated peers.

For more information on girls and education, go to the United Nations Girls' Education Initiative (UNGEI) at www.ungei.org. Also, check out the later section in this chapter 'Volunteering to empower girls around the world'.

Focusing on continuing education and worker re-education

One area of high-impact educational philanthropy is continuing education and worker retraining. With the world (in particular, the developing world) experiencing an unprecedented increase in useful lifespans, more workers may have multiple careers in one lifetime. As a result, mid-career retraining of the workforce is becoming a crucial area of education. However, little philanthropy focuses on funding mid-career workers to take time off, return to school, or upgrade their skills.

Major universities have done little to develop curricula for low-cost, high-value worker retraining, so this area is one in which private funding can help adult students obtain the tools to reach their full potential. In the UK and US, philanthropists often underfund and overlook vocational programmes. In America, community colleges and two-year institutions struggle to offer high-quality education at a reasonable cost, and even a small donation can make a huge difference. One huge problem today is a shortage of workers suited to existing jobs. Mull over your own skills and life experiences to see whether you can contribute. Think of ways in which you can spread your knowledge or make your work more accessible to the next generation. Here are a few ideas:

✔ Ask whether your employer allows you to take on an apprentice or summer intern.

✔ Write a blog or upload a series of videos on YouTube to explain how and why you do what you do.

✔ Check out your local authority (more than half of the over 150 local authorities in England have worker retraining initiatives in place or in development) or local tradesperson's union. The latter are often at the centre of retraining initiatives, especially in towns where factories or manufacturing businesses have closed in recent decades.

Supporting Educational Establishments

When you think of education, you undoubtedly think of schools – and with good reason: the hallowed halls of Britain's finest universities and preparatory schools have fuelled the popular imagination and inspired poetry by the likes of Gray and Swinburne. But other establishments – including lesser-known universities – make significant contributions to education as well. By supporting libraries, museums, universities, and so on, you help to preserve the educational and cultural foundation of a nation. In this section, we discuss such institutions, large and small.

Spreading literacy and knowledge via libraries

Shockingly, 1 billion of the fast-approaching world population of 8 billion can't read or write. As a result, they're locked out from humanity's printed and online knowledge. By supporting libraries of all sorts, you can transform these people's lives. Imagine the power you have to help bring them into the knowledge mix and bridge the digital divide; perhaps you'll find yourself funding the next Einstein or Nobel Laureate! The foundation of all lifelong learning opportunities is the spread of literacy.

But libraries are more than just collections of books you can borrow and old manuscripts you can look at. According to the Society of Chief Librarians, the five main categories of people who use libraries are as follows:

✔ **Career builders:** People who use libraries to prepare for job searches. They go to the library for help in writing their CVs and practising their interviewing skills.

✔ **Health detectives:** Those who use library resources to find out about particular health conditions.

✔ **Little learners:** Children between the ages of 5 and 10 who love reading.

> ✔ **Friend finders:** People who use the library as a place to meet others.
>
> ✔ **Research sleuths:** Those who use the library's resources to perform research on their own families or communities.

Add to this list the role that national libraries – repositories of nations' historical and vital documents – play and you can see that libraries are vital parts of local communities and national identity; they offer important resources for a country's citizens. Unfortunately, in the UK and elsewhere, libraries are being closed at an alarming rate due to budget constraints and the pressures placed on them by other methods of researching information.

Giving to libraries is more than just providing books; it's about spreading ideas and enabling even greater access to know-how. You can support incredible organisations such as the British Library and the US Library of Congress, as well as smaller research libraries and even your local public lending library, in all sorts of ways.

Libraries, whether physical or virtual, are homes to ideas. So use and support them. When you invest in knowledge, you and the whole world receive incredible benefits!

Lending a hand to national libraries

National libraries contain a nation's information – cultural and historical documents, rare and significant manuscripts, copies of all books published in that country, and so on. The nature of the collections means that these libraries are generally not lending libraries, though they do make their collections available to the public for viewing.

Whereas you go to your local library to borrow a copy of Shakespeare's *As You Like It,* for example, you visit the national library (such as the British Library in London) to view the original, valuable quarto edition.

The major national libraries in the UK are as follows:

✔ British Library (www.bl.uk)

✔ National Archives (www.nationalarchives.gov.uk)

✔ National Art Library (www.vam.ac.uk)

✔ National Library for Health (www.evidence.nhs.uk)

✔ National Library of Scotland (www.nls.uk)

✔ National Library of Wales (www.llgc.org.uk)

Each site includes a 'Support us' or 'Get Involved' link that offers ways you can help support the library and its mission through activities such as fundraising, 'adopt a book' programmes, volunteering, posting your own stories about what the library means to you and more.

A passion for spreading knowledge

The Kluge family is a major proponent of providing access to knowledge. Here John Kluge Jr describes his family's philanthropic quest through its efforts at the largest library in the world, the Library of Congress in Washington DC (whose collection holds about 150 million items with over 33 million books and is one of the greatest, yet among the most underappreciated, of all libraries):

'Like Benjamin Franklin, my father believed that an investment in knowledge paid the best interest. His scholarship at Columbia University unlocked the tools he would need in life, the greatest being access to knowledge and new ways of thinking. Two of his projects were helping to launch the Library of Congress's digitisation process and establishing the John W. Kluge Prize for the Study of Humanity, a $1 million grant for a lifetime achievement in the wide range of disciplines not covered by the Nobel Prize – think history, philosophy, anthropology, religion, politics, and so on – the most recent recipient being Fernando Henrique Cardoso, former President of Brazil.'

Helping out at your local library

Perhaps you're thinking to yourself that helping libraries is all about activities reserved for billionaires: endowing new buildings and donating rare collections. Well, we have good news. You can support and contribute to libraries in many different ways.

The most basic method is joining or leading a book drive. Many libraries are looking for good condition books to add to their collections. During these tough times, the budget for new book acquisitions has been evaporating. Book drives help offset this problem. Check with your local librarian to see which titles the library is seeking and then set out on a mission to secure them.

Another wonderful way to get involved with your local library is to join its volunteer reading programme. Often libraries have a scheme where you can go to the library and read literary classics to children. (Primary schools also need volunteers to encourage young children who may be struggling with their reading; for the UK, check out www.vrh.org.uk.)

These volunteer reading schemes are great activities for those in retirement, bringing knowledge and different generations together.

Perhaps the biggest gift you can give is funding the creation of children's books. Some developing countries have few children's books because they're expensive and considered a luxury good. By importing (donating) books in the appropriate language or working with literacy charities (which often license and translate popular children's and young adult literature), you can make a huge difference in the lives of children who otherwise have no access to appropriate literature in their earliest years of education. Orphanages and aid agencies that work directly with children often solicit for books – even one or two books can make an enormous difference to a child.

Don't worry if your budget is more modest than that of a billionaire. You can reach a massive scale, one library at a time.

Room to Read (`www.roomtoread.org/`), a leading literacy non-profit organisation, saw this need at first hand when operating in countries that had entire school systems wiped out from terrible regimes (such as Cambodia during the 1970s). It encourages local youths to write books and illustrate them, securing funding from donors to help get these books in English and the local language. This great project fosters creative thinking and cultural bridges and gifts children with books.

Room to Read's story shows that huge success is possible (check the nearby sidebar 'The success of Room to Read' for the full story).

The success of Room to Read

Room to Read started out ten years ago with five libraries in rural Nepal, 12 volunteers, and a budget of $10,000. It grew to reach 13,000 libraries servicing 6.6 million children and now has 10,000 volunteers across 56 cities worldwide. John Wood describes the turning point and quest to reach this super-scale:

'In 1998 during a trek through Nepal, I came across a school library devoid of books and returned home with echoes of the headmaster's prophecy: "We're too poor to afford education, but until we have education, we will always be poor." A spark was lit, and soon became a bonfire. A year later I returned to that library in Nepal with hundreds of books on the back of a yak and watched crowds of children and parents devour them with joy.

Education, the great equaliser, has the proven power to eradicate poverty. Research and practice demonstrates that when girls in particular learn, their families, communities, and societies benefit. Educated women are more likely to educate and, say, vaccinate their children and fuel their local economies, increasing wages and boosting a country's gross national product. Books and libraries are the ultimate hand-up, not hand-out. Of course no one can guarantee that every child is going to take advantage of them, but if we don't provide these assets, we *can* guarantee perpetual poverty.

A few numbers: Room to Read has placed over 10 million books into the hands of eager young readers in Bangladesh, Cambodia, India, Laos, Nepal, South Africa, Sri Lanka, Tanzania, Vietnam, and Zambia. Over 6 million children have access to the Room to Read network. A new Room to Read library is established every four hours! In the time that it has taken you to read this sidebar, Room to Read has distributed ten children's books. Each day we construct one new school in a country through our challenge grant model, enlisting community involvement through co-investment, and ensuring the psychological ownership and active participation of village residents.'

Preserving and sharing culture: Museums

Museums are a unique way to share, protect, and preserve cultural heritage. They're often the gateway for children to discover new cultures and are powerful places to spark curiosity and lifelong learning. Museums come in all sorts of types and sizes, and here we describe a very large and a very small one.

Meeting the mega-museum

Mega-museums are world-class museums with world-class collections, renowned curators, and programmes that reflect great achievements or events in world history. The classic mega-museum is committed to sharing a wide range of topics across various periods of history. Many have active lending schemes with other mega-museums around the world and sponsor touring exhibitions to introduce the museum's treasures to people around the country. Famous examples of mega-museums include the following:

- **The British Museum (London; www.britishmuseum.org):** Founded in 1753, this museum was the first national public museum in the world. It has ten curatorial and research departments and serves as a hub for social science historical research in England, Europe, and the Anglophone diaspora. Its collection is so large that less than 1 per cent of the collection is on display at any given time. It also has links to key research institutions, including Cambridge, Oxford, the London School of Economics, and the history departments of dozens of universities. It curates, preserves, and researches over 10,000 pieces and is considered the world's most important curatorial authority on historical English-language documents.

- **The Louvre (Paris; www.louvre.fr/en):** Since the Revolution at the end of the 18th century the Louvre has housed all the monuments of the arts and sciences, with other collections being added later. Today it houses the largest collection of many classes of art and has access (in its own or partner collections) to nearly 40 million items, artefacts, documents, paintings, and sculptures. Its collection is so large that the most recent cataloguing of the Louvre took nine years to complete. A searchable database of the collection exists, with information on most catalogued pieces and in-depth information on over 350,000 pieces (www.louvre.fr/en/moteur-de-recherche-oeuvres).

- **The Metropolitan Museum of Art (Met) (New York; www.metmuseum.org):** Established in 1866, its first object was a Roman sarcophagus. Today the museum houses over 2 million objects, tens of thousands of which are on display at any one time. Considered, along with the Smithsonian, the prime repository for art on the American East Coast (and the primary repository for art in New York City), the Met holds the largest collection for a thousand miles in any direction.

> ✔ **The Field Museum (Chicago; `www.fieldmuseum.org`):** Originally part of the Chicago World Fair of 1893, the Field Museum was continued through a significant donation by department store millionaire Marshall Field. Its mission is to accumulate and disseminate knowledge and the preservation and exhibition of artefacts illustrating art, archaeology, science, and history. Today, the museum houses a huge collection of over 21 million items.

Tough times hit mega-museums hard. They're expensive to maintain and often their budgets are the first to be cut during an economic downturn.

You can be a tremendous force in helping to maintain and preserve culture:

> ✔ **Donate your treasure or time:** You can donate to mega-museums directly or volunteer your time. For specific suggestions, visit the museums' websites. Each has some version of a 'Support the Museum' link that offers specific information about making donations, volunteer activities, and more.

> ✔ **Support the museum through your transactions and attendance:** Go to the museum as an outing. They make for great dates, time with children, and moments of quiet reflection. You can also become a member, which in addition to supporting the museum, also gives you the benefits of membership, such as discounts on special exhibit fees, extended hours, and more. Why not find that gift you've been meaning to send in the museum gift shop?

Charting the rise of the boutique museum

Boutique museums – small ones that zero-in on a sliver of time, geography, or theme – are on the rise. Examples of boutique museums include:

> ✔ **Historical sites linked to famous historical figures or events:** Charles Dickens Museum (London), Dickens's London home and collections of his artefacts; Monticello (US), home of third US president Thomas Jefferson; Fort George (Canada), headquarters of the British Army in North America during the War of 1812; and the Ernest Hemingway Museum, near the author's childhood home in Oak Park, Illinois.

> ✔ **Art collections:** Examples include the Rodin Museum (France), home and collection of French artist Auguste Rodin, and the Sorolla Museum (Spain), which houses a collection of Renaissance art.

> ✔ **Technology collections:** Museum of Ancient Greek Technology (Greece); Matsushima Orgel Museum (Japan), a collection of music boxes; and Experience Music Project (US), one of the largest collections of musical instruments and recordings.

Founding an art museum

Donald and Shelley Rubin, the founders of Multiplan, established a boutique museum. They're passionate about art and its role in inspiring others. Even when they were just getting started in life, they made supporting the arts part of their life. Here they share their story:

'We were walking in New York in 1975 when we saw two Tibetan paintings in a gallery and were mesmerised. We found that they cost $1,500 each and used a chunk of our savings to purchase the one we liked better. We were in love; in six months we returned and bought the other painting.

A number of years later we had 500 paintings and sculptures in our office and were conducting tours. We had to decide what to do with the collection and how to share it with the largest possible audience. We knew that if we gave it to a mega-museum, the art would be buried in storage with millions of other objects that the public never sees. We wanted people to see our collection in person, so we looked for a space and bought a wreck of a building from a bankruptcy sale.

We hired a world-famous architect and an award-winning graphic designer. We discovered a lot along the way and had to go back and redo things a few times, but we got it done, even though many people told us it was too complicated and we didn't have the money and expertise. If you have the drive, the imagination and the ability to pick yourself back up after making mistakes, you can make anything happen.'

These small, speciality museums offer you a great opportunity to support advancements or preservation in an area of great interest to you. You can do so through donations, attending programmes, or even working at one as a curator or volunteer.

If you find that museums are the right fit for you, and you're excited about a particular theme, search, visit, and establish relationships with a boutique museum. Who knows, you may even start your own museum one day!

Helping universities: Centres of excellence

Universities are the birthplace of new ideas, innovation, and deep learning. Whether public or private, they all seek benefactors, big and small. These funds help them support promising students who need financial aid and can later provide the university with the tools and environment to produce the next generation of leaders.

Universities in England and Wales have been under particular pressure to increase fundraising efforts since the end, in 2011, of the funding scheme whereby university-raised money had been matched with public funds.

In addition, although donations to universities have increased in the last couple of years, nearly half of the total donated amount went to Oxford and Cambridge. Therefore, many universities can use your help.

Funding a new university department

Establishing a new department at a university is a serious endeavour. It takes clarity of vision, a major funding strategy, and a team of advocates who are deeply passionate about realising the vision. But whether you're super-rich or part of the less well-off 99 per cent, you can participate in the capital campaign of a new university department or research wing. Every penny counts and it all leads to better, deeper, and increased research and learning.

If a particular illness has affected your family and you're keen to see breakthrough medical research carried out, you can participate in funding a new annexe at an appropriate institution.

An excellent example of people coming together around establishing a new school is the Said Business School at the University of Oxford. Wafic Said took on a vital role by providing a major contribution as an anchor piece of the funding strategy. The contribution was given in the form of a matching grant whereby Said would personally match funds raised from other donors. This commitment motivated the school to enlist other potential donors with all sizes of financial pockets.

Endowing a department chair

If your bank account doesn't stretch to creating an entire university wing, you can consider funding a *chair* (a professorship) at a university to help establish a foothold in a fresh area of academic inquiry. Such chairs fuel research and new classes, and permit the university to attract the best and brightest talent. Funding a chair can also spur other philanthropists to get in on the act and fund other educational options.

Sir Peter Moores endowed the Peter Moores Dean and Peter Moores Professor in Management Studies at Oxford. These posts set the stage for the business school to emerge and gave Wafic Said (see the preceding section) the confidence that he was working in a collaborative giving environment.

You can fund a chair for a period or indefinitely. Each university has a different structure on how it manages the funds allocated to a chair, and so be certain to understand the process in detail before donating.

Depending on the amount and duration of the endowment, you may receive naming rights for the chair. More important, however, is to ensure that you're funding a chair that resonates with your long-term quest for a better world.

Bank-rolling university research efforts

In the fictional world of *Indiana Jones,* Indy's mentor was Professor Abner Ravenwood of the University of Chicago, a learned man who pursued knowledge. His passion to get out into the field sparked the young Indiana to become the swashbuckling character that audiences love.

Well, real Indiana Joneses do exist, doing great work to expand human knowledge about, say, the climate and the ancestry of planet Earth, or about historical figures that featured prominently in nations' histories.

For example, the University of Leicester, in collaboration with the Richard III Society and Leicester City Council, uncovered the missing body of King Richard III, the last English king to die in battle (the Battle of Bosworth).

Many such projects – pursued by real-life Ravenwoods and Joneses – need your help. We discuss just one, the work pursued by Bernard Buigues and Professor Daniel Fisher.

Bernard is a French explorer whose passion drives him to endure some of the harshest conditions on Earth in Siberia. He works with the local tribes of reindeer herders as he strives to bring to light scientific insights hidden in the permafrost, which holds within it clues to the planet's last major climate change. Bernard has teamed up with some of the leading minds and universities in the world. One is Professor Daniel Fisher, who conducts his research on woolly mammoths at the University of Michigan's Museum of Palaeontology (see the nearby sidebar 'University of Michigan's Museum of Palaeontology' for more about Daniel's research).

The challenge today is that most university research departments are underfunded. So if you're passionate about learning from the past, discovering scientific breakthroughs for the future, or simply seeking to support endeavours that allow people to better understand the world, consider pointing some of your philanthropic efforts toward this meaningful form of research and discovery.

Many academic disciplines can use your help. To find programmes you want to support, enter the research project or topic followed by 'university research' (for example, 'cancer university research') into an Internet search engine. If you want to support the research programmes at a particular university, enter its name followed by 'research projects' (example, 'Oxford University research projects').

University of Michigan's Museum of Palaeontology

Daniel Fisher is a highly respected expert in mammoths. His research helps people understand the lives of these animals, explore the factors that drove them into extinction, and think about those issues to see what insights can be discerned today. He researches and explores these invaluable lessons in a university setting. The broader mix of the university allows an inter-disciplinary approach and helps spark the next generation of experts to continue the pursuit of this knowledge. Daniel Fisher writes:

'Palaeontology is the study of the history of life on Earth, and like any historical inquiry it contributes crucial perspectives to how humans view the present world. It does so not only by providing isolated glimpses of the past, but also by helping to clarify the nature and magnitude of changes operating over long time scales, enhancing understanding of processes at work in ecosystems of the past and present. My own research reconstructs the lives and environments of mammoths and mastodons (both relatives of elephants) in Ice Age ecosystems of Siberia and North America. I aim to shed new light on climate history, on human interaction with mammoths and mastodons, and on ways of monitoring the status of surviving elephant populations.

At the University of Michigan Museum of Palaeontology, we maintain a strong programme of graduate and undergraduate education and an extensive network of productive international collaborations. By focusing on the past all humans share, we offer an enhanced understanding of the present, providing the best platform for the decisions of tomorrow.'

Giving to your alma mater

At certain times of the year, university graduates receive letters, emails, or phone calls from their alma mater requesting donations (although it sounds like a 1930s singer, *alma mater* means their old university or college). Giving in this way allows you to pay your education forward. Endowments fund renovations, new buildings, student scholarships, and in tougher times they help underwrite operating expenses.

Bigger universities and colleges run specific fund-raising campaigns throughout the year, such as for a particular area of study, a new building, or a scholarship programme. When you're approached in this way, the key is to ask where the funding is going, how it's going to be used, and whether your gift is restricted or unrestricted funding:

- **Unrestricted funds** are a gift that can be allocated at the school's discretion.
- **Restricted funds** are more appropriate when giving a larger gift that you want allocated to a particular area of research or topic.

Consult with a solicitor or lawyer to make sure that you have a signed agreement reflecting your desired restriction (head to Chapter 17 to find out about the different designations). Giving a big or small gift puts money in the school's endowment, which is run like an investment fund. Universities make investments in public and private securities with the goal of reaching a target rate of return. They then parcel-out returns while doing their best to preserve their capital base. In falling stock markets, universities tap into the core capital to meet their operating expenses.

Make sure that the school has sound investment principles. After all, you worked hard for that money. Feel free to ask how the endowment is performing, what it's investing in, and how much of it is allocated on an annual basis. This information gives you a guide to how your contributions are being put to work. You can request these facts from the financial affairs department of the university's administration.

Creating Tomorrow's Leaders: Youth Groups

Today's youth are tomorrow's leaders, and education involves more than just formal academic attainment. You're in a position to be a positive influence on young people by giving the knowledge, experience, and mentoring that help them develop into ethical, good-hearted, well-trained, intelligent leaders.

If a youth cause or organisation speaks to you and you want to help, get in touch with it. Money is wonderful, and if you have it and want to share it, that's great. But if what you can share is yourself, people are going to be thrilled to hear from you.

Volunteering to empower girls around the world

Across the globe 250 million girls live in poverty. They face child marriages and limited access to healthcare, education, and employment for wages. Although they make up 52 per cent of the world's population, women and girls account for 70 per cent of its poor. Yet a very small amount of each international development pound (just 2 pence) is allocated specifically to them or the issues they face.

Guiding girls' futures

The US girl scouts (www.girlscouts.org) and the UK's girl guiding (www.girlguiding.org.uk) organisations are committed to building courage, confidence, and character in girls across the world. Today, millions of girls are supported by tens of thousands of adults. This area is one in which volunteering your time, energy, and experience is just as important as donating money. As Kathy Cloninger, CEO of the Girl Scouts of the USA, writes:

'Philanthropy isn't just about money, and it isn't just for rich people; it's for anyone who believes in a cause and wants to contribute to it.

Overwhelmingly, the most important philanthropic contributions we receive come in the form of the time and talent given us by our volunteers, who outnumber our paid staff by a ratio of about 107 to 1. If we had to pay those volunteers minimum wage for the hours they put in, it would cost us around $5 billion a year – seven times the size of the budget of the entire organisation! We couldn't do it, and we couldn't do what we do without them.'

By giving girls opportunities, such as education, access to healthcare, and microloans, you have a profound effect on not only one girl, but also on her family and community. Whereas an educated boy invests 35 per cent of his future income in his family, studies show that an educated girl invests 90 per cent in her family. She's also more likely to delay marriage, more likely to have fewer children, and less likely to be exposed to HIV/AIDS. In short, the most cost-effective way to lower poverty, uplift families, and help communities is to empower girls.

Increasing employment opportunities

Fostering self-sustaining employment skills is a high-impact charitable opportunity, which builds dignity, confidence, and sustainability. In the US *Trade schools* – also called vocational or career schools – focus on giving people the tools they need to enter the workforce.

Home Depot, the US home-improvement and construction product and service retailer, understands the importance of supporting a culture of craftsmanship. To that end, it runs a $1 million scholarship fund to help support students at leading trade schools. Home Depot is also keen to see the trade schools find innovative ways to help fund its students, and so the scholarships must be matched by the trade schools.

If you're involved in a field that relies on trade schools or are a leading craftsperson, think creatively about how you can inspire your organisation or industry to find ways to support and nurture young talent.

Spreading the Power of Education: Inspirational Stories

As we describe in the earlier section 'Going to the Head of the Class: Education Philanthropy', education is the ultimate gift that can change a person's life. But the challenge is to make sure that everyone has access to a high-quality learning experience. The opportunity for philanthropists like you is to figure out how to make that happen.

In this section, we give you a chance to explore some incredibly inspiring organisations that showcase ways in which you can get involved in education-related charities, therefore helping people across different cultural, geographic, and income divides. These exciting examples enable you to leverage all your giving powers, including your brain. The initiatives cover urban education, *next-generation open-learning tools* (essentially digital educational content available to all), emerging market opportunities (making museums and lectures from the finest universities available to people in rural areas through smartphones and other technologies), post-high-school ideas, and some reinventions of high school itself.

Renewing urban education

Urban education in disadvantaged neighbourhoods needs a serious makeover, and you can play an important role in improving the situation. At present, children in the most challenged areas can fall behind by the equivalent of one year or more of schooling.

You can make a difference in a number of different ways:

- ✔ **Join an afterschool tutoring programme.** Ask your local school about its schemes and how you can apply to become a tutor.

- ✔ **Become a Big Brother or Big Sister.** This organisation works with disadvantaged youth. You can register and find out more information for the US at www.bbbs.org. Chapters are springing up all over, too; for the international side of things, visit www.bbbsi.org.

✔ **Help support a student financially to get access to a private tutor; online private tutors exist as well.** Explore organisations such as www. tutor.com (in the US and Canada) to find a tutor for a disadvantaged student. Due to the international nature of the Internet, you can tutor a student in a faraway place (consider the success of Khan Academy, which we cover in the later section 'Providing free education to anyone anywhere: Open-source learning').

Many places offer tutoring services locally, too, such as Helping Hand Tutoring (Northern Ireland; helpinghandtutoring.co.uk) and First Tutors (UK; www.firsttutors.com). Think about how you can have the largest impact – with Skype and other technologies, you can tutor a child far away nearly as easily (or perhaps more easily!).

✔ **Volunteer at a local community organisation that takes a more far-reaching approach towards education.** Harlem Children's Zone (www. hcz.org) is one such organisation (find out more in the later section 'Pulling together to help an area's children'). Similar organisations exist in most major cities in the UK and US – End Child Poverty (www. endchildpoverty.org.uk) releases a report periodically that often mentions successful programmes.

✔ **Volunteer to create a course on an *open-software platform* (educational content made available for free to people via the Internet) so that everyone everywhere can benefit from your knowledge.** Khan Academy (www.khanacademy.org) is a powerful place to share your knowledge and skills. Check out the later section 'Providing free education to anyone anywhere: Open-source learning'.

✔ **Help young people to tap into their creative talents.** Flip to the later section 'Growing the creative class' for practical suggestions.

Pulling together to help an area's children

Sometimes more than a standalone effort is necessary to transform the educational lives of a child; it takes an entire community. Problems such as deteriorating housing, high crime rates, substance abuse, and low-level parenting skills combine to impact a child before, during, and after the classroom experience.

Lack of adult care and supervision at home and in the classroom can cause low attention spans and truancy issues. More serious acts such as drug dealing can sweep these children into crime networks and derail their opportunities to make an honest, decent living.

Programmes that address the multiple factors impacting a child's readiness to learn, remove distractions that impede the ability to stay focused, and provide ongoing support to bolster educational success are needed. The Harlem Children's Zone (HCZ) tackles these challenges head on (read the nearby sidebar 'Doing whatever it takes: Advice from the front').

Efforts are under way in the UK to create children's zones in the most dis-advantaged regions of the UK. These zones will adopt the HCZ's holistic approach, working with children over time and across all areas that affect their ability to learn and develop. During 2014, local governments and organ-isations such as Save The Children will be implementing zones similar to HCZs in the UK, beginning in London. Keep your eyes out and see whether you can get involved.

Doing whatever it takes: Advice from the front

Harlem Children's Zone provides a full range of educational, social, and health programmes that, when combined, create the conditions for positive, healthy, and fruitful education. It began in the early 1990s with one city block in Central Harlem, New York, and today spans 100 blocks and serves 10,000 children and 7,400 adults. It continues to innovate and collaborate with the community to generate new programmes and to deepen ties to that community, upholding its vision for a perpetual place of learning.

Geoffrey Canada, CEO of Harlem Children's Zone, writes:

'When I talk to philanthropists, I advise them to give from the heart and, of course, to give gen-erously. But I also advise them to channel their passion with clear-eyed intellectual inquiry, to make sure that they support people whose good intentions are matched by good results. "Return on investment" may seem like a cold-hearted business term, but it's equally important in the non-profit world. A well-run non-profit should be asking itself questions such as "what does it spend on administrative costs and what kinds of results has it achieved?", and so donors should do the same. Not every charity can easily quantify its impact in numbers, but potential donors shouldn't be afraid to scruti-nise an organisation.

Also, don't let scepticism overwhelm your impulse to donate. I've often been stunned by the dedication and talent of workers at the Harlem Children's Zone, and countless non-profits can do terrific work with your support. These organ-isations are literally saving lives and making life better for everyone, but they can't run on good intentions. They need books for kids and money to pay for the lights so kids can read those books. Therefore, let your passion for change guide you to making a difference and become a lifelong, generous, and smart philanthropist.'

For information about urban regeneration visit Creative Cities (`creative-cities.britishcouncil.org/`), a project providing information, contacts, and tools to make your town a better place to live. Research on making urban life safer, cleaner, and more enjoyable is an area of growing interest. The London School of Economics has an institute, LSE Cities, studying questions of urban life, city growth, and development – over the coming years, it plans to release research on these issues and what's working (and what isn't) in cities around the world.

Bridging the education gap

Imagine that you can educate children sustainably in sub-Saharan Africa for just £4 a month. Well, you can via Bridge International Academies. Instead of taking a non-profit approach, this organisation is working on building a for-profit social venture (of the type we discuss in Chapter 10). The first school is up and running in Kenya.

Bridge's schools leverage the best in technology learning platforms, mobile payment systems, and community collaboration in order to achieve the best quality at the most affordable price. They enlist, train, and support the talent within the communities they serve, which builds deeper and deeper levels of know-how within the community. This innovative social venture approach helps make the entity self-sustaining and opens up the prospects of reaching the hundreds of millions of children who are traditionally excluded from educational opportunities.

The opportunity here is for you to help fund scholarships that assist families in covering the cost. At such a low price, most individuals and families with means can help a family send their children to a high-quality school programme.

Along with other academies, Bridge continues to find ways to bring great education to those with minimal means, and you can help those students bridge that gap with scholarship support. Discover more at `www.bridgeinternational academies.org`.

Unleashing scientific minds

Many roads lead to Rome and the same goes for investing in children's futures. Although some thrive by going down the academic route, others become leading people in their fields by taking a less conventional, more practical and hands-on path in life.

Traditionally, bright students are encouraged through scholastic recognition, financial scholarships, and other schemes to continue their studies. But far less attention is paid to helping promising individuals become successful entrepreneurs, with most business schools giving away few scholarships. For an unusual programme that encourages talented entrepreneurs-in-the-making who can contribute to the future economy, create jobs, and make lives more enjoyable, check out the nearby sidebar 'Following the Thiel Fellowships'.

Have you ever thought about having your child skip the whole college thing and go straight to work? Perhaps you're cringing and conjuring up visions of a life of hardship, your child trapped in a low-paying job with few prospects for a brighter future. Well, an alternative version of this story exists.

Following the Thiel Fellowships

Peter Thiel, an early investor in Facebook and other ventures, recognised that the process of entrepreneurship often begins before (and independently from) college. He decided to invest in promising young people, but in different ways from the traditional scholarship funds or endowed libraries. Drawing upon his experience as a venture capitalist, Thiel realised that an incentive was needed for people to start working on their business venture ideas instead of taking a more traditional route and going to college and graduating school first.

The Thiel Foundation sponsors, among other programmes, the Thiel Fellowship, which offers no-strings-attached grants to young people so that they can focus on their work or research.

Founder Peter Thiel feels that the traditional bachelor's degree is up for a major makeover:

'The B.A. is a vague and outdated credential. It provides little value to employers, but the cost of acquiring one has more than quadrupled since 1980, on top of inflation [in the US]. Fortunately, there are more efficient and flexible ways to learn

than ever before. The Thiel Fellowship grants talented young people the freedom to pursue the next generation of tech innovation. The best way to learn how to innovate is to innovate.'

The Thiel Fellows programme is part of a larger area of prize philanthropy, which is rooted in the idea that extraordinary people and ventures exist that are outside the normal framework by which things are evaluated. These people don't meet traditional benchmarks, partly because they don't share conventional goals. By identifying people who are extraordinary and perhaps not oriented toward traditional goals (such as being the top student in their class), the Fellows programme identifies and nurtures people otherwise at risk of being bored, overlooked, or underused in a traditional undergraduate environment.

Take a look at www.thielfellowship. org to find out more about this extraordinary organisation and how it helps youngsters to follow their dreams of entrepreneurship and innovation.

Imagine completely re-envisioning your child's life journey as one in which a young mind is nurtured and cultivated all the way through to high school. And imagine that your child shows great aptitude for original thinking and innovation. Take it one step further and help her unleash that talent and make a contribution to society and build a successful venture.

If you think that this idea is crazy, remember that the formal education of one of the greatest inventors of all time, Thomas Edison, stopped after his home schooling. From a young age, he demonstrated scientific curiosity, tinkering, inventing, and drafting experiments. He worked at basic jobs and night shifts just to give himself the time to think during the day. Imagine if he'd been enabled to dedicate himself fully to creating inventions.

This path isn't for all children, but for those who show great promise, helping them through philanthropy may just discover and support the next Thomas Edison.

Think about how children in your own life and your own family can be encouraged to learn and explore in a more holistic way. Many people learn their most important lessons outside of formal classrooms, from friends or summer jobs or experiences in their neighbourhoods. Perhaps you can help cultivate this type of learning in the next generation.

Providing free education to anyone anywhere: Open-source learning

Open-source software developers test, grow, improve, and broaden their user base by providing universal access to their program code so anyone can modify and enhance it. Open-source learning applies this model to education, where educational content is made available online, free-of-charge, to be used, modified, and enhanced, as needed, by the different users.

This section highlights two efforts – the Khan Academy and edX – but you can embrace open-source learning in a number of ways. Helping to provide free education gives you the opportunity to combine your powers of talent, treasure, and time. Consider contributing to the following:

✔ **Share your skills via short instructional videos.** You can post them on websites such as Khan Academy (www.khanacademy.org). If you're a professor, ask your university whether it has plans to provide the coursework online for free. (Find out more about the Khan Academy in the nearby sidebar 'Civilisation requires free education'.)

- ✔ **Spread the talents of your local community at organised meetings.** Skillshare (`www.skillshare.com`) promotes people sharing their abilities.

- ✔ **Create an entire learning software program and have it on an open-source platform by using a tool such as Moodle.** Find out more at `www.moodle.org`.

- ✔ **Share your deep knowledge on a field of interest by building up a page on Wikipedia (`www.wikipedia.org`).** It's the world's largest open-source encyclopaedia.

You can share your knowledge and wisdom in so many ways that people seriously envision a world in which anyone, anywhere can learn anything at any time. All for free and at the pace that suits them.

Khan Academy

Salman Khan started this non-profit learning platform to inspire anyone with access to the Internet to participate in a culture of education. At present, Khan Academy serves around 5 million students per month, and numbers are growing. It has over 3,000 learning units (interactive videos, exercises, and simulations) that visitors can access at `www.khanacademy.org`. The usual format of a unit is 10 minutes long, so people can easily absorb the information.

Civilisation requires free education

Salman Khan, founder of the Khan Academy, writes:

'One of the biggest inflection points in history is starting: the Information Revolution. The pace of change is accelerating faster than any time in history. Given this fact, deep creativity and analytical thinking are no longer optional. Luckily, the same forces that make education an imperative are empowering new types of learning models.

The world can no longer afford only part of the population to be deeply educated. The Khan Academy's vision is to provide a free, world-class education to anyone, anywhere, and to create an institution that can last hundreds of years. We've already delivered 150 million lessons and are just getting started. We believe that students of all ages should have free, unlimited access to top-notch educational content on any topic and be able to consume and master this content at their own pace. A recent 30-day snapshot shows that we had 5,072,554 unique visitors to our website where people spent 1,357,377 hours learning.

Through our volunteer-driven effort, we already have content in Spanish, Portuguese, Bengali, Hindi-Urdu, Russian, Indonesian, and ten other languages.'

You can join in the mix as an educator, mentor, and coach. Also, if you're bilingual or multilingual, you can volunteer your translating skills to help dub or provide subtitles to broaden the accessibility of each learning unit (check out the nearby sidebar 'Civilisation requires free education' for more details).

MIT and Harvard edX

As the world moves toward an open-source mindset, The Massachusetts Institute of Technology, The University of California at Berkeley, The University of Texas at Austin, and Harvard University are leading the charge by offering course materials for free online to nearly all undergraduate and graduate classes. This joint venture is edX (www.edx.org), an initiative endorsed across all learning departments and a tremendous opportunity for people to supplement their educations and feed their curiosity.

Although edX isn't a degree-bearing programme, it's a powerful tool for those at universities around the world. In many places, universities are operating on thin budgets, making it difficult for them to service the needs of their many students.

In one uplifting story of edX, an engineering student named Kunle Adejumo from Nigeria was able to advance his studies through the course materials he discovered on edX. He helped bring these materials to his professor, which ultimately reached even more students.

These kinds of initiatives do well and thrive the more people use them, share them, and encourage others to do likewise. In effect, you can be an ambassador for open-source thinking when you use these platforms and of course when you help develop them.

If you have software abilities, get involved in an open-source initiative in your spare time. You can go to a code-athon and create something new or attend a hackathon and improve an existing open-source resource! You can also build a new app, a new section, or a new functionality that hasn't existed before. Many educational software and web resources need improvement; why not lend a helping hand?

Growing the creative class

If you're a creative person, you have something to offer. Perhaps you're an actor, musician, or dancer seeking to give something back but have limited resources. No worries. The early 21st century is a period of prolific creativity, and people want more and more of it. Shows such as *American Idol* and

X Factor engage millions of viewers in the quest for people of all backgrounds to showcase their best efforts. Citizens get in the mix by casting their votes to choose who wins the talent contests.

Although we applaud these shows as a means of talent discovery, another opportunity is for you to support or volunteer at a school committed to nurturing young talent at an early age. If you have creative gifts, you can volunteer or work at a place encouraging people to unleash their talents. Examples of such organisations include Action for Children's Arts (`www.childrensarts.org.uk`) and Creativity, Culture and Education (CCE; `www.creativitycultureeducation.org`). Creative abilities can be transformed into skilled job opportunities later in life. A wonderful example is the efforts of the renowned singer and painter Tony Bennett. He and his wife turned their love of the arts and friendship with Frank Sinatra into a place where young talent can thrive (see the nearby sidebar 'The Frank Sinatra School of the Arts').

The Frank Sinatra School of the Arts

Tony Bennett writes:

'Giving back through charitable work has grown increasingly important to me over the years. The cause most dear to me is arts education. To be a good artist one must first discover how to be a good student. We must never cease to study and practise the traditions and techniques of our crafts and humble ourselves to become dutiful observers of the world surrounding us.

Public education always suffers budget cuts during tough economic times, and so the arts are disappearing from schools at startling rates. Public access to a quality education is the great equaliser, and so we need schools to be great — for children of all means and backgrounds.

When my wife Susan and I first collaborated with the New York City Department of Education to found the Frank Sinatra School of the Arts, we simultaneously established our non-profit organisation, Exploring the Arts (ETA). We understood from the beginning that we needed a real infrastructure through which we could leverage long-term public/private partnerships. ETA helps us engage our personal and professional networks to raise both public and private donations to provide continued support to the school's arts programmes.

Inspired by the success of our non-profit's partnership with the school, we expanded ETA to support the arts in 13 additional high schools throughout the city. When Susan and I visit these schools and see the students hard at work and enjoying themselves in their arts classes, it fills us with tremendous joy. To find success in a career doing what you love is incredibly fulfilling, but to enable the success of others — that's the greatest reward of all.'

Playing 'games for good'

If you're into board games, video games, sports and the like and think that school was boring and needed a little more fun to it, the world of education (at least online) is coming around to your point of view.

Many people love playing online games. In fact, they love it so much that they clock up over 3 billion hours per week collectively worldwide. Now that's a lot of hours of adventure! Just imagine incorporating the same level of enthusiasm into the classroom. Game designer Jane McGonigal thinks you can. She believes that some of the world's biggest challenges can be overcome by using the same logic, passion, and commitment that people pour into getting epic wins in the gaming world. Read about her ideas in her book *Reality is Broken* (a brilliant read) or find out how she's applying them to improving health at www.superbetter.com.

Some champions are bringing this idea into the classroom, such as Elisa Aragon and Arana Shapiro of Quest to Learn (Q2L). Elisa and Arana are passionate about encouraging learning through the power of play. As a result, with the support of the MacArthur and Gates foundation, they've launched a school programme in New York based on the principles of gaming.

Whereas Q2L offers a classroom built around the game, an increasing number of games are available for organisations that offer up interesting platforms to help engage young people in their educations.

Keep 'games for good' on your radar screen. It allows you to give back, while knowing that children are learning *and* having an amazing time.

To discover more about these ideas, check out the following:

- ✔ www.mindbloom.com: Encourages holistic development in the classroom or at home.
- ✔ www.gamesforchange.org: Apply your talents in creating games for good and sharing them with others.
- ✔ www.worldpeacegame.org: For teachers, concerned parents, or students who want to increase awareness around peacemaking through the power of play and games in the classroom.

For more ideas on how you can use technology to spur philanthropic efforts, head to Chapter 11.

Chapter 6

Surfing the Age Tidal Wave: Helping the Elderly

In This Chapter

▶ Showcasing yourself as an active elder

▶ Understanding the needs of the elderly and their carers

▶ Appraising ways to help the elderly

*L*ife spans in Europe, North America, and the Far East now stretch into the late 80s and are surging into the 100s. This is great news of course, but it does mean that more than just a handful of people are reaching advanced old age. We call this a 'worldwide age tidal wave'. Over the next 10 years, more than 1.65 billion people are going to enter their senior years, a situation that brings with it many possibilities and many challenges.

You see, most societies are still parked in the past. Their economic and national social safety-net systems are built around the expectation that people retire at 65 and go to the great beyond at 67 – a scenario that's no longer the norm. Therefore, people have to re-envision how they're going to collaborate across the generations. Charity and philanthropy are sure to play an essential role in helping to build an inclusive future for all generations.

If you're a senior citizen or have senior citizens in your life, you have lots of philanthropic options available. You can discover opportunities within your immediate and extended family or become so passionate about being involved with elders and their carers that you reach beyond your family and into your community. In this chapter, we explain how changing your mindset can open up possibilities for getting and remaining active in life. Plus, regardless of your current age, we offer several suggestions for ways to get involved – which can be as simple as mowing a neighbour's lawn or visiting a retirement home with your friendly pet!

Building an Active Senior Giveback Lifestyle

Retirement is out. Reinventing yourself is in. You heard it here first!

You've been granted a bonus 20 years of life and the big question is: how will you make the most of them? One way is to expand your concept of retirement so that it includes purpose-driven activities and philanthropy. You have a chance to give back and share your life lessons. In this section, we outline some ideas for building an active giving lifestyle in your bonus years.

Redefining retirement: Pursuing an encore career

The old retirement dream goes something like this: you work hard, retire (after receiving a plaque or cake commemorating your service) and go on a permanent holiday. At first, the allure of exotic travel, golf-course membership, and visits with the grandchildren sounds appealing. After all, this is your time to kick back, relax, and enjoy the fruits of your labour. Eventually, however, if you're like most people, after a few rounds of golf you sink into your sofa and become a professional couch potato (watching your waistline expand and endless afternoon repeats on TV).

We'd like you to consider an alternative path: you work hard and retire (same cake and commemoration) but this time you embark on a purpose-driven life. You think about your passion, pursue meaningful and rewarding activities, explore fresh career possibilities, and integrate the work/life balance that you always wanted throughout your career. In this alternative version, life becomes an incredible opportunity to discover new things and to share with others the life lessons you've learned.

Everyone has a chance at a fulfilling purpose-driven life. Take it!

Volunteering your hard-earned skills

Volunteering is a wonderful way to give back by sharing the skills and insights you have accumulated over a lifetime. As an older person with a lifetime of experiences and capabilities to share, your talents can be vital to organisations that help others or make the world better.

Exploring your power as a senior: Civic Ventures

Marc Freedman, the founder of Civic Ventures, believes that everyone has a chance to be a powerful force as a senior citizen. He writes:

'Every 13 minutes, 100 people in the US turn 60. That's great news for philanthropy. In his book, *Drive,* management expert Dan Pink sees 60th birthdays as watershed moments, a time when people begin grappling with questions of mortality and possibility. "When the cold front of demographics meets the warm front of unrealised dreams," Pink writes, "the result will be a thunderstorm of purpose the likes of which the world has never seen."

That thunderstorm is here. In the US, 9 million people aged 44 to 70 are in encore careers that combine greater meaning, continued income, and social impact. And 31 million more want to be.

Today, people in the second half of life are:

✔ **Leading the field of social entrepreneurship.** Jenny Bowen was a screenwriter in her 50s when she saw a photo of a neglected girl in a Chinese welfare institution. By 1998, she'd adopted two girls from China and launched Half the Sky Foundation to change radically the way China cares for its 800,000 orphans. Today the organisation operates in 51 Chinese cities, providing infant care, pre-school programmes, free medical services for disabled children, and financial support for foster families caring for AIDS orphans.

✔ **Providing top talent to non-profits through Encore Fellowships.** Louisa Hellegers was a publishing editor for 40 years when she began looking for work with more meaning. She's now an Encore Fellow in New York City, working half-time for a non-profit that provides employment services for people recently released from prison. Intel, the giant chip-maker, recently announced that it would provide all its retirement-eligible employees in the US the chance to do Encore Fellowships for the greater good.

✔ **Going back to school for job training, not enrichment.** After 27 years with the national government, Mattie Ruffin retired. After a year's rest, she got restless and took a course at a Maryland community college to help her figure out next steps. She's now working at Prince George's Community College, helping adults revisit and expand their secondary-level educations. Scores of community colleges now help people retrain for encore careers in education, healthcare, social services, and the environment.

So happy birthday to all those turning 60. For tens of millions of you, the next decades will be full of work with purpose. For thousands of non-profits, it may be time to celebrate.'

The good news is that endless opportunities exist for getting involved to make a difference. In the following list, we explore some of those options:

✔ **Offering your technical and professional skills.** The first place to tap into your civic spirit is to volunteer your technical skills. In Chapter 13, we discuss how you can make use of your specific talents to help others or to support causes you believe in. Regardless of your background or field of interest – banker, accountant, lawyer, techie, mechanic, plumber, teacher, waitress, doctor, or whatever – you can become engaged in making the world a better place.

✔ **Volunteering with an organisation that helps seniors get involved in their communities.** These organisations include the UK's Royal Voluntary Service (www.royalvoluntaryservice.org.uk) and the US's National Corporation for National and Community Service (also known as Senior Corps).

If you're a senior in the US, check out Senior Corps. According to Dr Erwin Tan, Senior Corps' former director, Senior Corps offers programmes, such as the Foster Grandparents Program and RSVP, which give seniors direct opportunities to redefine retirement and what it means to be a senior:

- **Foster Grandparent Program:** Connects seniors with young children who're missing senior role models. It's an excellent opportunity for them to mentor young people and deepen the ties between generations.

  If you're specifically looking to help youth, consider this programme, which matches loving and experienced tutors and mentors to children and youth with special needs. Working one-on-one, Foster Grandparents provides support in schools, hospitals, drug treatment centres, prisons and young offender institutions, and child care centres. Among other activities, they review schoolwork, reinforce values, teach parenting skills to young parents, and care for premature infants and children with disabilities. Those who meet certain income guidelines receive a small stipend.

- **RSVP:** Lets seniors engage in a diverse range of volunteer activities, including tutoring children, building homes, assisting victims of natural disasters, and recruiting and managing other volunteers at local non-profits. RSVP volunteers choose how, where, and how often they want to serve, with commitments ranging from a few hours to 40 hours per week.

- **Senior Companion Program:** Allows seniors to help other seniors maintain independence by assisting with things such as shopping for groceries and paying bills; providing friendship and companionship; alerting doctors and family members to potential problems; and providing respite to family carers.

To sign up for any of these programmes or find out more about Senior Corps, go to www.nationalservice.gov/programs/senior-corps.

Sharing your experiences and stories

Over a lifetime you gather plenty of stories and anecdotes: simple, funny family stories, experiences that may be the missing pieces to a puzzle that can lead eventually to a scientific breakthrough or personal accounts of what life was like 'back in the day'. As you move into the sage zone, the time is ripe for you to share your stories.

Sharing your stories is an act of philanthropy that helps the planet become an ever-better place for everyone. Your stories can help the next generation feel connected to a common past, build relationships between generations, and reaffirm that all people have experiences that are unique and universal.

Every single person on the planet has a story to tell and that means *you* (imagine a poster with a pointing finger here!). So make sure that you share them. The good news is that many tools make telling your stories inexpensive, simple, and quick. You can videotape or audiotape yourself telling stories or write them out and pass them on in print. You can share your stories in a secure, safe, and private manner, or you can broadcast them at large. Whatever style or dissemination method suits your fancy, sharing your reflections on life is a powerful way to improve the world. In the following section, we share some of the organisations and tools that can help you save your stories for posterity.

Having a national conversation: The Listening Project

The Listening Project (`www.bbc.co.uk/radio4/features/ the-listening-project`) is a collaboration between the BBC and the British Library. Although not limited solely to seniors, it invites people around the UK to record their conversations with loved ones to preserve the stories for future generations. Some recordings are to be archived in the British Library.

Inspired by the US's StoryCorps, which you can read about in the next section, the Listening Project provides step-by-step instructions on how to record and upload your conversations.

Sharing your life experience with everyone: StoryCorps

StoryCorps (`www.storycorps.org`) is a brilliant non-profit organisation that helps you create professional recordings of your story and then share it with the world via the American Folklife Center at the United States Library of Congress. The organisation was founded on the principle that having people share their stories builds bridges between the generations and between people of different backgrounds.

StoryCorps has Story Booths in local communities. Originally, two facilitators held up to six 40-minute sessions a day and helped participants tell their stories, using professional equipment to record it. At the end of the session, participants received a free CD and a copy was sent to the American Folklife Center. Over the years, however, StoryCorps developed other tools and innovative ways of sharing the stories, including accompanying the audio with animated short videos. StoryCorps provides all the inspiration, tools, and guides to help you. StoryCorps works with NPR partners, including the BBC and CBC (Canada) to gather important audio stories from the Anglophone world.

To share your story through StoryCorps, make a reservation with the organisation in your community (go online at `www.storycorps.org`). If you're unable to find a local StoryCorps or you prefer the DIY approach, you can rent a StoryKit and make and submit your own recording.

Another way you can get involved is to expand this opportunity by facilitating a partnership with a local organisation that can set up a local Story Booth. Partnerships range from local libraries and museums to medical groups and others. Look at some of StoryCorps' current partners and see whether you can think of a great partnership in your community. After you identify a community partner, go to the 'Bring StoryCorps to your organisation' section and begin an application process that can help you activate this opportunity.

A word from Dave Isay, founder of StoryCorps

Every life is a story and for Dave Isay, the founder of StoryCorps, each life matters. Here, Dave shares the story of how this amazing storytelling organisation engages individuals and their communities:

'Since 2003, StoryCorps has allowed over 40,000 people around the US to share their stories with a family member, friend, or loved one. Each of these stories is recorded – a copy goes home with the participants and a second copy goes to the Library of Congress for future generations. In many ways, the act of interviewing someone is a way of telling them how much you love them and how much you value their life and story. Especially in this era of social networking, to stop, look someone in the eye, and tell them how much they matter by listening is a profound act.

The true power of this great body of American wisdom lies in sharing it with the public, which we do through our radio broadcasts, animations, books, and in the classroom. Through the simple act of listening, these stories reinforce people's shared humanity, help build connections between them, and, most importantly, weave into the fabric of our culture the idea upon which StoryCorps was founded – that each life matters equally.'

Creating Support Communities

Since the 1960s, the West has seen a massive shift from the traditional culture of a *nuclear family* (parents and children living in one home with events like relocation and divorce being rare and children living with parents until marriage) into the *scattered* family lifestyle (parents and children being individual units often undergoing constant geographical and lifestyle transitions). Whereas families used to share daily meals, family time, and multi-generational households, they now eat on their own, are overscheduled with activities, and rarely live together.

Although both family cultures have their pros and cons, the scattered family faces intense pressures when a family member enters very old age. The first cracks in the system show up in less and less available time. Ask anyone with small children and aging parents how much free time they have. The answer is nearly always zero! If you're part of this group, you carry the name of the Sandwich Generation (make ours a BLT!).

These challenges mushroom with the serious pressures of nurturing small children and falling into a reverse parenting role with your own parents. Exacerbating an already difficult situation are two current trends:

- ✔ **Household finances:** People are saving less and tend to live on expensive credit.
- ✔ **Living locations:** People often live vast distances from their parents.

This combination of time pressures, low levels of savings, increasing expenses, and living far away from family support systems produces a culture of incredible stress and serious health impacts. (Chapter 8 goes into more detail about how this situation affects carers.)

The good news is that you can redirect your path and avoid this mess. If you work really hard at it, you can even flourish and thrive, though it takes many acts of charity and philanthropy, big and small.

Building a tribe: Help for carers

A tribe is different from a family. You can be born into a tribe, but you can also choose to join a tribe. The modern world demands that we both integrate our identities into our work and adopt new identities as times change, as people age, and as our capabilities expand. Among the most important new roles people are learning to play are the roles related to supporting and enhancing the lives of elder members of the tribe.

A personal discovery: Michael Lindenmayer, founder of the Wisdom Flame

Michael T. S. Lindenmayer, one of the authors of this book and founder of the Wisdom Flame, is deeply passionate about carers, elders, and strong families. Here he shares his vision:

'Life is a journey and navigating the aging-to-saging zone can be turbulent. It makes you explore your values, tests the limits of your abilities, and offers everyone a unique chance to come together as a tribe.

During my early 30s, I lived in Rio de Janeiro. Adventure, friends, and meaningful work filled my sun-drenched samba-life in Brazil. Then my life path took a radical redirect with a brief visit to my family. They live in a small, beautiful lakeside town in the Midwest in the US. Yet all was not well on the home front. During my 14 years of international living, I had failed to see the brewing storm of parents burned-out with caregiving, a grandpa struggling to transform his aging into a saging experience, and an absentee third generation. The entire situation had put a serious economic, emotional, and health strain on the family.

So I packed my bags, said goodbye to Brazil, and moved back in with my parents. I was determined to help my family and all families find the strength, courage, and commitment needed to transform themselves into thriving tribes that respect their carers and invite their elders to be sages.

As I learned from my family, other families, and leading experts in the field of aging and caregiving, I wrestled with the question of why people ignored this issue until it smashed them over the head with a crisis. As I investigated further, I discovered the one major roadblock: the absence of a safe, welcoming, and supportive space to talk about the struggles that accompany this part of life's journey. And without that safe place to trade stories, learn new life skills, and build support networks, most people end up muddling through this life phase, going from crisis to crisis feeling misunderstood and alone.

That's why I founded the Wisdom Flame, an educational endeavour that runs workshops and lunches and provides materials to help people wake up to the issue, create a plan, and start building their tribe.'

The Wisdom Flame is a community-led initiative that helps families navigate the challenges of aging and caregiving. It helps bring about important conversations that help care for the carers and engage elders.

The Wisdom Flame is guided by a simple metaphor, the campfire. Anyone who has built a campfire knows that you need to feed it in order for it to last and burn bright; otherwise it burns out. The family is the campfire and by feeding your insights across the generations into that campfire, it can burn bright with wisdom. Building a campfire takes collaboration and vigilance and the Wisdom Flame offers the opportunity for you to expand your definition of family. Your family is a tribe composed of your immediate family, friends, and select professionals. The most effective tribes meet regularly, build trust, work through challenges, and celebrate together.

The Wisdom Flame encourages everyone to engage in this conversation, cultivate your tribe, and build a bright-burning wisdom flame that guides your family from generation to generation. To find out more, go to www. wisdomflame.com.

Encouraging a spirit of trust between the generations

Trust is important in the context of family relationships and caring. In essence, the conflicts between the generations can be summed up as the struggle to meet the demands of the elders, who are seeking maximum independence, and the needs of the carers, who want the greatest safety for their loved ones and respect for their efforts.

Family members are inter-dependent and people must find ways to collaborate, share resources, and be mindful of everyone's needs. To accomplish this goal, you have to build bridges of trust between the generations.

Such a bridge is possible when you talk about the tough topics, co-create a shared vision, and entrust each other to do their part in realising the plan. To entrust someone, you must have earned, accumulated, and protected enough trust through one good deed or kind act at some time. Here are some great ways to build trust between the generations:

- ✔ **Listen then speak:** Helps you understand each other's point of view.

- ✔ **Use 'I' phrases when expressing any challenges being experienced:** For example, say 'I feel hurt when this or that happens' and not 'You hurt me . . .'. The latter phrases open the door for the blame game and erode trust and bridge-building.

- ✔ **Share meals together on a regular basis:** Meals offer the opportunity for uninterrupted conversation, which is the building block for trust.

Think of trust as being like your bank account, into which you make deposits and out of which you make debits. You can grow the account or make choices that lead to bankruptcy. One of the most powerful philanthropic gifts is to leave a legacy of a trust account brimming with goodwill and wisdom.

Activating all the generations of your community

Most people know only a handful of people outside of their age group. How many people do you know, for example, who are 20 to 30 years over or under your current age?

The problem with maintaining this sort of mono-generational perspective is that it narrows your broader world perspective, limits your exposure to time-tested knowledge, and handicaps your ability to benefit from mentoring. It also straightjackets your conversations to the limited confines of your current environment. If you chat about homework with only your peers in school, swap work-related stuff only with your colleagues, or compare doctors only with others of your age, you miss out on the richly layered conversations that can emerge when generations mix it up together.

You have a chance to change this mono-generational culture. One of the first things you can do is to recognise whether you categorise, or pigeonhole, people by age (even unintentionally) – for example, all children report to school, all young adults to college, all middle-aged people to big, tall buildings for work, and all old people to retirement homes. With a perspective that relegates people to cookie-cutter roles and purpose based on age, you miss out on all the amazing ideas and opportunities a more open mindset has for collaboration with people outside your own generation.

You can find great value and unleash tremendous potential by bringing together the different generations. The lessons learnt from various generations' experiences are all valuable. When you blend them together, everyone's better for it.

Here are some ways you can expand your own interactions beyond your own generation:

- ✔ **Join a cause that taps into the talents of people from many generations.** Philanthropy is a great opportunity to bring the generations together. With so many different ways to contribute through your time, talent, treasure, and transactions, every generation can find a way to be part of a team effort.

  Local events centred on preparing food or enjoying music are great places for the generations to come together, for example, as they allow for individual creativity while offering a focal point for the community.

- ✔ **Involve multiple generations of your family in determining which cause to support.** Philanthropy is a way to explore your family's values. Sometimes this can be a feisty affair because people may differ on the best solution for helping others. Some lean towards government-sponsored programmes, while others prefer the civic and private sector as the main means of helping improve the lives of the less fortunate. Yet almost all generations agree that being charitable and philanthropic is the right thing to do.

✔ **Make your advisory board multi-generational.** If you're running a charitable organisation, consider having a multi-generational advisory board that can help provide the right mix of innovation, creativity, and experience.

Helping the Elderly

Interactions with elders give you a chance to exercise your compassion, ingenuity, and patience, valuable attributes that drive you from the heart, spark innovation, and help you develop the endurance to see things through in life. In this section, we outline some causes that help the elderly.

In addition to helping the elderly, seek to be a wise elder yourself and one day a sage. Lead by example through continued engagement in society. Retreating and waiting to fade out is the trend today only because most people no longer make the effort to bring the generations together to share their respective insights. So strive to open those spaces back up.

Volunteering at elder care communities

Although more and more centenarians are showcasing their youthful ways by climbing mountains or securing advanced university degrees, the hard truth is that, for most people, the last few years of life can be difficult. Illness can sink in its teeth, eventually requiring the services of assisted-living facilities.

Such communities that pay attention to the smallest of details and benchmark themselves to the highest standards deserve respect. But the vital ingredient that transforms these places from medical facilities and assisted-living residences into thriving communities is you.

Yes, *you* hold the key to transform a place into a true home for the elderly. One of the simplest things you can do is visit or volunteer for a care companion programme in your area. Most elderly people have few visitors. Their children live far away and are busy at work, and so older people spend most of their days alone in their rooms watching television. Your companionship changes that in a major way. You uplift their spirits, learn from their life stories, and cultivate the powers of patience and radical listening.

The gifts of patience, listening, and compassion come alive most when you spend time with people gripped by full-blown Alzheimer's. In most cases, when many of the memories are gone, pure compassion is what can connect with them; now, that's true unalloyed philanthropy.

Being supportive of elders

If you're on the younger side and passionate about your elders, you can contribute your energies as a volunteer in a number of significant ways. In the UK, Age UK (www.ageuk.org.uk) is a great organisation that helps you engage the senior community. To volunteer your energies and efforts, go to the website, your gateway to a world of philanthropic possibilities.

Some of the volunteer opportunities Age UK offers you include the following:

✔ **Befriender:** Many elderly people are alone and isolated. You can visit them in their homes, assisted-living facilities, or community centres for the elderly. They appreciate your energy and presence.

✔ **Fundraiser:** If you feel that you're better behind a desk working the phones, you can help with fundraising. If you have a technical skill to contribute, you can investigate volunteer opportunities at Age UK's headquarters as well (in London).

✔ **Gardener:** Everyone loves a beautiful garden, but for some seniors caring for and maintaining a garden is beyond their physical abilities. You can make their homes lovely by helping them in the garden. Dig up some weeds, plant flowers for the new season, or grow vegetables that you can rustle into a meal for them to enjoy.

✔ **Handyperson:** Many elderly people's homes or flats fall into disrepair because of difficulties related to doing heavy work or handling tools and concerns over expensive bills. If you have a knack for fixing things, lend a hand to a senior; they're sure to be grateful for the help.

✔ **IT coach:** Many seniors want to be on the information superhighway, but getting onto it can seem impossible. If you're tech savvy, you can help open a whole new world for the elderly by giving them access to email, social networks, online information, and more.

✔ **Store volunteer:** Age UK has a network of 470 charity stores stocked with donated goods and run mainly by volunteers. The position doesn't require any experience, just your great energy, hard work ethic, and common sense. All are welcome.

Feeding your elders

As elderly people retreat to their homes and assisted-living facilities, people outside that generation become less aware of their needs. One of the invisible crises that you can help fix is senior hunger.

Meals on Wheels is tackling this issue, providing meals to seniors who need them each day. Some programmes serve meals at locations such as care homes and extended-stay medical facilities whereas others deliver meals directly to seniors whose mobility is limited; many programmes provide both services.

Numerous volunteer opportunities exist at a Meals On Wheels programme near you, though specific openings vary from one location to another. Here are some options:

✔ **Drivers and delivery people:** Drivers pick up meals at a central location and then deliver the meals to Meals On Wheels recipients.

✔ **Meal preparation and packaging:** At many programmes, you can assist in the kitchen, preparing or packing meals for delivery.

✔ **Office help:** Many programmes can use your help to provide administrative and clerical support.

✔ **Special events:** All Meals On Wheels operations have events and fundraisers that require extra help – including planning and organising, publicity, onsite set-up, and staffing; ask your local programme about upcoming events.

Your interests and abilities can help at a local Meals On Wheels programme – whether you want to be hands-on or behind the scenes, and whether you can volunteer during weekdays, evenings, or weekends. Call your local organisation to find out how you can help. To find out more, visit `http://www.royalvoluntaryservice.org.uk/how-we-help/services-we-provide/practical-support-at-home/meals-on-wheels` in the UK or `www.mowaa.org` in the US.

A word from the founder of Meals on Wheels

Meals on Wheels serves millions of meals every year. Its founder, Enid Borden, is passionate about ending senior hunger.

'You don't see them at food banks because they're homebound and can't get out of their houses. You don't see them scavenging through dustbins. You don't see them begging on street corners. You don't see them at all. They live in a world so insulated and often abandoned that you don't know that they may be your neighbours down the street or down the hall. They live in a world of memories and little hope. They live in rundown tenements and in tract housing that they've shared with their grandchildren for years. They live in wealthy and poor areas. They live among us, yet miles apart from us. They all share something in common: they don't want you to know that they're in need – that they're hungry.

In 2005, nearly five million US seniors faced the threat of hunger. For 2010, just five years later, that number had soared to 8.3 million, increasing not only in numbers, as the population grew, but also in terms of percentage – from 1 in 9 to 1 in 7.

The Meals On Wheels Association of America is the oldest and largest national organisation representing local, community-based Senior Nutrition Programs in all 50 US states, as well as the US Territories. These programmes provide over one million meals to seniors who need them each day.'

Sharing your pets with your elders

You love your pets. Elderly people do, too! Unfortunately, many seniors who'd benefit from the love of a pet have to do without, because they can no longer care for or afford a cuddly companion or they live in facilities that don't allow pets.

Fortunately, you can give elders an opportunity to reconnect with animals by taking your pet for visits in assisted-living residences! Here are some things to keep in mind:

- Dogs tend to be the best and most welcomed at retirement homes. They have an intuitive way of emotionally interacting with people and their presence brings big smiles all round.

- Make certain that you call in advance to confirm that the facility is pet friendly. Also check which residents are open to having a pet visit them and the appropriate hours for bringing your happy pet to spend time.

Not every dog makes a good visitor. Well-behaved, calm, friendly, mannerly, and patient are the keys (and for your dog as well!).

✔ Make sure that your pet is appropriately groomed and up to date on all its vaccinations. Some of the elderly residents may have weakened immune systems and some facilities have requirements about the immunisations of visiting pets.

✔ Some organisations play matchmaker: FriendshipWorks in Boston, for example, has a specific programme called Paws, Pearls and Pals. You most likely have a similar programme in your community. Visit the organisation, meet the pets, and evaluate whether they're calm, clean, and appropriate for visitation with elders.

If no such programme exists in your community, consider it a great opportunity to take a leadership role and develop one. It's a joyful pursuit and one that makes everyone – the pet, the pet's owner, and the elder – happy.

If you want more than a temporary visit of a dog as a senior and you want to bring a furry friend into your life for companionship, great programmes are available for you, too:

✔ **Pets for People:** Supported by Nestlé, the owners of Purina dog food, this programme may be for you if you're over 55. Pets for People helps underwrite pet adoption. You can discover more information at www.petsforpeople.com, where you can explore the tab titled Purina Pet Adoption. Note: these programmes, often US-based, are constantly looking for opportunities to expand the concept to new places; why not start a Pets-for-People-type organisation in your community?

✔ **The Cinnamon Trust:** Sometimes an elderly person has a beloved pet, but is unable to help walk or take care of it. This UK organisation helps elderly people keep their pets or minds them if a client has a stay in hospital. You can find out more at www.cinnamon.org.uk.

✔ **The Royal Society for the Prevention of Cruelty to Animals:** This UK organisation encourages elderly people to adopt a pet as a great source of companionship. Check out www.rspca.org.uk.

Chapter 7

Nurturing the Planet's Children

. . . .

In This Chapter

▶ Assessing children's charities

▶ Providing opportunities for play

▶ Focusing on education challenges facing children and teens

▶ Providing environments in which children can thrive

. . . .

Children have been at the centre of receiving philanthropy for a thousand years or more and even a brief moment's consideration reveals why: nearly every culture across the globe views children as being a hope for the future. Even if the current working-age generation of a developing country is sick, illiterate, or without job skills, hope exists for the next generation. Everyone who wants to see a better society (and for those who don't we ask, 'Why on Earth not?') feels the impulse to influence positively the people who're going to populate (and lead) that society.

In this chapter, we take a look at the problems young people face today, focusing particularly on the importance of therapeutic play, good education for all ages, and safe places to grow up.

Getting Started in Children's Charities

The issues that children face today aren't new, but the inequality in childhood is large and growing. Children in some communities have vastly safer, more educational, and more nurturing childhood experiences than children in other communities – often ones that are only a postcode away. The present and future generations benefit from the building of environments in which children can enjoy safe neighbourhoods, academic excellence, and nurturing environments.

Choosing a children's cause or charity can be tricky, but to get you started here are a few questions to consider:

✔ **Where do you want to support children?** You can support projects around the corner in your own community, in your nation, or farther away in developing countries.

✔ **What form do you want your support to take?** You can support children in many different ways, from donating money, time, and skills, to fundraising for children's causes.

✔ **What type of charity do you want to support?** When answering this question, consider the following:

- **Who the charity targets:** Do you want to support individual children, groups of children, children's parents, or perhaps an entire community?

- **Size and scope of the charity:** Do you want to work through a large, well-known charity or a small-scale, local one?

- **What your preferred charity needs to provide:** If you're interested in children's education, for example, do you want to support a charity that provides educational facilities or one directly involved with educating children?

Check out the Internet to find a children's charity that ticks all your boxes. Three excellent websites are www.charitynavigator.org, www.charitychoice.co.uk, and www.timebank.org.uk.

Children are in need around the world and the costs of providing play areas, education, food, and shelter vary from country to country. You have to decide for yourself which children you want your philanthropy to benefit most directly, bearing in mind that your money may go further in different areas, depending on the current financial situation of the nation involved.

The charity you're considering should be able to tell you not only how much of your donation goes towards its programmes, but also what it accomplishes (for example, that a donation of £30 provides, say, a hot lunch to 25 children). Of course, not everything is easily quantifiable (the amount of care or play a child receives, for instance, is difficult to measure), but the charity should be able to provide some useful measurements, such as how many hours per week the volunteers play sports with children or how many trips to art museums and similar cultural attractions the organisation provides each academic year.

A word about child-sponsorship programmes

Child sponsorship programmes are ones in which you make a donation to sponsor a particular child in a developing country. These funds may be used in ways that benefit the child directly or indirectly, building a school or a medical centre in the child's community, for example. Often, in these programmes, you receive pictures of and letters from your child. These programmes are very popular and you may be interested in participating in one. If so, keep these things in mind:

✔ **Some higher-profile child-sponsorship organisations have been criticised for high overhead costs, including the use of expensive television advertising.** Some people argue, however, that these high advertising budgets are necessary to make potential donors aware of the organisation.

Remember, you have every right to ask an organisation what percentage of your donation goes directly towards helping children – looking at the organisation's budget is even better! Organisations with good accounting practices often show how much of their annual budget is spent on *media buys* (otherwise known as advertising) and direct mail.

✔ **Many child-sponsorship organisations are religious in origin.** Some welcome all children in need of help; others are outwardly evangelical or unwilling to help those with differing religious beliefs. If the religious beliefs of an organisation are important to you, look into how and why an organisation's religious affiliation may affect its behaviour.

The website `www.charitynavigator.org` rates charity organisations, including those using the sponsor-a-child model. It rates religious and non-religious organisations alongside one another, which can be helpful to donors balancing the priorities of maximising funding going to a child and the organisation's religious beliefs or affiliation.

✔ **Some child sponsor programmes have been accused of fraud or engaging in unethical practices.** Although many reputable organisations use the child-sponsorship model, some child-sponsorship organisations have been accused of committing fraud, sending fabricated updates from children, or using children unethically in their appeals, fundraising materials, photographs, or videos. Look into the history and practices of the organisation you plan to work with *before* sponsoring a child to avoid the fraudsters and exploiters. For information on checking out whether a charity is on the up-and-up, head to Chapter 4.

Creating Play Spaces for Children

The challenge of shrinking play spaces is immense, with many children no longer having the space at the end of the road or the playground next to the school. In many cities, substantially less public space is available than existed in the 1960s or 1970s. Even cities such as Chicago and London (which have set aside large areas for public use into the distant future) have seen these public places change in character due to increased crime, traffic, and other challenges.

When public space shrinks, play space often shrinks too, but disproportionately. This reduction is worsened by the recent patterns of cuts in the UK and US – children have less time to play outside during the school day and so playgrounds are put to other uses. A playground that may have been a vibrant area of exercise, socialisation, and creativity after school is destroyed because of a new school schedule.

A re-focusing on education in the UK, US, and elsewhere on doing well on tests instead of on things that are less-readily tested (but no less important) – such as developing co-operation, management, social and persuasive skills – play is less likely to be encouraged today than ever before. What was seen as a crucial setting for social development and growth is today often ignored or actively sabotaged as schools increasingly focus only on test scores.

Other aspects exacerbating the problem include the following:

- ✔ **Municipal budgets:** In hard economic times, city parks and other public spaces often suffer budget cuts that affect not only the upkeep of the parks, but also shorten park hours and eliminate programmes designed to attract families and children.

- ✔ **Trends towards suburbanisation:** As more and more people move out of mid-sized cities and into suburbs, community parks in urban areas are left with fewer resources and fewer visitors. Compounding the problem are neighbourhoods where the spaces between houses are themselves the size of small parks, thus eliminating the need for *community* spaces where children can congregate and play.

- ✔ **Growing divide between 'rich' and 'poor' neighbourhoods:** As neighbourhoods become economically segregated – with wealthier families living in some parts of town, poor families living in others and never the twain shall meet – economically disadvantaged neighbourhoods soon suffer the effects of neglect unless resources are dedicated to keep the parks vibrant.

But these challenges aren't insurmountable, and you can play a vital role through your philanthropy, as we describe in this section.

If you're thinking about getting involved in creating play spaces, consider potential projects carefully. Measuring and evaluating the impact of organisations that provide educational or therapeutic experiences to at-risk children is often harder than checking out, say, an organisation that erects tents for refugees or delivers a certain number of hot meals to the homeless. Nevertheless, still ask these organisations how they evaluate the impact they're making, because the answers tell you a great deal about their approach and which outcomes they view as successes.

Finding your project

Hundreds – perhaps thousands – of projects are addressing children's need for safe places. In some cases, the challenge is simply to provide a safe, accessible playground. In others, the goal is to use play to help children heal from potentially insurmountable trauma.

Many such projects, such as The Recreation Project (which you can read about in the later section 'Examining two inspirational projects'), are specific to a time and place, helping children in a particular region or area, for example, or focusing on children who've endured (or are enduring) huge challenges. Such restrictions don't mean, however, that these projects don't make a big difference or provide immense value to the children who participate. Nor do they mean that you can't duplicate these successful projects and scale them across cultures and geographies.

The first step in becoming active is identifying where a need exists. To discover areas of need in your own community, think about the neighbourhood you live in or the nearby communities you pass through but would never get off the bus in. What do you know about the people who live there? Is the community active and vibrant or one where children are seldom outside playing? If it's the latter, ask yourself why. Consider these reasons:

✔ **Lack of access to playgrounds:** To be used, playgrounds must be accessible to the children who live in the community: proximity is key. Fortunately, a playground doesn't have to be large or fancy; with work (and the proper permits), even empty or abandoned lots can be transformed into places for children to play.

  If your community has adequate playgrounds and green spaces and it borders a community that doesn't, an invisible barrier may exist between your communities. Ask yourself these questions:

  • **Where and why do borders exist between that community and yours?** What has your community been doing that creates, reinforces, or defines those borders?

  • **Does a way exist for children to cross those borders to play?** Think about the logistics (how can they cross the borders?) as well as the atmosphere in which they'd find themselves (would they be welcome?).

✔ **Playgrounds in disrepair or unsafe:** Children are infinitely resourceful and play in even the worst of conditions, but every child deserves a safe, well-kept place to play. Rubbish, broken equipment, ill-kept lawns, graffiti, and other signs of neglect doom a park and open the door for even worse behaviour.

Fortunately, these problems aren't insurmountable. By banding together with other citizens or getting involved with organisations that focus on play and playground projects, you can make a huge difference for the children in communities, near or far. To find out how, here's a list of organisations and useful resources to have a look at:

- ✔ **East African Playgrounds (EAP):** EAP believes that children need access to play and sports activities, alongside education, to reach their full potential. You can become involved with this charity in loads of ways from volunteering to fundraising (check out www. eastafricanplaygrounds.org).

- ✔ **Fair Play for Children:** This UK-based charity promotes the child's right to play in the UK and worldwide (see fairplayforchildren.net).

- ✔ **National Children's Bureau (NCB):** The NCB's mission is to improve the wellbeing of children across every aspect of their lives. It hosts play-specific organisations and networks dedicated to raising the profile of play (take a look at http://www.ncb.org.uk/what-we-do/play).

This list is only a tiny sample, of course. Surf the Internet to discover more inspirational charities and organisations dedicated to improving children's playing environments. Pick one that really appeals to you.

Examining two inspirational projects

In this section, you explore two examples of projects where new models replaced old play spaces, functionally and psychologically. Although located thousands of miles apart, both organisations operate in so-called play deserts (where children don't have safe, supportive environments in which to play, learn about themselves, and interact with their peers).

KaBOOM! – Building playgrounds at home

KaBOOM! (www.kaboom.org) is concerned with how urbanisation is killing play by impeding children's ability to engage in the exploratory, therapeutic experience that unstructured play provides. KaBOOM! is a national non-profit organisation that's dedicated to creating play spaces throughout the US with the participation and leadership of communities. KaBOOM!'s ultimate vision is to have a play place within walking distance of every child in the US. Check out the website for more information on the background of its amazing story and to get ideas on how you can build play spaces in your own community.

Don't be afraid to start small and dream big! Like many successful organisations, KaBOOM! didn't set out to be a national programme building thousands of projects. It started with one playground in Washington DC, as a neighbourhood project involving a few dozen volunteers, and then moved on to its next project. From its relatively small beginnings, the organisation has built over 2,000 playgrounds.

Kids chipping in to help

In KaBOOM!'s history of building playgrounds where they're needed most, more than one million citizen philanthropists, like the ones we feature here, have helped build great places to play:

- Kamilah Bryant (Maryland) was just 5 years old when she discovered the destruction caused in the US South by Hurricanes Katrina and Rita. With the encouragement of her great-grandmother, Kamilah made paper fans out of construction paper, decorated them with crayon drawings, and sold them at her church for $1 each. 'Kamilah's Katrina Fan Fund for Children Affected by Hurricane Katrina' was born and before long she'd raised $1,000. Kamilah donated that money to KaBOOM!, which used it to purchase a slide for one of the 136 playgrounds in its Operation Playground programme for hurricane-ravaged communities throughout the Gulf Coast.

- Girl Scout mother Barb Herrera (California) attended a conference in early 2011 where KaBOOM! staff described the organisation's efforts to map every playground in America. Barb's 16-year-old daughter enlisted her best friend and together the two created a comprehensive map of Santa Rosa playgrounds. The girls' map is now part of KaBOOM!'s nationwide Map of Play. They were honoured at the 2011 Find Your Passion event of the Northern California Girl Scouts Association.

The Recreation Project

One place in desperate need of positive, safe experiences for children is northern Uganda, a country that has seen its infrastructure damaged or destroyed by decades of war. Tragically, the war devastated more than buildings and roads. Hundreds of thousands of Ugandan children, some of whom were forcibly abducted by the Lord's Resistance Army, witnessed or took part in the atrocities of that war. Haunted by memories of battle or unable to explore safely the world around them, these children struggle to build and grow identities that are separate from the conflict. Without help, they risk being forever marginalised because of their experiences and wartime memories.

These children need a safe and therapeutic environment where they can relate to their surroundings, peers, and future. That's where The Recreation Project (TRP), founded by American Ben Porter, steps in. TRP uses outdoor adventures and sports to help children in northern Uganda reclaim their sense of self.

Ben's idea was to give northern Ugandan children the type of confidence-building, inspiring experiences that many American children have at a summer camp. He discovered that giving children such experiences outside of one-on-one therapy sessions helped them develop creative thinking and problem-solving skills, self-confidence, perseverance, and hope – which are all necessary to move forward after a conflict. To find out more about this charity and how you can play your part, go to www.therecreationproject.org.

Supporting Children through Education

Children are born with curiosity and a remarkable capacity to learn. Think of how, through infancy and young childhood, a child engages the world: absorbing information, mimicking behaviours (good and bad), and developing so quickly that each health-check visit involves the physician ticking off a series of major developmental milestones. Some children continue on this path throughout their lives: learning, growing, and striving to fulfil their potential. Other children, sadly, don't. The question is 'why?'

The lessons learned and events experienced in early childhood have a cumulative effect on the kind of person you become in later childhood, which affects the kind of person you become in your teenage years, which in turn affects the kind of adult you become.

Young children who aren't given the proper support or encouragement, or who face deprivations that undermine their ability to learn or develop, begin school at a disadvantage that's difficult to overcome. In addition, very few students who dislike school and perform poorly from childhood through secondary school go on to become fantastic university students, which is why supporting excellence at the preschool and primary school levels is so crucial. It makes achievement possible at higher levels of education.

Children and teens around the world miss out on education, drop out at school, or don't perform well for a whole range of reasons. A child born in a developing country may not be in school because she has to work to help provide for her family, or a teenager in a rundown city may drop out of school when he gets involved in youth crime. The causes are often complex, with factors such as health, sanitation, and economic and social circumstances all needing to be addressed to improve a child's opportunities.

In this section, we describe how you can help children and teenagers to reach for the stars through education and secure a better future for themselves. We focus here on childhood development and education: if you're interested in philanthropic endeavours that support general learning and universities, refer to Chapter 5.

Getting involved at the grassroots level

Whether your background is connected in some way to education – such as teacher, speech therapist, youth worker, or gardener at the local primary school – or education is simply a subject close to your heart, you can get involved in educational charity. Across the globe or right on your doorstep, you have lots of different options, from giving money to donating your time or skills.

Here are a few ideas to get your philanthropic juices flowing:

✔ **Can you spot services at neighbouring schools that aren't offered at yours?** You may be able to bring those services into your school by negotiating a partnership between a charity and your local school – the majority of these partnerships are negotiated by proactive groups of parents, not by schools!

✔ **Can your area's schools co-operate more?** Local schools may already arrange sport or other activities together but not collaborate on improving the curriculum or offering better nutrition at lunchtime. Often, schools simply need to be nudged in the right direction by members of the community.

✔ **Can you help an educational charity, perhaps by assisting its growth or offering your talents and time directly?** Can you then bring the benefits of your work back to your community and your children? Finding an educational charity that offers a service or benefit you believe in is a great way to get involved.

Public–private partnerships for schools exist in nearly every urban area in the developed world. Check with your community organisation, church, or employer to see whether they already have a relationship with a local school.

Schools need more than just partnership funding. After-school tutoring, sports instruction, or other offers of volunteer expertise are often welcome and much-needed. Helping the children of your community succeed is an investment in your community's future.

Supporting early childhood development

Certain countries have taken the lead on early childhood development, while others provide little state assistance to parents during the early years of their children's development. Philanthropists and private foundations partially fill this gap but work remains to be done. Something as simple as educating a parent about childhood nutrition or introducing a child to a nearby educational play option can make a substantial difference in a child's quality of life and in that child's later ability to learn.

Check out the following programmes to see how you can join in:

✔ **Sure Start:** Sure Start's mission is to give UK children a good start in life by improving childcare, supplying early education, and offering community outreach programmes focusing on health and family support. The more than 250 Sure Start centres throughout the UK are open to all parents and children, and many of the programmes are free. To find out more, go to `http://www.education.gov.uk/ childrenandyoungpeople/earlylearningandchildcare/ delivery/surestart`.

The UK's Sure Start programme is very similar to the US's Head Start, which enhances the social and cognitive development of children through educational, health, nutritional, social, and other services. Started in the US in 1965, Head Start sought to address the fact that low-income students weren't adequately prepared for a classroom environment. The US's Head Start programme was the first of its kind in the world. One of the best-known programmes created by Head Start is *Sesame Street,* the popular TV series that teaches children letters, numbers, and how to get along. Today, *Sesame Street* is broadcast in over 30 countries and over a dozen languages (`www.nhsa.org`).

✔ **Early Years Foundation Stage (EYFS):** The UK introduced this programme after the success of Head Start. Children prepare for school during their preschool years through social activities, structured play, and exploration of childcare and school-like environments.

The EYFS programme later expanded, today providing 15 hours of free early education to every young child in the UK for 38 weeks per year. The programme is funded through public and private grants and also provides advice for parents on preparation for school, nutrition options, and so on (`http://www.gov.uk/early-years-foundation-stage`).

Encouraging teenagers to stay in further education

Imagine a situation in which students from privileged backgrounds were regularly overlooked: quite rightly, you'd expect an outcry. Yet in disadvantaged communities that are underserved by further education, this event happens every single school year. Here we look at the causes of this problem and what can be done about it.

Tackling the barriers to attending college

Many people believe that the college-application process has become less uniform, less decipherable, and less fair over the years. Competition is fierce today: some 13-year-olds have CVs and parents choose after-school activities for their kids according to how they may look on their children's future college applications. Highly-paid editors help craft admissions letters and give advice on admissions strategy.

Very rarely (or never) can low-income students solicit this type of assistance: they don't have the funds to pay these experts and counselling and other services at the secondary-school level are unlikely to prepare them sufficiently for the college-application process.

The problem lies in the difference between local standards and national or international ones. Local parents or communities may have different expectations and different priorities, but top universities have strikingly uniform expectations when reviewing applicants. For this reason, a student may be top of the class at the local school and yet still not be accepted into the top universities.

In addition, parents and grandparents who didn't attend college tend to lack the social network needed to obtain good advice on college-admissions matters for their children and grandchildren. But the children of people who attended university are more likely to attend university, more likely to complete their degrees, and more likely to be employed at age 25 than their peers whose parents didn't attend university. But children don't control whether their parents attended university.

You can help with this situation in a number of ways. Here are just a few ideas:

✔ If you attended university, you can discuss the experience with students from a disadvantaged school.

✔ If you have expertise in financial planning or law, you can help parents plan for the financial realities of sending a child to university.

✔ If your teenager is interested in helping less fortunate peers, perhaps she may be willing to help one of her peers with coursework or in the university-application process (community organisations throughout the UK offer peer-to-peer tutoring relationships and many US school systems have youth-tutor programmes). Check out the following section for details.

Although not every student can attend a top university, every student should be able to aspire to excellence. Students can get inspiration from role models, high-achieving members of the local community, and even from encouraging friends within their peer groups. Simply taking time to think about questions like, 'what am I best at?' or 'what interests me at school?' can be important steps in the right direction.

Using peer support to help struggling students

Students who have a network of people to turn to when college becomes difficult are far more likely to succeed, receive good marks, and graduate. Many students lack a peer group or a family network and aren't knowledgeable about college and career questions. They aren't in a position to live on their own socially, financially, or otherwise. But your support can help.

If you think educational charity is just about mums baking cakes for the village school fete, think again!

A student peer group has two positive effects:

- ✔ **Social and psychological benefits:** Teens have someone to turn to; without such a group, they may feel as though they're facing educational and other challenges alone.

- ✔ **Functional or practical benefits:** In peer groups, students work together to do homework, prepare for exams, and so on. By performing these tasks in a group, the advantaged students model for the disadvantaged students the processes that successful students tend to follow. Also, a growing body of evidence suggests that students who discuss and debate academic materials with their peers come away with a better understanding of the material.

If you're a teenager, you can get involved big time and gather many benefits along the way. You can help your peers directly or organise great events, which is a fantastic experience that looks pretty good on your CV, too.

One organisation that helps students help their peers is DoSomething. org, which believes in young people and values their contributions. Go to www.dosomething.org for inspiration, hands-on action tips, and a lot of other stuff that may tickle your fancy. The website has lots about educational causes, from teaching literacy through storytelling to setting up your own tutoring programme. If you're not sure how to get involved, skip to the Action Finder page to locate an event that suits you down to the ground. The site also has a great app so that you can keep up to date with activities while you're on the go!

Helping students in other ways

If you're interested in helping struggling students, consider these activities:

- ✔ **If you live in a college town or near a university, consider volunteering a weekend to help students with career planning or financial planning questions.** Most students, in most countries, leave college with debt . . . and a lot of it!

- ✔ **Make a financial donation.** A small donation can go a long way in easing the financial strain of a college student, but recognising problems before they become critical is just as important. Look into the communities near you. Find out about students currently in college and see if you can make a difference – the best way to do so is to contact your university and ask whether a disadvantaged students funding scheme exists. Rising tuition costs mean that alumni are increasingly helping to fund needy students through sponsored studentships.

Gathering together a posse

In 2010, President Barack Obama personally donated $125,000 to the Posse Foundation (www.possefoundation.org), an organisation few Americans had heard of. Founded in 1989, it supports students often overlooked by traditional college recruitment and admissions mechanisms. It recruits seniors in high school and organises groups into a cohort (a 'posse') of ten students who support each other through their time in college.

The Posse Foundation isn't a small cause; it has awarded close to half a billion dollars in scholarships to remarkable students who, despite substantial challenges, thrive in a college environment (Posse's students have over a 90 per cent graduation rate). It also helps students understand the college admissions process early, which is crucial to success. Because community organisations and high schools refer their top performers to the Posse Foundation before the college admissions process begins, students can choose electives and strengthen weak areas prior to submitting their applications.

On campus, the Posse Foundation continues to work with students to support their needs as students, which may differ from the traditional four-year college students. This broader support system lets the Posse scholars programme be a conduit rather than a clique, allowing students who may never have gone to college the opportunity to thrive in elite communities and enjoy incredible opportunities.

Nearly half of Posse scholars are attending masters programmes or have already obtained advanced degrees. Others are using their education to do amazing things in their home communities or abroad.

Promoting Nurturing Environments and Safe Havens

Barriers to education can appear very early in children's lives: poor nutrition, lack of parental support, unsafe neighbourhoods, and extreme poverty are just a few of the things that can undermine a child's potential. Fortunately, a variety of charities are addressing these issues.

Tackling poor nutrition

Without proper nutrition, children suffer profound and long-lasting effects. Malnourishment affects a child's cognitive development (the ability to learn, problem-solve, think analytically, and so on), as well as social development (the ability to communicate, socialise, and adapt to new environments).

To live, learn, and grow, the human body requires vast resources – the three macronutrients (protein, carbohydrates, fat) and lots of micronutrients (vitamins and minerals), which people get from food. Without sufficient quantities of those essential building blocks, the body begins to make choices about where to expend its limited resources. It does so in this order: survival first, growth second, and then learning (brain development).

Recognising severe malnourishment in places facing famine is easy (distended tummies, lethargy, and so on), but malnourishment doesn't have to be severe to be a problem. Due to food deserts (areas where residents don't have access to healthy, fresh foods; head to Chapter 15 for details) and poverty in developed countries, malnourishment is a problem everywhere, even though its effects are more subtle: more behaviour problems, decreased attention, lower educational achievement, and so on.

Fortunately, early intervention can make a huge, long-lasting difference. Targeting interventions at preschool age children can lead to measurable improvements during adolescence and into adulthood. To address hunger and malnourishment, check out these organisations:

- ✔ **Enough Food for Everyone (`www.enoughfood.org`):** Organised by a group of British non-governmental organisations, Enough Food focuses on ways to protect communities that are vulnerable to hunger and to address childhood malnutrition.

- ✔ **Save the Children (`www.savethechildren.org.uk`):** This organisation addresses multiple issues affecting children: child poverty, children's rights, children's health, education, and childhood hunger around the world.

Offering a wealth of experiences

Without doubt, the broader a child's educational experiences, the better that child does in school. But what constitutes an educational experience? The answer is any activity that introduces children to the world beyond their own and engages them in discovery.

These adventures don't have to be expensive or far-flung: taking a day trip outside their city, neighbourhood, or village, going to museums and libraries, walking in the park or through a wood, attending neighbourhood ethnic festivals, learning new skills or hobbies . . . the opportunities to show a child that the world is an interesting and exciting place are nearly infinite.

Unfortunately, many children, due to poverty or lack of involved adults, live in a very small world indeed, being exposed to little more than what's shown on TV. A key way to remediate this deficiency is to support early childhood education; read the earlier section 'Supporting Children through Education' for information on these programmes and ways you can help.

You can also get involved by volunteering your time with intervention programmes that stimulate early cognitive development. After all, experiences are some of the most amazing gifts you can give children. If you want to help, check out the National Childcare Campaign's Daycare Trust (www.daycaretrust.org.uk), which has worked for the past several years on making positive early childhood learning environments more available, affordable, and popular.

Organisations that offer these types of experiences focus on 'match making' between children and activities or designing, building, and operating the experience themselves.

Addressing safety and care issues

All children deserve to live in loving homes, to have their physical and emotional needs met, and to be protected from harm. Sadly, the reality for many children is quite different. Whether the problem is abuse and neglect from parents or caregivers, living in neighbourhoods where poverty and crime are the norm, or living in war-torn or politically unstable regions of the world, too many children suffer in silence.

Children in these situations benefit from a variety of efforts, such as:

- **Having safe places for sport in a former war zone.** Refer to the earlier section 'Creating Play Spaces for Children' for organisations that build safe play spaces.

- **Being given scholarships to schools in a faraway place.** In addition to the benefits that education brings the individual and the community, the availability of such scholarships offers children a reminder that their futures can be bright and that they can participate in a global community.

- **Being able to discuss the hardships of wartime with sympathetic people from outside their village, culture, or family.** Such opportunities, in addition to helping the children cope and overcome their situations, also serve to remind them that safety and peace are possible.

Several organisations address safety and wellbeing issues affecting children. Here are just a few:

- ✔ **ChildHope (www.childhope.org.uk):** This international charity offers support for street and working children in Africa, Asia, and South America.

- ✔ **Hope for Children (www.hope-for-children.org):** Hope for Children seeks to improve the quality of life for and protect the rights of disadvantaged children in various Asian, African, and European countries, including the UK.

- ✔ **Kids Company (www.kidsco.org.uk):** Founded by Camila Batmanghelidjh, who was herself profoundly affected by a revolution in her native country, Kids Company seeks to help children who have been traumatised by abuse and neglect. You can read more about her story and Kids Company in the nearby sidebar 'Helping urban children: Kids Company'.

- ✔ **NSPCC (National Society to Prevent Cruelty to Children) (www.nspcc.org.uk):** Founded in the late 18th century as the London Society to Prevent Cruelty to Children, today's NSPCC works with local professional groups and agencies to keep children safe through various programmes and initiatives.

Helping urban children: Kids Company

Camila Batmanghelidjh founded Kids Company (www.kidsco.org.uk) in 1996, providing support to vulnerable inner-city children, by using the equity in her mortgage. The story of Camila's inspiration is itself inspirational.

She writes, 'Maybe being born two and a half months premature and not in an incubator made me stay in touch with the state between life and death, where only the most substantial truths survive . . . . The Iranian Revolution wrenched me from wealth and dropped me into poverty. My father was imprisoned. As a 14-year-old with political asylum, I came close to an understanding of rootlessness and craving for somewhere to belong that was threat-free. I've learned from abandoned children the impact of chronic childhood maltreatment, as well as the necessary interventions to promote recovery.

The source of my daily inspiration is the extraordinary courage and dignity of the children whose capacity for forgiveness in the face of abuse is profound and awe-inspiring. From them, I learned how much the brain changes to adapt to violent environments and the degree to which loving and consistent care can deliver reparations. Now the potency of love is being evidenced on a neuro-physiological level; abundance and absence are apparent on brain scans. It is so sad that something as fundamental as loving care requires evidence for others to invest in it when we know, behind closed doors in the privacy of our homes, that love is the reason we thrive. Most of us have been lucky to have been cherished. For those who haven't, reparation can only be generated through the care of another. It's kindness that restores dignity and hope.'

Chapter 8

Getting Healthy Together: Philanthropy and Healthcare

. . . .

In This Chapter

▶ Caring for the carers

▶ Providing and accessing healthcare worldwide

▶ Helping in specific areas

▶ Tackling health issues with technology

. . . .

*W*ithout good health, lives are severely compromised. Unsurprisingly, therefore, people go to great lengths to protect their health, and companies spend billions of pounds developing new techniques, drugs, and ideas to heal bodies. Despite these efforts, advances in treatment and prevention for many conditions are still a long way off, requiring the continued expenditure of time and money. Even when treatments are available, not everyone has access to them. For these reasons, donating in the area of healthcare makes a lot of sense. For example, you can support hospitals and clinics, fundraise for disease research, provide blankets, healthy food, mosquito nets and clean water, supply medicines, and more.

This chapter takes a look at several aspects of health philanthropy, including assisting personal carers, increasing provision in your own country and across the globe, helping in specific healthcare areas, and employing modern technology in the journey towards good health for all.

Looking into Healthcare and Carers

Once upon a time – in fact, not too long ago – hospitals were places where people went to receive treatment and recover. Even routine surgeries warranted a multiday stay and professionals (such as doctors, nurses, and others) were responsible for providing that care until it was no longer needed. Today, for a number of reasons, that reality no longer exists except for the most serious of health crises, and in-hospital recuperation is largely a thing of the past. Even people with serious health concerns and those recuperating from major surgeries often find themselves discharged into the care of family members.

Multiple factors have combined to create a situation in which complex diseases are now treated at home, making patient needs greater than ever before:

- ✔ The explosion of chronic (prolonged) conditions, such as diabetes, Alzheimer's and other dementias, heart disease, and so on, which require ongoing treatment but which, until a crisis occurs, don't require hospitalisation.

- ✔ The lengthening of lifespans and the limitations that often occur with advancing age (mobility issues, for example, or the ability to perform the activities of daily living such as preparing meals, taking medications, cleaning the home, and so on).

- ✔ The push by hospitals to return patients home as a cost-cutting measure to keep healthcare costs down.

The people providing the necessary care for such patients are spouses, children, parents, other family members, friends, and so on – all sorts of people who have to balance their family and employment obligations with the needs of the person that they're caring for and who aren't professional healthcare providers. In other words, carers are everyday people trying to do the right thing in incredibly difficult circumstances.

Recognising the challenges that carers face

Experts estimate that the number of informal carers in the UK is probably around 6 million, with one third of the population becoming a carer at some point in their lives. Often, people become carers because they're the only ones left who can help.

Many people assume the role of carer when a crisis occurs, or step in because no one else is available to help, and as a result they're unprepared for the difficult road ahead:

- ✔ **Lack of knowledge and training:** Due to the rising cost of medical care and the shortage of trained staff in most countries (including the US and UK), at-home carers are asked to perform tasks (such as cleaning feeding tubes, changing dressings, and so on) that nurses previously carried out in hospitals. These tasks go beyond simply dispensing medications, helping with daily chores, and keeping an eye out for problems. As a result, an increased demand exists for knowledge about the relevant ailments.

✔ **Poverty:** Caring is more than a full-time job – it's a way of life – and yet most carers are unpaid. According to the Princess Royal Trust for Carers:

- Around 60 per cent use their own income and savings to provide needed care and support for the person being cared for.

- Nearly 90 per cent consider themselves worse off financially.

- Nearly 40 per cent fear losing their homes as a result of the financial burden.

Surveys indicate that 1 in 5 carers eventually have to give up their jobs to devote themselves to full-time caring duties.

✔ **Social isolation:** The almost non-stop duties required of a carer, the lack of support services to provide a break from those responsibilities, and the inability of non-carers to understand how all-encompassing the role is, causes many carers to experience social isolation, even from people in their own families.

✔ **Often no ready replacement:** For carers to take a day away is hugely expensive, because they must replace themselves (often paying out of their own pocket) with a paid person or risk the comfort or life of the person receiving care.

✔ **Declining health:** The pressures of being a carer, the stress it puts on other relationships, and the almost single-minded focus on the needs of another person often result in the carer's own physical and mental health declining.

One of the biggest challenges about carers is that they find themselves defined by the hole they inhabit – a space left behind by limited funding, services, and policy.

Finding ways to support carers

Carers aren't generally organised as a group of people with a common identity, which means that they have difficulty finding and supporting one another. Three carers can be together at a social event or in a cafe and yet they're unlikely to talk about their shared caring experiences. Therefore, caring can become a lonely art that's practised in isolation.

Caring for the carers

Michael Lindenmayer, who had the experience of caring for his own parents, started Caregiver Relief Fund (www.caregiverrelieffund.org), which gives carers a chance to take a break from caring. This break can be anything from a voucher for a substitute carer, thereby giving the primary carer a needed break, to a mini-holiday away to rest and recharge.

The organisation addresses the major problem that carers are often chronically exhausted and have almost no time for themselves to 'recharge' psychologically away from their work of helping others. After a break, carers can return to the tasks of caring with renewed motivation, energy, and purpose. The Fund, based in the United States, supports carers who've been caring for a chronically ill, disabled, or elderly person for at least 12 months and whose annual income is less than US$80,000.

You can personally support a carer in a number of ways:

- ✔ **If you interact with, help, or depend on a carer, make an effort to reach out to that person.** Offer to relieve them for a couple of hours every week, for example, so that the carer can get a break.

- ✔ **If you have friends engaged in caring, don't be shy: ask about their support systems.** You may well be able to offer them some of the help they need, even if it's just an opportunity to discuss the challenges of their situations. You can also find support groups through www.patient.co.uk.

- ✔ **Volunteer with organisations that provide respite care or other support services for carers.** Several organisations, such as the following, work to help carers take care of their charges and themselves, providing respite care, support groups, and more:

    - www.carers.org
    - www.carersuk.org
    - www.carerssupport.org.uk

Providing opportunities to socialise and network

Carers have all sorts of different identities and so don't necessarily meet one another for mutual support. Building a dialogue and even a sense of community between carers is central to allowing them to support one another.

The Internet is a huge asset in this effort, allowing carers in different locations to interact for emotional and practical support. It also provides access to general advice offered by the medical community. Check out the National Health Service Carers Direct website (www.nhs.uk/CarersDirect) for general information about care and support, as well as information on peer support groups. Alternatively, use a search engine to look up 'carer support [your community name]' to find local support groups or 'carer support [health condition]' to locate groups that focus on providing support for those dealing with particular health conditions.

Many organisations, even ones more often associated with philanthropic activities overseas, now focus their attention at home. The Red Cross (www.redcross.org.uk), for example, provides different opportunities for carers to become more involved with other carers:

- ✔ It gives volunteers the ability to link up across many more activities than the occasional blood-donation drives or infrequent natural disasters.

- ✔ It encourages participants to stay in touch between events, including providing regional networks within which people can contact one another when certain expertise (such as drawing blood or teaching the carer to use speciality equipment) is needed.

- ✔ It makes local groups more welcoming to non-practitioner carers (relatives and friends without formal medical training) than they were in the past. Often, local Red Cross events provide sessions of training on routine and emergency-care procedures for carers.

Offering training opportunities

Carers have to carry out a wide range of duties and so training for these activities is becoming increasingly important. Not only does it give carers the information they need to perform the duties that have fallen on them, but also these training opportunities have become a central part of how carers meet and support each other.

Many community health organisations and clinics offer free or low-cost training for at-home carers. To find these courses and discover opportunities to get involved, check out these websites:

- ✔ www.sja.org.uk/sja: Here you can find information about the free Carers Support programme offered by the St John Ambulance charity and how you can help support the programme.

- ✔ www.childrenssociety.org.uk/young-carers: Nearly 170,000 children take on the role of carer for an ill or otherwise incapacitated family member. The Children's Society offers programmes designed to help such young people.

✔ www.vocal.org.uk/new-carers-training-website.html: CarersNet is a website for new carers, offering support and training for unpaid carers.

Increasing Access to Healthcare in Developed Countries

Despite the commonsense observation that everyone needs accessible healthcare, even in developed countries many people can't afford it. For example, over the last 30 years in the US, the cost of healthcare has gone up at a rate far higher than the increase in wages for the average American. The cost of prescription brand-name medications has risen at an even faster rate.

Even in the UK with the National Health Service (NHS), certain vulnerable populations – namely immigrants, asylum seekers, and people in disadvantaged areas – have difficulty accessing healthcare. The biggest problems are inadequate transport, inaccessible services, and healthcare staff treating members of certain groups less favourably than others.

To help alleviate such problems, you can support speciality clinics that target particular health issues or causes. This section has all the details.

Supporting speciality clinics in the UK

The NHS provides a number of clinics across the UK to care for the general health concerns of British citizens and UK residents. However, the system of priority the NHS uses is often less than ideal, especially when the need is chronic but not urgent (as is the case for many aging patients).

Free clinics are also available in the UK covering health services not provided by the NHS, such as dental surgery, ophthalmic and other eye-care services for the elderly, help with learning, to the use of animals for health problems such as guide dogs for the blind (www.guidedogs.org.uk), dogs for the disabled (www.dogsforthedisabled.org), and so on.

Unfortunately, with the current government's austerity measures, not enough public funds are available to maintain and expand hospital services. Hence, private donations to clinics and hospital projects have had to fill these gaps. Other major areas – including underserved areas of London – are beginning new campaigns all the time to improve health services at the clinic and hospital level. Check your local council's website to discover what's going on and how to get involved.

Supporting health clinics in the US

In the US, the need for free health clinics is widespread: free or charitable clinics are ones from which a person isn't turned away for lack of funds. These clinics can be urgent care facilities, but many are not. Most provide regular healthcare to people who, for one reason or another, can't afford to interact regularly with the pay-for-services healthcare system. These clinics offer such services as dental care, optometry or other specialist services; pharmacy facilities and access to discounted medications; and preventative care, check-ups, and access to medical advice.

Free and charitable clinics are vital to poorer communities. The largest role they play is in providing preventative care and maintenance of chronic conditions. Although these long-lasting conditions are expensive to manage, they're even more expensive when left unmanaged. For example, a diabetic who isn't properly cared for is substantially more likely to suffer blindness, amputation, or other preventable symptoms of the disease. People who take more than two medications regularly are more likely to ingest them improperly if they don't see a medical professional at least once a year.

To find out how you can support free clinics in the US, check out the National Association of Free and Charitable Clinics (NAFC; `www.nafcclinics.org`). The NAFC combats the problem of healthcare provision by providing accessible community healthcare. It's the only non-profit organisation focused directly on the needs of the approximately 1,200 free and charitable clinics in the US. The NAFC recognises that essential medical services and their delivery are the responsibility of everyone. It advocates on behalf of these clinics – and the clients they serve.

Improving access to UK health clinics

In the UK, the problem of accessing healthcare isn't due to an inability to pay or the lack of clinics (as in the US), but often lack of transportation: the inability of certain populations to travel to a healthcare provider. This lack of adequate transportation can exacerbate medical conditions. A poor patient without a vehicle and without a neighbourhood chemist, for example, is going to have difficulty filling or re-filling a prescription and may well go without medication.

Possible solutions to address this issue include creating mobile health services, encouraging physicians to set up practices in underserved areas, and creating a transportation scheme that helps patients make the journey to health centres and hospitals.

Going Above + Beyond: Helping cancer patients access care

Often, the first specialist available in the NHS system is located far away from the person in need, a problem in terms of expense and, very often, the frail condition of elderly patients. Private philanthropy tries to fill this gap by bringing the experts and facilities needed closer to the patients.

One example is the Above + Beyond fund (www.aboveandbeyond.org.uk), which noticed that many people in Bristol – despite its half-million residents – were having to travel substantial distances for cancer care. Often, people had to see specialist oncologists in London, which entails two hours of travel in each direction and a full day away from familiar surroundings. With the rising cancer rate in England (one of the fastest-growing cancer rates in the world), more oncology centres are going to be required in the future.

The Above + Beyond fund set out to raise the £6 million needed to provide care 'above and beyond what the NHS can provide', including providing top-rate facilities and care locally in Bristol so avoiding the necessity to travel two hours in each direction for a doctor visit in London. Improvements in major cities, including Bristol, Liverpool, Newcastle, and Nottingham have reduced wait times for patients substantially.

Here's how you can play your part:

- ✔ Offer transportation to someone you know who may need help getting to a medical appointment.

- ✔ Pick up medications or transport medical testing supplies for a person who can't drive (for whatever reason).

- ✔ Join a phone check-in service in your area to check on the elderly and make sure that they're okay and taking their medications.

- ✔ Volunteer with Scope (www.scope.org.uk), which posts volunteer opportunities to work with disabled adults, or Whizz-Kidz (www.whizz-kidz.org.uk), which lists opportunities to work with disabled children. Although based in London, both organisations have volunteer opportunities across the UK (over 9,000 people per year volunteer with Scope in England and Wales). If neither of these organisations is active in your area, check with local carer organisations to find similar opportunities.

- ✔ Donate time before or after activities at a local church or community centre to discover local families' needs and how you can help.

Promoting Health in the Poorest Regions of the World

Health can be a hard thing to measure, but life expectancy isn't. Looking at life expectancy by country, you're struck quickly by the obvious trends. Citizens of the following types of countries have longer life expectancy:

- ✔ Technologically-advanced countries
- ✔ Countries that haven't been at war recently
- ✔ Wealthier countries

People from poorer countries are firmly fixed at the bottom of the life-expectancy list. They're exposed to war, civil conflict, and endemic disease. Preventable diseases, such as malaria and yellow fever, largely eradicated in other parts of the world, remain common and deadly ailments in these regions. Lack of adequate or available care makes childbirth dangerous and death from vehicular and other types of accidents all too common. The healthcare infrastructure is often poor and made worse by poor sanitation systems. In addition, improving that infrastructure tends not to be a major priority of government policymakers.

These patterns aren't accidents. They reflect the unfortunate realities of modern healthcare: it's expensive and difficult (often impossible) to deliver the same quality of care in Burundi as in Birmingham. But some intrepid organisations are trying to do just that.

Eradicating malaria deaths: Malaria No More

Malaria No More has one of the most ambitious goals on the philanthropic landscape: eradicating malaria by 2015. As of 2012, the goal of near-zero malaria deaths by 2015 remains a dream, albeit an attainable one. The organisation uses a mix of prevention and education to combat malaria in high-incidence regions. For instance, in Okavango, Botswana, only 9.4 per cent of households had mosquito nets in 2007. Two years later, 91 per cent of households had nets – a huge achievement!

Malarial mosquitoes come out around 9 p.m. at night. Therefore, Malaria No More runs an advertisement called Nightwatch on many African radio stations to remind listeners that the malarial mosquito is a threat after 9 p.m. The voices of celebrities, musicians, and sports heroes deliver the message to get the attention of listeners.

In this section, we look at a number of ways people and organisations are working to improve the health of people across the world and tell you what you can do to help.

Beating the scourge of malaria

Malaria presents a huge challenge to those working to improve family life in the developing world because of its effect on children. A little less than half of the world's population (some 3.3 billion) is at risk of malaria and over 200 million people per year contract the disease; of those, about half a million a year die. Most malaria deaths (90 per cent) occur in Africa and 85 per cent are children aged 5 years old and under.

Despite these discouraging numbers, progress is possible. In fact, since the year 2000, the infection rate in Africa has fallen by one-third due to efforts such as the following:

- In one decade, over 100 million mosquito nets were made available.
- Low-cost diagnosis has become widely available, with a blood test yielding near-instant results that costs less than 50 pence in most of the world.
- Over 180 million courses of ACTs (malarial treatment) were distributed in 2010.

A number of organisations work to combat malaria and can use committed donors and volunteers. Here are just a couple:

- **Against Malaria Foundation (AMF;** `www.againstmalaria.org`**):** AMF provides mosquito nets to populations at high risk of contracting the disease.
- **Malaria No More (**`www.malarianomore.org`**):** This organisation seeks to eradicate malaria by 2015. Read more in the nearby sidebar 'Eradicating malaria deaths: Malaria No More'.

Tackling tuberculosis

The World Health Organisation declared tuberculosis (TB) to be a global health emergency in 1993. TB usually affects the lungs and many people are infected for months or years before symptoms appear. People may experience an incurable cough producing thick matter or blood. This material, spread by coughs and sneezes, transmits TB to others.

In addition to the health effects, TB also causes substantial social and economic problems. In India, for example, hundreds of thousands of children leave formal schooling due to the disease, and each year over $20 billion of economic productivity is lost to the Indian economy because of TB.

High-population areas allow medical projects to make big impacts without covering a large geographical area. More than 3 million of the 7 million cases of TB in so-called high-burden countries are in India and China, and so addressing the problem in these places positively affects many lives more quickly and for a lesser cost.

In the Millennium Development Goals, the United Nations set the goal of eradicating TB by the year 2050. You can play your part in the fight against tuberculosis by getting involved with, or donating funds to, organisations such as the following:

- ✔ **Operation ASHA (`www.opasha.org`):** Combats the spread of and suffering from TB in urban slums and poor, rural communities around the world. One of the organisation's most ambitious goals is to eradicate TB in India, which has one of the heaviest such burdens of any country. You can read more in the nearby sidebar 'Supporting Operation ASHA'.

- ✔ **TB Alert (`www.tbalert.org`):** A UK charity whose mission is to provide access to TB treatments for those afflicted and to control and eliminate tuberculosis in the UK and abroad.

Despite all the great work of these charitable organisations, TB is fighting back. In India, for example, a person dies from TB every 90 seconds and an estimated 100,000 cases of drug-resistant tuberculosis have been confirmed there, as have a dozen or more cases of XXDR tuberculosis, which is resistant to any currently available 'front line' treatments. So much work remains to be done.

Supporting Operation ASHA

Instead of implementing a centralised, hospital-based strategy, Operation ASHA uses local clinics to operate as outpatient clinics for the poor. The organisation has successfully treated nearly 20,000 patients and serves over 2,000 disadvantaged villages and communities. Today, over 5 million Indian patients, for example, depend upon Operation ASHA for their TB care.

Operation ASHA has been – and continues to be – a success story in India. Due in part to its educational efforts, a huge proportion of patients take their medications properly and complete their prescribed treatment. The detection and diagnosis rate for TB doubles when Operation ASHA begins operating in an area.

Putting the focus on prevention

In rural areas and developing countries, even treatable or minor conditions can become major health concerns due to difficulties in accessing treatment or medications. For this reason, as well as the fact that preventing a disease is often easier and less expensive than working to cure it, many charitable health organisations inject significant resources into disease prevention.

When thinking about targeting your health philanthropy, public health experts agree that *treating* an existing disease is 10–20 times more expensive than *preventing* that disease initially. For example:

- ✔ Building a water purification plant is expensive but cheaper than having an area inhabited by people constantly suffering from disease and in need of medical care.

- ✔ Providing mosquito nets costs a little initial money but provides great value compared to the loss of life expectancy, productivity, fertility, and other factors associated with malaria (see the earlier section 'Beating the scourge of malaria' for ways to tackle this disease).

One organisation, Partners in Health (PIH), formed by a group of healthcare practitioners and academics in the late 1980s, works with its partners to ensure that diagnosis and treatment are available free of charge to people living in poverty in the developing world. The hope is to popularise pre-ventative (rather than curative) medicine in the developing world, because although, say, making a sustainable plan to train 100 surgeons a year in Uruguay or Uganda is very difficult, preventing 10,000 people a year from needing surgery is possible.

For more information on PIH's work, see the nearby sidebar 'Building a healthcare infrastructure in Haiti: PIH'. To find out how you can help, visit the organisation's website at www.pih.org.

Addressing the dangers of pregnancy and childbirth

According to the World Health Organisation, every day 800 women die from complications related to pregnancy and childbirth. Of those 800 women, the vast majority – 99 per cent – live in developing countries and nearly all these deaths are preventable. Leading causes of maternal death include high blood pressure during pregnancy, severe bleeding during childbirth, and infection following childbirth.

EXAMPLE

Building a healthcare infrastructure in Haiti: PIH

The US-based charity Partners in Health (http://www.pih.org) has an ambitious project to build a new healthcare infrastructure in Haiti. The presence of its modern expansive facility, including a full-service hospital, is set to transform healthcare in the country, which has always struggled to reach any substantial part of the population. Serving a population of 1.2 million and employing over 4,000 people, the facility will soon provide surgery, infectious disease expertise, women's health services, ophthalmology diagnosis and treatment, and other services. Co-founder Dr Paul Farmer cites the emphasis on educating, training, and hiring local people as being key to the project's success.

The high risk of maternal deaths is due largely to the following factors:

- ✔ **Early pregnancies:** Complication in pregnancy and childbirth are the leading cause of death for girls aged 15 and younger.

- ✔ **Number of pregnancies:** Women in developing countries tend to have many more pregnancies during the course of their lives than do women in developed countries.

- ✔ **Lack of access to necessary care:** Many women in developing countries don't receive appropriate prenatal care during their pregnancies, skilled care during delivery, or adequate follow-up care after delivery.

GETTING INVOLVED

If you're interested in helping to prevent maternal deaths, you can choose which approach you want to take. As the preceding list makes clear, the problem is the result of a variety of contributing factors. By tacking any one of these issues – delaying pregnancies until after adolescence, facilitating family planning, or making timely management and treatment of complications possible – you can increase a woman's odds of having a healthy pregnancy. Here are a few organisations with these goals in mind:

- ✔ **Marie Stopes International:** This organisation provides family planning and reproductive healthcare to women around the world, with much of its work devoted to serving women in remote, underserved communities. To find out more, go to www.mariestopes.org.

- ✔ **Plan UK:** As well as many schemes designed to improve the blight of impoverished and vulnerable children around the world, Plan UK also sponsors programmes designed to eliminate the practice of forced child marriage. To find out more, go to www.plan-uk.org/early-and-forced-marriage.

> ✔ **RCOG Smile Appeal:** Sponsored by the Royal College of Obstetricians and Gynaecologists, the Smile Appeal raises awareness of maternal health issues and works with governments and world organisations to improve quality of care. For more information and to find out how you can help, go to www.rcog.org.uk/smile-appeal.

Getting healthcare to isolated communities

Although the last 50 years has seen a huge increase in the number of people moving to and living in large towns and cities, around half of the world's residents still reside in rural areas. Efforts to provide healthcare in such often isolated locations are logistically challenging, expensive, and sometimes unsustainable.

To help in such areas of the world, search the Internet for relevant organisations. One is the Rural Transport Network (www.virginunite.com/campaign/Rural-Transport-Network/). Its programme provides volunteer health workers in Kenya with motorbikes so that they can take medicines and medical supplies to rural communities.

Contributing towards a Variety of Other Healthcare Causes

Many people become interested in directing their philanthropy towards healthcare – whether it's giving financially, providing practical assistance, or raising awareness – following a personal connection or incident. Perhaps a family member, friend, or even yourself was (or is) affected by a particular illness – possibly one that you knew little about before – or an accident or other medical problem. Or maybe you want to support a particular hospital, department, or other charity or organisation that assisted you or your family during a difficult time. Perhaps your chosen focus is on research that can lead to cures.

In this section, we offer a variety of ways in which you can make a difference in the area of medicine and healthcare.

View the examples we discuss as just the tip of the iceberg and mine them for ideas and inspiration as you pursue your specific area of interest.

Providing aid to people suffering from paralysis

Depending on the extent of the condition and which parts of the body it affects, paralysis – the inability to move a part of the body (generally a limb) without assistance – can be an extremely debilitating condition.

Paralysis can result from severe injury to the head or spinal cord or serious health conditions such as stroke or multiple sclerosis. Although many causes for paralysis exist, the needs of affected people are strikingly similar and include the following:

- ✔ **Assistive technology:** These devices help paralysed individuals maintain their independence and include voice-activated environmental control units and computers.

- ✔ **Care and support:** Carers or service animals may be required for those who need personal assistance.

- ✔ **Mobility aids:** These items include wheelchairs and *orthotics* (devices such as braces that compensate for muscle weakness and help the limb function).

You can assist organisations whose main mission is to make care or assistive technology more available and those seeking medical breakthroughs to improve the prognosis and to find a way to repair the nerve damage and reanimate the paralysed limb(s). Here are just a few suggestions:

- ✔ **Spinal Research (`www.spinal-research.org`):** This organisation funds research around the world to develop treatments for paralysis caused by traumatic neck and back injuries.

- ✔ **SPIRIT (Spinal Paralysis & Injury Research & Training; `www.spirit-charity.co.uk`):** SPIRIT promotes education, training, and research into spinal cord injuries.

- ✔ **Walkabout Foundation (`walkaboutfoundation.org`):** The Walkabout Foundation has worked in the US and UK since 2009. In addition to donating wheelchairs, Walkabout funds important research into the causes and treatment of paralysis. It allows donors to 'adopt a scientist' working on issues important to paralysis and helps donors and healthcare workers understand the challenges of treating (and living with) paralysis.

- ✔ **Whirlwind Wheelchair International (`www.whirlwindwheelchair.org`):** This non-profit social venture seeks to make high-quality wheelchairs available to anyone in the world who needs one.

Re-inventing the wheelchair

Many people lose the use of their legs and need a wheelchair for transportation. Yet less than a quarter of people who suffer from injuries or disease that compromise their legs have the use of a wheelchair. Whether a hand-bike style (where users 'pedal' with their hands to drive a chain-driven wheel) or manual style (where users 'spin' two wheels at their side), wheelchairs are expensive to produce. At £200 per chair for a cost-conscious model, a wheelchair represents half a year's wages for people in many parts of the world.

In one scheme to address this problem, the Walkabout Foundation collaborates with Whirlwind Wheelchair International to donate the Rough Rider wheelchair. This chair is a complete re-think of the wheelchair, which has traditionally been a fragile, expensive, heavy device made of special parts. The Rough Rider is a wheelchair that uses bicycle parts, can be easily maintained with basic tools and is built to withstand operation on dirt roads and difficult surfaces – characteristics that make it suitable for people in the developing world.

Head to the nearby sidebar 'Re-inventing the wheelchair' to see how the Walkabout Foundation and Whirlwind Wheelchair International have joined forces to help paralysed individuals.

Promoting organ donation to save lives

Organ donation is one of the most powerful forms of philanthropy. Through organ and tissue donation, a single person can save or improve the quality of life for many others.

In the UK the number of people needing transplants is higher than the number of donors. Therefore, one of the most important contributions you can make is to become a donor yourself and to encourage others to do the same. Here are some ways you can help:

- ✔ **Becoming an organ donor after your death:** To do so, sign up with the NHS Organ Donor Register (www.organdonation.nhs.uk).

- ✔ **Donating before your death:** Following are some of the tissues and organs that healthy, living donors can give. Although kidney and liver donations are most often made by family members, donations can also be made between unrelated individuals:

- **Blood:** Despite decades of medical research, no synthetic replacement for blood is available, which makes the ready supply of usable, clean, screened, recent blood crucial. If you're a healthy person who hasn't travelled in an at-risk country or engaged in high-risk behaviour, we suggest you look into donating blood (contact `www.blood.co.uk` in the UK and `www.americasblood.org` in the US).

- **Bone marrow:** In this type of transplant, your bone marrow (more precisely, stem cells from your bone marrow) replaces bone marrow that's no longer capable of producing normal blood cells. To donate bone marrow, add your name to the British Bone Marrow Registry. Go to `www.nhsbt.nhs.uk/bonemarrow` for more information.

- **Kidney:** You have two kidneys but really only need one. Many studies show that a healthy person who donates a kidney enjoys a similar quality of life to a similar person with two kidneys. To find out more about living kidney donation, visit `www.livingkidneydonation.co.uk`.

The first kidney transplant took place about 60 years ago, but failed because the recipient's immune system rejected the new organ. Four years later, Nobel-laureate Dr Joseph Murray carried out a nearly identical procedure successfully (the donor and recipient were identical twins). Today, kidney transplants have been successful between donors and recipients of different ages, sizes, races, and regions.

- **Liver:** The liver is an amazing organ: part of it can be cut off and put inside someone else, and the original proceeds to heal itself. In the donor, the liver regenerates the donated portion, essentially regrowing to the size the body needs. To find out more information, go to the NHS organ donation website (`www.organdonation.nhs.uk/how_to_become_a_donor/living_donation/living_liver_donation/index.asp`).

Different cultural norms mean that the number of people willing to donate a kidney varies by region. For example, Spain and Italy have very low rates of kidney donation from living donors, while countries such as the US have high rates. Therefore, different countries have different needs as well as different laws and regulations governing organ and tissue donation.

Under current UK and US law, you don't own your organs. As a result, you can't leave them to others in your will or appoint a trustee to manage where they go. However, organ-donor systems in both countries allow people to designate themselves as donors. The system then allocates organs among potential recipients. Be sure you consult the laws of your country before making a donation.

Helping out hospitals and doctors

The plain fact is that the world has a shortage of hospitals and doctors. The doctors with the highest levels of training tend to live and work in areas of the world with the lowest rates of infectious disease. Similarly, doctors and hospitals engaged in research are often located far from the problems they're researching.

Several philanthropic endeavours seek to place doctors and medical facilities in the places where they're most needed. Some focus on constructing and staffing health centres in areas of need; others place doctors on the ground where and when they're needed.

Doctors Without Borders (Médecins Sans Frontières) is one such organisation. Founded in 1971, it offers medical care in regions and situations where traditional medical care infrastructure doesn't exist or can't cope with patient needs. The longest-running intense work of Doctors Without Borders is in Sudan, which has endured ongoing civil war, nutrition and water-quality problems for decades. Sudan is Doctors Without Borders's largest intervention, with close to 5,000 people in the field at times – more than the number of doctors in the militaries of Sudan and South Sudan added together.

If you're a doctor considering volunteering with Doctors Without Borders or want to work in the field in other ways, excellent! Go to www.doctorswithoutborders.org/work/field to find out what skills the organisation needs on the ground. If field work is beyond your ken, you can also support the organisation by making a donation to support its work at www.doctorswithoutborders.org.

If you plan to volunteer on the ground, be aware of the dangers of travelling in these countries. If you're new to such travel, consult the UK Foreign Office (www.fco.gov.uk) or the US State Department (www.state.gov) to understand the conditions you may encounter. If possible, speak with other volunteers who've recently visited the region, because up-to-date information on the situation is often hard to come by and yet invaluable.

After a natural disaster or in a conflict zone, access to nutrition, water, and sanitation are vital. Going more than one week without access to clean water and sanitation increases the risk of communicable disease by a factor of ten. To find out how to support efforts to improve sanitation and access to safe drinking water, head to Chapter 9.

Endowing research projects

Human knowledge in medicine and healthcare is improving all the time, but more research still needs to be done. Diseases, conditions, addictions, mental illness, and pain management are just a few of the many areas with secrets to unlock and treatments and cures to find. Whether you're interested in particular diseases or the frontiers of medical knowledge, such as unlocking the secrets of the brain or human genetics, you can almost certainly find scientists and researchers who have devoted their lives to making advancements in those areas.

Take cancer research, for example. Cancer is one of the most complex and difficult problems that scientists are working on. Although finding a cure for cancer is the gold standard of medical research, scientists are discovering that a single cure doesn't exist. The more they learn about how cancer forms, grows, and spreads, and how the body's biological processes respond to the disease itself and to treatments, the more they realise the complexity of the disease (see the nearby sidebar 'Combating cancer through early detection' for more details).

Even when a disease's mechanisms (how it develops, is transmitted, and so on) are fully understood, finding viable treatment options and even a cure are daunting tasks, requiring vast resources, the best minds, and private and governmental support. If you're interested in furthering medical research, consider visiting the Association of Medical Research Charities website at www.amrc.org.uk. The member organisations represent the leading UK charities that fund medical research.

Combating cancer through early detection

A multitude of different types of cancers exist, each with its own subtypes. In addition, no single cause of cancer exists: genetic abnormalities, environmental exposures, and viral agents can all play a role, but experts can't predict who will develop the disease. Some cancers remain dormant, some are slow-growing, and some reproduce and spread at an alarming speed, killing in a matter of weeks or months. So, although a lot has been discovered about the disease, a great deal is still to be learned.

What is known definitively, though, is that one of the best tools in the fight against cancer is early detection, which means frequent screening of patients. The Robert H. Lurie Comprehensive Cancer Center at Northwestern University (www.cancer.northwestern.edu/home/index.cfm) is one of the foremost research centres for oncology in America. The centre is a combination of patient treatment and cancer research, bringing together the latest knowledge about cancer and patients who can benefit immediately from recent discoveries.

In addition to treating over 10,000 new cancer cases every year, the Lurie Center spreads knowledge about how to best combat the disease through its affiliations with four teaching hospitals in Chicago. It offers screening for breast cancer, genetic cancer risk, prostate cancer, ovarian cancer, and skin cancer; patients who are diagnosed early have a greater range of available treatment options and better outcomes in their fight against the disease.

Raising awareness campaigns

One of the easiest and most common ways for you to get involved in health fund- and awareness-raising is via sponsored campaigns. The number of walks, runs, and bicycle races to support causes is dizzying and we don't even attempt an inventory here.

When you're considering organising a sponsored event for your chosen cause, check out similar occasions in aid of other diseases for ideas that combine a sense of community with a theme of philanthropic involvement (such as the one we describe in the nearby sidebar 'Walking away Alzheimer's'). These events can be great places to meet people, discuss ideas, and discover the newest efforts to advance your cause of choice. A website, www.charitywalksblog.com, keeps an updated list of walks and events for various causes. For more information on starting or participating in awareness campaigns, refer to Chapter 15.

A well co-ordinated healthcare awareness campaign needs to address the following three pillars with substantial and equal enthusiasm:

- ✔ **Care** is needed to allow those afflicted by disease to manage their condition.
- ✔ **Education** is central to the understanding and prevention of disease.
- ✔ **Research** is necessary to understanding and curing a disease.

Walking away Alzheimer's

The Walk To End Alzheimer's is one of the largest fundraising and awareness campaigns in the US. The Walk takes place in over 600 communities and contributes to the support and care of current patients and research to prevent Alzheimer's in the future. These Walks aren't only fundraising events, but also further the educational mission of the Alzheimer's Association, providing opportunities to learn about the disease, get involved with public policy initiatives, and find out about clinical trials currently underway.

The Walk To End Alzheimer's hopes to have 40,000 teams walking across America to end Alzheimer's. If you want to join, check out www.alz.org.

Using Technology to Improve Health

Technology's increasing role in and influence on people's lives is undeniable (in fact, perhaps you bought or learned about this book online – and look how much it's improved your life already!). Although not all the latest gadgets are beneficial, charities and philanthropists have been quick to take advantage of, for instance, the ease of organisation and improved communication that these innovations provide.

In this section, we get all high-tech and discuss the use of technology and the Internet in protecting and improving people's health.

Exploring online ways to improve health

The Internet is a huge learning tool for health improvement. From online healthy cooking classes and recipe books, to yoga groups and workouts, to triathlon and marathon teams who meet on Facebook, the health-improvement battle is shifting to the online space.

Staying healthy, maintaining a diet, or sticking at a workout programme is easier when you collaborate with others. Whereas people used to look to friends or peers for this support, more and more are going online. In addition, the Internet is beginning to play a role in self-diagnosis (beyond its use as a reference tool). WebMD (www.webmd.com) began as the online equivalent of a medical desk reference focusing on consumer education and patient safety, but it now allows patients to find information about diagnoses, pharmaceuticals, drug interactions, and drug recalls.

Online medical diagnosis is increasingly becoming a reality. Here are some examples:

- **Dermatology:** Patients can send electronically high-resolution photographs of moles or lesions and get immediate feedback on whether they need to visit a dermatologist.

- **Malaria:** Field-test kits now include scan-ready strips so that they're keyed to the time and place where the blood samples (or other samples) were taken.

- **Ophthalmology:** Webcam technology and eye-tracking software now allow untrained staff to discern people's eyesight prescriptions in the developing world.

- **Physician follow-up:** Doctors can follow up patients in displaced persons' camps and conflict zones via Skype, whereas before patients needed to see a field physician and then never saw the same doctor again.

> ✔ **Physiotherapy and rehabilitation:** Motion and body-intelligent capture technology (basically a way that a computer can watch and analyse your body's movement) such as Kinect is being used to store progress in patients and examine a range of motion limitations after road accidents and falling injuries, as well as identifying senior citizens most at risk of falls or losing balance.

Philanthropists and investors funded many of these initiatives, and new amazing things are becoming possible every day. If you want to become involved, use the Internet (what else!) to search for a technology company that invests in these intersections of technology and health and discover more.

Preventing tomorrow's health problems

Technology has become an integral part of the concept of fitness and health, from finding the best high-performance fabrics for world-class athletes to building the ultimate four-hour marathon song playlist. But technology can also play a role in everyday fitness and you can support these trends as a philanthropist.

One of the biggest health challenges today is childhood obesity, not only in wealthy countries but also in the developing world. For example, India is experiencing a particularly alarming rise in childhood obesity as fast foods and high-calorie drinks have become the norm in India's cities.

Although technology is often blamed for obesity – people are overweight because they work at computers, sit in front of televisions, or play video games – technology can also be a weapon in the fight against obesity:

> ✔ Nike + iPod debuted more than five years ago and combines a run's soundtrack with its distance, pace, and, in some instances, routes travelled while running.

> ✔ Jamie Oliver's 'Food Revolution' project (which we describe in Chapter 10) inspired several websites and apps that allow school administrators to evaluate school lunch options and parents to keep better track of what their children are eating.

> ✔ Employers, such as Google and Microsoft, use mobile technology and employee-communication apps to remind their employees of group runs or alert them (according to their GPS location) whether the weather is nice enough outside to cycle or walk to work.

Non-profit organisations working with the community – from food banks to car-sharing programmes – are using apps to help parents and community members understand how their programmes work. Initiatives to boost availability of services through the use of technology include (often real-time) updates of efforts to provide better nutrition, free health testing, or local government meetings. These innovations can be as simple as an app that reminds you when a blood-donation campaign is near your GPS location every 90 days, or as complex as a website that allows you to keep track of your family's prescriptions and healthcare needs.

Think about how your company, school, or community can better use technology to help people get things done – or simply get along. If you have the coding skills, attend a hackathon (you can read about hackathons in Chapter 13). If you don't have these skills, consider convening a session on what's needed and then finding a developer to develop the appropriate app or program. Often, overseas developers can create apps – particularly in India and China – for only a few hundred pounds while creating work for skilled young people in these countries.

Technology has a particularly crucial role to play as regards health in the developing world. As just one example, Rotary International supports ShelterBox, which uses technology to connect donors with its Big Green Box programme that provides a healthy, sanitary option for post-disaster shelter. The Big Green Box is a container that two people can carry. It contains a sturdy, semi-permanent tent that two adults can erect along with enough supplies to cook food and provide a safe place for a medium-sized family. The Big Green Box scheme features real-time tracking of each box to allow the organisation to perform a logistical audit of the aid process, as well as help donors and stakeholders to better understand the process and mechanics of the programme.

You can help by donating a box, fundraising for the overall programme, or volunteering on the ground. Take a look at `www.shelterbox.org` today. Don't forget to check back and watch your box travel to its destination!

Playing games for good health: SuperBetter

Dr Jane McGonigal, a leading game designer, academic, and expert on computer game design, has designed dozens of games and believes they can be a force for good in the world. When she suffered from a traumatic brain injury in 2009, she began designing a game to heal herself. Her game, SuperBetter, challenged her and turned her recovery into a fun adventure rather than an uncomfortable series of meetings with doctors and therapists.

SuperBetter is designed to help players become stronger, healthier, more resilient people. You enter your health goals, can add quests and adventures (tasks that help you achieve your goals), and have to watch out for 'bad guys' (activities that undermine your progress). As you complete tasks, you earn points for mental, emotional, physical, or social resilience. The game is free. To download it, go to `www.superbetter.com`.

For more information on the role games can play in philanthropy and how they can make the world a better place, head to Chapter 11.

Chapter 9

Becoming Eco: Protecting the Planet

In This Chapter

▶ Deciding on your eco interests

▶ Revolutionising water and sanitation

▶ Becoming a steward of the Earth's animals

▶ Having a positive impact on the planet

*Y*ou can direct your giving in many directions, but surely the one for which everyone shares a responsibility is the human home – Earth. The water you drink, the soil that nourishes crops, and the air you breathe – all these resources are incredibly precious. As a philanthropist, you can make an enormous difference by addressing the huge challenges facing your home. You have the power to eliminate pollution, protect the food supply, safeguard the forests, rescue animals, and purify the waters.

Whether you live in an urban jungle or the rainforest, on a mountain or by the sea, discovering your connection with the environment is one of the first steps to becoming a successful eco philanthropist. In this chapter, we explore some of the environmental issues facing the planet and explain how you can take them on headfirst.

Going Green: Finding Inspiration and a Focus

Eco philanthropy, like other forms of giving, takes many shapes and sizes, depending on your interests and what kind of assets you have in your arsenal – whether they're ideas, courage, compassion, or financial resources. Some eco philanthropists choose to travel across the globe to protect wildlife they care about; others make a difference closer to home – being smarter about what they buy from the supermarket, or using eco-friendly, reusable grocery bags, for example. The first step in finding that resonance is educating yourself about eco stuff. Intelligence can be your best weapon for defending your planet, and the best information comes from what you experience first-hand – what you see, hear, smell, touch, and taste; so get out there, open those eyes, and start taking notes!

Look around your home, garden, or city block. Is the local water safe to drink? Is there rubbish in the street? Does your produce come from your local farmer or from the other side of the world? Does your air smell foul? By asking yourself such questions you become aware of issues in your own backyard that can benefit from your philanthropic efforts.

The next step is making an informed decision about how to use your resources to create a flourishing planet and combat the key issues related to protecting the environment: adequate sanitation; the availability of clean, drinkable water; pollution; and caring for animals. Use these general areas (which we cover in this chapter) as inspiration and as guides on how to become involved and choose the kinds of causes you can champion.

Check out Chapter 4 for general information on becoming involved in philanthropic endeavours or organisations.

Taking small steps to generate big effects

You don't have to have celebrity status to protect the planet. But you can follow the footsteps of those you admire and who are making their gestures public in areas that matter to you. For some famous examples, read the nearby sidebar 'Saving the planet, the celebrity way'.

Saving the planet, the celebrity way

Here are some examples of the famous helping the planet:

- Intel founder Gordon Moore, former Burt's Bees owner Roxanne Quimby, and former Patagonia CEO Kristine Thompkins have joined forces to buy land and preserve it as national parks.

- Musicians such as the Black Eyed Peas, Jack Johnson, and U2 write environmental greening rules into their contract riders while developing programmes for their fans to offset their carbon footprints.

- Amanda Hearst, great-granddaughter of press baron William Randolph Hearst, and Georgina Bloomberg, daughter of New York Mayor Mike, teamed up with the Humane Society to rescue animals from puppy farms.

Make a list of your passions and think about how you can make a difference. Here are a few thoughts:

- **Keep eco-friendly, reusable grocery bags in your car or by your door for when you go shopping.** Have a few of them on hand because some inevitably end up in the kitchen only to be remembered when you're in line with your cart full of groceries!

- **Visit national parks.** The money you spend enjoying the land goes towards preservation.

- **Adopt a pet!** If you already have a houseful, offer to volunteer at the local animal shelter. Besides donations, shelters need hands-on help.

  Take your camera and see whether the shelter needs help photographing the new fluffy animals for its website. You'd be surprised at the myriad ways your talents can be put to use in a good cause!

- **Shop locally at farmers' markets for produce and other goodies.** In this way you not only support local commerce, but also reduce the carbon footprint created by transporting goods across the country . . . or even the world.

Teaming up to do good

If you have fire in your belly to take on a giant cause such as water or sanitation, you may want to consider teaming up. Although the Lone Ranger approach may seem cool, your chances of having a greater impact and higher success increase dramatically when you work with other philanthropists focusing on the same mission.

By joining forces with other like-minded individuals, you can compound the impact of your endeavours. A single person recycling at home is a great beginning; a neighbourhood of recyclers working in an organised way is even better.

Throughout this chapter, we highlight all sorts of organisations which have partnered with other agencies and individuals to great effect. Even small organisations can use this strategy successfully. Here are some pointers to get started:

- You don't have to be in the same location as everyone else to be a part of a collaboration team. With technology tools, such as Skype or other video-conferencing programs, social media, and others, working as a team can be done remotely.

- Find like-minded collaborators, and when a team is organised devise a schedule of events and a task force to make things happen.

✔ If you don't want to start from scratch, find a team that's organised already and see how you can join it. Think about what type of role you want to play on the team and make a list of ways you can fulfil that role. Remember to be open to other possibilities, too.

Coming Clean on Sanitation

We shall not finally defeat AIDS, tuberculosis, malaria, or any of the other infectious diseases that plague the developing world until we have also won the battle for safe drinking water, sanitation, and basic health care.

—Kofi Annan, ex-United Nations Secretary-General

One of the biggest opportunities for eco philanthropists also happens to be the dirtiest: sanitation.

But don't stop reading! Sanitation may not be the sexiest cause, but the impact is huge. If you have the courage (and the stomach), it's a worthy and noble endeavour for any courageous eco philanthropist. Increasing numbers of committed individuals and organisations are rolling up their sleeves to get down and dirty with sanitation.

Finding out the faecal facts

Shockingly, almost 40 per cent of humanity – that's 2.6 billion people – have no access to a latrine, toilet, or bucket, which is bad for them, bad for everyone else, and bad for the environment.

The fact is that poop is poison. It contaminates rivers, wells, and oceans. Ninety per cent of the world's sewage ends up untreated in drainage or run-off areas (watersheds) where the water becomes toxic and kills plants and animals. It also kills humans. Consider these facts:

✔ Just 1 gram of faeces can contain millions of viruses, bacteria, and parasites – a very nasty business that causes one out of every ten of the world's illnesses.

✔ Ninety per cent of diarrhoea is caused by faecal-contaminated food or water, and it kills a child every 15 seconds.

✔ According to the World Health Organisation, diseases from unsafe water and lack of basic sanitation kill more people every year than all forms of violence, including war. Children are especially vulnerable, because their bodies aren't strong enough to fight diarrhoea, dysentery, and other such illnesses.

Contaminated water isn't just a problem for the environment and health – it also affects education and even the global economy. For example, one-third of girls in sub-Saharan Africa drop out of secondary school when they reach puberty if their school doesn't have a toilet. If you help to provide the facilities, the chance of them staying in school increases dramatically.

Playing your part

Clearly, lack of proper sanitation is a big issue, but the good news is that a lot can be done to fix this problem and you can help in loads of different ways.

Every pound invested in sanitation yields at least a seven-times return on health costs averted and productivity gained. When latrines and hygiene education are provided to communities, 97 per cent of water-borne illnesses can be wiped away. Pretty awesome results!

In your own community, contact your municipality and ask whether they're in need of volunteer services – either hands-on, or using your professional skills if you are an engineer, for instance. As a volunteer, you have the opportunity to contribute towards the wellbeing of the community while gaining personal satisfaction and experience. Many communities have online applications you can fill out. Needs for volunteers are based on projects and whether or not a volunteer has a matching skill set.

If you prefer to help communities farther from home, consider donating money or time to organisations that address this issue:

- ✔ **IDEO (www.ideo.org):** IDEO teams up with non-profits, social enterprises, and foundations to create solutions to the world's most dire poverty-related challenges.

- ✔ **UNICEF's Sanitation and Water for All (SWA; www.sanitationandwaterforall.org):** A partnership of governments, donors, and multilateral organisations, SWA aims to ensure that all people have access to basic sanitation and safe drinking water, especially in countries where the needs are greatest.

- ✔ **Unilever (www.unilever.com/sustainable-living/healthandhygiene/bettersanitation):** Sustainability is integral to Unilever's mission. Among the organisation's goals are improving the health and wellbeing of over a billion people and halving the environmental footprint of its products.

- ✔ **Water & Sanitation for the Urban Poor (WSUP; www.wsup.com):** WSUP is a non-profit partnership between the private sector, nongovernmental organisations (NGOs), and research institutions focused on solving global problems such as inadequate water and sanitation in low-income urban communities.

WSUP? Working together is a great IDEO!

Jocelyn Wyatt, CEO of IDEO.org, writes:

'In 2009, IDEO, Unilever, and WSUP developed a partnership to design and build a sustainable enterprise to provide in-home sanitation in Kumasi, Ghana. The city of Kumasi has a population of 2.5 million people; 80 per cent lack access to in-home sanitation.

Currently, residents without in-home options pay daily for public toilets that are typically poorly managed and infrequently cleaned. There are high incidences of "flying toilets", where waste is discarded into the street, leading to contamination of water sources and diarrhoea.

The project started with a two-week research trip to Kumasi where the collaborative team conducted interviews with families about their sanitation practices and preferences. That trip illuminated the demand for a sanitation service where operators would collect waste from a toilet with a receptacle in the base (modelled after toilets used for camping or on boats).

In conjunction with WSUP and Unilever, an IDEO.org team worked on the design of the business model, service, and system of the new sanitation offering. The group returned to Kumasi to prototype opportunities with a variety of toilet models and branding directions. The insights gained from this testing led the IDEO.org team to design a urine-diversion toilet with a sealed waste container and the Clean Team brand.

The project has continued with a pilot test of 100 toilets, serving approximately 700 individuals in Ghana. In 2012, the team returned to refine the design of the brand and communications and the WSUP and Unilever teams plan to serve 10,000 families in Ghana by 2014.

Philanthropic support from Unilever, foundations, and individuals has funded the project and the work of two non-profits – IDEO.org and WSUP. Philanthropy has an important role to play in creating successful innovation and the Ghana sanitation project is a prime example of its impact.'

✔ **WaterAid** (`www.wateraid.org/uk`): WaterAid UK is a member country of WaterAid, an international nongovernmental organisation. Its mission is to transform lives by improving access to safe water, improving hygiene and sanitation in the world's poorest communities.

To see how three of these organisations are collaborating, check out the nearby sidebar 'WSUP? Working together is a great IDEO!'.

Water, Water Everywhere . . . But Is It Fit to Drink?

Water is the substance of life. Without it, humans and animals wouldn't survive. People drink it and use it to cook, clean, and power their homes and factories, as well as to do fun things like launch rockets. Even the human body is made up largely of water (60 per cent for the average adult male).

Clearly, therefore, everyone has a vested interest in striving for the availability of safe drinking water, the health of the Earth's oceans, and proper sanitation. With so many issues that need to be addressed, water can be an overwhelming cause to take on, making it difficult to decide where to even begin. Alexandra Cousteau, the granddaughter of legendary ocean explorer and inventor Jacques-Yves Cousteau, is continuing her family's 60-year legacy of advocating the importance of conservation and sustainable management of water. She has this advice for those who want to get involved:

✔ Find out where your water comes from.

✔ Take a field trip to a nearby fresh water source and look at use and conservation activities.

✔ Go exploring upstream and downstream of where you live, if you live near a stream or river.

✔ Visit your local drainage basin (watershed) and discover as much as you can about it.

By taking these steps, you understand more about your own connection to water and are better equipped to make decisions on how to use water and protect it. That field trip may just turn you into a serious water warrior.

Ensuring safe drinking water

Although oceans cover about 71 per cent of the Earth's surface, only 1 per cent of all water on the planet is drinkable. Therefore, safeguarding and preserving water are two of the most important tasks facing citizen philanthropists. Consider these challenges:

✔ **Availability:** Currently, 1.1 billion people don't have any access to safe drinking water.

✔ **Access:** Two billion people have to walk over a kilometre to access wells or other water sources. In Africa alone, people spend 40 billion (yes billion!) hours every year just walking to get or transport water. The ones who bear this burden are usually the women and children who walk long distances to the nearest source, which is often unprotected and likely to make them sick. The UN suggests that each person needs 20–50 litres of water a day to ensure their basic needs for drinking, cooking, and cleaning. Your philanthropic efforts can focus on providing water to those who don't have it or making life easier for those who must walk significant distances to get it. Organisations that provide this kind of help include the following:

✔ **One Water** (`onedifference.org/one-drinks/one-water/`): One Water was set up by UK philanthropist and entrepreneur Duncan Goose. One hundred per cent of profits from the sale of bottles of One Water are donated to fund water projects in Africa.

✔ **Voluntary Service Overseas (VSO; `www.vso.org.uk`) and Peace Corps** (`www.peacecorps.gov`): Both organisations (VSO in the UK and the Peace Corps in the US) send volunteers to work in host countries. These volunteers work on construction and other projects where they help organise and mobilise communities to provide health and hygiene education, among other services.

✔ **Water for People (`www.waterforpeople.org`):** Water for People is dedicated to helping people in developing countries improve their quality of life through the development of locally sustainable drinking water resources, sanitation facilities, and hygiene education programmes.

If you're concerned about problems in your own area, contact your local government offices to see what volunteer opportunities are available. Its website should have information, including volunteer needs, forms, and phone numbers to call for more information. If you live in a rural area with fewer needs, consider volunteering in a close-by city or town.

Helping water conservation efforts

According to London-based WaterWise, the UK has around 45 million toilets in homes. That means these toilets are flushing an estimated 2 billion litres of water every day! Approximately 30 per cent of total household water used goes down the toilet.

Of course, water is used throughout the home, and not just for drinking and bathing. In the kitchen, the tap and dishwasher make up 8 to 14 per cent of water usage. And outside, people wash their cars and water plants and flowers: your lawn sprinkler can use as much as 1,000 litres per hour.

Therefore, everyone can start protecting water supplies in their own homes. You can help conserve water by doing the following:

✔ Purchasing dual flush toilets, which have a split flush button giving you the choice of how much water to use.

✔ Putting low-flow showerheads in your shower to reduce the amount of water used. Don't worry, they still give you the feel of a normal shower.

✔ Using the dishwasher only with a full load every time.

✔ Running your garden sprinkler (if necessary at all) only in the early morning or late afternoon hours, when evaporation rates are lower than the middle of the day.

On a bigger scale, you can continue these efforts in the workplace, when you travel and when visiting family and friends. Educate others with the above data and information so that you get as many people as possible on board with water conservation.

Working to protect the world's oceans

According to Greenpeace's website (www.greenpeace.org) the oceans:

- Hold 80 per cent of all life on Earth.
- Drive the natural forces that maintain life on the planet.
- Create over half of the oxygen produced.
- Drive weather systems and natural flows of energy and nutrients around the world.
- Keep the Earth habitable.

Oceans 5: Building partnerships to help marine life

Oceans 5 (www.oceans5.org) is a 'global funders' collaborative... committed to protecting the five oceans of the planet'. The group's investments target large-scale campaigns designed to expand marine reserves and reduce overfishing. Board member and founder Tracey Durning says:

'I'm most passionate and motivated by collaborative philanthropy because I really believe that none of us will effectively move the needle (especially at the scale and speed it needs to move) on our own.

In 2010–11, I worked alongside a group of amazing philanthropists to launch an initiative called Oceans 5. We specifically focus our investments and support on large-scale, opportunistic projects and campaigns aimed at significantly expanding marine reserves and constraining overfishing because those areas are consistent with what marine scientists say are the highest priorities for the world's oceans.

What I love most about Oceans 5 is that it's an incredible way for philanthropists to collectively share and leverage their assets (knowledge, networks, funding, and influence) to support grantees and projects in much bigger ways than they would on their own. It's also a great way to really "walk the talk" around believing in the power of collaboration, which we look for often with non-profit organisations – and have already seen happening with most of the projects. For example, our first campaign, which aims to make the waters in and around Antarctica the largest network of no-take marine reserves on the planet, is an incredible collaboration of global nongovernmental organisations (NGOs), working with scientists, thought leaders, celebrities, and so on to that end. It's awesome to be a part of!

Oceans 5 is the kind of platform I've wanted to embark on since I first got involved in philanthropy about seven years ago. I've always believed there was a powerful opportunity for philanthropists to aggregate around issues they care about, build community, strategically share, and leverage their assets, and just become more involved, impactful (and therefore happier) givers overall.'

So they're worth looking after, to say the least! For over 40 years, Greenpeace has been doing just that. Another organisation whose mission is to protect the oceans is The Marine Conservancy Society (www.mcsuk.org) in the UK, which seeks to protect the seas, shores, and wildlife around the UK.

Protecting the Planet's Animals

No doubt at some point you've visited a zoo. But animals aren't just cute and entertaining; they're enormously vital to human survival, as they (along with plants) are part of the fragile network of organisms that sustains life on Earth. Looking out for their preservation and wellbeing is a cause that all eco philanthropists should consider championing.

As of early 2012, some 1.8 million different animal and plant species have been discovered on Earth, and even that only accounts for approximately 10 per cent of all living things on the planet. This isn't just an interesting fact: it speaks to the importance of biodiversity.

Biodiversity is the term used to describe the number and variety of species living on planet Earth: the greater the biodiversity, the more opportunities for economic development and breakthroughs in science and medicine. Abundance and variety of animals is extremely important for human survival and the health of the planet. But people's choices often put animals in jeopardy, sometimes leading even to extinction.

So of all the animals and their habitats, which one are you going to stand up for?

Animal welfare, like all causes, needs inspiring heroes: for example, Jane Goodall, who dedicated over 45 years to the study of chimpanzees and worked tirelessly on behalf of animal welfare; or the former state governor, Jon Huntsman of Utah, who signed a bill in 2008 creating a serious criminal penalty for abusing dogs or cats. Such people stand as remarkable examples of what can and should be done on behalf of animals. If you've ever considered being a hero for animals, now's the time to act.

Saving animal habitats

No real animal lover wants to live in a world where the only animals are those that live in zoos or other manmade enclosures. A key way to protect animals is to protect their natural habitats.

TECHNICAL STUFF

The Amazon: Facts and figures

The Amazon is responsible for producing more than 20 per cent of the world's oxygen (earning it the moniker the 'lungs of the planet') and for soaking up about one-fifth of the carbon emissions produced by burning fossil fuels.

Rainforests contain the greatest biodiversity in plant and animal life:

✔ Eight new species of mammal are found in the Amazon each year. The most recognised mammal is the jaguar, weighing up to 130 kilograms (about 300 pounds) and possessing the strongest bite of any cat species on the planet.

✔ More freshwater fish species live in the Amazon than in any other waterway in the world.

✔ Scientists estimate that the Amazon holds 2 million species of insects and arthropods.

In one tree alone, the famous biologist E.O. Wilson found 43 species of ants. Other notable critters found in the Amazon include the Hercules beetle, the strongest creature on Earth, capable of carrying 850 times its own body weight, and the blue morphos butterfly, whose wings are so iridescent that they can be viewed up to almost a kilometre away.

✔ The Amazon rainforest contains the highest number of birds in the world. Nine of the 14 species of macaw found in the Amazon are listed as vulnerable to extinction.

✔ Amazonian plants provide hundreds of cost-effective medical remedies for people. Despite this fact, less than 1 per cent of the Amazon's trees and plants have been tested for medicinal potential.

In this section, we have space only to examine one: the Amazon. Now there's a place no one wants to live without. Everyone on Earth benefits from its existence. Even though it may be far away from many people in Europe or the US, it's one of the most important places in the world to protect. To discover why in detail, check out the nearby sidebar 'The Amazon: Facts and figures'.

The Amazon is so incredibly vast that for many generations it was perceived to be invulnerable from the encroachment of humankind. Unfortunately, this isn't the case. Over 7,000 square kilometres of the Brazilian Amazon were deforested in 2010 and experts project that what's left of the Amazon will be gone in the next 40 years. In fact, 17 per cent of the Amazon rainforest has already been lost, and at the current rates of deforestation, researchers estimate that 55 per cent of the Amazon may be lost by 2030.

Scientists also believe that despite plenty of rain in the Amazon, if people keep cutting down trees the forest will become drastically drier, because deforestation can significantly reduce tropical rainfall far from the area where trees have been cut down. Air that passes over forests picks up moisture given off by trees and plants, which in turn fuels rains. Therefore, if or when those trees disappear, so will a good portion of the rain.

Watch the film

One of the Amazon's fiercest philanthropists is Sarah Dupont, president and CEO of the Amazon Aid Foundation. She spends so much time and energy on this cause because 'the Amazon has the most trees. Trees are life, homes to important plants and animals, and carbon champions of the world. And well, it is just plain beautiful.'

And she's right. Sarah Dupont has already witnessed the drying out of the Amazon. As a result, she produced a documentary film titled *Amazon Gold*, which shares her journey in witnessing the destruction of the rainforest due to illegal gold mining along the Madre de Dios River in Peru. You can watch a trailer at www.amazongoldfilm.com.

The destruction of the Amazon Rain Forest is a looming disaster, for the region's plants and animals, for you, for us, and for the world. Here are some ways for you to get started protecting the Amazon and its wildlife:

✔ **Help save the Amazon one tree at a time:** Contact Amazing Forest (www.AmazingForest.com). When you buy a tree through this organisation you get the following rewards:

- A personalised name tag that's tied around the tree's trunk (you get to choose the name of your tree!), made from eco-friendly stuff, of course, and a certificate of tree ownership, sent via email (so it's eco-friendly, too).

- A guarantee that 10 per cent of any profits made go to some worthwhile charities.

- Free access to your tree or any plantation site of Amazing Forest, in case you decide to go for a visit!

- Best of all, cleaner air to breathe.

✔ **Adopt an acre of land through the Amazon Aid Foundation's Acre Care programme** (www.amazonaid.org): For a relatively small donation, you 'adopt' an acre of land in the Amazon and your donation is used to generate interest in protecting the rainforest.

✔ **Fight wildlife trafficking through FREELAND Brasil** (freelandbrasil.org.br/en/): FREELAND Brasil seeks to eliminate wildlife trafficking while at the same time helping vulnerable communities become the first-line defenders of the Amazon (rather than the traffickers themselves).

FREELAND Brasil: Using science to fight trafficking

Juliana Machado Ferreira, Executive Director, FREELAND Brasil, writes:

'Wildlife trafficking is currently a major threat to Brazilian biodiversity. It is estimated that all kinds of wildlife trafficking – biopiracy; collectors and zoos; products and souvenirs; and pet trade – withdraw from Brazilian nature over 38 million animals every year (not including fish or insects), in an illegal business worth almost 2 billion dollars. The removal of numerous animals from their natural habitat on a regular basis has severe impacts on populations and on the environment. It can lead to decreased population viability, potential local extinction of the species, species' complete extinction, and even the unbalancing of the entire ecosystem.

FREELAND Brasil, in partnerships with other institutions, mainly SOS Fauna, aims to develop studies of population genetics to produce information on species history, guidelines on releasing rehabilitated animals, identification of wildlife trafficking exploitation hotspots, as well as investigative support for the local police. Our last but not least important goal is the setup of a Brazilian Independent Wildlife Forensic Genetics Laboratory, to provide high quality data on evidence analysis obtained from crimes involving wildlife, at no cost for the government.

I am personally very interested in using science to fight crimes against wildlife, especially wild bird trafficking to supply the pet market. What really drives me is the incredible amount of animals being caught, transported, and traded, and this activity's huge environmental impacts – the suffering that the animals go through is indescribable – and how widely this activity is accepted as part of the Brazilian culture.

Eradicating wildlife trafficking would mean not only an end to the suffering of millions of living beings whose lives have intrinsic value, but would also be a major step in protecting the very biodiversity we need to sustain life – including our own – as we know it.'

Rescuing animals in your home community

Giving your time, energy, or other resources to animals doesn't always have to be on behalf of entire species or their ecosystems. You can have just as profound an impact on the life in your local neighbourhood as you can in ecosystems such as the rainforests or the oceans.

If you've ever owned a pet – a dog, a cat, or maybe a boa named Bill – no doubt that pet had or has a loving, happy home; but not all animals are so lucky. Abandoned or born feral, stray animals live very hard, often tortuous, lives. They face hunger and exposure, disease and violence. Many are abused; those that are caught are often euthanised. Some face an even worse fate (as we explain in the nearby sidebar 'So who's the real animal?').

So who's the real animal?

Despite being outlawed in nearly all developed countries, dogfighting and cockfighting still secretly happen. In these fights, two dogs fight each other while onlookers bet on which animal will survive and which will die. If a dog survives a fight but doesn't win, it's often shot or left to die. Even though penalties for dog fighting and other related criminal activities have increased, it remains a multi-million pound underground industry. Certain dogs are bred and raised to be fighters. Other dogs – often strays or the least promising of a litter – are used to train the fighting dogs. All the dogs, whether the fighters or the ones sacrificed in training, suffer unspeakable abuse.

Dogfighting and cockfighting are illegal in all 50 of the United States and in the UK as well. In fact, England's 1835 Cruelty to Animals Act was the first such act to outlaw the practice.

Ironically, although the number of stray dogs and cats is still high, consumer demand for pets continues to grow and an entire industry has grown to meet the demand. Many people shop for pets at pet shops. Unfortunately, these stores often acquire their animals through brokers or middlemen that provide falsified pedigree documents for buyers. These animals are bred in industrial or large-scale commercial operations known as puppy farms, which favour profit and numbers of animals sold over animal wellbeing, health, and dignity. Puppy farm animals receive little to no medical treatment and are confined to small wire cages for their entire lives without socialisation or human interaction.

As depressing as the picture may seem, you can do a number of things to help, as the next sections explain.

Adopting an animal from a shelter

Adopting is one of the easiest ways to give to animals. By choosing to adopt from a shelter rather than buy from a pet shop, you decrease the number of animals who desperately need homes, you get to save a life that may otherwise be written off for euthanasia, and you reduce the consumer demand for puppy farms and mass-production breeders. Find a shelter near you by connecting with the RSPCA (www.rspca.org.uk) or by enquiring with your local council.

As smitten as you may be by that animal in the pet shop window, remember that you have the power to save a life by adopting an equally amazing animal at your local animal rescue organisation or shelter.

If you're set on adopting a pure breed animal, don't assume that a shelter doesn't have what you're looking for. Shelters occasionally take in pure breed dogs and cats whose owners can no longer care for them. Also consider these options:

✔ Contacting rescue organisations for the breed you're looking for. See the next section for details.

✔ Using reputable breeders and ensuring that they are caring for animals properly and not mass-producing animals that will not have homes.

Saving an animal not only rewards them with the gift of life, but also rewards you with years of unconditional love. Whether you prefer cats or dogs or love all types of animals, shelters and rescues are filled with enough to choose from. When you set out to bring a new pet home, consider these ideas:

✔ Where and how do you live? Make sure that your home is conducive to the breed you choose. A Maltese does well in a flat, but Jack Russell terriers, even though they're little, need more exercise. Research different breeds to find out which ones are appropriate for you.

✔ Puppies are always first to go from shelters, but older dogs offer a lot, too. Dogs with a few years behind them are more likely to be housebroken and able to go longer hours while you're at work. Some people worry that an older dog may have been raised with unwanted behaviours, but a good dog trainer can help with those matters, rewarding you with a fabulous furry friend.

Volunteering for or donating to a rescue organisation

Many rescue organisations specialise in rescuing animals from high-kill shelters. They also take in pets from owners who can no longer keep their pets for whatever reason, knowing that the rescue centre doesn't euthanise. Some rescues are breed specific and some take only small pets. But many take in all kinds of pets.

As a volunteer, you foster an animal in your home until it's adopted. These rescues help the overflow of pounds and shelters and are a great source for pet adoption and finding your next furry family member.

If your house is already full, you can volunteer in other ways. Shelters need all sorts of help, from walking the dogs to cleaning pens to photographing them for their website. Stop by and see how you can help make Felix's and Fido's stays a bit more comfortable.

Giving in other ways

Wendy Diamond, founder and editor of Animal Fair Media (www. animalfair.com), a company promoting animal rescue and welfare, offers some advice about organisations you can connect to help animals (read her story in the nearby sidebar 'Advocating fairness to animals: Animal Fair Media'):

✔ **Delta Society (www.deltasociety.org):** You can train your dog to comfort sick children and the elderly in your community as a therapy dog. One million people a year are positively impacted by the companionship of therapy animals.

- ✔ **Dogs for the Disabled** (www.dogsforthedisabled.org): Dogs for the Disabled works to pair disabled humans with canine companions across the UK.

- ✔ **Green Chimneys** (www.greenchimneys.org): Green Chimneys promotes 'the dignity and worth for all living things' by pairing children in need with abandoned animals.

- ✔ **The Humane Society** (www.humanesocietyny.org): The Humane Society of New York has cared for needy animals for over 100 years. You can volunteer at its shelter or give a rescued animal a forever home.

- ✔ **Support Dogs** (www.support-dogs.org.uk/): Support Dogs helps train and provide dogs to people with epilepsy, autism, and physical disabilities so they can live more comfortable, active lives.

EXAMPLE

Advocating fairness to animals: Animal Fair Media

Wendy Diamond, Founder and Editor of Animal Fair Media, writes:

'After rescuing Pasha, my Russian Blue, and Lucky the Maltese from a local New York City shelter, I felt compelled to start Animal Fair Media, the premier lifestyle media company advocating fairness to animals by promoting animal rescue and welfare. My animals provided unconditional love and loyalty, inspiring me to make a lifelong commitment to fight for disenfranchised animals across the globe.

When I launched my animal rescue mission in 1999, shelters across the country euthanised 12 million dogs and cats annually. Animal Fair Media and other amazing individuals and organisations raised public awareness of animal rescue and dropped this number to 5 million. Animal welfare awareness is here to stay until this number is zero, and there are no more homeless pets!

By bringing animal rescue to the forefront of public awareness, Animal Fair Media encourages responsibility amongst pet guardians worldwide. We have joined forces with politicians and media personalities such as Beyoncé, Brad Pitt, Halle Berry, Charlize Theron, and *Jersey Shore* star Vinny Guadagnino, lending our voices to help silenced and vulnerable homeless pets.

Our chief philosophy: Act locally! When passionate individuals get involved in their local shelters and organisations, they become a ripple of change that radiates out to the world at large, producing substantial results.

Donating money to local shelters or organisations helps, but so does volunteering time and energy. Find a local organisation that suits your lifestyle and roll up your sleeves! You can do anything from volunteering at a shelter to fostering pets in your home for a short time. The most rewarding way to contribute is by adopting a pet – shelters carry both pedigrees and mutts – and enjoy puppy love!'

Greening Your Community

In the past decade or so, you've probably heard the term *sustainable living* at least once or twice. This effort is really about reducing your negative output on the planet, which is commonly referred to as 'reducing your carbon footprint' or 'becoming carbon neutral'. That's fine if all you want to do is have a neutral impact on the planet, but if you want to make a positive impact, get ready to roll your sleeves up.

Combating pollution

According to the World Health Organisation, pollution is a major health concern. It affects the air you breathe, the water you drink, and the habitats that sustain life. Consider these facts:

- ✔ Air pollution and the resulting effects (particles from smokestacks and factories, the amount of ozone at ground level, and so on) pose serious risks to respiratory and heart health and are linked to incidences of lung cancer.

- ✔ Water pollution takes many forms: the accumulation of toxic compounds from industrial waste; the contamination of water by harmful organisms due to improper sanitation systems (see the earlier section 'Coming Clean on Sanitation'); the harm to marine life caused by these pollutants as well as depletion of the oxygen in the water (check out 'Working to protect the world's oceans' earlier in this chapter).

- ✔ Pollution – sewage, exhaust, agricultural, and lawn chemicals, and more – is a key contributor to habitat degradation. In worst-case scenarios, such destruction can render an environment unsuitable for the wildlife it used to support.

You can help reduce pollution and mitigate its effects by doing the following:

- ✔ Keep your vehicle well maintained, because a poorly maintained engine creates more air pollution and uses more fuel.

- ✔ Reduce the amount of time you spend on the road by combining trips, carpooling, and using public transport.

- ✔ Limit your use of petrol-powered lawnmowers, leaf blowers, and so on. Electric mowers or manual push mowers pollute less while saving you money on petrol.

Contact companies such as the European Environment Agency (www.eea.europa.eu) or the World Health Organisation (www.who.int) to find out how you can help reduce pollution and about the programmes they're involved with.

Reducing carbon emissions

The 2008 Climate Change Act established the world's first legally binding climate change target. In the UK, the aim is to reduce the UK's greenhouse gas emissions by at least 80 per cent (from the 1990 baseline) by 2050.

Carbon emissions result when you burn *fossil fuels* (gasoline, diesel fuel, kerosene, natural gas, and so on) and they're a key contributor to global climate change. According to the International Energy Agency (IEA), at the current rate of warming, the Earth's average temperature will increase between roughly 3 and 5 degrees Celsius by the end of the century. Scientists indicate that the increase must be limited to no more than 2 degrees increase to avoid catastrophic effects such as agricultural failure and melted glaciers.

Although the problem is a worldwide one – and one that's likely to get worse as government and citizens in growing economies adopt fossil-fuel burning technologies – you can help reduce pollution and mitigate its effects by doing the following:

- **Appliances:** When you replace electric appliances of any kind, do your research and check the EU efficiency label, A+++ being the most efficient and D the worst. (`ec.europa.eu/energy/efficiency/labelling/labelling_en.htm`).

- **Heating and cooling:** Perform regular maintenance on your heating and cooling system(s).

- **Insulation:** *Weatherstripping* (placing rubber or silicone strips to prevent the intrusion of outside air into the building), *caulking* (using a pliable or spreadable material to fill gaps and holes), and insulation work together to save you energy, improve the comfort of your home, make it quieter, and help you save money.

Websites such as `www.carbonfund.org` are good ones to visit and find out more information.

Creating a community garden

During World War I and World War II, neighbours in the US, England, Canada, and Germany regularly created local community garden projects. These 'victory' or 'liberty' gardens were designed to relieve pressure on public food supplies caused by war. By the mid-1940s, they were so successful that they were producing 8 million tons of food! After the war, many communities abandoned their gardens. Today, with increasing interest in sustainable living, these super productive gardens are back on the rise.

Community gardens have multiple benefits: they provide low-cost food; set aside green spaces; create stronger and healthier communities; and can even reduce crime! Talk about the power of planting!

To start your own community garden, follow these steps (adapted from a checklist provided by the American Community Gardening Association at www.communitygarden.org):

1. **Organise a meeting of interested people to determine whether a garden is needed and wanted, what kind it should be (vegetable, flower, both, organic), who it will involve, and who'll benefit.**

   Invite anyone likely to be interested: neighbours, tenants, community organisations, and representatives of gardening and horticultural societies, for example. Invite an official (such as your building superintendent) if the garden is to be in an apartment complex's grounds or a large number of tenants are involved.

2. **Form a planning committee.**

   This group can comprise people who feel committed to the garden, have the time to devote to it, at least at this initial stage, and have the skills to co-ordinate and form committees to tackle specific tasks such as funding and partnerships, youth activities, construction, and communication.

3. **Identify your resources by doing a community asset assessment.**

   Consider what skills and resources already exist in the community that can aid in the garden's creation. Contact local municipal planners about possible sites, as well as horticultural societies and other local sources of information and assistance. Look within your community for people with experience in landscaping and gardening.

4. **Approach a sponsor.**

   Some gardens 'self-support' through membership payments, but for many a sponsor is essential for donations of tools, seeds, or money. Churches, schools, private businesses, and parks and recreation departments are all possible supporters. One garden in the US raised money by selling 'square inches' at $5 each to hundreds of sponsors.

5. **Choose a site.**

   To discuss which sites might be available, you may want to contact the National Allotment Society (www.nsalg.org.uk) or local landlords with derelict or unused parcels of land. When you choose the site, be sure to do the following:

   • Make sure that it has an adequate amount of daily sunshine (vegetables need at least six hours a day) and available water.

   • Consider testing the soil for possible pollutants.

- Discover who owns the land and whether you can get a lease agreement for at least three years.

- Find out whether public liability insurance or an equivalent is necessary.

6. Prepare and develop the site.

In most cases, land needs considerable preparation for planting. Organise volunteer work crews to clean it, gather materials, and decide on the design and plot arrangement.

7. Organise the garden.

Members must decide how many plots are available and how they're to be assigned. Allow space for storing tools and making compost.

Don't forget the pathways between plots! Plant flowers or shrubs around the garden's edges to promote goodwill with non-gardening neighbours, passers-by, and municipal authorities.

8. Plan for children.

Consider creating a special garden just for youngsters – including them is essential. Children are less interested in the size of the harvest than the process of gardening. A separate area set aside for them allows them to explore the garden at their own speed.

9. Determine the rules and put them in writing.

The gardeners themselves devise the best ground rules. People are more willing to comply with rules that they have a hand in creating. Some issues that are best dealt with by agreed upon rules include subscription rates and how the money is to be used, how the plots are assigned, whether gardeners share tools and meet regularly, and how basic maintenance will be handled.

10. Help members keep in touch.

Community gardens are all about creating and strengthening communities, and regular communication ensures a strong community garden with active participation by all. Form a telephone tree (a list of people who call one another where A calls B, B calls C, and so on to spread news), create an email list, install a rainproof bulletin board in the garden, and have regular celebrations.

Chapter 10

Venturing into Venture Philanthropy

· ·

In This Chapter

▶ Introducing venture philanthropy

▶ Improving health through diet

▶ Making use of technology

▶ Investing in your interests

· ·

*Y*ou may have heard people use the term *venture capital,* which refers to investors providing finance to new business enterprises (so-called ventures) – and not as one hard-of-hearing friend of ours thought 'denture' capital (investing in the manufacture of false teeth).

Now, we know that since the 2007–8 financial crisis, investment and capitalism are dirty words to some people, but don't worry; we aren't suggesting you give your money to that most modern of cartoon villains – the fat-cat banker. No, we want to talk about the idea of venture capital being increasingly applied to philanthropy. In *venture philanthropy,* you invest in social businesses or projects that provide social returns to investors. Sounds better, doesn't it?

Venture philanthropy lets donors ensure that as much of their donation as possible is being put towards causes and projects that are effective, can be replicated to benefit lots more people, and are sustainable – that is, they can survive with their own profits, without further donations.

In this chapter, we introduce social venture philanthropy, describe some of the areas where it works well (food and mobile phone technology), and make suggestions for how you can join in. If you want to be more deeply involved with organisations you support financially, this chapter is for you.

Understanding Venture Philanthropy

Venture philanthropy takes the concepts and principles of venture financing and applies them to charitable philanthropy. So, we have to look briefly at venture financing first to understand venture philanthropy.

In venture financing, investors (often called *venture capitalists*) find small companies to invest in that have a great deal of growth potential and the ability to scale-up into stable, high-profit-making companies. In addition to making a financial investment (usually by buying equity in the company for a partnership stake), the venture investors also assume roles in managing the company – they sit on the board and are involved in key decisions about hiring, marketing, product development, and so on.

By influencing the decisions and direction the company takes, these investors take an active role in protecting their investment. When all is said and done, venture investors want to see a high return on their investment. For them, a good investment is one that returns high multiples of their original investment. If they invest £1 million, for example, they want multiple millions returned to them.

Venture philanthropists apply this model to charitable organisations. They look for small ones with the potential to do good, which can scale-up their programmes to reach large numbers of people or areas and have the organisational stability to promote their missions into the future. Often, these organisations lack the management ability to handle future growth, and so venture philanthropists often require that the management be changed or re-trained. The investors/donors give money to the organisation so that it can continue and expand its programmes. The investors/donors also become very active in how the organisation is run, the actions it takes to achieve its mission, and so on.

For venture philanthropists, a successful investment isn't one that produces a high financial return but one that has a sustainable, significant, positive impact in the world. In other words, they want the money used to the greatest effect, the organisation to be managed well, and its resources sustainably deployed over time.

Don't misunderstand the term venture philanthropy. Although the word 'venture' usually implies an element of speculation or risk, that doesn't mean that the people involved in venture philanthropy tend to lose out (spending so much time monitoring what's going on that they run out of time for other work or family) or that the organisation loses out by pursuing a goal that's too complex or succumbing to the 'Jack of all trades, master of none' syndrome, in which it functions neither as a successful charity (helping out) nor as a successful business (making money).

As the next section reveals, venture philanthropy can provide huge benefits for all involved.

Looking at the benefits

Recent research indicates that often no one misses out by participating in venture philanthropy. In fact, applying the key business principles to charitable programmes can be beneficial:

- ✔ Charities benefit from greater oversight. Charities with good governance practices tend to hire better-trained people and run on leaner budgets. Such organisations are generally better equipped to meet donor expectations.

- ✔ Social businesses are run more diligently because they know they need to meet interim benchmarks instead of merely looking good in annual budgets or photographs sent to donors.

- ✔ Donors are able to keep track of where their money is going and what it's achieving. Perhaps most importantly, they can see what's going wrong *before* it goes wrong and so reallocate their time, energy, and money to other outlets, instead of wondering where the money went.

More and more donors – even those who don't think of themselves as venture philanthropists – are demanding to see measurable results and more accountability from the organisations they support, something that venture philanthropy offers them. To find the people who're going to run the next big venture philanthropic enterprise, read on.

Understanding why venture philanthropy matters

According to Peter Thum, co-founder and CEO of Fonderie47 and co-founder of Ethos Water (find out more about these organisations in the nearby side-bar 'Building businesses with social purpose'), social ventures matter for several reasons:

- ✔ They generate social value. Although charitable giving may account for only a small percentage of a country's gross domestic product (GDP) (charitable giving by Americans, for example, historically hovers between 1.5 and 2 per cent of GDP), social ventures generate social value from the other 98 per cent.

- ✔ They create active interest by connecting people to issues for the first time or in a new and unexpected way. Many of these people would have no awareness of or connection to the issue without these brands.

- ✔ They integrate social mission into customer choice.

- ✔ They change industry competition through the natural adoption of their models (when commercially successful, of course).

If you want to support (as a customer or investor) or start one of these ventures, here are some characteristics that the good ones have in common and that you should look for:

- ✔ They're *startups,* which are organisations that did not exist only a few months or a year before. Generally, startups may have no employees at full wages or may have only a handful of employees. At this stage, it is not uncommon for the founders to take equity in lieu of pay, or for the core staff to take very low (below market rate) wages for the sake of the company, which would otherwise be starved by payroll obligations.

- ✔ The founder(s) have a personal, deep connection to the social mission.

- ✔ The team makes a living solely from the venture; it's not an ego project and failure isn't an option.

- ✔ The venture's mission and model can generate a change of awareness and action.

- ✔ The brand and its products or services are as good or better on key customer-buying criteria than their competitors.

- ✔ The business's economics optimise the balance between social purpose investment and the traditional emphasis on financial returns to ensure the sustainability of both elements.

Examining different models

In essence, three general types of venture philanthropy exist:

- ✔ **Traditional model:** A donor becomes intimately involved with the organisation and takes on a management role or heavily influences the direction of the organisation. This model often involves people taking positions on the boards of the organisations they support or businesspeople lending financial expertise to the management of a social business.

- ✔ **Delegated venture model:** Individuals or small foundations (typically) pool their resources into a fund that's managed by professionals (who may be financial experts or 'matchmakers'). These experts investigate opportunities and bring them to the organisation for funding.

- ✔ **Partnership model:** The investor or donor becomes a partner of the organisation, providing financing and management. In this model, the most donor-involved of the three types, the investor/donor becomes more like an active business consultant than a passive cheque-writer.

In this chapter, we focus primarily on the second and third models, because they're most likely to be the ones in which you can get involved.

Building businesses with social purpose

Peter Thum, Co-Founder & CEO, Fonderie47 and Co-Founder, Ethos Water, writes:

'When you buy something, you choose from a set of options; brands and products that have different features. In the 1980s, choice grew to include social impact. Companies like Newman's Own, Ben and Jerry's, and the Body Shop introduced products that embedded or were entirely built around a social purpose. Their products were made using ethical production practices, or their proceeds funded a mission, or some mixture of both.

Since then, many more of these types of brands have hit the market, all for-profit brands that entered as startups in existing industries. I've started a couple of these kinds of ventures myself, so I'm a clear proponent of this approach. Many terms are used to describe these companies, but I think that 'for-profit, social purpose venture' is the most accurate, even if a bit clunky.

Ethos Water (www.ethoswater.com), which Starbucks acquired in 2005, was one such venture. The idea was simple – drink water to give water. Sales of Ethos fund water and sanitation programmes for people in need around the world. After Ethos, I started Fonderie47 (www.fonderie47.com) in 2011, which transforms AK47s from African war zones into jewellery, the sales of which fund disarmament in Africa. As of February of 2012, we've destroyed over 10,000 assault rifles in Africa.'

When considering venture philanthropy, ask questions to understand how something works *before* offering your time, money, or expertise.

Finding venture philanthropy organisations to support

Most venture philanthropy organisations invest in big ideas – often ones that haven't been tried yet. Venture philanthropy funds tend to invest in small organisations with big dreams. Inevitably, not all these dreams come true and some of these organisations fail. But they have less to lose (in brand, credibility, staff, and so on) than big organisations, and so small ones are often more innovative and willing to try new ideas.

Every year many people with bright ideas attract international attention – all believe they can help in the fight against poverty, disease, malnutrition, infant mortality, and other ills. Some examples of areas attracting venture philanthropists' attention right now include:

- ✔ Housing, both in the developed and developing worlds (in particular demand is housing in urban renewal areas, affordable housing for seniors, and housing near new urban centres in the developing world).

- ✔ Medical protection such as inoculation, transportation, and so on (check out Chapter 8 for loads more on health philanthropy).

- ✔ Microbusiness/microfranchise, which are models where poor people can start businesses with small amounts of money, either on their own or by taking an existing franchise and expanding its reach (the later section 'Harnessing Technology with Mobile Mania' contains examples).

- ✔ Nutrition (we describe examples in the later section 'Providing Healthy, Nutritious Food').

- ✔ Sanitation (see Chapter 9 for more details on this area).

Discovering what to look for in an organisation

When you're searching for a venture philanthropy organisation to support, you want to be able to answer yes to these three questions:

- ✔ Does the organisation receiving your generosity have the ability to accomplish its goals?

- ✔ Is the organisation's management competent and does it have integrity?

- ✔ Does the organisation have financial stability now and into the future?

Unfortunately, almost no organisation from its beginnings has all these attributes in place. Some are stronger in one area than another and some need help in all three categories. But the great thing about venture philanthropy is that you don't have to search for the perfect organisation – you can select one and then through your involvement help make it better!

Going through an intermediary

Most people get involved in venture philanthropy through an intermediary – a middleman, broker, dealer, matchmaker, or talent scout. This intermediary can be a community investment fund in your city that's taking over poorly-run charitable efforts or a national initiative run by experts who make sure that money is used as well as possible to research a disease or a public policy question.

Most likely, someone is going to act between you and your venture philanthropy activities, so make sure that you're comfortable with the role this intermediary plays. For more details, read the later section 'Using intermediaries'.

Following the crowd

Venture philanthropy is an area where watching (if not following) the crowd can be worthwhile.

Global imperatives and businesses: Seventh Generation

Jeffrey Hollender, Founder and Former CEO, Seventh Generation (www.seventhgen-eration.com), writes:

'Imagine a world that creates opportunities for the wellness of people, planet, and all living things. At Seventh Generation, we use "global imperatives" to represent our role in the world that we dream of – the world at its best, most sustainable, and equitable state. Global impera-tives reinforce our belief that the corporation is the most powerful global institution in the world today, and that the role of business in society is one of the most important levers for change. These imperatives translate into objectives and strategies that can take 25, 50, or even 100 years to achieve. Although generally not the kind of timeframe within which business is comfortable thinking, that's what makes the pursuit of global imperatives so challenging, so important.

The development of Seventh Generation's global imperatives began with a question: "What is Seventh Generation uniquely able to do that the world most needs?" We spent time creating a working document that provides imperatives that were scary, inspiring, hopeful, impossible, and awesome all at the same time, but were designed to change the way we do business.

This document lays out our commitment to create a world of equity and justice, health and wellbeing; of more conscious workers, citizens and consumers; where natural resources are used and renewed at a rate below their rate of depletion; and to create a business where all our products' raw materials, by-products, and the processes by which they are made are not just sustainable but restorative, and enhance the potential of all life's systems.'

Thinking about how and why experts are focusing on certain projects or organisations is instructive. Ask yourself why the Bill & Melinda Gates Foundation or the United Nations is so interested in a new idea. Investigate why venture capitalists, known for spotting good ideas, are taking an interest in a small mobile-phone venture in Kenya (see the later section 'Making micro-marketplaces with mobile money') or that sanitation project in Indonesia.

To see the range of options that are available, take a look at some of these venture philanthropy leaders:

- ✔ **Alfanar Venture Philanthropy** (www.alfanar.org.uk): Alfanar markets itself as the first Arab venture philanthropy organisation and focuses on long-term investments in charities (which don't produce a return) and social businesses (which do create a return on investments) at an early stage, with the hope that they reach financial sustainability. Alfanar's criteria focus on how innovative, long term (sustainable), and enterprising/entrepreneurial an idea is.

- ✔ **Full Circle Fund** (www.fullcirclefund.org): This organisation focuses primarily on *engaged philanthropy,* which is a process of engaging the donor in every step of the decision, from the grant, through to the project's completion, and in any post-project analysis of its degree of success. Full Circle is regional (with a focus in and near San Francisco, California), but looks at organisations worldwide for inspiration and new ideas. Its heavy focus on building links between communities and developing strong leadership for those communities is unusual among venture philanthropy organisations.

✔ **Impetus Trust (**www.impetus.org.uk**):** Active for over ten years, Impetus Trust was one of the first large venture philanthropy organisations in the UK. Its model of venture philanthropy focuses on engagement, much as Full Circle Fund does (see above), and uses creative financing to its advantage, often combining grants with loans or education or other tools to allow organisations to meet their goals. Charities and social enterprises helped by Impetus have increased their incomes over 20 per cent while increasing the number of people they help by nearly 40 per cent.

This list isn't exhaustive or an endorsement of any of these organisations – just a list of options so that you can see the differences between various approaches to venture philanthropy.

Make use of the websites of the recipients instead of just those of the intermediaries. Often, from the recipients' comments (usually impregnated with varying levels of gratitude) you can read between the lines and see whether they felt supported. Perhaps some feel they received crucial help at an early stage whereas others feel they were bullied, overmanaged, or given unrealistic objectives. Take a look around and see what you find.

Planning your investment

To start thinking through a venture philanthropy investment, consider how you can lend a hand. Sit down with a piece of paper and carry out an inventory of your skills, contacts, and financial resources. Think through how your strengths and an organisation's weaknesses fit together.

Next, think about where the value (the money, the services, the consulting know-how, or just the materials) flows. In other words, how is what you're contributing adding value; what determines how large your social return on investment will be?

Consider how that value is used. Usually, venture philanthropy is a good fit for high-impact, low-overhead organisations. As a result, more of the money flowing through the organisation often goes directly towards accomplishing its stated goals than in a typical traditional charity.

This concept of identifying a need and matching it to a potential solution is nicely illustrated through the example of Grameen Danone Foods in the later section 'Joining needs and solutions together'.

As you plan your investment, keep these points in mind:

✔ **Social ventures needn't be charities.** These organisations can operate in a mix of ways. Some organisations use the funds to increase their outreach or fundraising capabilities; others use investments to pay a dividend or generate a cash return to investors. Be sure you understand whether the return on your investment is to be purely social or also financial. Note that any financial returns often create tax implications for you personally (see Chapter 4 for details). As with any financial investment, make sure that you understand the risks involved.

✔ **Venture philanthropy often involves social businesses, which have all the risks associated with other businesses.** Although getting involved in backing a new venture is exciting, be sure that you're confident that the people running the business are the right team for the job or – if they're not – that the investment team is aware of this problem and can provide the help they need. Money put into social businesses can lose value. To find out more about investments and the risks that accompany them, take a peek at Chapter 16.

Providing Healthy, Nutritious Food

Food creation and supply is an excellent area for venture philanthropy. Everyone buys food and cares (albeit to varying degrees) how safe, nutritious, and healthy that food is. Increasingly, consumers also care where their food comes from, how it's produced, and whether it's from nearby or far away. Here are just two reasons:

✔ **Improving food choices:** Medical studies suggest that more than a quarter of human health problems relate to diet and that poor dietary choices worsen existing problems. Experts are trying to influence what people eat, believing that positive change in this area has a wide variety of positive effects, such as:

- Lowering obesity rates

- Decreasing rates of cancer and heart disease

- Reducing the incidence of preventable chronic diseases

- Lowering healthcare costs for government and society

✔ **Focusing on a single product:** Often, a simple product is at the centre of the innovation. Whether it's small-batch granola or local non-pasteurised fruit juice, the creation, transport, marketing, and retailing of the product can affect its appeal to customers and its effectiveness as a social innovation. Therefore, a substantial connection exists between what customers want, what helps the community, and what makes business sense.

Social ventures exist at every stage of the food creation process, and venture philanthropists continue to invent new, exciting ways to support these ventures. In this section, we look at some venture philanthropy businesses that focus on diet, health, and the environment.

Joining needs and solutions together

In far too many places around the world, children have difficulty accessing nutritious food at accessible prices. Local businesses are aware of this problem (they see the results in their clients' children), and other firms have the technology to provide nutritious food at low cost but lack the local expertise or distribution network to get food where it's needed.

This position was the one facing the chiefs of Grameen Bank and Groupe Danone when they met at a restaurant in Paris in 2005:

- Grameen Bank knew that the people of Bangladesh struggled to provide nutritious meals to their children.
- Danone knew how to provide nutrients in the form of yoghurt.

Hence, Grameen Danone Foods was born. Grameen and Danone invested in a joint venture company that would be a social business where shareholders would receive a 1 per cent dividend (for more on dividends, see the nearby sidebar 'Giving twice over: Dividends') and the rest of the money would be reinvested to create new opportunities for poor people in Bangladesh.

In this example, Grameen and Danone are the donors and Grameen Danone Foods is the recipient – the social venture and beneficiary. Grameen and Danone lent not only their money and their powerful brand names to this joint venture, but also Grameen contributed its expertise about Bangladesh and Danone contributed what it had learned over decades of making nutritious yoghurt products.

Is your company looking for a partner or a way to increase its visibility? Why not find a way to partner and do business with that partner, rather than simply buying advertising or attempting to convince the partner to put its brand on your product? By working together, you can add more value to your brand and theirs – and make money in the process!

Giving twice over: Dividends

Sometimes, donors are willing to give up their right to a dividend or investment return if the venture does particularly well or has other benefits for the donors. The Grameen Danone Foods joint venture was so successful, and had such good effects for the bank and the food company, that donors agreed to return even the small 1 per cent dividend they originally asked to receive.

When you think of a dividend you may receive from a social investment, consider how it can best be used – sometimes, the best use is to donate it back to the venture.

Building awareness around healthy eating

Since President Obama was elected in 2008, one of the key issues his wife, Michelle Obama, has attempted to tackle is childhood activity and childhood obesity. While exercise and play are important, so is nutrition. And this has increasingly become a focus of national discussion in America – not surprising in a country spending years agonising over its huge healthcare costs and ballooning (pun intended) obesity epidemic.

Jamie Oliver has harnessed his celebrity status as a chef and an expert on all things culinary to try to change American eating habits and attitudes through his 'food revolution'. This project isn't just a TV chef's nod to social problems, but a broader philanthropic effort to shift the consumption of food to healthier choices.

At first, Oliver chose to focus on schools because:

✔ They're a central congregation point for the next generation.

✔ They're where children discover how to work, play, socialise, and eat!

✔ They're the easiest place to intervene and short-circuit the American path towards obesity and malnourishment.

The organisers quickly realised, however, that a deeper intervention was needed. Though improving school lunches was important, a broader deterioration existed in America's eating infrastructure. Americans didn't know how to cook – even the most basic preparation of food at home was seen as challenging, intimidating, and expensive.

So, Oliver adopted a broader strategy in order to:

✔ Improve school lunches and home cooking, including neighbourhood kitchens for people to learn how to prepare healthy food.

> ✔ Encourage corporations to partner with the project and take an interest in their employees' health and nutrition.
>
> ✔ View nutrition as a central priority for social improvement and innovation instead of an individual's series of consumer choices.

At the time of writing, the roll-out of this broader approach is underway. You can find out more about the Better Food Foundation and how to get involved at www.jamieoliver.com/foundation.

If you're inspired, consider making changes in your local schools. Research how much you know about the lunches provided by your child's school and scrutinise the availability of healthy options in the vending machines at the school or at nearby businesses. Perhaps an opportunity exists in a biology, physical education, or even an art class where children can learn and think about how food is made available to them. See whether you can integrate into your school's curriculum lessons on how foods are marketed (particularly unhealthy versus healthy foods) to help children become healthier, more informed consumers.

Creating all-natural brands

The question of what a brand means has historically meant how the brand appeals to consumers. Is it known for its low prices, for instance. However, today brands encompass values that are far more nuanced and interesting, like a brand known for its relationship to the environment or a brand known for hiring veterans from the armed services.

Brandan Synnott's desire was to provide a delicious, healthy product, a natural brand of food that, by itself, communicates the values of natural, healthy food. He hit on a huge success with Bear Naked, a granola brand that quickly became a household name in the US.

The Bear Naked story began the opposite way round to how most new products are launched. Instead of creating a product and then trying to market it as 'natural' or 'healthy', Synnott began with an idea to build a brand around nature. This decision to focus on branding and communication with customers worked as major retailers rushed to have Bear Naked foods on their shelves. The brand appealed to their customers and reinforced their image as a place to shop if you care about the environment, health, and value (the product is comparably priced to other products but offers more social, health, and environmental value).

The result was a win–win situation. Bear Naked's shareholders saw a 1,500 per cent increase in the value of their investment and the business has provided lots of positive social effects that reach beyond its customers, employees, and shareholders. By 2008, Bear Naked was a $65-million-per-year granola company helping tens of thousands of customers to have a positive impact while enjoying healthy, nutritious food. Part of Bear Naked's success came from the genuine relationship between nature and the company's products. It didn't just tack 'environmentally friendly' on its products as a mere marketing ploy. Instead, caring for the environment was integrated into the company's core.

As a venture philanthropist, consider how genuine the marketing claims are for the company you're supporting. Do the charities you care about add 'and friendly to the environment' as an afterthought or is the environmental impact truly central to their message and operations? Being genuine in your message – and supporting organisations that are genuine in theirs – creates an opportunity to do good and have better conversations with your customers, the organisations you support, and others who care about your cause.

Harnessing Technology with Mobile Mania

Technology is a great boon to people in the West, often supplying increased convenience and speed, but for people in developing countries it can mean so much more. Venture philanthropy is increasingly providing technology to the world's poor.

In this section, for example, we consider smartphones. The use of smartphones in the developing world (Africa is leading their adoption, the percentage of people with phones more than doubling each year) is a huge positive for many development initiatives. Not only do Africans in rural areas now access educational, healthcare, and services information that was previously only available via paper brochures or personal contact with NGO entities, but also rural Africans have relationships with hospitals, banks, and other institutions that were impossible before.

Using intermediaries

In the past, the world of philanthropy featured many intermediaries. To help someone in Kenya, say, a British philanthropist gave to a UK charity, which then found a Kenyan charity, which then found a local organisation, which then found someone who needed money. Today, the intermediaries in philanthropy are more savvy, less costly, and far more efficient. Best of all, they have business models that are better for donors and for recipients.

Created nearly ten years ago, Kiva Microfunds (www.kiva.org) links donors with entrepreneurs. The Kiva model is interesting, because it acts as a matchmaker, linking donors with people starting small businesses overseas. Often, these entrepreneurs have limited access to capital or only have access to regional or village moneylenders who charge high interest rates (sometimes in excess of 30 to 50 per cent annually).

Note the following if you're considering contributing to Kiva Microfunds:

✔ Kiva is an example of *crowdsourcing* (go to Chapter 11 for more), where a person can inexpensively appeal to a broad audience to fund an idea. Kiva works with about 150 microfinance organisations, which nominate entrepreneurs. An entrepreneur's pitch is made available on Kiva for a global audience of funders.

Many of these businesses aren't social businesses in the sense understood by Western entrepreneurs, in that the financial return may be far below market rate. This type of funding can be classified as venture philanthropy, however, because the recipients are often impoverished and many reside in the developing world.

✔ Through Kiva, you can fund small businesses directly. Yet, unlike venture capital models, Kiva funders don't receive a stake in the entrepreneur's business. Be sure you understand the arrangement you're entering into before you offer funding.

✔ Your involvement with the company you fund through Kiva is limited. Kiva represents a recent trend in venture philanthropy: the recipient is nearly invisible to the donor. In other words, although you have a sense of where your money is going, Kiva acts as a relatively opaque liaison between individual borrowers and lenders. Although arguments exist for and against this system, some involving privacy and efficiency, it interferes with your ability to interact directly with and counsel the venture you're investing in (something that's normally central to the venture philanthropy relationship). However, many supporters argue that the impracticability of true, direct donor-to-recipient interaction makes the Kiva model the most effective one possible with current communications and financial technology.

If you get involved in venture philanthropy, you have to decide for yourself how much intervention you're comfortable with. Most venture philanthropy uses an intermediary of some sort, but no matter how well this system is implemented it adds a layer between you and the people you're helping. You have to decide whether that's okay or whether you want to get more closely involved.

✔ You help entrepreneurs through Kiva by providing *debt* financing (as opposed to *equity* financing), which means that you're making a loan to a person starting a business rather than providing money in exchange for a share (ownership) of the business. Despite this important difference, debt financing schemes are generally discussed alongside venture philanthropy and social investment because just as some investors prefer to have the organisation owe them payments, others prefer to own a stake in the firm.

The numbers behind Kiva Microfunds

At the time of writing, Kiva is approaching $250 million distributed to people in the developing world with little or no access to traditional banks or financial tools. In 2008, despite the global financial crisis, Kiva's users still released $37 million to entrepreneurial ventures in low-income countries. These numbers are huge, but keep in mind that most of the money lent to entrepreneurs through Kiva comes from small donors just like you.

A great deal of misinformation exists about how organisations such as Kiva function. For instance, many people still believe that Kiva keeps the interest paid on loans given to entrepreneurs. As of 2012, this isn't true and Kiva funds its operations entirely with donations. If you're concerned about the practices of organisations you deal with (and you should be), ensure that you find out about each organisation's practices before deciding to do business. Chapter 4 tells you more about vetting organisations.

Communicating with micro-entrepreneur networks

The concept of micro-entrepreneurship is that people in poverty will not be lifted out of poverty simply by 'getting jobs.' People will instead need to create jobs for themselves, which often involves starting a company, running a shop, or vending goods on an informal basis.

In 1997, after seeing the potential of telecommunications ventures to lift people out of poverty, Grameen Bank started Grameen Telecom Corporation. Today, Grameenphone (a joint venture between Grameen Telecom Corporation and Telenor) is the largest telecommunications provider in Bangladesh with more than 30 million subscribers:

- ✔ Grameenphone provides prepaid service to poor people in Bangladesh who'd otherwise have no access to a mobile telephone service.

- ✔ Grameenphone also allows its users to use their phones to send money, pay bills, and visit Internet sites.

As part of Grameenphone's work to serve the poor and enable micro-entrepreneurship, Grameen Telecom operates the Village Phone system in Bangladesh. Village Phone gives Grameen Bank's clients access to mobile-phone technology at very low rates. These clients can then let others use their phones in exchange for a fee as a small business (in so doing, the person offering the phone becomes a 'phone booth' for local people).

Women all over Bangladesh have been brought out of poverty by starting a small Village Phone business. The phones are given to Grameen clients at low per-minute call rates and low prices. People who can't afford to buy the phones are financed with microloans from Grameen Bank. The Village Phone model has been cited as one of the most sustainable and imitated models for encouraging micro-entrepreneurship among the poor.

Whether low or high-technology, existing ideas used in a new context can have a huge impact in the world. Even the simplest tools – bicycles and lanterns – have been improved and optimised for use in the developing world, and the needs, wants, and day-to-day lives are different in different parts of the world. So keep in mind that your next big idea may not be something for a customer in the UK or the US, but rather for a customer in Kenya or Kazakhstan. Maybe you can help people in a different part of the world by adapting something from your place, work, or culture for use in a new context. Think on that next time you travel on business overseas or wonder why a business idea hasn't yet succeeded.

Tips for satisfying philanthropy

Alex Counts, President, Grameen Foundation (www.grameenfoundation.org), writes:

'Whether they give hundreds or millions of dollars, the most satisfied and effective philanthropists I know do their homework – online and in person – about the charities that interest them. Some of the most exciting work is applying the ethics and mission-orientation of the non-profit sector to business. Investing in social-purpose-driven businesses can be an exciting complement to traditional charitable donations.

Don't forget that philanthropy should be enjoyable. When you're engaging with organisations whose people stimulate, inspire, and appreciate you, in turn you become a fully creative collaborator, worth far more than your funding. When in doubt about where to invest, give the highest priority to finding deep enjoyment and a sense of meaning (not just a momentary thrill) – for *you* – through your philanthropy. Nothing is more satisfying than knowing that your hard-earned resources have truly helped solve a problem and changed lives, especially when the process also teaches you new things and introduces you to people who enrich your life.'

Making micro-marketplaces with mobile money

The growth of mobile phones has redefined life in the developing world. Often, in places like Vietnam and Uganda, a person who did not have a mobile phone ten years ago now has three. But phones are not only for placing calls and taking photos – new apps and other tools allow the poor to improve the management of their finances using phones.

Safari Communications ('Safaricom'; www.safaricom.co.ke) is a home-grown East African success story. In 1997, it was one of several telecommunications startups in East Africa. Today it's Kenya's leading mobile operator, with operations throughout the country and over 15 million subscribers.

Safaricom's rise from obscurity to success is due to its decision to provide services of value to the country's poor (as well as helping the poor directly through Safaricom Foundation). Here are two of its many innovations:

- ✔ **Flash texts:** A text-message service that helps poor Kenyans without sufficient credit to use their phones.

- ✔ **M-PESA:** A project that allows people to use a mobile phone like a debit card and to send money to another M-PESA user directly from the handset, without using a wire service.

Safaricom is a leader in Kenya's telecommunications business and in the broader discussion of how to build a business while serving the poor.

When considering your own philanthropic venture idea, remember that although you can always find ways to make something available in a new place, how that thing arrives in that place is also important. Consider whether to send an item overseas or train people there to make it. Or to take, say, a mobile phone provider to an African country or encourage that country's entrepreneurs to start their own mobile-phone company. These questions are at the intersection of investment and philanthropy and important to consider as you consider how to solve the world's problems.

Tying Your Interests to Venture Philanthropy

Connecting your interests to your philanthropy may be easier than you think. The environment and recycling/re-use may seem obvious causes to tie to venture philanthropy, but even a passion that seems at first glance unconnected to doing good – such as shopping, fashion, and looking beautiful! – can work, as we demonstrate in this section.

Transforming fashion into philanthropic passion

The fashion industry is heavily involved in issues such as combating AIDS and drug abuse and being anti-fur. Today, the business is increasingly embracing philanthropy as its central message. The popularity of items such as (PRODUCT)[RED] (www.red.org/en) shows this growing link between fashion products and philanthropy. Jump to Chapter 15 to discover more about how your next shopping trip can help improve the world.

Buying one, giving one

A growing area of retailing venture philanthropy involves the concept of 'buy one, give one', in which a firm makes a donation of some sort on behalf of the purchaser of its product. This can mean that a pair of shoes or eyeglasses is given away for every one purchased, or clean water is provided in Malawi when a bottle of water is purchased in Massachusetts.

Warby Parker (check out the nearby sidebar 'Seeing venture philanthropy more clearly') is one of the leaders in this area of philanthropy: for every pair of glasses the firm sells, it donates a pair to a person in need. Other examples of buy one, give one are Tom's Shoes (www.toms.com) and FEED Project (www.feedprojects.com). Some of these organisations give an item similar to what you buy: Warby Parker sells and gives eyewear; Tom's Shoes sells and gives shoes. Others donate something different from the purchase. In the case of FEED Project, the buyer gets a T-shirt or a bag and the recipient gets food. All these buy-one-give-one business models depend on interest in their products and interest in their model of philanthropy.

A shortage of glasses, shoes, or food represents well-recognised and urgent needs, and so consumers understand what these companies are doing and how they help people. This fact is true of all successful companies in this area: they address a well-understood need in a way people can understand.

Think about the effects of the goods you purchase. Who made them? Who benefits from them? What will you do when you're finished using them – donate the item, recycle it, put it into the landfill, find another use for it? Can you see a way to do more good: that is, make the product in a more environmentally-friendly way; give something to charity (money or items) each time this product is purchased; make the product's factory a more enjoyable place to work? Analyse and act upon these questions – find ways to do good while being a consumer.

EXAMPLE

Seeing venture philanthropy more clearly

Dave Gilboa, Co-Founder, Warby Parker (www.warbyparker.com), writes:

'We started Warby Parker because we love glasses but hated paying $500 for them. We thought it was absurd that the average pair of glasses in the US costs more than an iPhone. We found that the only reason for this expense is that a handful of massive corporations control the entire supply chain and mark-up glasses 10–20 times what they cost to manufacture.

So, in 2010 we introduced some innovation into the eyewear industry by creating our own brand, doing all the design in-house, sourcing the same materials that the big guys are using in their several-hundred-dollar pairs, having them made on identical production lines, and selling them direct to consumers online for $95 including prescription lenses.

Beyond the prospect of disrupting the eyewear industry and transferring billions of dollars from large corporations into the pockets of consumers, we were interested in creating a for-profit company that has a positive impact in the world (we're also 100 per cent carbon neutral). In our first full year in business we distributed over 100,000 pairs of glasses around the world.'

Spreading awareness of breast cancer

You can't miss the omnipresent pink ribbons at charity walks in cities such as London and New York, and yet in much of the world breast cancer is still a taboo topic. Women have difficulty seeking healthcare and often are provided with incomplete or low-quality care. Sometimes embarrassment is the issue in a culture of male doctors; sometimes the problem is reluctance to hear bad news or fear of asking about breast cancer. Sometimes the cost or lack of necessary intervention prevents families from taking care of healthcare needs.

The Estée Lauder companies are active in associating women's issues with fashion. Its brands, including Clinique, DKNY, and Jo Malone, have been powerhouses in the worlds of fashion and philanthropy, helping to spread the word about women's health issues. Co-branding lends the credibility, comfort, and trust that consumers already hold for a given brand to a new product, experience, or charitable cause.

DKNY's efforts to spread breast cancer awareness in the Middle East are savvy in three ways:

- ✔ It uses a strong brand to associate fashion with health awareness.
- ✔ It incorporates a women's health component into major events frequented by influential celebrities and tastemakers.
- ✔ It talks about women's health in regionally appropriate and culturally sensitive terms, in parts of the world where women's health has often been underemphasised compared to other awareness topics.

Relating effectively to the audience is vital in any advocacy-focused philanthropy. You need to understand the cultural, educational, and geographical context of the campaign and assess its likelihood of success within that framework.

Understanding the broader politics of a situation is important as a citizen, consumer, or philanthropist. For instance, many humanitarian philanthropists praise the work of DKNY and other brands in raising awareness about health issues, but are critical of parent company Estée Lauder's (and Lauder heir Ronald Lauder's) support for Israel. If you have humanitarian and political concerns, you need to weigh a company or campaign's effects in several dimensions and decide for yourself whether the organisation has positive or negative effects.

Protecting women's health in the Middle East: The Zahra Association

Millions of women every year are affected by treatable diseases that go undiagnosed due to poor access to care, cost of testing, or other factors (even though the cost of testing for many of these conditions is less than the cost of a cup of coffee in London). Breast cancer is a particularly disastrous disease when left undiagnosed, where the survival rate becomes substantially worse with each year. In the Middle East, despite substantial government healthcare subsidies, many women don't receive regular check-ups and women tend to get full medical examinations infrequently, often without breast-cancer screening. The Zahra Association in Saudi Arabia is using savvy marketing, help from corporate sponsors, and knowledge of the local healthcare system to change this by educating women in Saudi and elsewhere about breast cancer.

Reema Bandar al-Saud, Zahra Breast Cancer Association of Saudi Arabia, writes:

'We were founded in 2002 by Dr Souad bin Amer whose own mother, the Zahra for whom the organisation is named, was one of the victims of this disease. Tragically, Zahra isn't alone. She represents one out of every five Saudi women from the Gulf region who develop breast cancer.

But we're changing the tide. We're pushing for the medical and cultural changes that ensure early detection and the swift intervention that comes following the diagnosis. Our main goal is generating awareness and endorsing educational measures. We're actively reaching women from rural villages to the cosmopolitan cities. We won't stop breaking records, as we did in 2010 with the largest human awareness ribbon, where 3,952 gathered shoulder-to-shoulder in the A Woman's Stand campaign.'

Think about the relationship between your consumerism and your philanthropy to become a more involved, more conscious consumer *and* philanthropist. Do the causes you support and those of the companies you support align? If you have an idea for a cause your favourite brand should support or a company your favourite charity should approach, speak up. Often, partnerships are ripe, unspoken ideas just waiting to happen!

Searching out natural, healthy, and sustainable beauty ingredients

Since The Body Shop came on the scene in the late 1970s, more and more people have become sensitive to where their beauty products come from. Today, hundreds of brands use product attributes such as 'not tested on animals' or 'not containing petroleum products' to differentiate their products and draw consumers' attention. But how can you fit the ingredients you smear on your body with your philanthropic agendas?

One of the biggest challenges is creating a class of luxury beauty and personal-care products that shows concern for the scarcity and location of their sources, while not turning to synthetic sets of ingredients. In general, consumers aren't willing to pay premium amounts for synthetically manufactured, primarily petroleum-based products. Therefore, people are venturing (no pun intended) into the forests and prairies of the world to look for ingredients and the last few years have seen several items from Asia enter the beauty vocabulary.

The search for new ingredients in cosmetics is a global quest. You can help by investing in products that contain locally and sustainably harvested ingredients and use agricultural and labour practices that you agree with. For example, you can avoid companies that use ingredients not typically used in Europe or which use child labour. If products have to be brought from abroad, you may want to consider the transport cost of those ingredients as well. Many fair-trade labelling initiatives integrate some or all of these concerns; research them and use the research of others to help guide your decision-making as a consumer.

Being thrifty is hip

Although recycling is cool, re-use is even better! You may be surprised to know that recycling a plastic bottle requires far more energy than making a new one. With current technology only recycling aluminium and glass saves energy, with glass being the most easily recycled material by far. Recycling paper and plastic are energy-intensive – if you can re-use that plastic bottle or office paper instead, do it!

Charity and thrift shops have become fashionable, thanks to a global recession and retro consumer tastes. As a result you'll probably see more popping up in the coming years – even for causes that haven't traditionally run retail shops – and philanthropists like you can buy cool stuff while helping out others (for more on this subject, turn to Chapter 15).

If you see one of these shops, go in and look around. You just may find that perfect thing to buy (or that perfect cause to support).

Seeking sustainable packaging options

Most people burn or bury their rubbish. Even those who don't physically set fires or dig holes probably give their waste to people who then burn or bury it. Yet little thought is given to the biodegradability or clean-burning characteristics of most waste.

Take packaging, for example: most consumers don't pay attention to what happens when they throw it away. As a result, packaging is a hidden environmental cost of buying nearly anything. Given the rise in online shopping, Amazon.com has spent a substantial amount of time, effort, and money on researching and developing better packaging options for its goods. But many companies aren't so thoughtful in this regard.

A concept called *lifecycle design* is taking hold, though slowly. For example, German automaker Audi produced the Audi A2, a lightweight, low-fuel-consumption car in which nearly every piece of the car was stamped with a recycling code. The car can, literally, be recycled when it's no longer usable. This kind of thinking should – and will – make its way into the small, disposable products that litter people's lives.

Even though many people separate their recycling from their rubbish, often the latter still fills several heavy bags whereas the recycling is a lightweight collection of cans, bottles, and packages. Flipping this ratio would be better, to make most of what a household produces useful or at least re-useful! Many manufacturers are looking at making this happen, and you can support them by choosing products with a positive end-of-life plan. To find a list of companies that use sustainable packaging, check out the global Sustainable Packaging Coalition at `www.sustainablepackaging.org`. Want to know what's up in the world of sustainable packaging and who the innovators are? See `www.packagingeurope.com`.

Chapter 11

Solving Problems through Innovation and Technology

. . . .

In This Chapter

▶ Connecting technology and philanthropy

▶ Using technology to address basic needs

▶ Competing and collaborating to bring about radical change

▶ Gathering experts together

. . . .

*C*haritable giving is currently undergoing a major shift as innovation and technological advancements allow people from around the globe to pool their talents and resources to achieve amazing things. Technology is increasingly being used to bring people together to help solve huge problems; charities can now broadcast their mission and needs much farther and wider than ever before, attracting larger numbers of individuals and organisations to their causes. Plus, technology serves as a platform through which groups can co-ordinate and collaborate in their efforts to achieve a shared goal. Often, technological solutions are themselves vital resources for cash- and resource-strapped charities.

Throughout these pages we emphasise that technology promotes social connectivity and drives new industry, and in so doing has a philanthropic *multiplier effect* (an idea from economics where an increase in spending produces an increase in national income and consumption greater than the initial amount spent). For example, when a charity provides housing or food or job-search help for the unemployed, it often stimulates other positive activities in the vicinity, creating a win–win in a community.

In this chapter, we focus on the creative ways in which charities are using design and information technology (IT) to tackle housing needs and disaster relief. Giving committed volunteers the right tools and access translates into more resources, more expertise, more creativity, and more involvement – all vital components for tackling the world's large-scale problems. We also describe how two apparently conflicting ideas, competition and collaboration – when combined with innovation and technology – can be used to improve people's lives.

Thinking about Technology's Role in Philanthropy

Innovation and technology have changed our lives. We make restaurant bookings differently, we buy things differently, we find our way to our destinations differently. Everything is different from a generation ago. When was the last time you turned the pages of a telephone directory to find a telephone number? Well, technology is also changing philanthropy!

Providing the Most Basic Needs with Technology

Learn by doing – it's a simple phrase you've no doubt heard a thousand times. Certainly, working on a given task is what inches people ever closer to excellence and this truth certainly applies to the realm of innovative, sustainable design and outreach to the developing world.

Tackling the problems that face your brothers and sisters around the world along with others who have experience is the best way to use your skills to the greatest effect (for examples, think of Doctors Without Borders and the schemes we cover in Chapter 13). The last ten years or so have witnessed new developments that expand on this great original idea, from telecommunications to smartphone applications letting people ask for help, diagnoses, or transport. These new innovations allow people with all sorts of skills to get involved in different kinds of projects around the world that, in their own way, make a huge impact on the lives of the poor or disadvantaged. In this section, we take a look at just two: housing and disaster relief.

Even when you *do* want to travel and work on-site to help people in need, at times you can do more good (and do it more efficiently) by lending your expertise and time in your home country, a strategy that has the added benefit of allowing you to devote time for charity continuously while maintaining employment (Chapter 3 has suggestions).

Housing the world's most vulnerable populations

One example of hands-on-from-home philanthropy is the field of innovative, sustainable, and *smart design* for buildings, especially for impoverished or displaced communities. Smart design often involves making places, spaces, and things more durable, more upgradeable, or more functional. By bringing together experts in any field with experienced planners who know how to effect change and work with local officials, you can truly harness the resources of the global funding community to complete meaningful projects that make a real difference.

Currently, one in seven people live in a refugee camp or slum. More than 3 billion people – nearly half the world's population – don't have access to clean water or adequate sanitation.

Building shelters for the poorest of the poor: The $300 House project

The $300 House project embraces the challenge of producing shelter at a very low cost. Rather than the mud huts and tin shacks that many poor people live in throughout the world, $300 House seeks to create safe, affordable housing. Housing is the basic building block of community. It is difficult to cultivate a healthy community if people cannot be protected from the weather, have their treasured belongings invulnerable to theft, and consistently have a place to sleep through the night in safety.

Based on the belief that a safe, affordable, sustainable home is a first step towards overcoming poverty, the $300 House project (www.300house.com) brings together three groups to achieve its goals:

- ✔ **People who'll live in the houses.** Many of the world's poor are homeless or live in self-built houses in slums. The $300 House project aims to create simple dwellings that keep these families safe from the elements and offer them night-time privacy and safety.

- ✔ **People who design the houses.** Designers can be anyone – individuals, student groups, professional architectural and design firms, and so on – who come up with a workable solution.

- ✔ **Organisations that, when a suitable design is formulated, can reproduce the design at scale.** Given the nature of this task – mass producing and selling of the winning design – this group consists of non-profit organisations, governmental agencies, and private and public businesses capable of performing this task.

The fact that residents pay for their homes (through creative loan solutions, such as microfinancing) and are responsible for the home's upkeep, makes the $300 House project more than just a charity. It provides an immediate need and gives the owners a path out of poverty.

In addition to housing the world's homeless, the concepts used and lessons learned in creating these homes can inform and be applied to the green housing movement in developed countries.

You can become involved in the $300 House project in a number of ways: check out `www.300house.com/participate.html`. The site has information about how a variety of individuals (students, teachers, designers, architects, and so on) and organisations (universities, profit and non-profit businesses, institutions and foundations, and NGOs) can participate.

Building better: Architecture for Humanity

Architecture for Humanity (`www.architectureforhumanity.org`), founded in 1999, is a non-profit design services firm. By tapping a network of more than 50,000 professionals who want to lend their time and expertise to help those who'd otherwise be unable to afford their services, the organisation takes design, construction, and development services to where they are most needed.

The innovation in architecture is both functional and cultural. After the earthquakes in Japan and Haiti and the hurricane in New York City, Architecture for Humanity helped bring improved designs, more liveable spaces, and safer buildings to people in the wake of disaster. In replacement homes, gathering spaces, and workplaces, the community can rebuild culturally and socially.

Architecture for Humanity states that thoughtful, inclusive design creates lasting change in communities by:

- ✔ Alleviating poverty and providing access to water, sanitation, power, and essential services.

- ✔ Bringing safe shelter to communities prone to disaster and displaced populations.

- ✔ Rebuilding community and creating neutral spaces for dialogue in post-conflict areas.

- ✔ Mitigating the effects of rapid urbanisation in unplanned settlements.

- ✔ Creating spaces to meet the needs of those with disabilities and other at-risk populations.

- ✔ Reducing the carbon footprint of the built environment and addressing climate change (see Chapter 9).

The organisation has built structures for more than 2 million people in 46 countries around the world. Advocacy, training, and outreach programmes impact an additional 50,000 people annually. Architecture for Humanity manages its building projects from concept to completion, including all aspects of the design and construction. Clients include community groups, aid organisations, housing developers, government agencies, corporate divisions, and foundations – a pretty impressive group to join!

Suppose, for example, that you're an architect working on constructing some of the largest and most impressive bank headquarters around the world – a career that provides you with a comfortable living and exposes you to the discrepancies between rich and poor in worldwide society, from lack of safe housing and access to clean water to the dearth of schoolhouses in poor and rural communities. Although you donate money to charity, you want to contribute in a more tangible way. Architecture for Humanity may be just what you're looking for.

You can submit plans for various projects around the world, giving impoverished communities access to a top-flight architect (you). In addition to helping others, you also have a chance to work on different challenges than those typically facing the skyscrapers to which you currently devote most of your time – win, win!

Of course, you don't have to be an architect to contribute to Architecture for Humanity. One unique way to get involved is to join its design fellowship. This provides a chance to gain new experiences while honing design skills and serving a like-minded purpose. Opportunities, when available, vary from project to project, and fellows are matched to projects according to their skills. Keep in mind that these fellowships usually last from six months to a year depending on the project. Although the position includes reimbursement for travel and other out-of-pocket expenses when possible, design fellows volunteer their time. If grant funds are available, fellows may receive a stipend to cover cost-of-living expenses.

Another option is to work with the Open Architect Network, which is supported through Worldchanging, an online, open-source community dedicated to improving living conditions through innovative and sustainable design. Here designers of all persuasions collaborate with other professionals and community leaders to address specific design challenges and manage design projects from concept to implementation.

These options are great for people interested in housing projects. If you believe in the cause and want to contribute financially, you can donate at `architectureforhumanity.org/donate/sponsor` and `openarchitecturenetwork.org/support`.

Disaster relief: Helping during crises

A lot of people want to volunteer for causes such as natural disasters: they feel a strong urge to help clean up the rubble, hug the people affected, and start the rebuilding process, but they have no idea where or how to begin. Perhaps the need to get in your car and just drive to the location to see how you can instantly help is foremost in your mind. Or you may search the Internet for organisations that co-ordinate and provide help after natural disasters. Maybe you dial a number you see on TV and give your credit card number. Perhaps you're left feeling hopeless because you don't know what to do beyond watching the news and praying for the best.

Technology plays a vital role in helping, with ongoing research into digital technologies and services for disaster planning, preparation, rescue, and recovery. Although they can't prevent a natural disaster from hitting, these technologies help emergency services better *manage* them and minimise the disasters' effects on communities, infrastructures, and the environment.

One of the most crucial aspects of innovative smart design (that we discuss in the preceding section) is the role it can play in the lives of refugee and displaced communities: it can affect their temporary housing and provide safer, longer-lasting shelters that are more likely to withstand an uncertain future. This section delves more deeply into how people around the world come together to offer aid in times of natural disasters.

The world needs innovative, more effective solutions to the problems of refugee housing and sanitation. Ask yourself how you can help. The next great humanitarian idea will come from a unique and fresh answer to a question that has probably been asked a thousand times. Of course the best way to arrive at a new solution is by getting together with others who share your particular passion or expertise. Whether you help facilitate the connections or participate in the discussion, everything counts!

Helping out in Afghanistan: Shelter for Life

Technology now plays a huge role in allowing people to participate and give aid from a distance and also to get down-and-dirty in hands-on improvements as regards rebuilding after earthquakes, floods, and so on. Having technology at the forefront of these innovative ideas means being able to rebuild in ways that are far more effective than ever before.

When an earthquake rocked Afghanistan in 2002, Shelter for Life International (www.shelter.org) provided emergency shelter to some 30,000 people. Rather than immediately opting for winter tents, the group paused to think about the long-term needs of the community it had been called on to aid and used its experience in the area to build permanent housing.

For roughly the same cost of a winter canvas tent, the group was able to build 5,000 shelters in 76 villages over the course of a four-month period. Better yet, they worked side by side with the villagers, enlisting the help of earthquake-affected families in construction and transferring new skills. During the project, community members were also offered training on seismic awareness and earthquake preparedness.

Considering disaster relief closer to home

Disaster relief isn't just a need in the developing world. The floods, tornados, and hurricanes that affect developed countries every year pose the same challenges to disaster relief agencies and aid organisations. Examples include the 2012 Great Britain and Ireland floods and, in the US, the east coast's suffering from Hurricane Sandy in October of 2012: many towns and communities are still recovering almost a year later.

Natural disasters have increased in severity and frequency in recent years; in 2010 alone, 385 natural disasters affected 217 million people worldwide at a cost to the global economy of US$123.9 billion.

Lending a hand after a natural disaster

Technology advancements have allowed us to interact differently with natural disasters. We use satellites to spot hurricanes. We do seismic surveys to estimate earthquake risk. But after a disaster occurs, technology can help, too. Technology can recruit volunteers, co-ordinate relief efforts, build new maps that reflect flooded roads and destroyed buildings, and help victims find family members.

The tricky part about responding to natural disasters is making sure that your efforts to help don't end up ineffective or inadvertently making matters worse. A community left reeling after a flood, for example, may not be able to withstand an influx of well-meaning but poorly-organised volunteers when basic services still need to be brought back online.

The following list outlines some ways to make effective contributions:

✔ **Contribute money:** A lot of times giving money may be the only or the best way you can help. Despite lacking the hands-on quality that many people crave, it's a terrific way to help. After you decide on a charity (Chapter 4 offers tips on choosing a charity), be sure to inquire whether or not the organisation has a specific fund set aside for the relief effort you want your donation applied to.

✔ **Donate food, clothing, or other supplies:** Some people have the resources to give away food, clothing, cleaning supplies, tools, and other necessary items. Instead of the staging areas, which often can't manage large donations and can be chaotic, look into whether local schools, churches, and community centres are accepting donations: they're the ones that often conduct food and clothing drives. Also, if you can, find out which items are the most needed before donating.

Donating blood can also be a great way to help!

✔ **Give time and labour:** The key when pursuing this route is to make sure that your efforts are co-ordinated and address the needs of the community you're going to. Organisations such as FEMA (Federal Emergency Management Agency) and the National Guard in the US and the Territorial Army in the UK, as well as some charitable organisations, have response teams and protocols to step in when disasters strike.

Government organisations and charities, such as the Red Cross, that specialise in disaster relief have workers who're trained and know what to do when they go into disaster areas to perform tasks such as search and rescue. In many situations, an untrained individual can end up becoming another person in need of rescue. Don't let this be you! If you decide to volunteer during a natural disaster, co-ordinate with the trained responders. Find out how you can help and be an asset, not a hindrance, especially in a way that risks your life, too.

Competing for Good in the Virtual World

Social networks and massive multiplayer gaming are new industries driven by technology and they can have a powerful version of the philanthropic multiplier effect. Writers, tech gurus, and philosophically inquisitive people are beginning to ask how the unreality of gaming and the impersonal – yet hyperconnected – world of social media platforms can be used to bring about change in the real physical world.

Tapping into the allure of games

Games are everywhere. They enable you to practise challenges you face in the real world and function as a diversion from those same trials. In fact, you can find yourself playing games without even knowing it. Take, for example, your tendency to create little reward scenarios in your head to help you finish tasks more quickly, or the way you invent fun ways to make a boring project more enjoyable. You play these games alone, but team games build camaraderie, help you understand group mentalities, and give you a chance to experience supporting and leadership roles in myriad scenarios.

A powerful resource: Internet gaming

Imagine you harnessed all the hours devoted to gaming – by professional gamers and the staggering percentage of the population that devotes immense amounts of time to their gaming lives – to tackle the problems facing the world today. What would that look like?

Jane McGonigal's book *Reality is Broken* (see Chapter 5 for more) addresses this question in an attempt to discover how to avoid a vacuum left in the real world as young people flock to the virtual world to seek fulfilment. Games now offer a level of sophistication and customisation that simply didn't exist before. They also exist virtually rather than just in the field and they're evolving to mirror people's lives more closely (the extreme being something like Second Life, where a person has a virtual existence through a fictional online character) while simultaneously pulling people away from the physical world.

Imagine being able to change the world by gaming: a huge challenge of course but what potential rewards are on offer from this extraordinary resource.

The world is full of eager heroes: the trick is getting them to fight and win real-world battles, providing clean water to a real community for example, rather than leading an imaginary army to conquer a virtual realm.

Looking closely at how games motivate players

Part of the appeal of gaming is that the rewards are obvious. Often, success is more clear-cut than in life and the problems you're trying to solve are laid out in front of you. This clarity of purpose and effect is one way that the gaming world differs from the real world, where people who want to make a difference must struggle to figure out exactly what they want to take on and then need to calculate how much of a difference just one person can make.

Real-world challenges are never going to be as clear-cut as the challenges of the gaming world, but in both worlds one person can make a huge difference; by harnessing the power of communities, you can multiply the power of the individual. After all, gamers are already motivated to overcome challenges.

Challenging gamers to tackle real-world problems

To understand how gaming principles can be applied to real-world problems, consider the challenges facing the education system. As you discover later in this section, gamers can help.

As the metaphors in gaming have become more specific and more compelling, the game developers have been laying the groundwork without realising it. Microsoft recently sponsored the Imagine Cup Competition, an event that had a pool of 74,000 entrants from high school through graduate school. The three winners came up with these compelling ideas:

- ✔ Using a portable device to help visually impaired students with note-taking.
- ✔ A digital strategy game that challenges children to improve the environment through clean energy.
- ✔ A game for your smartphone in which players fight deforestation to earn points.

The next step is to bring the simulation back home. The team at the Imagine Cup Competition from Tribeca Flashpoint Academy that developed the award-winning environmental game, Spero, (Latin for 'hope') used 9- to 12-year-olds as testers. They found that a full-on gaming experience, even with all the challenges, visual feedback, and fun that gamers expect, also led to learning. When the game had engaged the children, the team told judges, 'They wanted nothing less than to save the world'.

It's time for the games to find their way back to reality – just as games once mimicked reality, a better reality can be improved and imitated through games. This is the return of authenticity. The great part is that when this happens, you can play too! Gamers become world changers and world changers start playing the largest, most important game of all!

The problem: Considering the lack of authenticity, customisation, and more

Jesse Schell, a game designer and professor at Carnegie Mellon, wants to remind people that 'The Future is Beautiful'. And it looks to be that way because everyday products are beautiful – even phones are so beautiful and useful that people wait for days in line to fetch the latest one.

But where, for example, are these beautiful new ideas in education? Shouldn't education be beautiful, authentic, and individualised? Yet classrooms are ugly and programmes, textbooks, and tests are all standardised. Sharing is rarely a priority, and certainly not to the extent being extolled socially and in the highly networked arenas of the business world. Plus many classroom lessons have an inauthentic quality: rather than a bona fide expert standing before a classroom of engaged and curious students, a pseudo expert stands before a classroom of students pretending to care.

The solution: Applying core principles and tenets to real-world scenarios

To solve this problem, some of the same principles used elsewhere need to be applied to education.

Take customisation, for example. Jesse mentions a teacher, Lee Sheldon, who reimagined the grading system. Instead of an averaged grading system, Lee laid out a grid where you begin with no experience points (an 'F'), and as you progress, you gain experience points on each assignment and 'level-up' a grade. Everything is forward motion, the motivation is constant and the fear of failure minimised. This solution is an obvious gaming metaphor, but that metaphor came from the real world. After all, experience usually dictates success, and it certainly correlates to proficiency.

This system is great for keeping the reward system of education in line with the reward system children experience in games and go on to experience after school. Of course, students face discrete tests in the real world and moments of failure, but like this system life is all forward motion. This gaming, grading metaphor rethinks the problem with a unique solution.

Endeavours such as this one have to find a balance between structure and customisation. You can't customise everything, of course, certain universals always exist. But to the degree that learning can be tailored to the individual and each changing generation, people can expect to reap the rewards of a veritable torrent of untapped potential from the children in classrooms. We believe that if you present students with unique tools and put them in teams where they have to work together to get the most out of different resources, you can just sit back and watch the sharing happen.

Be on the learning end or the teaching end of this technological revolution. Teach an online course on a topic you know about. Learn a new skill or a new language online – participate in this sharing of talents and knowledge.

Putting the 'you' in YOUmedia

The YOUmedia project in Chicago (www.youmediachicago.org) takes on customised learning by bringing digital art education to inner city teenagers. Instead of standardising the process and forcing children to interact always using their knowledge within a rigid structure, the programme takes its cue from the three ways teenagers often interact with learning:

✔ They start by hanging out on the periphery of a new challenge or topic.

✔ Then they begin messing around with it.

✔ Eventually, if you reach them, they begin to geek out and really get into it.

Jesse Schell's team at YOUmedia designed their learning space to match these three stages, and they've had a lot of success and are looking to expand the programme, which boasts the following attributes:

✔ **Youth-centred:** Design and programming embrace youth preferences, interests,

practices, and attitudes. The youth voice is essential.

✔ **Interest-driven:** Programming is driven by youth interests and is meaningful and relevant to their daily lives.

✔ **Reflective:** Youth review and critique their own work to hone their skills.

✔ **Making and doing:** Programming centres on hands-on, active engagement. Youth don't simply consume media or information, they're producers of content and projects to share with a broader audience.

✔ **Collaborative:** Youth work regularly with others from different schools, backgrounds, and areas of interest and expertise.

✔ **Interdisciplinary:** A variety of content and perspectives from multiple disciplines are incorporated into programming and workshops.

Tackling mega challenges with mega prizes: The XPRIZE story

Competition and large-scale prizes motivate and influence giving, galvanising individuals, corporations, and communities to innovate and create new ways to tackle problems. This section highlights an organisation that uses the power of technology and competitive spirit to encourage such solutions to problems that have long plagued humanity.

XPRIZE (www.xprize.org) is a global leader in the creation of prize competitions whose mission is to spur radical technological breakthroughs that benefit humanity. XPRIZE designs competitions to address seemingly insurmountable issues and offers large monetary incentives for individuals and organisations to participate. The parameters of the competitions are devised by the Prize Development department, and the large monetary prizes are made possible by grants or donations from businesses, foundations, and other contributors. The winners are the first teams to achieve the specified goal.

Expressing surprise at an XPRIZE prize!

Here are some examples of the unusual XPRIZE competitions:

✔ **Ansari XPRIZE:** The original XPRIZE competition to create a private spaceflight vehicle.

✔ **Archon Genomics XPRIZE:** A genomics competition challenging teams to sequence 100 human genomes within 30 days or less.

✔ **Google Lunar XPRIZE:** A competition to put a robot on the moon.

✔ **Northrop Grumman Lunar Lander X CHALLENGE:** A competition to build precise, efficient, small rocket systems.

✔ **Progressive Insurance Automotive XPRIZE:** An engineering competition designed to create a fuel-efficient clean car that gets 100 miles per gallon.

✔ **Tricorder XPRIZE:** A competition to create a portable medical diagnostic device.

✔ **Wendy Schmidt Oil Cleanup X CHALLENGE:** A competition inspiring a new generation of innovative solutions to speed up the cleaning of seawater surface oil resulting from spillage from tankers, ocean platforms, and other sources.

XPRIZE is different from other philanthropic organisations in that it doesn't directly fund research itself. Instead, its efforts go towards incentivising others to take up the challenge and race to find a winning solution. For some examples, read the nearby sidebar 'Expressing surprise at an XPRIZE prize!'

You can become involved in XPRIZE in a number of wonderful ways:

✔ **Join the Vision Circle:** Vision Circle members are the largest contributors, fuelling XPRIZE's capacity to add prize competitions and enhance educational outreach. These members are XPRIZE's core shareholders and their input is vital to its long-term focus and success.

✔ **Become a member of the Innovation Board:** These philanthropists engage actively with Foundation Leadership on strategic topics such as defining the annual Grand Challenges and areas of focus for the Board of Trustees' Visioneering. The Board also works closely with the Foundation to identify strategic partners and opportunities.

✔ **Become a Spirit of Innovation member:** Spirit of Innovation members are a small group of donors who provide the seed capital used to design, fund, and launch XPRIZEs and XCHALLENGEs. Becoming a Spirit of Innovation member also allows you to participate with your ideas, passion, and connections. What a great way to become involved!

✔ **Join the Entrepreneurs' Circle:** The Entrepreneurs' Circle is a select group of innovators who've partnered with XPRIZE by contributing private stock in their companies in the hope that in the future their contribution may provide the critical capital to support the ongoing mission of the foundation. The Entrepreneurs' Circle has representation from several companies, among them: GNS Healthcare, Group4Labs, Prodea Systems, Tervela, Inc., Facebook, and Space Adventures, Inc.

✔ **Donate:** You can donate funds at `www.xprize.org/donate` and keep up to date at `www.facebook.com/xprize`.

Collaborating for a Better Tomorrow: Crowdfunding

In the preceding section, we describe how competition and large-scale prizes can motivate and impact giving, but collaboration can be just as effective. In this age of social media and interconnectivity, a new kind of crowdsourcing can be applied to all sorts of fundraising to achieve amazing results! That's what crowdfunding makes possible.

Crowdfunding is a collective effort of individuals networking, often through the Internet and social media, to pool their money to fund a common interest project or a cause. Think of it as a more sophisticated version of the slit-topped collection jar; the difference is that you can potentially reach millions rather than hundreds of people. Collaboration is king, and crowdfunding is another way to get where you want to be faster.

Crowdfunding can help communities come together around the needs of individuals and also be applied to communities helping communities. With crowdfunding, one person's mission can quickly become the cause of many. In just a couple of minutes spent on the web you can find hundreds, even thousands, of like-minded individuals who are just waiting to take up your cause! Crowdfunding is like the little pebble that rolls down a snowy mountain, gathering snow as it becomes an avalanche for good.

Putting the crowd to work

In years past, charities spread the word about their missions and raised their impact – and their fundraising potential – by hosting large galas or planning-intensive events that drew deep-pocketed contributors. Now crowdfunding allows people to come together and raise funds and awareness without the need and expense of such events.

With crowdfunding, you can immediately champion a cause from the comfort of your home and around your busy schedule. It also enables you to work more easily with people from all over the world on a cause. Wow!

Consider these great reasons to get involved with crowdfunding:

- ✔ **Galas aren't your thing.** Maybe you hate the idea of giving as an expression of social status. To you, the cause is the thing, not the event.

- ✔ You want to leverage the power of microfunding and the broad participation through small donations that many people around the world can participate in.

- ✔ The Internet allows you to bypass the overheads of traditional marketing and public relations associated with charity-event planning. By avoiding these expenses, the money raised can be put to use rather than maintaining the overheads.

- ✔ **Your cause is personal and you're unsure exactly how broad your potential audience may be.** Crowdfunding lets you get your idea out among the people with a chance of achieving results far beyond your expectations.

If you decide to participate in crowdfunding (whether initiating the cause or donating to another one), work only with established crowdfunding sites to ensure that your activities comply with laws governing fundraising and donations. Do a little research and find a company whose approach is most compatible with your set goals. Doing so also helps you best align your efforts with the pool of potential donors you want to reach.

Finding a crowdfund project to support

Crowdfunding is a great way to give to a cause you believe in, and you can do it from your laptop. When considering a crowdfunding site, pay attention to the following:

- ✔ **Check for secure encryption on all transactions using Transport Layer Security (TLS) or, at a minimum, secure socket layer (SSL) technology.** This provides a secure communication and makes sure your computer is 'talking' in a secure conversation.

- ✔ **Look for 'https' (rather than just 'http') at the beginning of the website address.** This protocol, which adds 'secure' to the familiar 'http' is the addition of TLS (see above) to the normal hypertext transfer protocol.

- ✔ **Read the crowdfunding site's statement about its policies, including its terms, conditions, and privacy policy, *before* donating or entering your credit card information.** Doing so helps you understand how your donation and your personal information will be handled.

After you find a site, you can peruse the listed projects or search for a specific type of project to support. For example, if you love the idea of supporting budding landscape photographers who support green environments, you can search under the arts or photography genre.

Crowdfunding sites offer varying levels of support and your donations can be as low as a few coins in your pocket or at much higher, life-changing levels. Gifts for donating can be anywhere from a Thank You for Your Donation to much higher value gifts, such as tickets to attend galas and events.

Starting your own campaign

You can create your own crowdfunding campaign to raise money for a particular cause. A successful campaign takes dedication and time before, during, and after, but the effort is worthwhile when you see the funds starting to accrue. Here are a few tips to help your campaign succeed:

- ✔ Create a video that clearly states your cause and the reason for raising money.
- ✔ Have creative and well-thought-out thank you gifts, because they often drive a project. Ensure that the cost doesn't dig too deeply into the pockets of the funds though.
- ✔ Line up donors willing to fund the campaign before it starts to ensure a successful launch.
- ✔ Use social media to share the campaign.
- ✔ Follow up with all donors by sending 'thank yous' and their gifts.

GiveForward: Raising funds to cover medical bills

In the US, millions of uninsured people are unable to afford the care they need, or insurance that would cover the care they need. While the US is unusual among developed countries, this is a common problem around the world. More than five billion people do not have health insurance and more than this lack access to both routine and catastrophic care. In the United States, one in three bankruptcies is related to medical costs, and this is a growing problem globally as the cost of care rises more quickly than wages.

GiveForward (www.giveforward.com) is a crowdfunding site dedicated to raising funds to help pay medical bills. The company's goal is to alleviate the financial burden of a medical crisis and help answer the question so often on the minds of friends and loved ones: 'What more can I do?'

GiveForward offers personalised fundraising pages specifically geared towards a variety of situations; online coaches with expertise in fundraising for cancer, medical equipment, transplants, and diabetes; a blended approach that features broad, anonymous donor reach and personal attention to individual beneficiaries; and an entire team of support staff to help you get on the road to recovery.

As a result, families facing medical crises can more easily do the following:

- ✔ Update friends and family on progress.
- ✔ Invite friends from Facebook, LinkedIn, and Twitter to participate.
- ✔ Post event information.
- ✔ Leave words of encouragement.
- ✔ Link to other blog sites.
- ✔ Make a broad network of sympathetic people accessible, no matter how far away they are.

All in all, GiveForward is a great example of how business and altruism can come together!

GiveForward believes in fee transparency, making clear how much it deducts from each transaction. As a supporter, you can choose to donate a little extra and cover the fees, and most supporters do. Therefore, GiveForward's fundraising fee is effectively only 2.6 per cent on average, making it the least expensive crowdfunding platform for helping those in need.

Kick starting a new mission: Kickstarter

Kickstarter (www.kickstarter.com) is one of the most popular crowdfunding sites and offers opportunities to fund and support creators and projects – everything from films, games, and music to art, design, and technology. Kickstarter is full of projects, big and small, that are brought to life through the direct support of donors and contributors. Since launching in 2009, more than 4.6 million people have pledged over $743 million, funding more than 46,000 creative projects.

Anyone can launch a project on Kickstarter as long as it meets the organisation's guidelines. If people like a project, they can pledge money to make it happen.

Artists are drawn to Kickstarter because they have complete control over and responsibility for their projects. Project creators even set funding goals and deadlines. Some people find this a downside, others see it as a positive, but funding on Kickstarter is all-or-nothing, which means that a project must reach its funding goals to receive any money. All-or-nothing funding may seem scary, but it's amazingly effective in creating momentum and rallying people around an idea. To date, Kickstarter boasts that 44 per cent of projects have reached their funding goals.

Kickstarter is a for-profit company based in New York. The staff answer questions from backers and creators and find new projects to share. If a project is successfully funded, they apply a 5 per cent fee to the collected funds. You receive a token gift for your donation (as long as the project is funded).

CrowdRise: Tapping into the power of a fanbase

CrowdRise (www.crowdrise.com) is known as the go-to crowdfunding site for celebrities who want to champion a cause while simultaneously tapping into the entire breadth of their fanbase and avoiding the time-consuming black-tie events that reach only a relative few. But CrowdRise isn't solely for household names. A group named 'Robin Hood', for example, had an incredible fundraising team in the New York Marathon, and Molly and Matt (photographers in Florida) created a Charity Wedding Registry for causes they both support and raised over US$13,000.

Much as Kickstarter allows anyone to fund large-scale art projects through goal-oriented micro-donations, CrowdRise helps make giving fun! Like friends on Facebook, potential benefactors to your cause can follow you and make use of social media's multimedia marketing opportunities. CrowdRise offers competitions and prizes for achieving fundraising goals. Take a look and start bringing together a new community of donors for your cause today.

CrowdRise is entirely free to use and you can create as many fundraisers as you want. When you or anyone else donates to a fundraiser or charity through CrowdRise, the organisation takes a transaction fee to cover credit card fees (to stay in business). These fees are competitive and charities are offered three plans so that they can choose the best pricing option for them. Plus you don't need an account to make a donation and donating to a project takes less than 30 seconds!

The rise and rise of CrowdRise

When Robert and Jeffrey Wolfe sold their business, they wanted to turn their attention to making a positive social impact. They were struck by a grassroots fundraising model used by Barack Obama during his presidential campaign, which leveraged micro-donations and a new generation of social-media-conscious participants to achieve amazing results.

They believed that this approach could work in the world of charity, too, and the result was the creation of CrowdRise. Teaming up with old friend Shauna Robertson and her fiancé Edward Norton, the four launched a trial. With Norton planning to run the New York Marathon in support of the Maasai Wilderness Conservation Trust, the group launched a campaign that tapped into the actor's fanbase. Over about six weeks, they raised an astonishing $1.2 million, largely from small donations.

Calling All Experts

Some people's unusual level of dedication, resources, and creative vision change the world in profound and lasting ways. Expertise is needed, however, to take ideas and turn them into projects, charities, and reality. Whether someone is willing to lend a bit of expertise can make or break a project, or determine whether it will happen over or under budget.

Social entrepreneurs: Making change happen

Social entrepreneurs are individuals with innovative solutions to society's most pressing and difficult social problems. They're considered society's *change agents,* because they create innovations that rock the status quo and transform the world.

You can identify social entrepreneurs who are bringing positive changes to the world and then empower others to join them through social media, fundraisers, media campaigns, and other grassroots efforts to raise awareness, thus expanding their reach and deepening their impact. The end result is a fundamental change in society and the ultimate goal of global improvement.

Great social entrepreneurs

Social entrepreneurs come up with new solutions to social problems and then implement them on a large scale. Here are some examples of innovative social entrepreneurs:

✔ **Vinoba Bhave (India):** Founder and leader of the Land Gift Movement, who caused the redistribution of more than 7 million acres of land to aid India.

✔ **Dr Maria Montessori (Italy):** Known for developing the now popular and successful Montessori approach to early childhood education.

✔ **John Muir (US):** Naturalist and conservationist, who established the National Park System and helped found The Sierra Club, a major environmental organisation.

✔ **Florence Nightingale (UK):** She established the first school for nurses and fought to improve hospital conditions.

Investing in social entrepreneurs: The Skoll World Forum

The Skoll World Forum on Social Entrepreneurship (www.skollworldforum.org) was founded in 1999 by Jeff Skoll. Its mission is to apply entrepreneurial approaches and innovation to solving the world's problems. Skoll identifies people and programmes that are already creating positive changes in their communities and around the world and supports and empowers them to expand their reach, thereby deepening their impact. This goal is accomplished through grants and awards.

To date, Skoll has awarded more than $358 million to social entrepreneurs, including investments in 97 remarkable social entrepreneurs and 80 organisations all around the world. To add to these impressive numbers, through its grants Skoll funds a $20 million+ portfolio of programme-related and mission-aligned investments.

Each year, the Skoll World Forum hosts a symposium featuring the leading innovators and thinkers from around the world to brainstorm ideas on how to find innovative solutions to the world's most pressing social issues, such as human rights, peace and human security, deforestation, and more.

You can become a member of the Forum's online community where technology and innovation come together to help people connect from various locations around the world. You can access streamed sessions from the meetings, blogs, and videos. Skoll is involved in social media through YouTube, Facebook, Twitter, Google+, and its blog.

In addition, many of the programmes that Skoll supports use technology to serve their cause and to make a difference in new ways. Programmes such as 'Why Sprint Wants That Cell Phone You Don't Use Anymore' are pushing to recycle technology that's out of date. Finding such programmes and donating your old mobiles is one of the easiest ways to get involved.

Meeting other masterminds of change: SOCAP

Social Capital Markets (SOCAP: www.socialcapitalmarkets.net) is an annual event that brings together leading global innovators, including investors, foundations, institutions, and social entrepreneurs, with the goal of supporting the growth of market systems that have positive social impact. For example, the theme of the SOCAP 2013 event was health, and one area of the focus related to showing how market decisions that promote good health result in a measureable return on investment.

Social entrepreneurs are invited to the annual event and you can join in by volunteering to help it run smoothly. This is a wonderful way to be in the thick of the excitement and discover more about the entrepreneurs involved.

Harnessing the power of ideas: Ted Talks

TED (www.ted.com) is a non-profit organisation that gives a forum to guest speakers with 'ideas worth spreading'. Originally, TED was a conference that brought together the three worlds of technology, entertainment, and design, but it has broadened its scope greatly. It still holds conferences each summer but also includes the award-winning TED Talks video site, the Open Translation Project, and TED Conversations, the inspiring TED Fellows and TEDx programmes, and the annual TED Prize. The goal of TED is to foster the spread of great and inspiring ideas around the globe by providing a platform for the world's smartest thinkers, greatest visionaries, and most inspiring teachers to an audience of millions. The hope is that, by gaining a better understanding of the most pressing issues facing the world, people will be motivated to help create a better future. Central to this mission is a belief that the greatest force for changing the world is a powerful idea, which when received by a prepared mind can have extraordinary impact. It can reshape that mind's view of the world, dramatically alter the behaviour of the mind's owner, and cause the mind to pass on the idea to others.

Since Sapling, TED's parent company, acquired TED in November 2001, it has been searching for ways to exploit the extraordinary passion and inspiration created every year at conferences to influence beneficial change in the world. TED says that this now happens in several major ways:

- **TED Prize:** Takes a great idea each year and seeks to achieve goals of global impact. The 2013 winner was Sugata Mitra's School in the Cloud (www.ted.com/talks/sugata_mitra_build_a_school_in_the_cloud.html). His goal is to recruit technology, architecture, creative and educational partners to assist in designing and building the School in the Cloud, which is, in fact, a physical building in India.

- **TED.com:** Allows the great ideas shared at TED to be easily accessible anywhere in the world, in more than 70 languages.

- **TED Fellows programme:** Brings extraordinary new voices into the TED community. Fellows benefit by attending TED or TEDGlobal Conferences, participating in Fellows pre-conference activities, participating in the coaching programme, and more.

- **TEDx:** Supports the creation of independent TED-like events in communities around the world.

The profits made by the TED conferences are directed towards their powerful initiatives. Here's how you can help TED and support its initiatives:

- Support the desires of the TED Prize winners and help them distribute their ideas.

- Contribute to TED or the Sapling Foundation.

✔ Promote TED Talks through social media and so on. Join its Facebook fan page or follow it on Twitter and share posts and tweets with your followers.

✔ Consider helping a TEDx prize winner. Some suggestions:

- Try out a Self-Organised Learning Environment (SOLE). Visit the Ted website to download the toolkit.

- Support the School in the Cloud. You can join the school's network of educators, make financial donations, or help build the school (email sugata@ted.com for information).

- Spread the word via Twitter: #TEDSOLE.

Supplying social ventures and charities with IT

Technology can be donated itself and not just act as a conduit for accessing info or setting up collaborative models for charities. Here are two examples:

✔ **Aspiration Tech (`www.aspirationtech.org`):** Aspiration helps non-profit organisations and foundations access and use software tools to more effectively carry out their missions. It serves the causes as ally, coach, strategist, mentor, and facilitator to make more impactful use of IT.

The best way to help Aspiration Tech is to donate on its website or spread the word by joining its social media sites and sharing posts with your own following. Additionally, look into the projects it supports and see which ones match your interest and how you can volunteer.

✔ **TechSoup (`www.techsoup.org`):** TechSoup is a non-profit organisation whose mission is to make technology available to non-profit or public libraries. TechSoup partners with hardware and software companies (Microsoft, Adobe, Symantec, and others) to achieve its goals.

Sign up on TechSoup's website and participate in the community blog and forums. Check out Donation Eligibility and peruse the organisation's donation programmes and products. Also, register or associate your organisation to participate in these programmes and products.

Part III
Delivering on Your Good Intentions: Practical Ways to Get Involved

Top Five Things to Think About when Getting Involved

✔ Instead of spreading yourself thinner and adopting more and more causes, determine whether there are causes with which you're already involved where you could find more, better or smarter ways to help.

✔ Do you know anyone who's really good at doing what an organisation isn't very good at doing? A great bookkeeper, for example, who cares about animals and an animal charity who's books are a disaster? Perhaps the best donation you can make is an introduction.

✔ Rather than worrying about the sustainability of an organisation far into its future, why not examine its current initiatives and what needs to be done to achieve them? It's no use worrying about whether the organisation will be around in ten years if it'll be unable to finish its projects planned for the next five.

✔ Consider how your personal relationship to an organisation changes your perspective, and perhaps makes you more likely to fund things you otherwise might not. We all have strong emotions surrounding our hometowns or our universities, but is building a new expensive library really what either most desperately needs?

✔ Think about your time as though it were your money. Do you really want to spend your time volunteering for a cause you wouldn't donate money to or donate money to a cause where you feel volunteers are misused, disrespected or not valued? In philanthropy, you're using all of your resources to achieve your goals – the organisations you support should be too.

Go to www.dummies.com/extras/charityandphilanthropy for free online bonus content.

In this Part

✔ Look at how you can donate your time, use your talents, share your treasure and engage in transactions - and help the world by doing all of the above!

✔ Consider the best way to get involved and the most efficient way to share what you have with others.

✔ Learn how your valuable skills are transferrable from your professional life to your life as a philanthropist

✔ Listen to stories from inspiring people with fortunes large and small who have found ways to make an impact on the world around them.

✔ Discover how to broaden your understanding of investing to include philanthropic investments and identify which of the hundreds of companies that are trying to make the world a better place are ones you want to support or invest in.

Chapter 12

Donating Your Time to Help Out Others

....

In This Chapter

▶ Thinking about donating your time

▶ Helping with housing

▶ Feeding those in need

▶ Becoming a great citizen

....

*P*erhaps you want to give but feel that your bank account is rather thin at the moment. No worries. You still have a precious gift to share with others: your time. Donating time is a powerful act of charity and philanthropy through which you can create immediate benefits for those you're helping and long-term good for society.

In this chapter, we describe some great practical examples of how you can give your time to good causes. In the short run, you can help solve a pressing practical problem, such as helping to build a roof over someone's head, feeding a hungry person for the day, or helping people of all ages. In the longer term, you can help guide an at-risk child towards a brighter future or plant trees in your community and make a healthier and more sustainable environment for the next generation.

Although several other chapters cover similar subject areas to this one, here we focus in particular on volunteering your time, rather than the equally generous approaches of donating professional skills or treasure (see Chapter 13 and 14, respectively). We use plenty of cross references to where you can find further details on specific subjects elsewhere in this book.

Considering Time-Giving Ideas

Donations of time are essential because most charities run on volunteer power. Volunteers make every donation given to an organisation go so much further. The ability to have a person quickly and competently address an issue is enormously valuable – often charities are understaffed and have a shortage of time to deal with things.

This shortage of time is by design. Donors ask charities to do as much as possible with a limited amount of money, and ask that charities spend as little as possible on overhead (which includes paid staff). As a result, there is a chronic shortage of time at most charities, since there is a shortage of people, and this shortage is often reinforced and even encouraged by donors.

To get the most out of your volunteering experience, try to find a match between what you're seeking and the needs of the organisation where you plan to donate your time. This matching could be of your interests and the charity's mission, the amount of time you're willing to donate and the role to be filled, or the geography or population you want to work in. The great news is that loads of possibilities for volunteering your time are available and so you're sure to find a good fit. You just need to do a little homework.

Before you commit your time, make sure that you check and understand the following aspects:

- ✔ Whether the volunteering experience is a one-time deal or demands an ongoing commitment.

- ✔ Whether it requires technical skills or is a low- or non-skilled opportunity.

- ✔ Whether the time commitment comes along with a required financial obligation.

Providing Housing for People in Need

Everyone needs a safe and secure home. The challenge is that billions of people live in sub-optimal shelters or, even worse, have no homes at all.

Hard times can force an eviction or drive poor families into tenements. A war or natural disaster can displace people and cause them to become refugees. Closer to home, domestic violence and mental illness can force people into becoming homeless. For loads more on housing issues, turn to Chapter 11.

The good news is that you can help address these problems by contributing your time to help build or secure housing for those in need.

Most charities involved in building housing will train you – even if you know nothing about carpentry and haven't swung a hammer in a decade, they'll show you what to do and how to do it. It can be a valuable learning experience for the volunteer and a valuable contribution to the organisation.

Exercising your muscle power to build homes

A number of organisations help build safe and secure housing for families. Their work can take the form of building a home from scratch or simply doing a home makeover, and they need volunteers to help them accomplish their mission. So, this weekend, skip going to the gym and instead get your workout by helping to build a home!

The typical organisation finds the family and location and secures the building materials, technical planners, and required permissions to erect the house or complete a renovation. What they typically lack is the labour to get the job done. With some focus and sweat, volunteering to help build a house can be great fun.

The rewarding work includes clearing a site, moving building materials around, and ultimately picking up a hammer or paintbrush and pounding some nails or laying down a coat of colour. Who knows? You may even get to wield a sledgehammer and behave like the Incredible Hulk, smashing through walls to make way for new plumbing, wiring, and ventilation!

Building a home or renovating an old one is one of the most satisfying ways to spend your time. If you go with friends, you build new bonds and have fun. If you go by yourself, you have the potential to make new friends. The best reward of all is meeting the family or person in need and knowing that you made their lives dramatically better.

Selecting a reputable organisation

When considering donating your time in this way, you need to work with a trustworthy organisation. Read its website, talk to prior volunteers, and search on the Internet to ensure that it's in good standing.

You can find local organisations as well as international ones. Good places to find recommendations for local programmes are with faith-based organisations. They often sponsor programmes themselves and are in touch with families in need.

One of the most respected organisations helping thousands of families is Habitat For Humanity. Check it out at www.habitat.org and www.habitatforhumanity.org.uk. Opportunities tend to come in two general groups:

> ✔ **Long-term service.** If you're passionate about helping to secure homes for the disadvantaged, volunteer opportunities are available at Habitat's headquarters, which usually run for 2 to 6 months.

✔ **Extended trips.** If you have a bit more time, opportunities exist to help re-build in disaster-relief zones.

If you have less time available, some organisations offer similar volunteering trips from just two weeks to places in the developing world, such as through the UK's Christian charity Mission Direct (`www.missiondirect.org`).

Habitat For Humanity and similar organisations offer several volunteer opportunities:

✔ **Local:** You can find a project near your community where you can volunteer your time to help a home.

✔ **Veterans:** If you're a veteran, explore this option for volunteer opportunities and homeownership programmes.

✔ **Women:** If you're a woman and want to develop building skills alongside other women, this is a great opportunity for you.

✔ **Youth:** Opportunities are available if you're aged 5 to 25, along with teachers and youth leaders.

Taking necessary precautions

Well-run organisations provide you with protective glasses, hard hats, and thick gloves. But you can also take the following actions to make sure that you're protected and ready for the work at hand:

✔ **Be aware of potential health issues:** Working on building a house or a renovation project is hard work. Make sure that you're in good enough health to do light-to-heavy lifting. You should also be attentive if you have asthma or any airborne allergies, which construction materials and dust can exacerbate. Plus, always make sure that you look to see whether a first-aid kit is onsite.

If you're volunteering on a renovation location, inquire about the possible presence of asbestos, lead paint, or any other harmful items. Disturbing these substances can cause serious health issues.

✔ **Dress appropriately:** Wear old clothing or something you don't mind getting dirty and potentially torn. In every case, be sure to wear the thickest shoes or boots you have to avoid a nail in the foot or smashed toes.

✔ **Seek medical attention when warranted:** If you find yourself with a cut, a rash, or any feeling of being dizzy or unwell, stop immediately to rest. If the condition continues or, in the case of a cut, you have difficulty stopping the bleeding, seek medical attention as soon as possible.

Rethinking Hunger and Health

All humans need energy and the best way to recharge yourself is by being nourished with fresh, healthy, and nutrient-rich foods. But food is also much more than just powering up your body: it's the fundamental building block of being healthy. Yet many people struggle to know when or where they'll secure their next meal. (We devote Chapter 8 to issues of health and healthcare.)

The key to bringing food security to everyone is making sure that healthy, sustainably grown food is accessible and affordable. In this section, we outline some of the many options available if you want to donate your time to make a meaningful impact in this area.

The great news is that the key ingredient in accomplishing this goal is investing your time in making meals, growing healthy foods, and mentoring others on healthy living. You can also get involved in how food is grown and produced. If you tackle this challenge in an organic and sustainable way, you also help improve the environment (check out Chapter 9 for more on eco issues).

When it comes to hunger, think outside the box. Hunger, food insecurity, and poor nutrition don't just afflict poor children in drought-devastated countries. They're also problems for populations closer to home, such as the elderly, time-deprived new parents, the homeless, and people who're nutrient-starved but obese.

In this section, we include material on feeding vulnerable locals and new parents with great healthy food. If you want to know more about the particular issue of feeding the elderly, skip over to Chapter 6.

Combating hunger in your hometown: Working at a soup kitchen

According to a 2013 report by Church Action on Poverty (www.church-poverty.org.uk) and Oxfam (www.oxfam.org.uk), half a million people in the UK can't feed themselves or their families. The most urgent and important action you can take with your free time to address hunger is to help people get a meal today.

In every big city or small town, the easiest way to help others eat is to volunteer at your local soup kitchen, a vital and vibrant part of all communities. These kitchens are the frontline warriors that help the neediest. Soup kitchens always need three basic types of volunteers:

- ✔ Those who secure food for the food bank by running food drives.

- ✔ Those who do the cutting, chopping, stirring, and so on to prepare the food.

- ✔ Those who serve the food and stick around for clean-up duty.

Most faith-based organisations run community soup kitchens. Some soup kitchen organisations also serve as places to help train people with new skills and get them on the path towards employment in the food services sector. DC Central Kitchen (www.dccentralkitchen.org) is a great example of this kind of soup kitchen organisation that builds skills and meets the needs of the hungry in the community. The American Church in London also has a progressive programme (discover more at www.amchurch.co.uk/soup_kitchen.htm).

Here are some points to keep in mind when you volunteer at a soup kitchen:

- ✔ **Working in a soup kitchen is hard work.** It involves handling food, sharp knives, and hot pots and pans. If you choose to help prepare the meals, make sure that you're comfortable working with the tools and equipment of the kitchen.

    If you have a cold or are feeling under the weather, stay home. You don't want others to get sick. You can always come back another day when you're feeling better.

- ✔ **Be respectful to all the people served.** Some of the guests of the soup kitchen may have mental problems or live on the street. Although most guests are thankful for the meal and are friendly, others can be grumpy or erratic. Just keep that sunshine energy you brought with you to the effort and know that you're helping them to get through a tough day. If a situation arises where you're uncomfortable, seek out the leader of the soup kitchen for advice with the challenge.

Here are two great ways to play your part in a soup kitchen:

- ✔ **FareShare (www.fareshare.org.uk):** The UK's leading charity that helps secure high-quality, low-cost, or free food for hunger relief organisations in Britain. Through its 17 locations, it helps provide 900 community member organisations with food, training, and advice. The food it contributes helps to deliver over 10 million meals per year.

- ✔ **Feeding America (www.feedingamerica.org):** America's foremost domestic hunger-relief organisation and fourth largest charity (according to Forbes). Through a network of more than 200 food banks and 61,000 local food pantries, kitchens, and emergency shelters, Feeding America provides more than 1.35 billion kg of food and grocery items to 37 million people each year. You can contact the organisation's website to find the best way for you to contribute as a volunteer in your community.

Feeding new parents

With the arrival of their little bundle of joy comes an unexpected impact: hungry new parents. Changing nappies, feeding the baby, and still continuing with their day jobs can throw a spanner into parents' daily routines. One of the first and most basic needs to get disrupted is being able to take time to make a fresh, nutritious meal.

As a result, many new parents' diets take a nosedive. They end up ordering takeaways, which becomes expensive really quickly when the food is high-quality and nutritious, or very unhealthy when the food is of the fast-food-and-pizza variety. Alternatively, many new parents just end up eating whatever random items find their way into the refrigerator.

You can help new parents out with your time in two basic ways:

- Volunteer to cook them a meal and drop it off at their home. Apps are sprouting up that help groups of friends become superheroes to parents of newborns by co-ordinating who's responsible for dropping off meals on which days.

- Collect the groceries and drop them off at the new parents' home. Assisting with the shopping is a major help, because just getting to and from the shops can sometimes seem on a par with climbing Mount Everest.

Tackling hunger through community gardens and local farms

If you're a disaster in the kitchen (burnt water, anyone?) but have green thumbs, you can still donate your time to help tackle hunger.

Growing sustainable food locally

Producing sustainable local food is a big deal. Community gardens can play a pivotal role in promoting food security, while they reduce dramatically the carbon footprint involved in transporting food around the world.

Rebel urban farmer: Ron Finley

One superhero doing incredible urban environment food work is Ron Finley (www.ronfinley.com). His work can inspire you to start your own initiative in your community. He's reclaiming unconventional areas of growing food that showcase the importance of healthy food and access to it.

Having grown up in a food desert in South Los Angeles, American Ron Finley tried a novel approach to have, as he says, 'a carrot without toxic ingredients I didn't know how to spell'. He planted vegetables in the curbside strips of dry dirt outside his home. Then he started planting vegetables in the neglected dirt areas elsewhere.

City officials didn't take too kindly to his solution – the city owns the parkways – so they charged him with gardening without a permit; but Ron fought back. He petitioned the city to give him and others the right to grow food in their own neighbourhoods. The petitioners won, the city backed down and Ron's guerrilla-style of urban gardening is turning food deserts into food forests around the US.

At the simplest level, you can join a community garden. You can till the soil, cultivate the garden, participate in the harvest, and then share the bounty with local soup kitchens and families in need. We talk more about creating community gardens in Chapter 9.

Community gardens aren't just for leafy posh neighbourhoods. You can create one almost anywhere, even in hyper-urban environments, which are often most in need of fresh produce when they become *food deserts* (neighbourhoods dominated by convenience stores whose main supplies consist of chips, sugary drinks, and other types of junk food: see Chapter 15 for more details).

The upsides of an urban community garden are making new friends and knowing what goes into the food you eat.

To make fresh, healthy produce available to these areas, you can help install community gardens in plots dedicated to that endeavour or go the way of Ron Finley and reinvent abandoned plots and grassy sidewalk medians as areas to grow fresh fruits and vegetables (for more information, head to the nearby sidebar 'Rebel urban farmer: Ron Finley'). Every major city has urban gardening projects: search the Internet for possibilities. Some cities even sponsor programmes that you can volunteer for, so make sure to check out your city government's website for potential opportunities related to community gardening. You can also check out these organisations:

✔ **Federation of City Farms and Community Gardens** (www.farmgarden.org.uk): Encourages gardening as a community activity throughout the UK, particularly as an intergenerational social activity and as a revitalisation activity in urban areas.

✔ **Royal Horticultural Society (www.rhs.org.uk):** Approaches gardening as a skill that can be taught as a lifelong endeavour. Offers advice, online resources, and classes to improve the novice gardener's skills.

Helping out on a farm: WWOOF-ing

If you love the countryside or live in it, you can donate your time and become a farmhand. The practice is called *WWOOF-ing,* which is nothing to do with noisy dogs but stands for Worldwide Opportunities on Organic Farms or Willing Workers on Organic Farms. The usual trade is room and board for labour. Farms all around the world participate in this network.

The benefits of WWOOF-ing are the same benefits as good old-fashioned labour: you get trim pretty quickly, sleep deeply at night, and gain the invaluable skill of farming.

These three websites help you explore WWOOF-ing:

✔ **WWOOF International (www.wwoofinternational.org):** A website exchange at which you can identify opportunities to work on organic farms around the world.

✔ **WWOOF UK (www.wwoof.org.uk):** The membership charity for UK WWOOFers.

✔ **WWOOF USA (www.wwoofusa.org):** America's leading online website to find opportunities for volunteering your time on an organic farm in the US. Contact the website to find the best match for you.

Preparing Your Own Care

Save up: retirement and old age are expensive. By now, you've no doubt heard this mantra from your parents, high-school counsellors, and advertisements on the television, radio, and Internet. The message is simple: save up and life's better for you.

The challenge is that even the most disciplined and committed savers are unprepared for one of life's major investments. People have difficulty saving for their care for a number of reasons. Here are just two:

✔ Many people live payday to payday and lack the extra income that makes saving for something beyond the next car repair or dental bill difficult or impossible.

✔ Many people assume that the government will swoop in and help you out as you get older. But the reality is that, according to HMRC data, pensions fall well below working income levels. Although the average income in the UK is £19,000, the average pension amount is a little more than £11,000. This discrepancy means that you have to gear up to take care of yourself and your loved ones.

One problem is that nobody is leading the conversation on saving for your own care, which is where you come into the mix. You can help kickstart this vitally important conversation.

Become familiar with organisations such as Prepare Your Care (prepareyourcare.org) in the US or end-of-life planning organisations affiliated with the NHS (www.nhs.uk/Planners/end-of-life-care). People involved in end-of-life planning help companies, faith-based organisations, community organisations, and individuals get this conversation started. You can sign up for training and certification programmes and then volunteer to lead conversations in your community.

When selecting an organisation, make sure that you understand whether it provides education or formal advice. Education is the main way to go as a volunteer. If you find that you're passionate about helping friends, family, and colleagues get care prepared, you may consider pursuing it as a profession.

Understand the difference between giving educational advice versus giving professional advice. To give professional advice, you must have certain certifications, and registration with professional and governmental organisations may be required. To stay out of trouble as a volunteer, we recommend you focus on educational opportunities.

After getting trained, the next step is to become an advocate within your community and workplace, with the goal of starting conversations about getting care prepared. The organisation you volunteer for most likely has presentation materials and speaking notes; the best also have strong supporting partners on standby to help families answer their professional needs in this area.

This volunteer opportunity is one of the most rewarding experiences and best uses of your time. Witnessing families becoming stronger and your workplace becoming care prepared is a powerful experience.

You can volunteer for programmes that educate young mothers and parents on the benefits of proper nutrition. Look for local organisations that offer training, nutritional classes, and community outreach in this area. After you're trained (or if you're already a nutrition professional) you can sit with families, engage them in a dialogue about healthy food choices, and give them that boost needed to switch from unhealthy diets to ones that are tasty and healthy.

Offering Medical Help to the Urban Poor

If you're a nurse, doctor, public-health advocate, or someone passionate about the health of your community, you can contribute your expertise to making a difference to people's health. The health needs of the urban poor run the range from educating people on preventative care to helping those with health issues to gain access to professional services. On the preventative side you can apply your talent and time to building awareness around the prevention of spreading infectious diseases.

Infectious diseases take a heavy toll on the urban poor. The great news is that many of these diseases are preventable. The key to stopping HIV, AIDS, and other infectious diseases is strong community outreach about the importance of both prevention and testing. You can be part of this community outreach.

The urban poor typically gain access to health information through four basic access points:

✔ Grassroots community outreach events

✔ Hospitals and clinics in their communities

✔ Mobile health units

✔ Stand-alone walk-in clinics

A wonderful example of a mobile health unit is the Night Ministry in Chicago, which has been in operation since 1976. Its full-length bus has been retrofitted with a rapid HIV-testing unit, and the programme offers a safe, secure, and reliable place to do testing and to supply free preventative materials. You can find out more information on the Night Ministry at www.thenightministry.org.

If you're a professional healthcare worker and you want to apply your know-how and time, this is a great area of philanthropy to consider. Also, if you're a gifted marketing, branding, or communications expert, you too have a role to play in helping spread the message of prevention and testing.

Whether you have professional skills to contribute or general skills you want to put in the service of others, you can find channels to help you donate your time and talent to a mobile health clinic by searching online and asking within your community. Many faith-based organisations are active and may have opportunities for you to volunteer as well. You can also check with the hospital and medical groups in your community and see whether they have grassroots efforts where you can volunteer your time.

Make sure to review the programme and organisation. You want to ensure that it adheres to the highest standards of hygiene, professionalism, and ethics.

Contributing Your Time to Being a Great Citizen of the World

We believe that a central duty of all human beings is to make the world a better place for other people and those who come after. One of the greatest goals to which you can devote your time is living demonstrably as an ethical, compassionate, involved citizen.

In this section, we describe two ways to do so: devoting a whole gap year to helping others and becoming a mentor and guide to at-risk children.

Taking a gap year to help, learn, and share

So, you've finished school and are gearing up for university: congrats! The challenge is that you don't know what you want to pursue as a career.

If you don't know what you want to study, consider exploring the world, helping others and making an impact by taking a gap year. It'll change your life forever.

You experience more than you can imagine and your potential for contributing now and in the future grows dramatically, because you develop a deep understanding from firsthand experience of the challenges that you witness and experience. You're also likely to make interesting friends on your journey and the year is sure to enrich you culturally.

Gap years aren't only for those leaving secondary or high school; they're also for after you graduate from college and university. Some people even take these gap years *during* their university experience. (The latest version of the gap year happens right in the middle of your professional career, a sort of mini-retirement with meaning.)

Depending on where you are in life's journey, a variety of programmes are on offer. Check out these organisations:

✔ **Global Citizen Year** (www.globalcitizenyear.org): Unlike other programmes that require a college degree, Global Citizen Year taps the potential of American secondary school graduates. Read more about the programme and its founder in the nearby sidebar 'Being a global citizen: Abby Falik'.

✔ **Volunteer Service Organisation** (www.vso.org.uk): VSO places university-educated British volunteers in countries to help with local development, based on a match between the volunteer's skills and the need expressed by local partners.

Inspiring and guiding children

Think back to when you were a child. If you sit for a minute and reflect on the important people in your childhood, you're certain to recall the names of particular adults who inspired you or helped guide you to expand your horizons, pick up new skills, and become more independent.

EXAMPLE

Being a global citizen: Abby Falik

Global Citizen Year is a perfect example of an organisation that has a great programme for you if you're considering taking a gap year. Founder Abby Falik shares her vision here:

'I'm the founder and CEO of Global Citizen Year, an award-winning social enterprise that re-envisions the path to college as an extraordinary – and untapped – opportunity to unleash the potential of America's next generation of global leaders. Each year we provide a diverse corps of high-school graduates with a Peace Corps-style experience across Africa, Latin America, and Asia, preparing them to approach college and careers with passion, perspective, and purpose.

Whereas the Peace Corps expects volunteers to have a college degree, Global Citizen Year provides a transformative experience *before* college – a critical moment for helping young people understand themselves and their potential as leaders.

Through an intensive 10-month programme, our fellows live with families in rural communities in the developing world where they work as apprentices in schools, health clinics, farms, and technology centres. Hands-on experience with the realities of life outside America, combined with a world-class training that provides exposure to social entrepreneurs, NGOs, governments, and donors awakens passions, expands potential, and affirms a sense of purpose.

At the same time, the experience enables our fellows to approach their college years with intention, focus, and motivation.'

Now that you're all grown up, it's your turn to be an inspiration or guide to the next generation. You may have children of your own, you may be in the pre-parent stage of life but love kids, or you may be someone whose children have flown the nest and you're looking for a way to help other youngsters. Now is your chance to transform your time into a powerful act of philanthropy. You can team up with organisations that play a pivotal role in the development of children and your community. You can help spark the next generation of citizen leaders, as the next sections explain. (For more information on other ways to help children, head to Chapters 5 and 7.)

Mentoring at-risk children

You can play a vital role for a child at risk. One of the best ways to volunteer is to become a caring role model for a youth. One of the best organisations working in this space in the US and in several other countries around the world is Big Brothers Big Sisters. It operates in many countries (www.bbbsi.org) and is starting a chapter in England as this book goes to press.

Big Brothers Big Sisters may just be the perfect fit for your volunteer time. For more than a century, this organisation has helped children who may come from a single-parent home, face chronic poverty, or have incarcerated parents. These children are at risk of repeating this cycle unless they have caring role models to show them an alternative pathway forward. You can be that caring role model, by sharing all kinds of activities with your donated time.

If you donate your time as a volunteer, you're called a Big and the child you help is called a Little. Although you're given basic guidelines on how to share your time with a Little, see this as an opportunity to stretch your imagination and come up with fun and simple activities, such as learning a new sport, reading books together, or going to a museum. The key is that you're present to help the Little and show that alternatives exist in life.

This volunteering often results in friendships and directly helps to reduce the chances of Littles making decisions that reduce their future prospects.

You can apply directly online to Big Brothers Big Sisters (www.bbbs.org in the US and www.bbbsi.org internationally). The online application covers four basic steps:

1. **Fill out your online application.**

   Select your post (or zip) code to identify the local branch of the Big Brothers Big Sisters organisation in your area. You then see a simple online application to complete.

2. **Have a one-on-one interview.**

   This interview helps to ensure an appropriate match between you and a Little.

3. **Undergo a background check.**

   Big Brothers Big Sisters is vigilant and wants to make sure that volunteers have a clear background before being put in contact with a family.

4. **Get matched with and introduced to a family.**

   Although you don't need any special degrees or background to be a Big, a good match is necessary; this means matching up on location, personality, and preferences. Then you're introduced. Big Brothers Big Sisters provides ongoing support via a Match Support Specialist. You can count on this person to help navigate any challenging situations that may arise.

Providing leadership and role models for children

If telling stories around the campfire and helping to build life skills in young boys or girls sounds fun to you, consider becoming a volunteer leader in your country's scouting or girlguiding programmes.

These organisations are geared towards empowering children to develop a wide range of skills through a series of challenges. Successful completion of these tasks secures them a badge. Collect enough badges and you earn the chance to take on ever more challenges. The core value is building confidence, commitment, community goodwill, and leadership skills.

If you're a parent, you inevitably find your child tugging on your shirt and asking to join one of these organisations or something similar. As a busy parent, you may find that this is the perfect opportunity to spend more time with your child and to inspire other children.

You can step up and volunteer your time for these organisations as follows:

- ✔ **To serve as a powerful female role model for girls, sign up at** www.girlguiding.org.uk **in the UK or** www.girlscouts.org **in the US.** At the Girlguiding site, you find a Get Involved section with links to information and registration instructions. At the Girl Scout website, click the For Adults tab to get access to volunteer information. By following the instructions, you find yourself on the path to being in front of a room filled with girls excited to learn about the world and be inspired by your example.

- ✔ **To serve as a powerful male role model for boys, sign up at** www.scouts.org.uk **or** www.scouting.org **in the UK or US, respectively.** Click the Get Involved tab and enter your post or zip code to find the scouting organisations in your area. The options range from being a supportive father of your son's troop all the way up to leading a den. (If you elect to become a den leader for the Boy Scouts of America, you must engage in formal training to equip you with the know-how and skills needed to help implement the organisation's programme and education curriculum.)

Chapter 13

Making Use of Your Specific Talents

· ·

In This Chapter

▶ Volunteering your skills effectively

▶ Banking on your financial talents

▶ Employing your legal expertise

▶ Displaying charitable creativity

▶ Getting all techie

· ·

*W*hen you think of people using their talents to support a cause, perhaps you picture a rock star playing a charity concert or an amazing surgeon volunteering with Doctors Without Borders (an organisation we cover in Chapter 8). But everyone has talents that they can use to help others. In this chapter, we describe how you can volunteer your personal and professional skills to charitable or philanthropic organisations. We provide some general pointers for you to note when donating your work skills and also cover the specific areas of banking, the legal profession, creative industries, and computing skills.

Although we focus on these well-known occupations, with a little imagination you can put to philanthropic use just about any skill, however unusual or niche (so all you cruise-ship unicyclists and ice-cream testers can play your part too!).

Part of the value in volunteering your own skills is to spread those skills, particularly in environments where people may have limited exposure to what you can offer. Therefore, you make a difference not only by doing, but also by teaching. When you donate your specific talents in a way that helps others learn to do some of what you do, you build an organisation's strength and sustainability. True, the teenagers who work after school at your local charity aren't going to become amazing computer programmers simply from watching you set up the website, but letting them help you may give them new skills, pique their interest in computers, or even change their career path down the road.

Working at Good Works: Considerations when Donating Your Talents

Your time and expertise have value. Whether you're volunteering at a neighbourhood food bank or doing your normal work for free, you're providing a service that the philanthropic organisation would otherwise have to pay for. So both types of volunteer work are important and beneficial to charities.

But when you donate professional skills, you need to be aware of some additional considerations beyond just wanting to help others. Here are a few points to bear in mind:

- ✔ **Employer rules and policies:** Professionals may be constrained by rules specific to certain employers or firms. Be sure to check with your firm's human resources department to find out what you need to know.

- ✔ **Professional ethics and codes of conduct:** Many professions have codes of conduct or ethics that continue to apply, even if you aren't being paid. Before accepting a volunteer project, be sure to review your profession's rules of professional responsibility.

- ✔ **Tax implications for donated professional services:** Find out in advance how and whether your donated professional services have tax implications for yourself and for the charity you're helping.

In addition, be aware of volunteer burnout, which is all too real and a problem for many organisations. If you want to support one that depends upon volunteers, make sure that it has a way to use its volunteers in a responsible, limited, and reasonable way. If not, it's likely to go through the supply of volunteers at a very fast rate.

If you can, give the organisation as much notice as possible when you plan to volunteer, particularly if it depends heavily upon volunteer staffing. Doing so lets the organisation use your volunteer labour as strategically as possible and increases your impact.

Don't aim simply to give away your services but to make a real impact with your work. Think in terms of who gets the most out of your services and whether you can provide what they need.

Bringing in the Bankers and Accountants: Providing Financial Services

Although the term *financial security* may conjure up images of wealth, if not luxury, it simply refers to being able to control and manage financial affairs in a way that secures wages, saves and builds up wealth, and provides access to funds when the vicissitudes of life send opportunities and unexpected expenses your way.

Helping people escape poverty through access to financial tools

Financial tools – bank and savings accounts, access to credit, and modes of making financial transactions safe and efficient – are important components of financial security. Research suggests that simply having access to these tools helps lift poor people out of poverty more quickly and enables them to retain financial gains that may accrue.

Those without access to these tools or services exist on a cash basis. They receive their wages in cash; conduct all transactions using cash or assets (such as jewellery or livestock), which is difficult to store and move; and rely on informal providers, such as pay-day loans, when emergencies occur. The fact of the matter is that living on a cash basis, by its very nature, is expensive and difficult and leaves poor families even more vulnerable.

For more information on this issue, check out Banking on Change (www. plan-uk.org/what-we-do/banking-on-change), a partnership between Barclays, Plan International, and CARE International UK that gives millions of poor people access to basic banking services.

Volunteering in the financial services industry

There is a huge range of skills in the financial services industry that isn't present or common in society generally. For those of us who have worked in investment banks, it's hard to remember that not everyone knows how to sort out financial information or how to understand interest rates.

This creates a wonderful opportunity to take skills that you may have or take for granted on a day-to-day basis and donate them to people who haven't had the opportunities you've had.

If you're a financial professional you can volunteer your services at organisations such as Ladder Up, which provide financial services to the poor.

Ladder Up (`www.goladderup.org`) is a new model for volunteering in the financial services industry. It offers professional financial services, including tax preparation and financial planning, to people who are *unbanked* (don't have a traditional relationship with a retail bank) or close to the poverty line (many of these clients are members of the American working poor). These people can't afford professional tax planners, accountants, or financial advisors, at least not at the rates these professionals normally charge.

Ladder Up's volunteers help thousands of people understand, prepare, and file their taxes, which for the poor or the economically insecure is more than just a matter of bookkeeping. Since its creation in 1994, Ladder Up has helped 148,000 clients find about US$300 million. That means more money in the hands of private individuals, and more money for their families to climb out of poverty (for some numbers, see the nearby sidebar 'Ladder Up provides real financial returns').

Ladder Up provides real financial returns

A poor person paying US$1 of taxes in the US system is likely to return about US$0.30 of benefit to herself, her household, mortgage, children, and so on. Therefore, a poor person in the US who doesn't overpay and gets to keep that dollar enjoys three times the benefit!

In addition, a quarter of Ladder Up's Tax Assistance Program (TAP) clients are single parents with annual incomes of less than US$15,000. As a result, Ladder Up's work doesn't just affect working parents; it affects their children, too. By finding maximum benefits

available for each household, Ladder Up's TAP programme helps families plan for the future.

For example, a majority of high-school seniors in Chicago public schools have zero college savings – that's not just among TAP clients; it's true across the school system. Without a full scholarship or government assistance, these young people won't be able to continue their educations. Finding that tax credit or financial aid opportunity can enable families to send their children to college.

Ladder Up provides training to its volunteers and asks for a reasonable, consistent amount of participation from them. On a Saturday morning, each volunteer helps out three or four families with tax questions and other queries. If you aren't trained in preparing tax returns or prefer to help in other ways, Ladder Up has additional volunteer roles you can perform.

Unfortunately, although efforts are underway to duplicate Ladder Up in the UK, nothing has launched yet and probably won't until 2015. If this area interests you and you think that an organisation such as Ladder Up would benefit UK households, lend your voice in support of these efforts – start a local volunteer programme that attracts professionals or work with a local organisation to do 'matchmaking' between those with financial skills and those who may be less financially literate.

Summoning All Lawyers: Helping Out the Little Guys

Lawyers are among the highest-paid professionals in the UK and the US. Many of these lawyers are some of the top philanthropists – not simply in terms of amounts donated, but also in public service and volunteering.

Many lawyers forego high salaries at top firms to volunteer in elected or non-elected positions in government, to run community organisations, to help startup companies or to sit as judges. Others use their legal knowledge in advocacy, helping their communities or the poor. Many of the most famous members of the legal profession are defined by their work on public-interest cases and on behalf of defendants unable to afford the services of large law firms at standard billing rates.

In the UK, Inns of Court traditionally provided some services to the indigent or those who could not afford representation. Today, social services agencies and private charities often take the lead, but many fall through the cracks. Many who are injured do not know how to access the remedies available to them; many who are entitled to government benefits are unsure how to claim them; and many who are involved in divorce or child custody proceedings find the situation confusing and demoralising. The availability of law assistance that has been heavily discounted or donated is important for these clients.

Apes go to trial… and win!

One of the most famous lawyers and cases in the US are Clarence Darrow (1857–1938) and the 1924 Scopes trial. This trial pitted Darrow, representing defendant John T. Scopes, against the state of Tennessee and the Butler Act, which forbade the teaching of Darwin's theory of evolution in US schools.

For inspiration, read or see the play *Inherit the Wind,* a dramatic retelling of what came to be known as the 'Scopes Monkey Trial' – Kevin Spacey played Darrow in the Old Vic theatre's most recent performance of the play.

Lending your legal expertise

In the UK you can volunteer time at the LawWorks Clinics Network (`www.lawworks.org.uk`), an organisation sponsored by the Law Society that offers free legal advice in clinics throughout the UK; members include nearly all the major law firms in England and Wales.

In addition, Inns of Court, legal associations for barristers in England and Wales, provide opportunities to help non-profit and low-income clients and often maintain lists of volunteer opportunities.

In the US, your state Bar Association can recommend volunteer opportunities. Also, many law firms have *pro bono* initiatives that can link you to charities or needy clients who may most benefit from your help.

Building your pro bono legal practice

As a solicitor, you can donate your services to clients free of charge by doing *pro bono* work (that is, representing a client free of charge).

Many people think of a *pro bono* practice as centring on criminal law, because *pro bono* criminal lawyers are often the centre of attention and protect the liberty (or even life) of a defendant. But attorneys in other areas of practice can have an equally dramatic effect in civil law, family law, and so on.

People in the UK and US depend upon the legal system in their daily transactions, but are rarely familiar with the subtleties that lie within it and so benefit greatly from committed, informed legal counsel.

You have a luxury in *pro bono* work that's not enjoyed often enough by criminal *pro bono* lawyers – you get to choose your client! So why not choose someone you believe in, trust, and want to work with? Find someone who's starting a business, a charity, or a local school, for example. These entrepreneurs must navigate corporations, contracts, employment, and tax law and other areas to get an enterprise off the ground – areas often deemed worthy of years of study in law school. Too often, they end up with mediocre services from uninterested counsel at high billable rates.

You can even offer your services to someone who's starting a lawsuit. You may end up as an advocate for citizens whose drinking water has been made unsafe by corporate dumping, or as counsel for a class-action lawsuit against a pharmaceutical company that didn't adequately test its product, for example. (Be careful, however, to review the professional responsibility rules in all jurisdictions in which you're licensed before taking on any clients).

Choose wisely and you can discover the most rewarding work of your career. Many attorneys who do *pro bono* work on behalf of very poor defendants, community organisations, or young entrepreneurs say that the work is some of the most engaging, interesting, and meaningful in their careers.

If you're a younger or less experienced attorney, volunteering your services can be a great way to take the lead in a complex matter or to be the point of contact with a client. These experiences are often 'off limits' to younger attorneys in their first two or three years as an associate in a large firm, and *pro bono* work is a great way to get these experiences earlier in your career!

Finding clients to help

As a lawyer, the first step in finding someone to help is to make yourself available. Talk to your firm, your fellow associates and partners, and your local bar association. Go to events where you're likely to meet people who can make referrals and, preferably, people familiar with your rules and boundaries about volunteering your services.

Needs testing is a hot topic currently in legal communities discussing *pro bono* work. Although the debate requires more depth and breadth than we can give here, consider which situations merit your help. If you believe that very poor (*indigent*) clients are most in need, you may want to approach organisations that help this population. If you believe that highly innovative entrepreneurs or courageous community organisations deserve free legal help, consider offering your services to these types of clients.

Setting expectations for pro bono work

Professional and ethical rules on *pro bono* work normally don't require that a client be *unable* to pay. The client who would need to sell her car or remortgage her home to pay for legal services may be just as desperate for help as the client who has nothing at all. Be sensitive to the fact that you have a rare skill that costs a great deal of money to obtain. Be sensitive to the inability for most people to afford market-rate legal services.

Non-lawyers aren't generally familiar with the professional responsibility rules governing the profession, and so take time to discuss these rules with your prospective clients. Do the following to clarify the client's (and your) expectations:

✔ Provide a brief education on what the rules are and what your relationship is with a *pro bono* client.

✔ Be honest and forthcoming about your boundaries and realistic about your commitments: underpromising is preferable to overpromising.

The *pro bono* client is in a vulnerable position and one that's different from the position of a paying client who retains your services. Respect this position by laying out what you can and can't do for the client.

A Cuban *pro bono* revolution: Legal counsel for Guantanamo detainees

During the George W. Bush administration, many prisoners were sent to Guantanamo Bay (or 'Gitmo' for short), a naval base in the Caribbean on the island of Cuba, for potentially permanent detention. Many, upon reaching Gitmo, hadn't been formally arrested, and most weren't represented by attorneys. Seeing the threat this situation posed to the rights of those detained at Gitmo, Chicago law firm Jenner & Block immediately established a section of its website to prepare defence resources for Gitmo detainees. The web presence established a central location to announce recruiting, news, and needs related to Gitmo detainees.

After the Gitmo cases, Jenner's work in public service continues. In 2011, Jenner & Block

attorneys donated an average of over 150 hours each to *pro bono* work: that's well over 50,000 hours per year across the firm! The firm publishes a *pro bono* newsletter, entitled *The Heart of the Matter*, which discusses both firm-wide and individual attorney projects in the area of *pro bono* legal work and community service. You can read more at jenner.com/publicservice/called_to_serve.

This situation isn't unique; even mid-sized (and small!) firms nowadays have ambitious goals in terms of *pro bono* work. This can be great experience, strengthen your firm's links to the community, and even bring visibility among new potential (paying) clients.

Calling All Creative Types: Moving People to Take Action

It is the function of art to renew our perception. What we are familiar with we cease to see.

—Anais Nin

Art is the lie that enables us to realise the truth.

—Pablo Picasso

The creative industry in all its forms (film, music, architecture, painting, writing, and more – even advertising) has long been allied with social causes. Whether the work is intended as social protest (such as Dickens's *Hard Times* or US author John Steinbeck's *The Grapes of Wrath*) or as journalistic reflections of reality that spur change (the iconic photographic images from the Vietnam War, for example), art has the ability to move people in ways that statistics, reports, and sometimes even personal anecdotes don't. In this way, the creative arts can be a powerful force for change.

Media are at the centre of modern life and so think about how you can play your part. Do you create content every day to send out into the world: a short story on a blog, a poetic status update on Facebook, a retweet of a poignant quote on Twitter, or a photographic record of an event on Tumblr? Through media relationships, people make friends, share ideas, change perspectives, and communicate their passions.

In this section, we look at ways in which you can use your own creative abilities to bring about change. If you don't think that you have a creative bone in your body and computers are more your thing, consider using your tech-savvy to help other creative types to get their messages out (as we describe in the later section 'Rallying All Techies').

Sharing great untold stories

In 2007, a team of filmmakers secretly filmed the killing of dolphins in Japan. Using high-definition film cameras disguised as rocks, champion divers and stealthy above-water filmmaking techniques, the team gathered some of the most emotional, compelling, and controversial footage ever captured of dolphins being hunted and slaughtered.

The footage was edited into the film *The Cove,* which won Best Documentary Feature at the 82nd Academy Awards. (You can read about Deborah Bassett, who participated in a paddle-out ceremony to expose the slaughter of dolphins in Japan, in the nearby sidebar 'From girl-next-door to philanthropist'.)

Of course, stories don't have to be Oscar-worthy to make a difference. Nor do they have to be clandestinely recorded. They just need to be shared. You can share your experiences and concerns through your own personal network of friends, family, and peers or by broadcasting them to a wider audience through social media. In the following sections, we offer some ideas to inspire you.

From girl-next-door to philanthropist

Deborah Bassett writes:

'I had travelled extensively throughout Thailand in 2002 where I was engulfed by both the kindness and the humility of the Thai people. When worldwide headlines broke about the Asian tsunami on Christmas Day in 2004, I knew in a heartbeat that I needed to go there to help. At the time I was "living the dream" as an avid surfer in Hawaii and certainly didn't have the funds to do much monetarily, but that did not stop me. I canvassed local establishments with jars adorned with the photos from my trip to Thailand to rally pocket change to support my efforts. Within 10 days, I had raised enough money to send myself to Thailand to take part in the tsunami relief efforts through a programme in Monterrey, California. From there, I volunteered for Habitat for Humanity in El Salvador, building homes for families who had gone without roofs over their heads for several years due to harsh natural disasters.

Although my experiences on the ground were personally gratifying, it was on my return home that I was able to extend my impact by sharing images and writing that encouraged others to become involved in these causes.

In the year that followed, using money I had won by competing on the TV series *Are You Smarter Than A Fifth Grader?*, I self-funded my position at an organisation that couldn't afford my services and attended numerous global conferences, including The Clinton Global Initiative, which was really a crash course in philanthropy.

I also travelled to Taiji, Japan, to raise awareness about the annual dolphin slaughters, volunteered at an orphanage near Cusco, Peru, and documented a jaguar conservation project in the heart of The Selva Maya Rainforest in Mexico. During that time, I became more passionate about ocean conservation and joined the Sea Shepherd Conservation Society. Over the course of several years, I helped organise various fundraising events and participated in direct action campaigns, some of which were later highlighted on the television channel Animal Planet and in the Academy Award winning film, *The Cove*.

Today I spend the majority of my time working as a consultant for nonprofit organisations which need representation in the areas of fundraising, publicity, and outreach. In my spare time I help to promote important environmental and social issues as a blogger, photographer, and writer. Although I don't consider my work to be heroic or even out of the ordinary, I do enjoy inspiring others to get involved with causes they believe in. Everyone has something to contribute and if a regular "girl-next-door" from Connecticut can be considered a philanthropist, anyone can.'

Creating public awareness

Creativity is at the centre of awareness. We notice things that are clever, interesting, or unusual. The things that are typical, mundane, or plain simply roll by as part of our scenery – after years of walking the same path, there are thousands of details we fail to notice. The art of advertising and other related areas of media draws us out of this trance, allowing us to focus in on our surroundings and listen to new messages.

The UK and US both have rich histories of using art and advertising to create greater awareness, whether through posters on the Underground in London or through clever campaigns on the taxicabs of New York City. These traditions are rooted in the recognition that encouraging people to listen comes both in *what* people are being told and *how* they are being told.

Imagine if one person with a great story could benefit from the funding and resources of another person who knew a lot about how to tell that story.

The Ad Council uses this revolutionary concept: it allows causes to focus on finding effective ways to tell their stories, while letting another party fund, maintain, and expand the conduit through which those stories are told.

Finding the right tool to spread a message can often be nearly as important as finding the right message to send.

The Ad Council (www.adcouncil.org) is a non-profit organisation that distributes public awareness campaigns in the US. It's unique internationally in that it doesn't generally produce content. Instead, it takes content from contributors (charities, government entities, awareness campaigns, groups of celebrity advocates, and so on) and creates opportunities for this information to be disseminated to a broad audience.

Getting the message across

The Ad Council began as part of the American propaganda effort during World War II. It showcased advertisements that encouraged people to support the war effort, to gather scrap metal for wartime recycling, and to buy war bonds. Rosie the Riveter, a cartoon depiction of a woman working in a factory during the war, remains one of the Ad Council's most iconic images.

After the war, the Ad Council focused on peacetime issues such as environmental stewardship, heart disease, urban crime, education, drunk driving, and seatbelt usage. Today it continues its work delivering critical messages to the American public.

Although you may not be able to work directly with the Ad Council or have an organisation similar to the Council in your area, you can become involved in awareness campaigns; Chapter 15 has the details. You can also go to the Ad Council website for inspiration on what successful campaigns look like. Study a few of the Council's classic or contemporary announcements to see how sound, images, and content are combined to create compelling calls to action.

In addition, the London College of Communication (www.lcc.arts.ac.uk) periodically publishes or brings attention to award-winning advocacy campaigns. MediaCom (www.mediacomuk.com) and other large ad agencies in London also publish their output, including public-interest work, online and these pieces can serve as great inspiration.

Donating your intellectual property

Intellectual property (IP) refers to the right you have to something that you create: a logo, a song, a photograph, and so on. It may also be an invention or a story you've written. Intellectual property has value, and it can be bought and sold.

As a philanthropist, you can donate your IP to causes you believe in. Consider these examples:

✔ **Donating the rights to that great photo.** Suppose you took a beautiful picture at the pond a few years ago. If people running an environmental campaign to save the pond are looking for a shot to use on their postcards, posters, or websites, you can give the organisation the right to reproduce and use your photo in its campaign.

Be careful when using photographs that feature people, especially if they participated in a professional capacity, as an actor or model, for example. You may not have the right to donate the photo without obtaining a model release or similar document for the people depicted in the photo. Whether you're a professional photographer or an amateur, make sure that you have a good model release form to use with the subjects of your photos. Local arts organisations or university art departments can often help you find the standard form in your jurisdiction.

✔ **Donating a song you created.** Music IP, particularly performance IP (a recording of you playing a song, for instance), is an amazing asset. Just because that song didn't land you a big record deal doesn't mean it should be gathering dust on your shelf (or, nowadays, on your laptop). Consider letting a local charity, political candidate, or student filmmaker use it!

In one of the most effective donations of a song, Natalie Merchant allowed select events and campaigns to use her hit song 'Wonder' to promote their causes (the song is written as a first-person account of a person with a debilitating disability, though the song leaves ambiguous whether the condition was caused by disease). Through this donation, these organisations were able to produce advertisements and other media that grabbed the attention of people who otherwise may not have paid attention to their advertising.

Make sure that you do indeed own the rights to the property you're considering donating. For example, if you perform a cover for a ballad written by another artist, do you own the rights to the ballad (no!) or the musical rendition (possibly)? For information about IP rights, check out the Intellectual Property Office website at www.ipo.gov.uk.

Making music festivals with a mission

In 1971, George Harrison and Ravi Shankar organised their Concert for Bangladesh, the purpose of which was to raise awareness of the plight of, and find relief for, refugees from East Pakistan. Widely seen as the first of the large-scale rock benefits, the concert took place at New York's Madison Square Garden in front of an audience of 40,000. It was followed up with a best-selling live album, the proceeds of which also went to refugee relief. Since then, several other notable benefit concerts have occurred:

- ✔ **Farm Aid:** In Champaign, Illinois, in 1985, a concert was held to benefit American family farmers. It was a huge success, raising in excess of US$9 million, despite coming in the wake of the severe early-1980s recession.

- ✔ **Lilith Fair:** Nearly 15 years after Live Aid (see the next bullet point) and Farm Aid, the Lilith Fair reinvented the genre of charitable mega-concerts. A female-led annual festival co-founded by Sarah McLachlan, it raised over US$10 million for women's charities in its first three years.

- ✔ **Live Aid:** This dual-venue concert, organised by Bob Geldof, occurred simultaneously at London's Wembley Stadium in the UK and at JFK Stadium in Philadelphia, Pennsylvania, in the US. Its purpose was to help raise awareness and funds for famine-ravaged Ethiopia. Arguably the first mega-concert, Live Aid had a global audience of nearly 2 billion in 150 countries and raised £140 million.

Benefit concerts have a dual purpose: to raise awareness of a problem and to raise funds through viewer donations. Next time the summer concert and festival season comes around, consider visiting an event that helps fund a cause you believe in.

Transmitting Your Tech Talent

Technology skills aren't evenly distributed around the world – or around a country – for a variety of reasons. Some children are exposed to computers at a young age, while others aren't; certain professions demand a level of technical skill that others don't.

Although familiarity with technology is one of the most unevenly-distributed assets on the planet, like wealth, technical skill can be donated. Done carefully, technical assistance can be an amazing and high-impact method of philanthropy.

Joining a hackathon

Hackathons are small, focused periods of code creation. Compared to larger, structured projects of collaborative programming, hackathons have several advantages:

- ✔ They allow a small group to work organically in creating software that accomplishes a particular task.

- ✔ They encourage performance-focused development, instead of software that looks pretty but may not function well.

- ✔ They tend to bring together people from varying backgrounds, creating a group that, as a whole, is better equipped to troubleshoot and 'bugstomp' code than groups limited to people who are accustomed to working together. This aspect often encourages rapid innovation and code abbreviation.

In addition to the advantages, however, hackathons have a couple of challenges as well:

- ✔ **Although well suited to developing purpose-built software on very short timelines, they aren't well suited to developing more complex software.** The person managing the hackathon should ensure that the goal is reachable in the provided time and that the skill sets of the programmers involved match the roles needed.

  An increasing number of hackathons encourage people to sign up in pairs for *pair programming*. Though a good way of managing volunteers (people are more likely to sign up with a friend), it may not lead to maximum productivity among expert programmers. An in-depth study published in 2006 suggests that experts, when paired, aren't substantially more productive (or less bug-prone) than experts programming alone.

✔ **The software developed in the hackathon process (or as *print process,* a short hackathon) tends to be aimed towards sophisticated users.** Though fine for an application to be used by fellow programmers, it may result in applications that average computer users find unapproachable or cumbersome.

If you're a programmer, use your talents by participating in a hackathon. To find upcoming events, check out www.meetup.com/UK-Hackathons-and-Jams or lanyrd.com/topics/hackathon.

Supporting a small charity's IT systems

Even large businesses have trouble with information technology. For instance, a large bank may have to run five or ten different pieces of software for the same purpose (particularly because many large banks used to be five or ten smaller banks). Large utilities and government offices often have different computer systems for different tasks, with many other tasks still completed with pen and paper. As disorganised as this sounds, it's efficient compared to the computer systems at most charities.

When managers at non-profit organisations try to make the most of small budgets, technology is often at the bottom of the to-do list, a situation that has many negative consequences. For example, as more and more donors (particularly ones who've read this book!) look to a charity's website for important information, the quality of the website can impact on whether they donate. A website that looks antiquated (or hasn't been updated in months or years) is a red flag to a savvy donor – the potential donor may wonder what's going on at the organisation. A charity that fails to post last year's annual report or the newest financial information on its website risks looking disorganised or, worse, dishonest.

Many charities simply don't have the money or skills to keep a website updated. Even if a charity is able to manage its Internet presence, it may not be able to manage important databases or upgrade its systems. A charity focused on hunger or healthcare, for example, is unlikely to have a lot of technical expertise among its core group of volunteers, a situation that makes improving the charity's technology situation costly. Outside professionals charge fees that are generally unaffordable and, even if the fees are affordable, they take money away from the charity's main mission.

Even in today's world, computer skills are rare. Donating your computer skills, even for a weekend (or after work for a few week nights) can make a huge difference in an organisation's ability to use technology. Donating your technical expertise benefits an organisation in a couple of key ways:

✔ It makes the organisation more presentable on the Internet and more efficient in the office.

✔ It saves the organisation the money it would otherwise spend finding, hiring, and paying a consultant to fix its technology problems.

By offering these services for free, you allow the charity to direct its energy and funds towards accomplishing its primary mission.

Many well-meaning volunteers have set up complex software or new systems for charities and then returned a few months later to find these systems in disarray or disuse. Technology is only as good as its users: if you're going to change or update how things work, be sure to train someone (or, ideally, more than one person) to use the new stuff.

Contributing to an open-source platform

In the past 15 years, the concept of an open-source platform has changed. Originally, *open source* meant sharing source code and even, in some cases (for example, with Linux OS) sharing all aspects of the operating system and its applications. Usually, these bits were shared as raw source code to people who'd edit and improve the software. Sharing source code is the computer equivalent of letting the audience read (and edit) your screenplay rather than allowing them to see only the completed film.

Today, the open-source model reaches far beyond software and computers. Now, it also refers to sharing how stuff works. For instance, a business model or process can be open source.

Maybe you have a startup model that works well for entrepreneurs in Africa, or a way of performing a task more efficiently than commonly used methods. When applying the open-source model, you make your startup model or the efficient process available to other organisations so that they can use and modify it to their situation. Unlike traditional businesses that guard these advancements or efficiencies in order to protect a competitive advantage, social ventures and philanthropic organisations share them in order to maximise the benefits beyond their own missions.

The primary strength of open-source platforms is that they allow people to take quickly what they need and adapt it to what they're doing. Thinking in terms of open source allows organisations to be inclusive rather than secretive, to share rather than hoard, and to co-operate rather than compete.

This concept has strengths and weaknesses and may not be suitable for all areas, but for some problems – those that are so complex or massive that individual organisations working in isolation struggle to generate an impact large enough to make a difference – it makes sense. Huge philanthropic and scientific projects, such as perfecting the structure of great research universities (which were modelled on German academies, and then on Oxford and Cambridge, and today on top research departments at various universities) or sequencing the human genome (which was a competitive race, but also a collaborative effort among top scientists who shared techniques, information, and insights), have had 'open source' aspects driving their success.

You can get involved in open-source initiatives in any community. Opportunities for building open-source platforms for sharing information exist whatever your interest, from environmental conservation to spreading healthcare information to building ways for parents to communicate about education (see Chapter 5 for more details on open-source learning).

Here are just some of the many formats available:

- ✔ **Rating systems:** Allow people to rate services they've received or express their opinions – great for things such as healthcare providers or educational tutors where the quality of the service may be crucial.
- ✔ **Updatable databases:** Great for lists of resources.
- ✔ **Wikis:** We discuss these in the next section.

Sharing your knowledge freely: Wikis

One of the most amazing platforms for knowledge-sharing today is the wiki. A *wiki* is a collaborative effort to build a knowledge base in a given area using the Internet. The largest and most ambitious wiki project is Wikipedia (en.wikipedia.com), but thousands of other wikis exist, covering topics from kite-surfing to knitting.

Wikis allow users who don't know each other to help build a common pool of knowledge from which everyone can draw.

Originally, some people argued that wikis wouldn't work, believing that the result would be too much incorrect, erroneous, or self-promoting information. This information, some argued, would crowd out valid stuff. Others thought vandalism would destroy wikis over time, because few users would have time or energy to patrol constantly for wiki vandals. However, despite these challenges, wikis have become a huge success.

Wikis are a type of open-source approach. Everyone can see what's current, what existed in the past, and how edits have occurred. By making all this information available, a chain of accountability evolves. Identifying top contributors, vanquishing vandals, and refining content becomes easy.

Think about the cause you want to support as a wiki:

- ✔ What knowledge do you want to see shared?
- ✔ What tools can assist people in collaborating better?
- ✔ What information is missing that would be important to add next?
- ✔ How can people be convinced to co-operate and share the wealth of knowledge they've built?

Think about how you can use shared interest in a cause to motivate people to improve and spread information. To find out how to create a wiki page, go to `en.wikipedia.org/wiki/Wikipedia:Your_first_article`.

If you don't want to build a page in Wikipedia itself, you can create your own Wiki universe in which people can share their knowledge. To learn more about originating your own wiki, visit `http://www.wikihow.com/Start-a-Wiki`.

Chapter 14

Sharing Your Treasure

In This Chapter

▶ Introducing treasure donation

▶ Making a difference with treasure of any size

▶ Multiplying the impact of your charitable endeavours

*O*ne of the most useful things you have is your *treasure:* the cash you've saved, the assets you've accumulated, and the investments you've made. This treasure, in whatever form it takes, gives you security and options. What do you want to spend it on? Cash in particular, because it's so readily available and so easy to transfer, is extremely versatile. You can do nearly anything with cash, and so choosing to give it away is a remarkable act of selflessness. In this chapter, we explain how you can give, whether you have big treasure, small treasure, or no treasure, and how to multiply your contributions via employer matching schemes and company/charity partnerships.

This chapter is by no means solely for wealthy people, just as Chapter 12 on donating time isn't only for people with loads of spare time. Our goal is to help you understand the different kinds of treasure that you can donate, how organisations use these donations, and how you can give your treasure strategically, effectively, and responsibly.

If you prefer to enjoy your money rather than give it away – but you still want to have a positive impact while doing so – read Chapter 15 to find out more about spending while doing good!

Donating Money and Assets: A Few Things to Know

Each person's treasure is different, in size and in content, and determining how much and what to give is a matter of apportioning what you have. You may be thinking of donating your car instead of selling it, donating some shares of stock rather than cashing out and taking your profits, or donating the cash lying around in your 'rainy day' account. In each of these cases, you're apportioning your treasure.

Regardless of the manner in which you donate assets – whether they're cash, property, items, or securities – keep the following points in mind:

- **Before donating, check the laws in your local jurisdiction.** Special rules govern what benefits you can receive for making a donation. Donating physical objects, such as cars and clothing, is dealt with differently from donating stocks or bonds. Check with your tax advisor if you're confused or have questions – the rules can be complex, especially for large donations.

- **The amount you paid for something is often different from the 'amount' of your donation.** Typically, the *fair market value* (more common in American and European law) or *merchantable value* (more common in British and Commonwealth law) is used to determine the value of an item. A tax advisor is valuable in understanding what you can claim for the value of items donated. Often, a formal appraisal isn't necessary – unless you're donating something of substantial value, as we explain in the next item in this list.

- **If you're donating something of substantial value, like art for a charity to auction, hire an appraiser familiar with the applicable laws.** Some auction houses offer such appraisers for hire at reasonable rates in the hope that you use their auction house to dispose of the asset. If you go this route, however, never sign a contract that forces you to use the services of an auction house because you used the services of its appraiser or appraisal service.

Making a Big Difference with Small Treasure

The piggybank. The change jar. The bank account that's been sitting since the previous time tight jeans were cool.

Most donations come from small donors. In 1998 (the year with the most complete survey data available), over 70 per cent of American households gave to charity and the average household gave over $1,000; charitable donations have grown in almost every year since. In the UK, despite fewer incentives to give to charity, many taxpayers still support their favourite causes. In fact, middle-class people in England give £3–5 (the amount varies from year to year) for each quid the upper class contributes.

In short, millionaires don't give the vast majority of donations each year: that honour goes to ordinary people with ordinary lives and livelihoods. How that money is put to use decides whether the treasure has an impact on communities, the environment, and the world.

Still, most communities benefit from a mix of philanthropy. Although large donations from wealthy donors (which we cover in the later section 'Going Big: Big Treasure, Big Responsibility') can help build an endowment or erect a building, the day-to-day costs and salaries are usually covered with help from small donors. In addition, innovative fundraising efforts of recent years where donors 'buy a brick' or 'pay a day', allow smaller donors to pool their resources to achieve big goals and sustain organisations effectively.

In this section, we take a look at how people with ordinary resources can make a difference. (If making even a small donation seems beyond your abilities, hop on over to the later section 'No Treasure? No Problem: Seeing How You Can Still Give', where we explain how even those with very limited resources can still make a significant difference.)

Devising an effective donation strategy

Although most people agree that throwing money at a problem is generally not the best or most effective way to solve anything, that still seems to be the strategy many donors – especially small donors – take. Whereas rich donors often have legal and financial advisors and other experts to guide them on how to set up and manage their charitable contributions, small donors generally have only their good intentions.

In philanthropy, as in every other endeavour, good intentions aren't quite enough. You also need to think strategically and pragmatically. True, doing a cost–benefit analysis of your donation's impact may seem rather cold-hearted (aren't all hungry children deserving? Isn't preserving historical architecture always a worthy goal?), but you can do more good for more causes for a longer period of time if you let your head, as well as your heart, in on the decision-making process.

Setting your expectations with hypothetical questions

To start forming a strategy, change the way you think about your donations. Instead of focusing on the general intent ('I want to make children's lives better', for example), think in terms of return on investment: how can you maximise the positive outcomes/impacts with a donation of X amount?

Consider what a good measure of your treasure-sharing may be and then test it with hypothetical questions such as the following:

- ✔ 'If I have only £50 to give away, what can I do that positively affects the lives of at least five people? How about the lives of 50 people?'

- ✔ 'If I decide to give away £1 every day, what's the highest impact thing I can do in my community? What if I gave away the £365 for the year in one day – would I make a different choice?'

- ✔ 'If I want to touch the lives of 1,000 people with my philanthropy, how much money do I need? Can I find a way to do it for less than that? What if I want to touch the lives of 10,000 people?'

These 'small gift' questions can be hard, but asking them is a useful exercise whether you have hundreds or millions to give away. First, thinking in terms of small donations imposes a discipline that working with 'the sky's the limit' numbers typically doesn't. Second, thinking about such questions – and inventing your own – helps you to build more realistic goals and expectations about how to make an impact with your treasure. Third, it helps you figure out how to use your resources as efficiently as possible. Remember, every pound not wasted is one you can use to influence the causes you care about.

Perhaps the greatest benefit of asking yourself these hypothetical questions is that it prepares you to ask very targeted questions of the charity you decide to help. Maybe you want to give to clean up a local park. When you talk to the park district or parks organisation, you can ask questions such as 'Can the park be cleaned up for £300, and if not, why not?', 'What costs are associated with park clean up?' and so on.

Considering your giving options

Today, philanthropy is less expensive, relative to salaries in the developed world, than ever before. A key reason for this change is that wages have risen while philanthropic causes themselves have become more efficient. As a result, the range of options available to philanthropists has expanded dramatically:

- ✔ You can donate a small portion of your salary every month and it's likely to be used far more effectively and efficiently than 10 or 20 years ago.

- ✔ You can set aside a portion of investment returns each quarter or each year and decide which charities the amounts can benefit. This allows you to have substantial impact one to four times per year.

- ✔ You can talk with a charity whose long-term goals you support about automatically deducting a donation from your account each month. This reassures you that you're always supporting this charity without having to remember to write a cheque each time.

Thinking about giving as a daily budget item

Many people give in the moment: a natural disaster occurs somewhere in the world and they call the helplines to donate money or collect items to donate to the survivors. This impulse to help in the moment is a generous one, but if it's the primary way you give to charity, you're missing the opportunity to do good beyond the immediate need.

A better strategy is to think about giving as a category in your daily budget. Planning your donations as a regular expense rather than as an impulsive, sporadic event, benefits you – and your causes – in an important way: it lets you look farther into the future and structure your gifts in ways that are more interesting, accountable, and impactful.

Consider street begging as an example. When you pass a beggar, street musician, or someone else soliciting money, do you drop a few coins into the hat or tin can or do you pass by? It probably depends on the kind of day you're having, whether you have some loose change in your pocket that you can easily retrieve, and whether you find the recipient particularly appealing.

Yet if that person's wellbeing were any other item in your personal budget, you'd ask questions, such as whether this purchase is good value, and you'd consider competing products. If you begin to ask those same kinds of questions about philanthropy and do the same kind of calculation, the answers shape your analysis and inform your behaviour. In the begging example, you're likely to discover better ways of supporting that person than a direct gift of cash.

Mobilising your network to give

You may be modest in treasure but rich in friends. If so, you can maximise your giving power by empowering the people in your social network to get involved and give to causes you all believe in.

Recently, online social networks have become more closely related to philanthropy. People increasingly use sites such as Facebook to promote causes, find volunteers, and schedule fundraising events. Apps that help gather treasure – such as Causes, ChipIn, FundRazr, and Fundraising – have made this process easier for fundraisers and donors.

As you mobilise your network, don't limit yourself to the people you connect with online. You also have a social network that doesn't reside inside your computer. Your real-life networks may include classmates, friends from work, friends from your travels, and other people you've met.

Mobilising your network is an art form, with no set 'best' way to do it. But the next sections give you some ideas.

Keeping your network connected

A social network isn't a wheel with you at the hub and spokes joining you to your friends. It's a spider web of wheels, each connected to the others through people who know each other. By reinforcing your relationships and helping others to build relationships with each other, you can grow your network (and your impact) into an entity that can engage in activities together, address problems as a group, and fund causes that no single person in the network could fund alone.

A network is more likely to give to causes everyone cares about if the different members feel connected to one another and to the group as a whole. To create this feeling of connectedness, effective networkers use the best tools available, online and in face-to-face. Although the best tool may occasionally be sending a mass email, more often it's gathering people together after work, for a picnic or for dinner.

Don't become complacent with your social network simply because you have Facebook or another tool to keep track of your acquaintances. Maintain your network with emails, phone calls, letters, and periodic get-togethers. Doing so brings you closer to the people you know – and they may be people you want to collaborate with in the future!

Spurring your network into action

Keeping your network connected isn't enough to mobilise it for action. You also need to inspire the group to take action. To help you do so effectively, ask yourself these questions:

- ✓ **What excites the type of people who'd be excited about donating to your cause?** For instance, you may already be part of a group that cares for local land, made up of people who're concerned about the environment. By tapping into other groups of people who've already been identified as wanting to help the environment, you're more likely to have a sympathetic audience for your thoughts. Also, you're more efficient in using your resources, because the people you're appealing to wouldn't be members of these groups if they weren't at least somewhat interested in hearing from people like you!

✔ **How can you harness enthusiasm for your cause within the group you've chosen?** Creating enthusiasm is difficult – so why not harness the enthusiasm that already exists? The best way is to figure out what really drives the passion of the group you're appealing to. Is it an upcoming decision about the local factory, a concern about the lack of teachers at the school, or a larger worry about the youth unemployment problem? By understanding why people are enthusiastic, you can begin to understand how to use that enthusiasm to bolster your cause.

If you can create a compelling message and call-to-action, you're likely to be on the path to social-networking, treasure-combining success!

Being aware of the costs of mobilisation

Sometimes the cost of mobilising your network is high relative to the rewards: chances are you won't raise a lot of money if your mobilisation plan is to get a lot of college students together on campus to discuss how penniless everyone is. But if you can match the event with the crowd and be creative in how you pull it together, you can keep the costs low and still bring in substantial donations: for example, an after-work event in Chicago in late 2009 raised tens of thousands of dollars by getting people together in a donated venue to try some reasonably priced wines.

If you're mobilising your network through online venues and apps, be aware that fees for using fundraising services change constantly, including social networking applications. Check the fees related to fundraising apps and the transaction websites the apps use (including PayPal). Otherwise, you can end up paying a lot of fees just to raise a small amount of money.

Going Big: Big Treasure, Big Responsibility

Some lucky people have big treasure. In the course of writing this book, we've met several such people, with all sorts of stories. Sometimes their wealth came from a wealthy uncle or grandparent who passed away. Other times, they discovered a piece of art or an old sports car in the garage that turned out to be worth millions. Often, their stories shared this beginning: 'I had this friend in college who started a technology company no one thought would succeed...'. One woman was an early Starbucks employee (more accurately, a 'barista') who went on to be very wealthy thanks to Starbucks stock options.

No matter where your treasure comes from, think about this question: 'Do I, sometimes, in some ways, have more treasure than I need?' If the answer is yes, go on to ask this question: 'Am I interested in helping the world by sharing that treasure with others?' If the answer is still yes, you're reading the right chapter of the right book.

When making a big donation, you can find that thinking in terms of ratios is helpful:

- ✔ How big is this donation relative to other big donations the organisation has received (and how well did it manage those other large gifts)? This helps you to understand the role you play and the stake you hold in the organisation's work.

- ✔ How big is this donation compared to the organisation's monthly or yearly budget? Knowing this helps you keep perspective on the kind of impact you can make and how you might be able to affect or assist the organisation.

- ✔ How big is this donation compared to how much the organisation will spend on its next major project? This allows you to see whether you can push a specific initiative or project along.

- ✔ Are others able to match this donation in part or in whole (and, if not, why)? This information helps you to understand if your impact can be multiplied or amplified with the help of others.

By running through these questions, you can quickly assess the donation's size and figure out what types of planning need to be done. For example, if you're donating to a large institution, such as a university or hospital, the organisation probably has a development officer or, in many cases, a major gifts department that deals with large gifts. A smaller organisation, where you're an unusually large donor, however, may be unfamiliar with structure, accounting, or legal questions – exercise patience while they examine how to best work with you (you've given them a very good problem to have, but they may not have answers for you instantly).

If you have questions, the best idea is to get legal advice before any money changes hands.

Our friend Liesel Pritzker has big treasure and discovered that it brings with it huge opportunities and responsibilities. Having given away millions of dollars before her 25th birthday, Liesel quickly became an expert at deploying her treasure to address the issues she's passionate about. (You can read about her philosophy in the nearby sidebar 'Unlocking human potential: Liesel Pritzker Simmons'.)

EXAMPLE

Unlocking human potential: Liesel Pritzker Simmons

'The room was small, dark and dusty – certainly not a good setting for a preschool. The only daylight came through a few holes in the corrugated tin roof. But a preschool it was, and in this room in the Dharamṣala valley in Himachal Pradesh, India, I met Nikil. I think he was about 2 and a half years old, but it's hard to say because malnutrition had stunted the growth of most of the children I was looking after that summer when I was 22.

One day I noticed Nikil pawing at something on the floor. Instead of playing with the beaten-up wooden blocks, he was hunched over, fascinated by something I couldn't see.

Worried that it was a dangerous bug of some sort, I raced over, but quickly realised that it was a spot of light. The sun was shining through one of the holes in the roof, creating a perfectly round spot of light on the dusty rug. Nikil was trying to pick up that little coin of light with his hands. I smiled at his earnestness and watched as he furrowed his brow in frustration. So I cupped his little hand in mine, and we carefully 'scooped' the ray of light into our hands. He squealed with delight, and started to giggle when together we 'dropped' the light back onto the floor. Hearing his laughter, the other toddlers wandered over and became entranced in this surprising game.

For weeks, the children waited for the time of day when the coins of light would appear on the rug and play the light game. But then one day, I noticed Nikil didn't join them. He was standing, staring straight up at the dirty roof. His young and nimble mind had worked out that the light didn't come from the floor but from the sky. And from that moment, every day at around 11 o'clock, Nikil was no longer looking at the floor, but craning his neck and reaching his fingers up to those holes in the tin roof. He had figured it out.

Watching a child discover the world is inspiring and humbling. Sure, I had given him a little guidance and help, but his curiosity and tenacity ultimately solved the riddle. And that's when I felt my own definition of philanthropy come into being. For me, the purpose of philanthropy is to unlock the human potential that's already there but is perhaps hindered by economic or social barriers. Two years after I met Nikil, I took a large portion of my own money to create the IDP Foundation, Inc., with a focus on international education. Whenever we think about potential grants to fund, we keep Nikil's spirit in mind. What is the problem to solve? Is the community already trying to solve it? What are the barriers that are keeping those community-led solutions from working, and what tools (time, talent, grants, or investments) can help remove them?

To me, impactful philanthropy is achieved by listening, watching and then taking action with respect.'

No Treasure? No Problem: Seeing How You Can Still Give

What if you don't have any treasure? You look at your bank account and it contains money you need. You look around your home and it's full of stuff you like, love, and don't want to give away. You need your car to get to work. Can you be philanthropic without treasure?

Absolutely!

You can donate your time or your talent. Chapter 12 explains how the gift of time is an indispensable commodity for cash-strapped charities and Chapter 13 delves into different ways to donate your skills and expertise.

Nicole Buffett: Giving the most valuable thing you possess

Nicole Buffett, artist and Warren Buffett's granddaughter, has little money, but she considers herself a philanthropist. She donates her time and talent generously. As an artist, she can create treasure to donate or auction for a good cause. Nicole also donates things that cost nothing but have a value, for instance by giving her voice to a cause. She says:

'Philanthropy is *not* limited to how much money you may or may not have, make or have access to.

Philanthropy exists to make the world a better place. In my own personal efforts and struggles to find my own identity in light and dark of my grandfather's wealth, I have continually become more and more aware of what is most real. Realness is a way of configuring the things

that have true value – not just the value of how many dollars you have but the value of how much positive impact and effect you have on a daily, moment-by-moment, basis.

The most valuable thing I give the world is my creative energy. Every time I complete a painting or work of art of any kind, I am sharing the most valuable thing that I possess. Instead of trying to write the most impressive grant, build up my resume, or stay seated on a Board to win the approval of my family so that I might be deemed 'suited' to give, I choose to give radically and spontaneously at every moment, every day, by living my life as an artist and making my life one that stabilises itself through the proliferation of all that is creative.'

Creating a Multiplier Effect

Treasure is created in a variety of ways and usually needs to be gathered together. The essential concept behind fundraising or donating is that, when you put many little treasures together, you end up with a big treasure pile. By thinking of treasure as something that can be gathered, combined, and grown, you can develop a different perspective on how to put your treasure to work.

In this section, we look at two ways of increasing the effectiveness when you donate your treasure: employer matching programmes and company/good cause partnerships.

 Nearly every philanthropic experience using treasure is a mix of using others' services and your money, because unless you're going to hop on an aeroplane and deliver the money yourself, people are bound to be between you and the recipient of your generosity. By choosing these services well, you can make life easier for yourself and make your donations more effective.

Looking into matching programmes

Matching is one of the most powerful treasure concepts and it works in two main ways:

- ✔ **Matching gift programme:** A corporation or business implements a programme in which it matches its employees' charitable donations. This match can be like for like (pound for pound or dollar for dollar), half the amount (£0.50 per £1), or even double the amount. Some firms set a match ceiling, in which the matching gifts stop after the ceiling is met (so make your donations early!) – mind the match amount, it may be a maximum per employee or a maximum for all employees put together.

- ✔ **Matching grant programme:** An individual or corporate donor makes a matching grant to a favourite charity. The donor gives a like-for-like amount for what the charity can raise within a certain period of time. The matching funds may apply to everything raised within the fundraising hour, for example, or anything raised by the end of the year.

 Companies offer matching gift programmes because they have a positive impact on giving. Research demonstrates that when employee contributions are matched, all measures of success are positively impacted including employee satisfaction, employee participation, and average gifts. Bear that in mind if you find yourself trying to persuade your company to set up a matching programme.

Supporting matching programmes

Thomas Bognanno from Community Health Charities of America itemises five reasons why you shouldn't miss a chance to participate in your matching gift or grant programme:

✔ They're among the most efficient and effective ways to fundraise for charities.

✔ When your company matches your gift, your favourite charity receives more money than if you gave outside your employer's programme.

✔ More money for your favourite charity means more money to fund the work of its mission.

✔ Charities gain tremendous value for the gifts they receive through such workplace campaigns, as these companies are also a fantastic source of future support, enthusiastic volunteers for events, and so forth. Charities may also lack things that your company has a surplus of – you may have a conference room that sits unused much of the week, but the charity has no place to hold a board meeting or a negotiation with a major donor, for instance.

Participating in employer matching programmes

Thousands of companies in the US have matching programmes, including most Fortune 500 companies. Some major corporations in the UK, especially those with headquarters in the US or Canada, now also offer such programmes. But you don't need to work for Google or Amazon to have an employer matching programme. Over 75,000 small and mid-sized businesses in the US have charitable matching programmes and many smaller UK companies offer them as well.

Ask the human resources (HR) department of your company whether a matching programme exists. Alternatively, you can find out if your employer offers such a scheme by going to the International Justice Mission UK website: www.ijm.org/content/company-match. Often, simply filling out one or two forms can double the treasure you donate!

Here are some things to keep in mind:

✔ **Know the boundaries of the match and its rules.** For many companies (particularly those headquartered or doing business in the US), any donation to a charity or non-profit organisation in the US (refer to Chapter 4 for details) is eligible. For others, donations to any domestic organisation with tax-deductible status (different, in some cases, from the charity or non-profit organisations) may be eligible. Still other employers consider matching employee donations to international causes or projects. Head to the later section 'Activating your employer's matching programme' for details on the kind of information to ask for.

Don't assume that matching programmes are just for senior employees. For instance, through the Starbucks Foundation's 'Choose to Give' programme, Starbucks matches all gifts by its baristas totalling between $20 and $1,000 to eligible charitable organisations.

✔ **Know the form that your donation must take.** The donation may not need to be in cash. Some corporations match donations of securities, for example, basing the matching contribution on fair market value. Make sure that you're clear on what kinds of donations your company accepts.

Microsoft has matched charitable donations like for like for years, but also expands on this concept by donating $17 for every hour an employee volunteers. Microsoft employees gave about $45 million in donations to non-profits in 2011 and, adding in the volunteer match money, Microsoft matched nearly $50 million of employee charitable activity in just one year!

✔ **Know the kind of proof you must submit to trigger the matching funds.** Employer matching programmes often require that you present proof of your charitable donation, and sometimes credit card statements aren't sufficient. Be sure to keep the original slip or receipt the charity provides you, for your employer and your tax records. Provide a copy to your employer, but keep the original.

If your employer requires that you give donation receipts to your HR department by the close of the calendar year, you may only have a few days to submit proof of those holiday season donations! Plan ahead or you may miss out on the matching offer.

Multiplying your effect by taking advantage of gift and grant programmes

The best situation is where you can combine the different types of matching programmes to really multiply your giving. Suppose, for example, that you bought a share of stock in a corporation at £50 a share and it's now selling for £100. If you sell your stock now, you pay taxes, and so you decide to donate the stock to a worthy cause.

You can simply donate the stock (after determining that your employer matches donations of stock, of course) and get the matching funds from your employer, or you can do some investigation into whether any of your favourite charities also has a donor who's matching gifts. If you discover that another donor has indeed offered a matching grant of, say, 100 per cent of donations for this month, you can multiply your original £50 investment eight-fold. Here's how:

1. **You donate the stock worth £100 to the charity.**

2. **Your employer chips in another £100 because of its matching grant programme.**

3. **The anonymous donor makes a matching £200 donation, totalling £400.**

Through smart giving and matching funds, you turned a £50 investment into a £400 gift to your favourite charity!

Such a scenario isn't uncommon. A little bit of research can multiply your impact and make a big difference to a cause you care about.

Activating your employer's matching programme

Many employees don't participate in employee-giving programmes because they don't want co-workers to know about their charitable activities, they don't like dealing with the HR department, or they fear a mountain of paperwork. Although these may be real sources of anxiety, they aren't good reasons not to approach your employer for matching funds.

If your employer has a matching programme and you're considering not using it, think about this: is doubling your donation to an organisation you love and care about worth a little extra paperwork or a little inconvenience? If the answer is yes, drop an email to your HR manager!

But we recognise that the process is intimidating to some people, and so to help we've created a guide to get you started:

1. **Checking things out with your HR department.**

   So that you can plan your gift to ensure that your donation qualifies for your employer's matching programme, have a chat with your HR department and ask these questions:

   - Which donations are eligible for matching? What kinds of donations are *not* eligible for matching? If I give stocks or bonds, for example, am I still eligible for the match?

   - Does a lower or upper limit exist for which donations are matched?

   - What's the time limit on claiming a match?

   - What paperwork is needed and when must it be submitted?

   When you figure out the answers to these questions, you're ready to plan your gift.

2. **Planning your gift.**

   Many people find that the easiest way to begin this process is with a simple question: How much good does £X do? As Chapters 4 and 10 show, many causes can help you quantify this equation. Maybe £20 is enough to provide clean drinking water for a certain number of people for a certain period of time, or to provide mosquito bed nets to five families.

After you determine how much benefit your gift alone brings, figure out how much benefit doubling your gift brings. Consider these examples:

- If £25 pays for half of a toilet to be installed (including the pit, the outbuilding, the toilet basin, a handwash station, and training for local people) in Malawi, your employer's £25 match can pay for the other half of the toilet project.

  Even better, why not publicise the project with co-workers or on your company's Facebook group to have more toilets donated?

- Donating £350 can provide a refurbished small-displacement motorcycle for an African entrepreneur to start a motorcycle taxi service. Plus, £350 is needed to maintain the same vehicle over the next three years, thanks to poor roads and the harsh African environment. So you can provide the motorcycle while your employer provides the maintenance plan.

Not all types of philanthropic donations qualify for employer matching funds. For example, imagine that, rather than give a motorcycle to the taxi startup, you prefer to lend the money because, you reason, the moped taxi driver would be able to pay back the money (possibly with interest), which you can then use to help another entrepreneur. This is a great idea, and many organisations focus on exactly these types of small loan arrangements (head to Chapter 10 for details). The problem from a matching-donation perspective is that your employer will almost certainly not match your loan to the entrepreneur the way it matches a grant.

So decide how you can make the greatest impact for your cause. If the method you choose is one for which matching gifts or grants are an option, great. If not, that's fine, too. You can also make an additional impact by telling others about your gift, giving early so that others in your network can give gifts during the same campaign, or giving other items (such as airline miles, for instance) to the charity alongside your financial donation.

Encouraging your company to engage in do-good partnerships

Here's a simple question: why do you think that companies have the type of matching programmes that we discuss in the preceding section? The answer isn't simply marketing or public relations; companies are also interested in building fruitful partnerships.

Showing an interest – financially or otherwise – in the causes that employees care about is good for business. And, sometimes, it can even contribute directly to the bottom line.

You can encourage these relationships, because, contrary to what you may think, these initiatives often start from people innovating within the organisation rather than from the CEO. Therefore, keep an eye out for interesting partnerships for your company – you may be able to combine your work and your philanthropy! As you consider the possibilities, keep these points in mind:

- ✔ **Think about how the people or groups work together in other areas.** What values do your employer and your favourite cause share? What do you enjoy about working for Company X and volunteering at Charity Y? Asking these types of questions can clarify how and why the two organisations may benefit by partnering up.

- ✔ **Think about why working together makes sense for this cause and your employer.** Although everyone likes to do nice things for others, before you propose a particular partnership to your employer you need a strong business case supporting the partnership. Think about why your partnership idea is interesting, strategic, and worthwhile. Would it be more effective than the same time and money spent on marketing? Would it reach people who typically don't interact with your products or who may not understand the value in them?

In the following three sections, we describe three companies and organisations that create such partnerships. You can use their stories for information and examples of how such partnerships help businesses, as well as people in need.

Using skilled workers in developing countries: Samasource

In the new economy, employers have lots of technical work to be done, but it comes in bursts, meaning that employers must make a choice: hire and fire people constantly or find a sustainable-but-temporary source of people who can take these jobs.

That's where Samasource comes in. Founded in 2008 by Leila Janah, Samasource's mission is to alleviate poverty by addressing what Janah considers 'the greatest ethical battle of our time': disparity in access to opportunity to work. It represents a new kind of philanthropy: a hybrid of non-profit mission and business methods that helps clients and beneficiaries.

Samasource (*sama* means equal in Sanskrit) gives *microwork* – basically tiny consulting contracts – to highly skilled people in the developing world. Specifically, Samasource brings dignified, computer-based work to women and youths living in poverty. Employers save time and money, and the most

Sourcing work to skilled workers in developing countries

Before founding and becoming CEO of Samasource, Leila Janah worked at the World Bank as a management consultant. There she realised that traditional forms of foreign aid and economic development weren't going to lift people radically out of poverty.

Samasource provides a much-needed service to businesses and through its wages combats poverty in the process. Here's how it works: through its technology platform, the SamaHub, and its innovative model of small digital tasks that can be completed using low-cost computers and free software, Samasource gives women and youths the skills and resources necessary to deliver in-demand digital services to companies around the world, services such as image tagging, data entry, transcription, and content moderation.

In three years, Samasource has paid more than $1.6 million in real wages to over 2,100 trained workers, benefitting tens of thousands in impoverished areas. On average, Samasource workers double their income within a few months of joining the network and support up to five family members with their earnings. Leveraging its technology platform and enterprise clients, Samasource is tapping the brainpower at the bottom of the pyramid – alleviating poverty and pioneering a new approach to economic development.

marginalised people in developing countries are empowered to contribute to the global economy. Samasource enables them to become breadwinners and, as such, to access new educational, health, and social opportunities for their families and communities. Find out more about Samasource in the nearby sidebar 'Sourcing work to skilled workers in developing countries' or go to www.samasource.org. You can also follow it on Facebook (www.facebook.com/samasource) and Twitter (@samasource).

Building direct partnerships: Grameen Danone Foods

An example of a direct partnership is Grameen Danone Foods, a social business in Bangladesh. Danone has expertise in delivering packaged, safe, inexpensive yoghurt that contains vital nutrients. Grameen has expertise reaching the rural populations of Bangladesh and delivering financial services, but its clients also need nutritious diets (the typical diet in rural Bangladesh lacks several key nutrients).

A new company, Grameen Danone Foods, began operating in Bangladesh to provide affordable, nutritious food to Bangladesh's rural population. The partnership set a goal to build 50 dairy processing facilities in Bangladesh over ten years. These factories are of substantial size (producing over 10,000 kilograms of yoghurt daily) and create jobs for local populations. The pre-packaged cups of yoghurt are now available in rural and urban Bangladesh.

Both businesses benefit from the arrangement. Instead of simply making a donation, Danone was able to study and make improvements to its manufacturing process – lessons it can apply to other low-income markets. Grameen was able to have banking clients who were happier and healthier – and, as a result, more likely to be able to work and repay their loans.

Tapping into consumer concerns: Toyota Manufacturing UK

Toyota Manufacturing UK partners with environmental charities in the UK. By donating the use of Toyota vehicles to projects helping to clean up natural spaces, Toyota gets visibility as an environmentally-friendly product. Its sponsorship of environmental education further enhances the link between Toyota and environmental friendliness.

One of the most interesting aspects of this partnership, however, is that it's driven by consumer concerns and not monolithic corporate strategy. Toyota Manufacturing UK invites its customers to bring charities to Toyota's attention, a tactic that not only increases Toyota's exposure to customers and potential customers, but also acts as an early warning system, alerting Toyota to customer areas of concern. For example, are consumers more worried about CO_2 emissions, road congestion, or a perceived lack of high-quality small cars?

By having the public actively engaged in nominating causes for Toyota to partner with, the company can engage more effectively in its partnerships and address consumer concerns more quickly.

Chapter 15

Making an Impact with Your Transactions

*T*hroughout this book, we talk a lot about teamwork, and for good reason. The power possessed by a motivated, organised group that shares a coherent vision can move mountains – and often it starts with one person and one idea. Why not you?

Every second of your life offers you the chance to do something special, but within that notion of possibility is a simpler truth: every little thing you do has an impact and is a choice that represents how you want to live and the example you want to set. These transactions are the standards you choose for yourself, the ideals you uphold and declare to be most dear, and the bricks and mortar of social change. When a lot of people start to change the way they do a few small things, huge changes occur that can shift the course of human history. Positive change has to start somewhere: it starts with you.

In this chapter, we look at the ways you can use everyday transactions to make the world a better place. We introduce you to purchasing power and awareness campaigns, and we also discuss making a difference when (and how and to where) you travel and when you buy life's essentials of food and clothing.

Recognising the True Cost of Your Purchases

Each time you make a purchase, you're voting with your wallet. Of course your purchasing decisions are personal, but whether you're satisfying a need for food or clothing, or buying a material good or a service, you're likely to have a range of different options for filling that need. You can buy this brand or that brand, opt to shop at this retailer or that one, and pay price X or price Y. In the end all these decisions boil down to one question: where do you want your money to go?

This decision has ramifications beyond getting what you need as a customer. Whether you intend to or not, where you spend your hard-earned pay and what you spend it on sends a message that you support the business practices of the firm you're patronising. For this reason, your purchase becomes about more than just the 'what'.

Every time you buy something, you aren't just choosing the 'what', but also the 'how', the 'who', and the 'where'. As the global economy has evolved and markets have sought out greater efficiencies, consumers have been presented with more and more ways to get their goods for less. Although this may be good for your wallet or purse (at least in the short term) the effects are far reaching, because a cost comes with these efficiencies. Sometimes that cost is intolerably high: the use of child labour or the subjection of workers to unduly harsh working conditions. Other times, the cost is simply the inevitable closing of small retailers who can't compete with the large chains or superstores.

Choosing to incorporate idealism each time you open your wallet can cost you a few extra coins, and so figuring out where you stand and then paying attention is important. In this section, we offer three general suggestions that apply to all your purchasing decisions. For specific ideas regarding particular kinds of transactions, check out the later sections 'Travelling with a Heart: Where to Go and Where to Stay', 'Reducing Your Carbon Footprint', 'Helping the Planet One Meal at a Time: Food Shopping' and 'Keeping the Shirt on your Back: Shopping for Clothes'.

The savvy consumer is most likely to win out. Shopping isn't just about getting the best deal; it's also about knowing that you're buying from a company or producer that holds itself to a higher standard – just like you!

Reading the labels

When you want to make a difference through your transactions, you can start with something as simple as reading labels. Pay attention to things such as the following:

✔ **Where something is made.** How far does the item have to travel to reach your shop? What do you know about the work conditions of the manufacturers in that region of the world?

✔ **What it's made of.** Are the ingredients or the raw material acceptable to you?

✔ **How it's made.** Know what a label means when it says 'organic', for example.

You can use this kind of information to make decisions about whether you're comfortable supporting this business through your purchase.

Advertising and marketing are geared to take advantage of anything that motivates consumers to pay a little extra, whether because of perceived luxury or socially or environmentally-conscious methods of production. Therefore, you need to look inside the product to find its value, which may not be the main 'selling point' from its advertising or packaging. Simply because a product is not marketed for its good environmental effects or its lack of animal testing does not mean it does not have these favourable characteristics.

Thinking about the product in a larger sense

As well as making a point to read food labels, clothing labels, and so on, as we describe in the preceding section, you can also interpret this recommendation to mean finding out about the product in a larger sense.

Ask yourself what larger impact, if any, this product has on the areas you care about:

✔ Is it inherently dangerous?

✔ Is it harmful?

✔ Does it exploit vulnerable groups?

A particular brand of cigarette used to have a mascot that research showed appealed to adolescents and teens, a group that tends to engage in riskier behaviours. If you understand that people who start smoking when they're young are more likely to become addicted, life-long smokers, you begin to see how this seemingly 'innocent' mascot was in fact a subtle way of advertising to children – an activity that ran afoul of US law. Perceptive consumers reacted to the brand individually, but it wasn't until initiatives to combat the practice itself arose that the mascot was removed from view. Think about the impacts of all aspects of a product, from its manufacturing to its distribution to its marketing to its impact on society.

Checking out the company

You can extend your investigation beyond a product to the company itself:

✔ Does it engage in ethical practices?

✔ Does it treat its workers fairly?

✔ Does it engage in environmentally friendly (or even environment-neutral) manufacturing processes?

A good place to start when checking out a particular company is your country's Better Business Bureau (www.bbb.org in the US and Canada). The UK analogues are the Office of Trading Standards or Trading Standards Institute (learn more at www.tradingstandards.gov.uk) and the Office of Fair Trading (www.oft.gov.uk). This resource is just a jumping off point, but accreditation requires that a company has met a set of guidelines for honest and ethical business practices.

Certainly, this sort of checking helps to guard against dealing with fraudulent merchants, but in this section we show you how to look further into a company's labour and environmental practices to help you decide where you want your money to go.

According to Scott Cooney, author of *Build a Green Small Business: Profitable Ways to Become an Ecopreneur,* a business is described as 'green' or 'sustainable' if it matches the following four criteria:

✔ Incorporates principles of sustainability into each of its business decisions.

✔ Supplies environmentally friendly products or services that replace demand for non-green products and/or services.

✔ Is greener than the traditional competition.

✔ Has made an enduring commitment to environmental principles in its business operations.

To discover whether a company fits these criteria, take these actions:

✔ **Look for certification.** In the UK, all Green Deal organisations must be authorised and are recognised by the quality mark. Also check for the Forest Stewardship Council (ic.fsc.org/index.htm) logo on wood and paper products. In the US, look for the Energy Star label (www.energystar.gov) on appliances and electronics, the organic seal (www.ams.usda.gov/nop/indexNet.htm) on food and cosmetics, and the Green Seal (www.greenseal.org) (in Canada, the EcoLogo: www.ecologo.org) on household cleaning products. The advocacy group Labelling Matters (www.labellingmatters.org) is active in the UK, EU, and worldwide trying to improve labelling of food and food-related products.

✔ **Do your research before you head out shopping.** Some useful sites include Consumer Reports (www.greenerchoices.org), Greenercars (www.greenercars.org, which covers models available worldwide), and the Electronic Product Environmental Assessment Tool (www.epeat.net). These sites help you sort through manufacturers' claims on larger 'green' items. The Environmental Working Group (www.ewg.org) and Responsible Purchasing Network (www.responsiblepurchasing.org) can supply helpful information on smaller items such as cosmetics (see also www.ewg.org/skindeep), cleaners, and food. In recent years, the UK has been critical of 'green labeling' on non-green products, and the Department for Environment, Food, and Rural Affairs routinely updates the site here with information about how products must be labelled: http://www.gov.uk/environmental-claims-and-labels-guidance-for-businesses).

Buying into Awareness Campaigns

The goal of all awareness campaigns is to inform the public of an issue that the campaign sponsor deems important. These campaigns can be sponsored by industries (to stop music or video piracy, for example), advocacy groups (address poverty or education programmes), health and governmental organisations (to stop smoking), and so on.

They're meant to raise awareness, involvement, and money for the causes being highlighted. In this section, we look at a few of these campaigns, explain how you can begin your own, and discuss what to look for before you support any particular campaign.

Supporting campaigns you believe in

As anti-slavery campaigner William Wilberforce famously said: 'You may choose to look the other way, but you can never say again that you did not know.' When an awareness campaign touches your heart, you may wonder what you can do to support that campaign.

Here are some suggestions:

- ✔ **Share the information:** The idea is that as a campaign increases awareness of a situation, more people become involved and exert an influence that can eventually bring about much-needed change. For example, before breast- or colon-cancer awareness campaigns, many people didn't talk about these diseases because of their personal nature. This situation delayed discovery of the tumours, made positive outcomes less likely, and left sufferers feeling isolated and alone. Today, especially with breast cancer but increasingly also colon cancer, that situation is no longer the case. The campaign did what it was intended to do: to use public awareness to shine a spotlight on a situation that, when left in the dark, would continue to kill millions needlessly.

  Therefore, one of the most meaningful steps you can take in support of a cause is to help shine the spotlight. Start with the simple message to your friends, family, and others in your network that alerts them to the cause. Pass along articles, stories, social media posts, and other information.

- ✔ **Give:** Many awareness campaigns are sponsored by advocacy groups that need funds to support their missions. By donating money, expertise, supplies, or other resources, you can help them accomplish their goals and feel connected to a cause that matters to you.

Viewing an example of a successful anti-slavery campaign: The Somaly Mam Foundation

Slavery, human trafficking, and non-consensual labour are related issues that involve millions of people around the world as victims, perpetrators, and even unwitting consumers who buy goods or consume services provided by people who have been trafficked. The issue, far from the minds of most on a day-to-day basis, is huge in its scale, both economically and from a human perspective.

Like many successful awareness campaigns, the founding of the Somaly Mam Foundation was made possible by circumstance, when trafficking survivor and activist Somaly Mam crossed paths with Jared Greenberg and Nicholas Lumpp, two Americans determined to build global awareness and support the fight against child slavery.

When the three met, the sex slave trade had developed into the second-most-profitable criminal industry, trailing only narcotics, and international governments had yet to combat the problem effectively. To make matters worse, often corrupt government and law enforcement officials protect this vile industry.

Somaly Mam, a victim of the sex trade herself who escaped, made it her mission to rescue, rehabilitate, and reintegrate victims. The result was

AFESIP (*Agir pour les Femmes en Situation Précaire,* which translates to 'Acting for Women in Distressing Situations'), an organisation that has transformed the lives of thousands of victims.

After speaking with Somaly Mam, touring the facilities, and meeting some of the rescued young women, Jared and Nicholas wanted to share their life-changing experience with the many people around the world who didn't know that this terrible industry even existed. Raising awareness and funding organisations such as AFESIP was clearly paramount to combating the illegal trade. Somaly laid out her vision for a US-based organisation that would take her life's passion to the next level: the result was the Somaly Mam Foundation (SMF).

To get involved with the SMF or AFESIP:

- ✔ **Make a donation:** Like other charities supporting disenfranchised populations, the SMF and AFESIP try to raise money in a variety of ways. They state that £7 ($10) provides a week's worth of food to a survivor in one of the shelters in Cambodia and they also offer for sale a £10 ($15) survivor-made Akun bracelet from www.empowermentstore.org (Akun means 'thank you' in Khmer). It is important, as a responsible donor, to understand how organisations are raising funds and support and to ask questions when you have them.

- ✔ **Volunteer:** The SMF's Project Futures global network of passionate volunteer activists uses what they know and who they know to raise awareness and funds in their communities. Visit projectfutures.somaly.org to see examples of the innovative grassroots events and campaigns, and download tools to get started.

In her own words: Somaly Mam

Somaly Mam, Founder of the Somaly Mam Foundation, writes:

'I'm a survivor of sex slavery, the second largest criminal industry in the world. I was sold to a brothel when I was 12 years old, and was a victim of rape and abuse for nearly a decade. But I escaped, and couldn't live knowing others were left behind.

Since 1996, I've assisted more than 7,000 victims of human trafficking and sex slavery to escape the brothels and private homes where they're held captive; in our shelters, they can recover, rebuild their lives, and ultimately become a part of the solution. We measure success one life at a time: because if we save one girl, she can save ten, and those ten can each save ten more. We give survivors a voice in their lives, and empower them to create and sustain lives of dignity.

Remember that life is love: with your passion and compassion, you can help others to heal from these wrongs and put an end to sex slavery once and for all.'

You can find out more about Somaly Mam and her organisation at www.somaly.org and by reading her memoir, *Road of Lost Innocence.*

Being a savvy consumer-philanthropist

As you think about the larger implications of your purchasing transactions and take steps to align your values with your purchase decisions, you start to see all kinds of opportunities for using that power to send a message to merchants and to engage in philanthropic campaigns through making special purchases – which is a very rewarding experience.

As you make decisions about which campaigns you support and the form that your support takes, consider the current needs and how they can be best addressed, as well as how much of the proceeds generated for the campaign go direct to its mission.

Consider the breast-cancer awareness campaigns. They've been highly successful and supported by numerous healthcare organisations, advocacy groups, and businesses, increasing preventative screening, early detection, financial support for research, and more.

During October (Breast Cancer Awareness Month) in the US, National Football League (NFL) players wear and promote pink gear and equipment that's later sold as a fundraiser for breast-cancer research and awareness. The NFL auctions off the sweaty, pink gear worn during games and sells a variety of new attire online.

Sounds great, right? Well, the catch is that only 5 per cent of the sales of these items goes to the American Cancer Society.

As a result of concerns, the organisation Breast Cancer Action launched the 'Think Before You Pink' initiative, which encourages people to pay close attention to where proceeds from pink products go. Executive director Karuna Jaggar says:

> *If we could shop our way out of this epidemic, we would have done it. We don't need more awareness; we need solutions… We're looking for progress that makes a difference in addressing and ending this breast-cancer epidemic.*

Make sure that the business you support isn't one that's just using charitable campaigns for the primary purpose of bolstering its own sales and not seriously helping the advertised causes. Some degree of suspicion about the level of support these campaigns actually offer the beneficiary charities is not only okay, but healthy.

Creating your own awareness campaign

No matter what your cause, most likely many more people are waiting for someone to rally behind. With a little hard work and a sense of conviction, that person can be you!

If you want to start your own awareness campaign, here are a few suggestions to help you gather others who share your desire and raise awareness of an important issue:

- ✔ **Research your cause:** Think about how your issue affects people locally and worldwide. A lot of resources are available related to diseases and social issues that you can take advantage of – such as poverty, education, housing, or clean water access.

- ✔ **Investigate what else is happening relevant to your cause:** If other organisations or efforts are already addressing the issue you've identified, see whether you can integrate your efforts with theirs.

- ✔ **Figure out how you want to present your data:**

    - See whether you can get quotes from experts who specialise in research relating to your cause: call universities, NGOs, and government agencies. Also, talk to people affected by your cause, because real stories are powerful!

    - Use pictures because they often make a stronger impression than words. Get striking images that help raise awareness and motivate people to get on board.

    - Expert speakers can have an incredible impact and are the best way to educate your audience on the issues surrounding your cause. After all, an awareness campaign is about achieving change through education and public awareness.

- ✔ **Build your team:** The ideal team helps you gain momentum and expand the reach of your campaign. Team members need to share a passion for your cause, be able to commit to the process, and have appropriate and friendly people-skills to bring others on board.

- ✔ **Be open to different strategies:** For an effective campaign, you may need to vary your strategy to create a message that resonates with the many diverse groups you hope to reach. For example, the message of helping the environment may attract some people, while the social message of helping people who live in or near that environment may attract others. By combining these messages in honest, direct ways, you can find more support for the cause.

- ✔ **Pick the moment to kick off your campaign:** Find out whether a month is devoted to your cause. Are people more likely to respond to your cause at a particular time of the year? Summer is probably not the best time to raise awareness for providing warm coats to the homeless, for example, but it's a great time to discuss childhood hunger (many school-age children on reduced and free lunch programmes at school go without regular meals during the summer breaks).

Travelling with a Heart: Where to Go and Where to Stay

Every adventure has an impact on the environment, but you can play your part by thinking carefully about where you visit and where you stay after you arrive.

Exploring culture: Visiting eco-friendly cities

Different places worldwide are taking action to incorporate sustainable practices. By spending your tourism (or business-travel) pounds in places that make eco-friendly decisions, you send a message to those cities – and others – that environmentally responsible locations are attractive to travellers. Here are some cities that offer wonderful cultural experiences and environment-friendly planning:

✔ **Copenhagen:** Secured by its leading position within green, regional growth, Copenhagen Capacity, Copenhagen's inward investment company, has been assigned the role of lead partner in a new Organisation for Economic Co-operation and Development (OECD) project. Copenhagen's Cleantech Cluster (www.cphcleantech.com) is to be used as a case study on green growth and creating green jobs.

With ten participating countries, Copenhagen was the first to host the international workshop in late 2012. The OECD project 'Measuring the Potential of Green Growth' has the goal of looking at the indicators needed to measure progress on how to adjust low-carbon activities and create sustainable green activities in industries, firms, and regional and local ecosystems. An international network of regions, cities, and local areas where robust development strategies for transition to a greener economy are taking place is to be formed.

✔ **London:** Under the eco-microscope of the world, London was under a lot of pressure to provide sustainability goals as it prepared to host the 2012 Summer Olympics. By most standards, they succeeded remarkably, improving the city's systems for residents and tourists alike – changes that have continued beyond the games and include a massive new cycling infrastructure, a new rubbish system that focuses on recycling and more (see the nearby sidebar 'A city transformed: London' for details on these changes). London made a clear effort to draw tourists and residents to an improved quality of life and it's unambiguously a better place to visit and live than before the Games. So, if you're booking a trip, consider visiting London for a pedal around Big Ben (check out the later sidebar 'A city transformed: London' for more.)

✔ **Vancouver:** In 2012 Vancouver, Canada, announced its ambitious action plan at `http://vancouver.ca/files/cov/Greenest-city-action-plan.pdf` to become the greenest city in the world by 2020. Sporting green streets is part of the plan. Technically, a *green street* is a street where walking or biking is prioritised over cars. As far back as 1992, Vancouver got the ball rolling when a group of landscape architects and others who supported the walking environment formed an Urban Landscape Taskforce. They looked at designing a system of streets called 'greenways'. These streets contain pavements, pedestrian ramps at each corner of the sidewalk, pedestrian-activated intersection controls where needed, infiltration bulges, public plantings, benches, water fountains, and even some public art. Much like London did for cyclists, Vancouver prides itself on making the city more walking-friendly.

EXAMPLE

A city transformed: London

Following the London Summer Olympics in 2012, London is continuing to carry the Green Torch and is being recognised as the most prominent metropolitan example in the world of a city willing to address climate change. Here are just some of the key changes:

✔ **A massive new cycling infrastructure that transformed the transportation culture in London.** This new approach to transportation, designed to be simple and safe, and to have a low impact on the environment, reduced carbon emissions and energy consumption.

✔ **A new rubbish system.** This system is on track to recycle, reuse, or compost 70 per cent of the city's waste.

✔ **A cooling, heating, energy, and blackwater recycling system that saves water and energy.** This major effort addressed the biggest concern facing London: its lack of modern insulation (incentives were offered for homeowners to replace windows with double-glazing and to refit homes to use less heating). To conserve local water supplies, London's Olympic Park and Village used recycled sewage water for indoor toilet flushing and landscape irrigation.

This innovative *blackwater* recycling programme, along with other water-saving measures such as using efficient fixtures, helped the summer games reduce its use of drinking-quality water by 58 per cent – exceeding its initial target of 40 per cent.

Even though the Olympic Games are behind him, London's Mayor has a long list of sustainability proposals. The most popular and by far the most dramatic is his cycling initiatives, which transformed London from a traffic-congested quagmire to a cycling mecca. Consider that the number of active cyclists has doubled since 2000, and more than 540,000 bicycle trips are taken per day in and around London. All these cycling locals and tourists mean that sustainably-minded folks now find it easier than ever to hop on a bike and ride to all the green spaces, historic monuments, and pubs they can pedal to. As more and more Londoners identify themselves as cyclists, the city continues to invest even more in maintaining and improving the cycling infrastructure.

Despite a few bumps (potholes!) along the way, London was remarkably successful in achieving its sustainability targets – a goal that the city has committed to for the future as well.

Taking the LEED: Eco-friendly lodgings

Green credentials have become a must for organisations. Multinational companies strive to show that their business is green and sustainable, including their buildings – although environmental assessment in this area is nothing new. The UK's BREEAM (the Building Research Establishment Environmental Assessment Method), appeared in 1990 and has since expanded by leaps and bounds, with a 19-page report with 27 credits growing to a detailed 350-page technical guide with 105 credits.

For nearly 20 years, BREEAM dominated environmental assessment of UK buildings. The US has now caught on with its Leadership in Energy and Environmental Design (LEED) programme. LEED is now spreading to the UK, and many US hotels, whether ritzy or not-so-ritzy, have climbed aboard the green bandwagon. To be considered 'green', hotels have to earn specific accreditations. The LEED certification is highly regarded, and hotel owners and managers are striving to achieve this goal.

Portola Hotel & Spa: Silver Certification

The Portola Hotel & Spa in Monterey, California, received its Silver Certification from LEED back in 2011. As a part of its journey to attain this certification, the Hotel & Spa completed a variety of enhancements that included remodelling its guestrooms in the following ways:

✔ Using bath amenities, which are completely biodegradable and low-flow water fixtures.

✔ Using Green Label Plus carpet in all guestrooms, which is certified by the Carpet & Rug Institute for low volatile organic compounds (VOCs), which are less likely to cause allergies or other health issues.

✔ Using low or no VOC paints.

✔ Using environmentally friendly, custom-designed mattresses from a local mattress company.

✔ Including energy-efficient televisions and refrigerators.

✔ Using Forest Stewardship Council (FSC)-certified wood products, internationally recognised standards that deliver environmental services to local and global communities, including clean air and water, and contribute to mitigating the effects of climate change.

Janine Chicourrat, general manager of the hotel, says 'The green experience at Portola Hotel & Spa is reflective of our commitment to the environment and preserving our coast's extraordinary natural beauty. Guests appreciate the everyday sustainable practices, which is very rewarding, and locals appreciate our commitment to the community. Achieving Silver LEED Certification is an added testament to our passion and efforts and we are proud to be an environmental leader in Central California and across the state and country.'

The US Green Building Council is the nation's foremost coalition of leaders from across the building industry working to promote buildings that are environmentally responsible, profitable, and healthy places to live and work. The LEED Green Building Rating System is a voluntary, consensus-based national standard for developing high-performance, sustainable buildings. Members of the US Green Building Council representing all segments of the building industry developed LEED and continue to contribute to its evolution.

If you're travelling, check and see whether the hotel you're staying in has LEED Certification or other Green Accreditations. In the UK, interest in LEED is growing. The Green Building Certification Institute's website records 66 LEED Accredited Professionals in the UK (the fifth highest national total behind the US, Canada, UAE, and China).

The brands most represented on the certified hotels list include Marriott, Starwood, and Hilton, but many are added to the list annually. You can visit www.GreenHotels.com to search for green hotels.

Checking out other tips for the caring traveller

Eco-friendly travel starts right away. Here are some things you can do before you leave home:

- Adjust your thermostat so your heating and cooling aren't triggering on and off while you're away.
- Unplug your electronics: even in standby mode they consume power, with plasma TVs, microwaves, and chargers being the worst culprits.
- Fill up some re-usable containers with the products you need instead of buying additional sundries.

While you're on your trip:

- Many hotels ask you to let them know whether or not you want your sheets and towels washed daily. If you're staying more than a night, you can save water by letting the hotel staff know you don't need these items washed daily.
- Turn off the lights and air conditioning when you leave the hotel room.
- Depending on where you travel, stretch your legs and choose to walk instead of renting a car. See if your hotel has a shuttle or try the local public transportation. If you have to rent, ask for a hybrid, or better yet, see whether a Zipcar is available (head to the later section 'Zipcar: Car-sharing programmes' for more).

Reducing Your Carbon Footprint

If travel beckons you, be considerate of the environment and the *carbon footprints* you leave (this includes CO_2 from your air travel, but also, for instance, your rental car). Fortunately, you can shrink the footprints from Big Foot-sized to Tinker Bell-sized by being thoughtful about your habits. Whether you're going by plane, train, or car, travelling is exciting and adventurous and you can make it even more so by adding a green approach to it. This section explains how.

If you're travelling by car and own a gas-guzzler, consider renting a hybrid model for long trips. Doing so saves fuel and produces far less carbon monoxide emissions.

Introducing the idea of smart transport

Smart transportation can mean a lot of different things, but the goal is all about providing better, broader, more sustainable access to goods, services, and opportunities. The traditional transportation model featured the romantic notion of a car in every family's garage and the freedom that comes from the open road. The 21st century reality is, however, less romantic. In 2010, the number of cars in the world exceeded 1 billion – a number that foreshadows an eerie future with billions of fossil-fuel-burning cars, clogged highways, and barely breathable air.

Still, the car and transportation industries are evolving, thanks to government initiatives and consumers concerned enough about the cost of fossil fuels and their negative impact to demand more fuel-efficient options. The key question is then: how do you improve ways to get to where you want to go?

Smart transportation isn't just about electric cars or car alternatives. Crucially, it's also about providing transportation to communities that lack paved roads with access to healthcare, education, and better economic opportunity. That's smart indeed!

Picking a mode of transport that reduces your carbon footprint

Air travel often accounts for the biggest slice of the pie in a person's carbon footprint. If you're a road warrior or love to travel on holiday, this section offers a variety of suggestions for tempering your impact on Mother Nature.

Counting the cost in CO$_2$

Aviation contributed 649 million tonnes of CO$_2$ to the atmosphere in 2010. The effects of the pollution caused by air travel are unique because these are harmful gases emitted directly into higher layers of the atmosphere and may have more negative effects than ground-level pollution of the same quantity or composition.

One simple solution is to keep travel to a necessary minimum. When face-to-face meetings aren't vital, teleconference!

Teleconferencing is often a viable alternative to business travel. Unlike the early days of video chats, today's conferencing tools are staggeringly advanced, allowing screen sharing, multiplexing, and an array of collaborative tools that rival what you can spread out on the surface of the best boardroom table. Skype and other online tools are awesome, whether you're keeping in touch with a field team or hammering through deal points. So take advantage of technology that can help you save the planet, one business meeting at a time. Get your green geek on!

If you have to fly, try to book a direct flight to save on fuel consumption.

Zipcar: Car-sharing programmes

Urban centres and suburban communities can cut down on their carbon footprints in many ways. Public transportation is a great option, but its availability and practicality varies widely from city to city. For urban dwellers, one solution is car-sharing programmes.

Sharing is caring, plain and simple. You may already be familiar with ride-sharing programmes – the ones that let you find ways to make use of the carpool lane on your daily commute by riding with someone and taking an extra car off the road (and we're not talking about cutting 10 minutes off your ride time with the assistance of a sharply dressed mannequin riding shotgun). With a car-sharing programme, however, you're not just sharing a ride; you're sharing the actual car.

Zipcar is a membership-based car-sharing company providing reservations to its members, billable by the hour or day. You pay a one-time application fee, an annual fee, and a reservation charge. Petrol, parking, insurance, and maintenance are included in the price.

Here's how it works. Often *having* a car in a city would be really handy, but *owning* a car is usually far from convenient, cheap, or practical. Zipcar – and other car-sharing plans – offers the goldilocks solution (one that's neither too hot nor too cold, but *just right*): place lots of self-service Zipcars five to ten minutes from car-sharing members across cities, college campuses, and residential and commercial developments. The members can reserve Zipcars online or by phone at any time, even up to a year in advance. Members have automated access to Zipcars using an access card that works with the car's technology to unlock the door, where they find the ignition keys inside. Zipcar has a neat mobile app that members use to honk the horn in order to locate their assigned Zipcar and unlock the doors.

Zipcars live in 50+ cities across North America and the UK, though such programmes were pioneered among the congested streets of European cities. In the UK, visit www.zipcar.co.uk to enrol or find out more about the five towns and cities involved.

To make transportation greener, everyone has to remember that getting from one place to another needs to be more about practicality than ego. A giant SUV or luxury barge to ferry a sole passenger to and fro is an excess from another time. Take pride in the economy of your motor's carbon footprint rather than its road presence; the planet thanks you for your sensible priorities.

Pedalling power

People spend a lot of time talking about smart transportation of the four-wheeled variety, but what about all the green greatness of that old two-wheeled standby, the bicycle? Pedal power has the potential to change the world and not just because bike riding is green. Bicycles are also cheap, light, and off-road capable, and they require a minimum of maintenance that can be easily taught to willing mechanics worldwide.

So brush off your bike and get pedalling: to work, the shops, or even out for a weekend adventure. If, for whatever reason, bike riding isn't possible or practical, consider donating to organisations that use pedal power for good. The following sections highlight two such organisations: Peace Pedalers and World Bicycle Relief.

Here are some inspiring facts about bikes and bike-riding:

- ✔ Riding a bicycle regularly and being healthy increases your lung capacity by up to 3 times compared to a sedentary cigarette smoker.
- ✔ Over the same span of time, you can ride a bicycle four times the distance you can cover on foot.
- ✔ The British Heart Foundation has discovered that cycling at least 20 miles a week reduces your risk of heart disease by 50 per cent.

Inviting the world to ride: Peace Pedalers

Founded in 2002, Peace Pedalers (www.peacepedalers.com) is a 'Worldwide Invitation to Ride'. The organisation took two-seat tandem bikes on an around-the-world adventure through 81 countries with a unique approach: riding on the *front* seat and leaving the rear seats open to *invite people*.

Lead riders were prepared with extra riding clothes, helmets, and camping equipment to share with local strangers (who soon became friends after accepting the invitation and making a few pedal strokes on the tandem!) The lead riders often shared a meal at the end of the road and always supplied their willing guests with money for the return trip. Over 1,000 people accepted the invitation to ride, proving that language, cultural, and religious boundaries can be crossed by anyone, anywhere.

This kind of smart transportation is all about cultivating the bonds formed by travel. Technology has evolved in lots of ways so that people can minimise face-time, even though, undeniably, the world has never been so connected. Efforts such as Peace Pedalers serve as reminders that transportation isn't just about commuting or the practicalities of getting where you need to go. It also has the power to foster personal connections, broaden your horizons, and enrich your life and the lives of others. The founders put it very well: 'It represents an intention for balance and courage to simultaneously live our personal passions, make contributions to our global community, and love unconditionally' – core principles that everyone can get behind!

Seeing the multiplier effect in action: World Bicycle Relief

World Bicycle Relief (www.worldbicyclerelief.org) was founded by SRAM Corporation in 2005 in response to the Indian Ocean Tsunami. World Bicycle Relief partnered with aid organisations on the ground in Sri Lanka, distributing over 24,000 bicycles to assist in the rebuilding efforts and provide access to education and healthcare while reconnecting workers to their livelihoods.

One fundamental idea behind World Bicycle Relief is the multiplier effect a bicycle has on human utility. A bicycle can be the difference between a local who can get to a clean water source and one who can't. Bicycles can be the tool that helps a young girl realise the dream of access to education. And in a continent racked by the AIDS epidemic, they can provide a crucial link in the chain of access to medical care.

After the programme's success in Sri Lanka, aid organisations working in sub-Saharan Africa approached World Bicycle Relief to assist with volunteer healthcare programmes in Zambia, where 40 per cent of the population was suffering the effects of HIV/AIDS. In partnership with local aid organisations, World Bicycle Relief provided 23,000 specially designed, locally assembled, rugged bicycles to healthcare workers treating HIV/AIDS patients. In a further effort to foster local labour and industry, the organisation trained local field mechanics to build, maintain, and repair bicycles. The programme in Zambia led to further work in microfinance, education, social enterprise, and field mechanics training schemes throughout Africa.

Since getting started on the continent, World Bicycle Relief has changed lives across Africa, putting roughly 100,000 bicycles in the field and training more than 750 field mechanics. The organisation has supplied bicycles in Kenya, Mozambique, South Africa, South Sudan, Tanzania, Uganda, Zambia, and Zimbabwe.

You can discover more at world bicyclerelief.org/pages/programs

Lowering your carbon footprint by how you shop

You can adjust your lifestyle in myriad ways to minimise your impact on the environment.

Shopping locally

One of the best, easiest, and most familiar ways to get green is to go local. This simple philosophy revolves around directing your pounds to local communities. In an age of globalisation, the payoffs can be huge. Local patronage offers these benefits:

- ✔ Fosters regional resilience by increasing local investment options while simultaneously providing a source for revenue and growth within the community.
- ✔ Decreases the use of fossil fuels.

You may even find yourself investing in *carbon credits* (an investment that lets you invest directly in reducing your carbon footprint) if you want to offset things such as frequent air travel. Carbon credits, depending upon their type, may be available from your usual investment advisor.

Choosing restaurants that support local farmers

Find out which local restaurants support local farmers. The less distance your food travels to get to your plate, the less carbon your dinner puts into the atmosphere. You also benefit from fresher ingredients that are unlikely to make use of flash freezing and preservatives to maintain their flavour. Family-owned farms are also more likely to farm sustainably – avoiding heavy pesticides, using crop rotation, contributing to the biodiversity of the ecosystem, and bypassing engineered crop strains in favour of organic seeds and harvesting methods.

Helping the Planet One Meal at a Time: Food Shopping

A lot goes into the food you eat; perhaps more than you realise. Most days you probably don't think beyond 'do I really fancy that biscuit/doughnut/croissant… no I mustn't… oh, go on then'. But if you want your diet to have an impact beyond your stomach, you also need to consider the wider impact of your food:

- ✔ Did it come from small, independent farmers or from a large factory farming conglomerate?

- ✔ Is it organic (and what exactly does *organic* mean)?

- ✔ Do the farmers engage in harvesting practices that make the most of the soil or that deplete it?

- ✔ Is this food healthy – not just for you but for the planet as well?

Taking a closer look at your food items and how they're grown

The way the developed world eats changed during the 20th century with the arrival of convenience foods, pre-processed foods, and chemically enhanced foods. When you look at your shopping cart, you may want to ask yourself this simple question: is this really *the best food for me*?

Check out the nearby sidebar 'Thinking about what you're eating' for more details.

Thinking about what you're eating

Nutritional science is great for understanding what your body needs every day and how different nutrients affect you. Foods with naturally occurring vitamins and minerals are always healthier than enriched products containing supplements that are never present in nature. Likewise, many people now feel that voting with their wallets for things such as free-range eggs (from non-battery-farmed hens) or grass-fed beef is important. Sometimes these choices are motivated by humane concerns for the animals, other times by health fears relating to hormones that may be present. The choice is a personal one, but worth thinking about.

In addition to thinking about the food itself, also consider the farming practices of the farm where it's grown. Crop rotation is a means of maintaining healthy, rich soil. Modern farming often relies more heavily on pesticides, enriched fertilisers, and chemical engineering to obtain a large produce yield on a consistent basis.

This approach has pluses and minuses: with a population of billions of people, modernised agriculture allows us the ability to produce enormous amounts of food; however, the price of this production is often inferior nutritional values for the foods produced. Small farms can never deliver the quantity of food that factory farms are responsible for, but a strong case exists for supporting smaller, sustainable farms that use methods such as crop rotation instead of chemical engineering where possible.

Supporting your local farmers by shopping at a weekly farmers market is a good place to start. You can also look for supermarkets that carry produce and meats from smaller farms.

Choosing where to shop

Supermarkets and food shops are your links to food producers. You may not have a lot of choice in your neighbourhood or town, but if you live in a location with several supermarkets within a short distance, consider the following questions when deciding which shop deserves your money:

- ✓ **Does it engage in sustainable and ethical business practices?** For information on LEED certification, refer to the earlier section 'Taking the LEED: Eco-friendly lodgings'.

- ✓ **Where does it source its supplies?** If it promotes sustainable practices but buys supplies from companies or farmers that don't, you can inadvertently support businesses whose practices don't align with your values.

- ✓ **What about its energy use?** Does it use only energy-efficient lighting and EnergyStar-certified appliances?

Plenty of companies – some established and some just starting up – are tackling the problems of how to get sustainable, healthy foods on to the tables of families living in communities near and far. Seek out companies in your area interested in healthy food – this creates two benefits: the food is better for you and has a lower carbon footprint associated with it, as it was not moved from a farm halfway around the world.

Deciding what to buy

In addition to comparing shops' business practices (see the preceding section) you can also impact the products it sells by making deliberate decisions about the brands and items you buy. Ask yourself these questions:

- ✔ Are the products made, grown, or otherwise produced in a way that treats workers ethically?

  In the late 1960s and early 1970s, table grape growers in California refused to pay their workers the federal minimum wage. When consumers across America boycotted the grapes, eventually a deal was struck between the growers and the United Farm Workers of America (which fought against inhumane working conditions and treatment of farmworkers in the US). This bit of history shows the power of your spending decisions to affect business practices.

- ✔ Are foodstuffs grown, raised, or produced in a manner that protects the environment or that treats the animals in an ethical and humane way?

  Starting in the 1980s, the natural foods industry took its first steps towards the supermarket format. One of the products of that evolution is Whole Foods Market, a certified organic grocery. For info, head to the nearby sidebar 'Helping yourself to Whole Foods.'

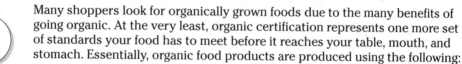

Many shoppers look for organically grown foods due to the many benefits of going organic. At the very least, organic certification represents one more set of standards your food has to meet before it reaches your table, mouth, and stomach. Essentially, organic food products are produced using the following:

- ✔ Agricultural management practices that promote healthy ecosystems and prohibit the use of genetically engineered seeds or crops, sewage sludge, long-lasting pesticides, herbicides, or fungicides.

- ✔ Livestock management practices that promote healthy, humanely treated animals by providing organically-grown feed, fresh air, and outdoor access while using no antibiotics or added growth hormones.

- ✔ Food processing practices that protect the integrity of the organic product and disallow irradiation, genetically modified ingredients (GMOs), or synthetic preservatives.

USDA organic certification demands that food is grown and handled without persistent toxic chemical inputs and according to strict procedures. They have to contain 95 per cent organic ingredients. (Labels that state that a product was 'made with organic ingredients' requires that only 70 per cent of the ingredients be organic).

Helping yourself to Whole Foods

Whole Foods began as a partnership between four local business people in Austin, Texas. Now it has markets throughout the US and across the Atlantic in the UK. Whole Foods was, in fact, the first nationally certified organic grocer in the United States. It describes organic agriculture as a production method that emphasises the use of renewable resources and the conservation of soil and water to enhance environmental quality.

In addition, Whole Foods was the first retailer to offset 100 per cent of its energy consumption with wind energy credits, an action that effectively reduced the company's carbon emissions by hundreds of millions of pounds. Although Whole Foods hasn't had a perfect record as it expanded, part of its mission continues to be to use practices that serve the planet while remaining profitable.

An organic label doesn't prohibit synthetic inputs, mean that the food is locally produced, or indicate that it comes from an independent rather than a factory farm. Many of the large brands such as Heinz, Dole, ConArga, and ADM have organic subsidiaries, and organic products produced on this kind of scale doesn't mean as much for biodiversity, but it's still a step in the right direction! After all, as efforts are made to shift the means of food production towards sustainability, corporate accountability is something to look for.

Recovering food deserts

A *food desert* is an area in which residents have little or no access to food shops offering food items such as fresh produce, unprocessed meats, or healthy grains, which are vital components to healthy diets. People who live in food deserts – mainly the poor in inner cities and depressed rural areas – suffer from malnutrition because they tend to rely on unhealthy food options (salt- and sugar-laden snacks and drinks, processed meats, and so on) available from convenience stores and fast food outlets. These foodstuffs are often seen as cheap and easy alternatives when going far afield for healthy ingredients, or having the time (or knowledge) to prepare them, isn't an option.

These deserts exist in some of the world's wealthiest countries, including the US and the UK. If feeding the hungry is a cause that inspires you, acting to eliminate or remediate the existence of food deserts is a cause well worth your time and effort.

Putting good food at the fingertips of members of the community is essential to combating growing health epidemics stemming from obesity and poor nutrition. Here are some ways to play your part:

- **Round people up to help:** You may need to have a fundraiser and equipment-gathering event to get launched, but this is a great way to educate your community about the need while giving you the chance to round up volunteers. Holding such an event gives you the chance to explain your ideas and entice people to participate. Make it entertaining and informative.

- **Identify beneficiaries:** The organisations you choose to support ought to serve people within the food desert. Remain open to suggestions from volunteers and hold a number of events slated to serve new, as well as repeat, organisations.

- **Find a kitchen:** Seek an industrial kitchen in your community that will share its space with you. Places that don't need their kitchens on certain days or during certain hours are ideal.

- **Learn from local farmers:** If you're not an expert on farming, reach out to those who are and see what help and information they can offer you. You may be able to receive donations from farmers as well, or be able to go to farms and collect the fallen crops.

- **Enlist some help:** Sometimes you just have to ask for help! Examples of volunteer tasks include sorting and cleaning, cutting, cooking, canning, and storing and delivering the food.

Fixing the grocery gap: Stockbox Grocers

One Seattle-based startup company is looking to 'fix the grocery gap in a neighbourhood near you'. Stockbox Grocers (www.stockboxgrocers.com) wants to put a miniature grocery inside reclaimed shipping containers placed in car parks of existing businesses across the US. The idea is to offer the essential grocery items and fresh produce to communities that don't have easy access to that kind of food.

Stockbox is all about practical access. The company hopes to combine the appeal of brick-and-mortar dependability with the low overhead of a food truck model. It focuses on perishables, which addresses the typical family's needs when shopping for strictly food items while also cutting down on inventory, keeping overheads low. Often Stockbox competes against stores that favour stocking junk food over fresh items. Stockbox's challenge is changing the conception that food shops need to be supersized supermarkets that offer nappies and mouthwash alongside bananas and poultry. This new offering hopes to be the convenient grocery that supplements the convenience store.

Keeping the Shirt on your Back: Shopping for Clothes

One of the most mundane activities you engage in every day is deciding what to wear: 'what shirt do I wear for the meeting?' 'Should I get that new dress?' But these ordinary, everyday tasks offer you a chance to shake things up, providing you with the best opportunities to make a fundamental impact on the world through the daily choices you make.

Paying attention to issues that matter: Going organic

Every item that can be manufactured can be manufactured in ways that follow principles of sustainable business practices. Clothing is no different. When making decisions about your clothing purchases, think about which of the following issues resonate with you and look for companies that engage in the practices you support:

✓ **Materials used:** Organic fabrics such as cotton, wool, silk, and hemp must meet regulations set by the North American Organic Trade Association regarding fibre processing, production, dyeing, and nontoxic handling.

✓ **Manufacturing processes and locations:** As a rule, chemicals used in the manufacturing processes of organic cloth – knitting, weaving, cleaning, scouring, dyeing, and finishing – must conform to the process requirements to ensure environmental sustainability and mustn't be carcinogenic, mutagenic, teratogenic, toxic to mammals, or an endocrine disrupter (ouch, sounds nasty!).

Check out `organicclothing.blogs.com/my_weblog/2006/04/certified_organ.html`, which provides a lot of international, valuable information that helps you sort through buying organic clothing.

Understanding what the labels mean in the fashion world

People often have a hard time understanding the meaning behind a 'green', 'eco', or 'sustainable' label in their clothes. Does such a label mean that the clothes themselves are made of eco-friendly material? Or that the company recycles accordingly? Currently, the fashion world is still trying to define these terms.

According to Rachel Miller, who teaches Sustainable Design in the Department of Fashion Design at Pratt Institute in New York, the term *sustainable design* can mean a number of things:

> *It could be about preserving the environment, it could be about ethics and fair wages, it could be a designer that has an interest in designing with organic materials, or it may be recycling what's already there, using recycled materials to create something new.*

Accusations have been made that companies are riding the 'green' label wave as a marketing tool. Of course, just because some firms use the label more as a marketing approach doesn't mean that legitimate green brands that *are* doing their part to help preserve the planet don't exist.

To discover whether a clothing manufacturer truly embraces sustainable design, ask whether your favourite clothing company has signed a commitment pledging to cut its carbon footprint.

Just recently, Tesco, Marks and Spencer, and the UK government's Department for Environment, Food and Rural Affairs (Defra) were among the High Street retailers, charities, recyclers, and other major players in the clothing sector that committed to eco-friendly practices by signing a pledge to cut their carbon, water, and waste footprints by 2020. The Waste & Resources Action Plan developed a guideline for a footprint calculator that enables companies

Green clothing: Ferel Childe

One company that integrates a sustainable business model with clothing design is Ferel Childe. Based in New York and California, and headed by Moriah Carlson (Brooklyn, NY) and Alice Wu (Oakland, CA), this bicoastal company is known for its one-of-a-kind pieces and its use of sustainable fibres. Ferel Childe clothing is manufactured in New York and earns the 'green' moniker by disposing of production waste by donating remnants to schools or sending them to a textile recycling facility. To prevent excess inventory, Ferel Childe produces by the order and provides transparent reports about its sourcing and manufacturing techniques upon request by customers.

Some people have the impression that if you're buying eco-friendly clothes, you must be a hippy. But that's not true. Feral Childe's collection has a range from quirky to nerdy to elegant, making the company's lines suitable for a variety of customers who want to support a company that supports the environment.

Dig a little deeper and you're sure to find other companies following green guidelines.

to quantify and report the total global impacts of the clothes they make, sell, and recover in a consistent way. The baseline data gathered in 2012 will help signatories identify and agree upon targets for carbon, water, and waste savings, to be delivered by 2020, and identify the next steps to reach the goals.

Some of the other companies onboard are: Arcadia Group, ASOS, British Retail Consortium, Centre for Sustainable Fashion, Clothes Aid, I&G Cohen, John Lewis, Next, Sainsbury's, Salvation Army Trading Company, and the Textile Recycling Association. Many more are expected to sign the pledge.

Chapter 16

Investing Financially in a Brighter Tomorrow

*A*pathy and scepticism are two great enemies of philanthropy and charitable endeavours, and the current climate of suspicion surrounding big businesses and global banks doesn't help. In the world of investments, however, this wariness can be a plus, because an alternative exists to the traditional institutions in the form of ethical investments.

If, like an increasing number of people, you don't want to invest your money in ways that create a financial gain but keep you awake at night with guilt, you have an alternative: put your money to work through new investment tools and products that provide a financial return but also align with your philanthropic passions. This approach is called *impact investment* and is part of the wider tendency of *socially responsible investing* (SRI), one of the fastest-growing areas of investment management.

In this chapter, we explain how to invest while maintaining a clear conscience and still enjoying a healthy financial return. We describe looking into companies to discover their values and decision-making, and introduce you to the state-of-the-art investment options available. We discuss why removing certain companies from your portfolio and replacing them with firms whose policies you agree with is worthwhile, interesting, and profitable.

Understanding Socially Responsible Investing

All businesses have obligations to the broader community and those that make proactive, positive efforts to be more aware of these responsibilities are said to display *corporate social responsibility*. Such socially responsible firms look at aspects other than providing maximum short-term returns to shareholders. (We focus mainly on this type of effort and not so much on corporate social responsibility relating to advertising and marketing – the efforts that companies make to publicise their social awareness, such as 'social responsibility' notices or conspicuous labelling.)

When you engage in SRI, you use the power of your own investment decision to make a positive difference in the world in numerous forms:

History of corporate social responsibility

Socially responsible investing emerged in the US in the 19th century. After the Civil War, some university endowments reconsidered their investments, refusing to invest in war-related or overseas companies. Even following the repeal of prohibition in the 1930s, others continued to avoid investments in grain alcohol manufacturers and breweries. In the early 20th century in England, some university investment managers and industrialists objected to manufacturing and shipping monopolies that exploited resources and people. They sought alternative investments or imposed limitations (such as only dealing with companies that instituted a minimum wage).

As Cold War military spending climbed in the 1960s, and social issues became prominent in American politics, corporate social responsibility entered the vocabulary of businesspeople after several scandals and as the media took a hostile stance towards American corporate governance. Business schools began discussing the concept

of 'stakeholders' alongside that of 'shareholders'. In the UK and US, issues such as environmental pollution, racial equality, and gender bias also contributed to questions of whether large companies were acting responsibly.

Corporate responsibility became national news in the US after the 1977 Ford Pinto car scandal. Someone at Ford knew about the potential hazard of Pinto drivers being hit by burning fuel from the petrol tank. Ford carried out a cost/benefit analysis and found that fixing the problem would cost more than paying lawsuits from dead or injured owners. It decided to save money and sell the car with a faulty petrol tank design, figuring that saving the lives and suffering of customers wasn't worth the $11 cost per car. Among dozens of others, 13-year-old Richard Grimshaw was severely burned by motor fuel. This behaviour outraged consumers and called into question whether multinational firms really cared about their customers.

✔ You invest in companies that best represent your values.

✔ You use your power as a shareholder to influence the corporation's policies or decisions to make it a better corporate citizen.

✔ You invest in companies that do business in communities, at home or abroad, that are underserved by 'mainstream' companies.

Caring about returns – financial and otherwise

As a socially responsible investor, you may need to change your mindset of what constitutes a 'good' return. Whereas for traditional investors a good return is one that yields the highest financial gain, people interested in SRI take a broader view. For them – and for the companies they invest in – a good return yields financial gain whilst also having a positive impact on people and on the environment. (Head to the later section, 'Paying attention to the triple bottom line' for more details.)

In addition, you can shed the idea that doing good and doing well are mutually exclusive propositions, not least because ideas of investments being 'good' or 'profitable' are highly subjective. Instead of comparing these two aspects and subtracting 'good' from 'profit', you're better served by adding them together so that the equation is more like the following:

> Good things that happened because of the investment I made + money I made = total good stuff

Thinking about profits and positive impact in tandem allows you to figure out the total upside on an investment. Don't ask, 'how much is the investment good for me as against good for the world?' You're part of the world. An investment can be really good for you and super for the world!

Putting together a financially competitive portfolio of SRIs is simple these days, with many companies and businesses running socially responsible policies and programmes to help you build a portfolio of firms whose practices align with your values. Plus, some recent studies indicate that SRI portfolios do as well as, and in some cases better than, traditional investment portfolios.

Bringing business sense to social problems

Historically many organisations and charities were too mission-focused (for example, 'We want to save whales') and failed to be project-oriented (for example, 'We want to halt one particular Japanese whale hunt in a specific region of the world'). In many cases, the results were missed deadlines, half-completed goals, and frustrated donors. To help address this issue, people imported the idea of project management from the business world to 'do-good do-well' investments (*project management* means the ability to supervise, from start to finish, a project that solves a particular problem.) In this section, we discuss how a business culture of deadlines, accountability, and audit mechanisms is often just what non-profit or charity organisations need.

One of the advantages of social investments is that every enterprise has a guiding principle embedded within it. If a business owner believes that his company is accomplishing good in the world, contributing something and participating in positive progress, he wants it to stay in business. Unlike charities, most companies need to turn enough of a profit first to keep the lights on at a minimum and hopefully enough to satisfy the investors.

When figuring out how to turn a profit whilst also making the world better, you need to use other calculations. In general, these calculations tend to be good for the world and include the following questions:

✔ How can the company be more efficient and less wasteful?

✔ What do we do to make the most of every relationship and opportunity?

✔ Do we cultivate employees with potential and make sure that we keep employees with talent?

✔ What would inspire the firm's partners, excite stakeholders, and impress competitors?

✔ Why is our firm's vision of the future the right one, and how do we play a role in shaping that future?

Companies that ask such questions generally have a better rate of success and create positive effects on their goal to maximise profits for shareholders *and* on their long-term planning. In general, companies (and people) with long-term plans tend to care more about the future. As a result, a company that plans to be doing business 50 years from now needs to think about the condition of the environment in 50 years, where its employees are going to live, where it can obtain the natural resources needed for its manufacturing, and so on.

Avoid companies that ask, 'How can we make Joe work harder for less pay?', 'How many weekends can we use the corporate yacht before the shareholders ask questions?' and 'Can we survive another six months or six years?' They aren't thinking long term and are likely to be less successful.

Screening for Socially Responsible Companies

All investors choose from a vast array of investment options. Perhaps you already sort your investments according to the traditional concerns of risk and return, future plans for the money (how long you plan to hold the investment), and so on. Well now you can add corporate social responsibility to that list of considerations. Today, many investors choose organisations based on their innovation, culture, and track record for living up to their promises and projections – financial, social, and (in some cases) environmental. These concepts are relatively new corporate attributes but seem to influence heavily how companies act in the future.

Look at the world of investments as a vast clearing with flowers to discover and not as a large minefield with dangers to avoid. Investments can sponsor positive corporate practices as well as avoid negative behaviours. The search for well-run, thoughtful, forward-looking companies is more rewarding and more profitable than the search for ethical flaws in your current portfolio's companies.

Investing in the 'good' or avoiding the 'bad': Types of screening

You can screen companies in two general ways:

✔ **Look for and avoid companies that produce a product or engage in practices you disagree with.** In its simplest form, SRI means not investing money in companies whose products, policies, or impacts you disagree with (for example, tobacco or alcohol). People in the financial industry often call these *negative screens,* because they say what the portfolio can't have in it rather than what it can contain.

✔ **Seek out and invest in companies that promote the policies or produce products that have a positive impact in the areas important to you.** Your support can be hands-off – investing in companies already aligned with your values and whose missions you believe help the company fulfil its objectives, or hands-on – actively seeking to influence corporate decisions.

Investing or divesting?

The concept of screening investments arose in the 1980s, where people decided not to invest in what they considered 'bad' firms (negative screening) but instead chose to channel money into companies doing 'good' things (positive screening). For example, people opposed to white minority (apartheid) rule in South Africa didn't want their investments to benefit firms

there. Eventually, this campaign of *divestment* (disassociating with the firm) damaged South Africa financially and was part of the reason for the peaceful transition to democracy. Today, the focus has shifted towards helping firms doing good rather than simply divesting from firms doing bad.

Paying attention to the triple bottom line

Many companies manage to produce social or environmental gains while maintaining or creating profits. To achieve this aim, they're increasingly including other factors in their business decisions and activities in addition to profit – looking at their total social (or social and environmental) impact instead of simply focusing on the money profits. These companies don't stop serving shareholders' interests or stop trying to maximise shareholder profits, but they do repurpose their research and innovation efforts around the company's responsibilities and function in society.

Businesses focus closely on their *bottom line* (which is an ultimate outcome and not a crease in your trousers from sitting for too long). Until fairly recently, they focused on the financial bottom line: does the business make money or bring in a profit for investors and owners? Socially responsible companies, however, realise that their policies, products, and conduct produce more than financial outcomes: they also impact people and the environment. A company's financial, social, and environmental impacts are called the *triple bottom line.* You hear this term (or double bottom line for two of the three items) a lot in the world of SRI.

Businesses making an impact: Microfinance

In the microfinance industry small business loans are made available to entrepreneurs in poor countries. Microfinance banks are the developing-world equivalent of high-street bank lending.

Small entrepreneurs (increasingly called *micro-entrepreneurs*), farmers, and others borrow money from microfinance institutions. The idea is that these loans enable people to start businesses, grow crops, or engage in other activities that provide the income necessary to build more secure futures for themselves and their children, and to have a positive impact on their communities. The access to loans allows borrowers to consider how to grow their businesses and make longer-term investments.

In turn, microfinance banks make money on the interest paid on these loans.

If microfinance piques your interest, check out the following websites for inspiration and ideas:

✔ **Choose by company:** MIX Market (www.mixmarket.org) rates and evaluates microfinance institutions around the world, helping donors such as you to understand the complex numbers in firms' annual reports and press releases.

✔ **Choose by geography:** To explore your philanthropic interests in a particular part of the world, you can look into microfinance institutions according to their geography:

- **Accion** (www.accion.org) is active in 31 countries.
- **BRAC** (www.brac.net) operates in 11 countries.
- **Fonkoze** (www.fonkoze.org) is the leading firm in the troubled country of Haiti.
- **Grameen Bank** (www.grameen.com) is active globally.
- **Opportunity** (www.opportunity.org.uk) is active in 20 countries.

Businesses that engage in innovation

To find socially responsible companies, pay attention to the philanthropic challenges that spur innovations addressing the issues you're concerned with. If you care about nutrition, invest in a grocery chain that provides nutritious options at reasonable prices in underserved areas. If you care about healthcare and accessibility, invest in pharmaceutical firms with a broad mission to provide products at discounts or free of charge to the poor. If your concern is the proliferation of arms, revise your investments to avoid investing in companies that produce and broker weapons.

Consider the specific cause of sanitation. Seven billion people live on the Earth, but many don't have toilets (for example, less than a third of India's households have access to one). The reason isn't hard to figure out: toilets are expensive to purchase, transport, and install, and people in poverty may not have the skills or tools to install a toilet themselves. But FINISH (www.ideaken.com/finish), for instance, developed a contest to develop sustainable rural toilet systems.

Innovation in sanitation: Winning traits of leading systems

The following common traits exist among today's leading sanitation systems:

✔ The system sets up toilets in densely-populated areas.

✔ The waste from the toilet is treated and baked (in some models, microwaved), turning it into fertiliser that's sold to local farmers.

✔ The community gets access to toilets where otherwise they'd use fields or primitive (often overflowing) pit latrines.

✔ The farmers get access to affordable, safe fertiliser.

✔ The villagers get toilets paid for by the fertiliser company.

✔ The fertiliser company makes a profit on the fertiliser it sells to the farmers, because the raw materials to manufacture the fertiliser are obtained cheaply and locally.

This solution is beneficial for people and the Earth: people get working and sanitary toilets (helping to fight disease and the spread of infections) and it's environmentally friendly by using the treated, safe waste to fertilise farmers' lands.

Noting the company (or companies) that participate in or win such challenges gives you an idea of which ones make problem-solving innovations a priority and which, because of this focus, have the potential to make significant returns on investment as well as significant improvements in people's lives. Most large corporations make substantial engineering investments in solving interesting problems or showcasing their abilities (see the nearby sidebar 'Innovation in sanitation: Winning traits of leading systems' for more).

Many websites, such as Water Charity (www.watercharity.org) and WaterAid (www.wateraid.org), act as clearing-houses for smaller sanitation and water-related projects. For instance, as we're writing, several projects are available at www.watercharity.org that require less than £150!

Toyota usually supports environmental charities (part of its push towards very low and zero-emission vehicles), but also has a great deal of expertise in making things efficiently. It sent its top engineers to the Food Bank of New York City, which feeds 1.5 million people every year. The results were striking (see the *New York Times* article on improvements such as reducing the time to pack boxes of supplies for Hurricane Sandy victims from 3 minutes to 11 seconds at www.nytimes.com/2013/07/27/nyregion/in-lieu-of-money-toyota-donates-efficiency-to-new-york-charity.html?pagewanted=all&_r=0).

Many such efforts win awards and feature in the media – keep a look out for companies undertaking these efforts and find out who's having success.

Looking into a company's decision-making

When considering an investment in socially responsible corporations, you don't focus just on a company's financials (income, balance, cash-flow statements, and so on). To determine whether a company is a good fit in your investment portfolio, you look at other things as well.

By understanding the management's future goals for a firm, you gain a better understanding of the companies in which you're investing. As a shareholder, you own the business, and as an investor, you want to own businesses with plans for the future that you understand and agree with.

In this section, we describe looking into a firm's management and checking its decisions so that you invest only in companies that produce social gains.

Investigating management decisions

How a firm's management makes difficult choices tells you a lot about its policies. When you're deciding whether to invest in a company, check its decision-making and whether it's ethical and in line with your own ideals.

Although you may hear the vague phrase *corporate governance* thrown around, we prefer to use the clearer term *decision-making*, because this is key to corporate responsibility and corporate social impact.

Examine key decisions of a company's history (hiring decisions, policies towards employees, manufacturing choices, and so on) to help gain an understanding of how it's managed and see whether you agree with the choices. Ask yourself these questions:

- How did management make this decision?
- How did it follow through on the decision or strategy afterwards?
- What are the consequences of the decision for the company as a whole, its employees, and the communities in which it operates?

Examine not only how the decision was made but also its consequences. Who was affected and how? Were the people affected given a voice in the decision-making process?

Finding answers to your questions about decision-making

To answer these questions, you can use loads of valuable resources. Your inquiries when examining companies aren't substantially different from your inquiries regarding charities (as we discuss in Chapter 4). Check out:

- **Accounts:** Such as board meeting minutes (often available from a company, at least in excerpted form, though usually not published on the investor-relations part of the website). These are legally required and disclose how decisions are made including whether a vote was taken, how many people voted, whether a discussion was held, and so forth.

- **Supplementary documents:** Studies done, people interviewed, and so forth.

The annual report is the *least* useful way to judge a company's attitudes, outlook, and direction. Publicity people, accountants, and lawyers prepare this glossy document with a lot of pictures of happy people, and it's the firm's key piece of yearly storytelling. Even a factory that makes asbestos using child labour can look good in an annual report!

The most important thing for a potential investor to do is to observe an organisation over time. Can you get answers from the company when you call or email? Do updates to the website or other materials clearly state what issues it hopes to address in the coming months or years? Do the leaders seem committed to the company's mission, or was the mission simply drafted by an advertising agency and placed on a shelf?

Assessing the quality of a firm's decisions

After you discover what decisions the company has made, you can assess the decisions themselves. Consider not only the outcome, but the intention behind the decision as well.

Contrast the disgraceful Ford Pinto scandal we relate in the earlier sidebar 'History of corporate social responsibility' with the 1955 disaster at the Le Mans car race in which a Mercedes race car flew into the crowd and caught fire, causing more than 80 deaths – the worst accident in motor-racing history. The company board held an emergency meeting immediately and withdrew from the race out of respect for the victims and later from motorsports completely, focusing instead on safety and other areas of automotive research, despite the fact that racing was the primary form of auto advertising in the 1950s. Mercedes kept its pledge for decades before returning to racing in Formula 1 as a constructor in 2010.

When assessing a firm's decisions, look at these things:

✔ **Its ability and willingness to address the issue.** Not every company has the corporate governance mechanisms in place to hold an emergency meeting like Daimler-Benz did (and make such a sweeping decision). The ability of a company to make quick, sound decisions is important for its business success and its role in the wider community. You want to see indications that the company takes its responsibilities seriously. Safety was a key part of the Mercedes brand, and withdrawing until safety was improved showed concern for the company's reputation, future, and position.

✔ **Whether the decisions are ethical.** Yes, every company that hopes to stay in business must be concerned about its financial health, and a cynical (or realistic) argument can be made that companies engage in socially responsible behaviour not because they want to do good but because doing good increases their profits. Nevertheless, socially responsible companies seek to balance the calculation out, recognising that not all gains or all costs are monetary ones.

During a company crisis, someone makes an ethical decision between two options: for example, 'Do we save money by making exploding Pintos?' or 'Do we stop racing even though it's our most effective advertising effort?'. When you evaluate a firm's decision, ask yourself whether it's defensible from an ethical standpoint.

When choosing between two companies in the same industry (in this case, auto manufacturers), appraise their behaviour when the pressure was on to check corporate policy and management ethics.

✔ **How the company responds to crises regarding its product or service.** Some companies' decisions result in responsible actions, based on objective assessments of the situations or dangers; others default to a defensive posture, deflecting responsibility to maintain market share. For an example of the gold standard of corporate behaviour in a crisis, see the nearby sidebar 'The Tylenol scare in 1982'.

When considering your investments, a pattern of defensive reactions to valid concerns may make the company ill-equipped to address valid concerns in an open manner. Defensiveness in decision-making is often a sign of a company in decline. Recent corporate failure stories (including Hewlett-Packard and Kodak) were preceded by dozens of defensive press releases. So not only is the company unable to make sustainable, ethical decisions that support its social and environmental bottom line, but also its financial bottom line is probably in jeopardy.

The Tylenol scare in 1982

Johnson & Johnson was faced with a public-relations nightmare when someone in Chicago began poisoning Tylenol painkilling capsules. The company quickly issued a nationwide recall of over $100 million in Tylenol-branded medicines and swapped any Tylenol capsules for hard Tylenol tablets. This swift action is credited with preventing at least three more poisoned bottles from reaching customers and saving the value of the Tylenol brand — thereby saving lives and millions of dollars of shareholder value.

Students study this gold-standard corporate reaction to a product liability issue in business and law schools and it's highly regarded by advertising and public-relations firms.

Not every company, however, performs to this high standard when faced with an emergency. Some companies see any criticism of current practices or products as an attack.

Determining whether your vision and the company's practices are in sync

Look to whether the practices of a successful business are likely to be aligned with the change you want to see in the world. When you close your eyes, what does your desired future look like? Does the company you're considering investing in have products, services, and attitudes that work well in your imagined future world? Can it help that future happen? If so, perhaps that firm's worthy of your investment.

When you're researching the investment, include so-called soft signals as well as 'hard' numbers. Read recent quotes from the CEO and notice what the company talks about most often (and what it seemingly doesn't want to talk about). These signals are often just as important as the accountancy on the final pages of the annual report.

Find out the experts who make a living by analysing a particular industry. If you're interested in solar panels, for instance, a wealth of knowledge is already available on which technologies seem most promising and which companies are involved. Many banks make analyst reports and other documents available on a monthly or quarterly basis. Government think-tanks and agencies can be an excellent source of information as well: for instance, the American government's National Renewable Energy Laboratory (www.nrel.gov) publishes papers on technologies, companies, and philanthropic or social efforts in the renewable energy sector.

Providing power

Mike Lin of Fenix International (`fenixintl.com`) investigated organisations trying to make the world better for the 1.5 billion people without electricity, but he found few solutions. He realised that the electric grid failed in developing nations because centralised power generation is costly and prone to corruption and breakdowns. Using his engineering and entrepreneurial experience, he started Fenix, a business focused on solving the energy problems of the world's poor. The company's key product, the ReadySet, is essentially an intelligent battery unit that lets people charge small devices such as mobile telephones even without access to a reliable power grid. They can charge the ReadySet with a solar panel or even with a bicycle.

The UK government is aiming to meet the EU 2020 target (15 per cent of its energy to come from renewable sources by then). The initiatives needed to meet these goals are researched primarily through the United Kingdom Energy Research Centre (`www.ukerc.ac.uk/support/tiki-index.php`). Solar energy is just one example: the same analysis and resources are available in other areas, from clean water to urban issues and housing.

Taking a More Active Role: Impact Investing

Whereas socially responsible investing (see the earlier section 'Understanding Socially Responsible Investing') can be limited to investing only in companies whose products and missions align with your values and eliminating those that don't (such as manufacturing tobacco, testing products on animals, having a poor safety record, and so on), some investors want to take a more active stance with their investments. They seek a more proactive and affirmative portfolio management activity.

The result is *impact investing* – the idea that investors can create positive change in the world through the actions of the companies they support. So impact investors invest in companies that they believe are going to make the world a better place as they grow. They invest in organisations that are more likely to have positive effects in the hope of accelerating these changes while reaping financial rewards in the process. Impact investing aims to anticipate and influence the decisions that companies make. As an impact investor, you choose your investments, at least in part, based on the current (or potential) positive social or environmental impact of the company's activities. A mixture of the company's financial, social, and environmental performance – with its areas of research, hiring practices, management, and so on – influences your decision to invest (or not).

The impact-investment industry has grown quickly. A 2009 study by Monitor Group anticipates that impact investing will grow from a $50 billion industry in 2009 to a $500+ billion industry in 2019. For comparison, at the time of the report Apple and Google were each worth about $100 billion.

Here are two key assumptions behind impact investing:

- ✔ As an impact investor, you measure investment performance alongside the effects you're having on the world. You evaluate the success of your investment on financial and positive impact terms.

- ✔ Companies have a positive or neutral impact on the effects that you observe in the world. By allocating capital to these firms, you increase the positive impacts (or decrease negative impacts) on the world.

All your investments have an impact of some sort. The issue of building a specifically impact-investment portfolio is a question of maximising the positive impact the world enjoys from your investment strategy.

Seeing the wood for the (Amazon's) trees

Amazon.com sells (or re-sells) nearly everything imaginable and its products constitute a substantial portion of all packages delivered to residential addresses in the UK, the US, and many other countries. In the wake of this enormous success, environmental groups criticised Amazon for its packaging practices. By 2007, customers and shareholders were discussing the issue.

A year later, Amazon joined Microsoft and other companies in committing to a plan to use easy-to-open, less bulky packing materials.

As a result, Amazon is able to save money on shipping costs (by using smaller, lighter packaging), provide a better experience to customers (by having easier-to-open packaging), and address environmental concerns (by contributing less shipping material to landfills). Perhaps most importantly, Amazon took concerns about packaging as an invitation to forge new partnerships, innovate, and deliver a better service to customers.

Identifying the areas you want to impact

You can translate all sorts of values into a plan for impact investment. Does the investment's *value* come just from money? No, it also comes from how well the investment's *values* match your own. Having trust that an investment will perform well in both a financial and social sense gives you more than peace of mind: it gives you a better investment strategy. Consider these examples:

✔ Investing in a manufacturing company with a plan to create jobs in a particular economically-disadvantaged geographical area.

✔ Investing in companies that make worker education a priority through such measures as continuing training, on-site language courses, tuition reimbursement, and broader educational benefit plans.

✔ Investing in pharmaceutical companies that prioritise research into certain diseases or don't test their products on animals.

Acumen Fund (www.acumenfund.org) is one of the longest-running, brand-name organisations focusing on impact investment and aims to build financial *and* human capital in the impact investment space. It oversees debt and equity investments of tens of millions of dollars in half a dozen markets. Its fellowship programme creates the pool of professionals to manage Acumen's investments (and investments in the broader impact-investment industry) as interest and investment in this area grow.

Working where your passion lies: Gita Drury

Gita Drury had considered her investment decisions as being separate from her interests in philanthropy and social responsibility until a meeting with her financial advisor. Now, her work, philanthropy, and investments are more closely related.

Gita writes: 'I learned about socially responsible investing when my financial advisor explained about applying social and environmental screens to my trust fund portfolio; and yet simply weeding out weapons, tobacco, animal testing, gambling, and so on felt dissatisfying and passive. But the experience led to my current passion: helping

to grow and democratise the field of impact investing. The high minimum initial investments required by many impact-investment funds effectively limited who could take part. I joined the team at ImpactAssets (www.impactassets.org), whose strategic vision addresses these challenges, ultimately working to expand the flow of capital to the most promising emerging companies and social entrepreneurs. We're nearing the tipping point when all interested parties and even idealistic 18-year-olds (or 68-year-olds) can invest their assets in companies that truly reflect their values.'

Establishing your impact-investment criteria

Evaluating investment impact can seem like a chicken-and-egg problem: you want to invest now before the impact happens, but you need to be sure that the impact happens before you invest. Fortunately, you don't have to wait forever to make the investment because an entire industry of people is thinking constantly about this problem. And they've become reasonably good at working out which companies have a realistic plan to create positive change in the near future.

Here are some examples of questions to ask when making impact-investment decisions:

- ✔ If I invest in this paper company moving towards non-wood and sustainable paper manufacturing, along with recycling existing paper, will I make a positive impact or merely increase the number of trees killed in the short term before it changes its practices?

- ✔ If I invest in a company that makes healthy, but expensive, food, am I increasing or decreasing the accessibility of healthy food for everyone? Is more healthy food being available a good thing if 90 per cent of people can't afford to buy it, or does that simply stoke society's nutritional class warfare?

- ✔ If I believe that fewer cars are the goal, but that most people won't abandon their own soon, should I invest in a company that makes cleaner cars, hoping that more of those will be less polluting?

Of course, we can't give you 'right' or 'wrong' answers to these questions; they're simply the kind of thought-provoking questions to ask yourself when you're interested in having investments that reflect your values.

Choosing where your money goes

In addition to investing in firms with positive environmental and social records or encouraging other companies to take up better practices, impact investing includes a range of practices and concerns. Here's a list with a couple of examples in each area:

- ✔ **Supplying loans or credit to help poor families or areas:** Oikocredit (www.oikocredit.org and The Calvert Foundation (www.calvert-foundation.org).

- ✔ **Banking with community development banks and similar institutions that support underserved communities:** Move Your Money (moveyourmoney.org.uk) and Urban Partnership Bank (www.upbnk.com).

✔ **Investing in clean energy projects:** Triodos Bank (www.triodos.co.uk) and Climate Investment Funds (www.climateinvestmentfunds.org).

✔ **Helping to provide housing options:** Habitat for Humanity (www.habitat.org) and Shelter (www.shelter.org.uk).

✔ **Providing medicines, food, and disaster relief:** Bridge Capital Fund (www.unicefusa.org/news/news-from-the-field/the-unicef-bridge-fund.html) and Operation Blessing (www.ob.org).

✔ **Increasing incomes for women-led agricultural co-ops:** Root Capital (www.rootcapital.org) and Shared Interest (www.sharedinterest.org).

To begin an impact strategy, start with simple criteria and a list of 'help' and 'hurt' items. In your 'help' list for a paper company, for example, you can include forests and workers (if the company sustainably replants the forests it uses in paper production and employs workers on fair terms and at fair wages); in your hurt list put things you value but believe the company jeopardises through its business.

Say you want your investments to help grow forests and impact negatively as few environmental resources as possible. You know that Brazil has a major forestry management challenge, because parts of the Amazon are disappearing daily, and so you decide to make the Amazon a focus of your new impact strategy. Through research online and reading recent news articles on the Amazon and the impact of multinational corporations in Brazil, you discover that a lot of forest destroyed in western Brazil is levelled to make room to graze cattle. You take this into account when looking at companies to add to your investment portfolio, considering the impact of agribusiness and other industries and not only the impact of logging and paper companies.

Therefore, your 'help' and 'hurt' list may look like this:

Help	*Hurt*
Ranchers (ranches get bigger)	Forests (being cleared for cows)
Consumers (cheaper paper)	Tourism (less Amazon to enjoy)
Consumers (cheaper beef)	Small farms (sold to large companies)

One of your chief goals is to help, not hurt, forests and so you're unlikely to invest in this company.

All investors, large or small, have a range of options – not just in stocks and bonds, but in a wide array of products. By looking carefully at the choices you make, and what they mean for the future, you become more aware as an investor of your investments and the effects they have.

The logic behind impact investing

John Goldstein of Imprint Capital Advisors (www.imprintcap.com) is a veteran and innovator in impact investment, who was building impact-oriented portfolios for clients long before the concept reached the mainstream. Here he describes the rationale behind impact investing:

✔ **The money is available:** Impact investing is targeting $100–200 trillion in investable assets, which is 500–1,000 times the amount of charitable donations.

✔ **The resource is renewable:** When given away, money is gone, but invested money returns and allows people to have an impact *and* the choice of spending that money, donating it or investing it again for more impact.

✔ **The method works:** People who made their money in business and finance want to harness the potential power of enterprise and investment models to maximise their impacts on chosen charitable issues and causes.

Evaluating your investment impact

Measuring impact is notoriously difficult, particularly compared to measuring financial investment performance. If you buy a stock for £10 and sell it at £11, measuring your financial performance is easy. But if a company makes nutritional improvements to the school lunches it serves or stops marketing its cigarettes using cartoon characters, how do you measure that impact? Luckily, a whole industry of financial experts, statisticians, and consultants is measuring the good being done (such as Mission Measurement, www.missionmeasurement.com, which serves as auditor and repository of good ideas and best practices to all sorts of clients including the Bill & Melinda Gates Foundation.

Of course, most private investors don't have the time, money, or patience to hire a firm to perform studies, but past analyses (often published free of charge online or made available as a supplement to annual reports) can be highly informative. Here's where you can find out more about measuring the impact your investment has without having to hire an expert:

✔ **Boston Consulting Group:** Occasionally publishes case studies and material showcasing how to improve practices in the philanthropy world (www.bcg.com/about_bcg/social_impact/philanthropy).

✔ **McKinsey & Company:** Produces a well-written and informative quarterly newsletter often with information on philanthropy (articles free at www.mckinseyquarterly.com/Nonprofit/Philanthropy).

✔ **New Philanthropy Capital (NPC):** Works with charities on impact measurement and helps them become more successful in achieving their missions. Check out the website and downloadable publications on impact measurement (www.thinknpc.org).

✔ **TPG Companies:** Performs studies on all sorts of topics, including a case study on philanthropic impact at www.whatmattersmost.com.

Measuring impact has a lot to do with your personal expectations (which is what you measure corporate performance against), but here are a few quick tips to bear in mind:

✔ Working out the mission of a small company with one big project is easier than figuring out the mission of a large company that's in a large number of different businesses.

✔ Calculating the impact of a company that makes only, say, sandwiches or sells only books is obviously easier than for a company that makes, say, bulldozers, industrial rubber products, and pharmaceuticals.

✔ Figuring out the long-term social agenda of a company that recently changed its CEO or offered shares to the public is difficult, because the inner workings of the firm may have shifted substantially.

For more tips on balancing positive impact and income, flip to the later section in this chapter 'Matching philanthropic purpose and profits'.

Inspiring impact investing: Kristin Hull

Kristin Hull is an investor who recently shifted her money into impact investments:

'I discovered impact investing in 2008 along with the concept of Whole Portfolio Activation Toward Mission. Hearing stories of other participants' experiences inspired me to activate my portfolio towards social and environmental justice. Our family foundation already grants at least 5 per cent of our endowment every year to cutting-edge non-profits and I work with impact investors to further its goals while bringing market-rate returns. I invest in companies making the changes we want, such as lowering emissions for the trucking industry, encouraging women-owned businesses, and funding new urban charter schools. I've moved our foundation assets to being 100 per cent fully mission- and impact-invested.

I want companies to be rewarded for their care for the environment and treatment of customers and employees. Orienting my investment portfolios to support companies that share my values helps me further my philanthropic mission. More broadly, looking at and investing in corporate performance helps you to increase your philanthropic impact and maximise your portfolio's performance.'

Doing Good while Doing Well

Lots of people want to be involved in companies that make the world better while making a profit. Over the last 30 years or so, and particularly the past decade, the focus has shifted from investing in companies that do less harm to investing in companies that do more good in the world.

Doing good while doing well (that is, while making money) is a pretty easy concept to discuss but a harder one to put to work in the real world of tax planning, retirement accounts, and personal finance. Identifying and locating do-good do-well ventures is a critical part of impact investing (which we define in the earlier section 'Taking a More Active Role: Impact Investing'). After all, having an investment budget that's doing good in the world is all very well, but the resulting income also needs to, say, help you retire someday or supplement a college fund. As we explain in this section, you can realistically do both.

Integrating impact investing into your financial life

To clarify your thoughts, write out some of your philanthropic and financial goals under the following headings:

Investing in peace to gain wealth

John Kluge Jr has spent years figuring out his role as philanthropist and impact investor:

'In the spring of 2011, four families from the US, Germany, and Saudi Arabia started a new kind of company to capitalise, build, and operate for-purpose (do-good) for-profit (do-well) ventures. We named the company Eirëne, after the Greek goddess of peace and prosperity, and established a few rules, which you may want to consider for your own venture:

✔ Each venture must address a problem that affects at least one billion people.

✔ Each venture must be profitable.

✔ Each venture must have radical positive externalities. Our businesses are designed to generate positive social costs, with multiple layers of benefit to human beings and the planet as part of the business model.

✔ Each venture must be able to scale. We start small and grow and are willing to invest at least ten years per venture.

✔ We have to have fun. If we're not having fun, something's probably wrong.'

✔ **Directly related to each other:** For example, investing in a company that creates jobs in your city may make your own plans to retire to the city rather than the countryside a little more comfortable. You'd write something like:

> 'I want to invest in at least one company that creates jobs in my local area to make sure that the area is still doing well financially when my children reach adulthood.'

✔ **Indirectly related:** You may hope that your children don't have to worry about certain illnesses and want to support companies doing research into those diseases. You'd write:

> 'I want to support at least one company that does research into heart disease, which runs in my family; I realise it may not find a cure in my lifetime, but I want to support this effort.'

✔ **Related to other people:** Perhaps you visited a place where a new privately-owned water purification plant or power plant is improving life. For example:

> 'I want to invest in a company finding a way to make water clean cheaply. I visited Kenya and was horrified to see people drinking dirty water. The problem doesn't directly affect me or my family, but I feel that investing in people who're doing this research and the company they work for is the right thing to do.'

For more inspiration on do-good do-well ventures, read the nearby sidebar 'Investing in peace to gain wealth'.

Business practices and employee happiness are intimately connected: many businesses with good business practices and happy employees are also some of the most valuable corporations in the world. The simple fact is that employees don't want to work at a place where they're likely to be robbed in the car park after work, or have to tell the children that what mum or dad did that day helped kill the rainforest or deprived thousands of children in Asia or Africa of clean water.

The interaction between corporate behaviour and corporate success – that used to be controversial – is today difficult to deny.

Matching philanthropic purpose and profits

Don't look for a 'right' mathematical ratio that relates doing good and making money; that's the wrong approach! Instead of asking '*Should* I be willing to take lower profits on an investment if the company makes the world better?', ask '*Am* I willing to?' (The 'should' implies being judged if you give the 'wrong' answer, when one doesn't exist.) If you're not willing to take lower financial performance, seek out an impact investment that's expected to perform at (or even outperform) market rates of return. If you are, you have a wider range of investments available to choose from.

You don't need to be an 'investment martyr' and sacrifice your ambitions for profit to create positive change. Investing in companies that do good doesn't mean that you're going to make any less money on your investments. If you receive contrary advice or are told that you need to expect a vastly lower rate of return, consider changing investment advisors.

If you're willing to receive a lower rate of return from your impact investments, consider debt investments, or bonds, contracts in which you lend money to a corporation for a fixed period of time at a fixed interest rate. Many companies in the impact-investment space aren't large enough to issue publicly-traded bonds but may have lending arrangements for interested investors (perhaps via their website or by post). This type of contract allows you to lend money to the company directly without having to buy bonds on a public exchange. You can often negotiate with the company, particularly if it's a startup. Be creative! Often, non-standard terms (tailored to your needs and expectations) work best for you (lender) and the company (borrower).

This option can be a good way to get a predictable rate of return while supporting a do-good company. Often, you can make arrangements in which you offer only a portion or small percentage of the total money needed, with some minimum investments on offer at as little as £500.

Keep track of the investments you make for positive impact purposes. Doing so allows you to check them periodically and compare the rates of return against other investments, and lets you assess your decision-making process, so that you can make better decisions in the future.

Chapter 17

Getting Strategic in Your Giving and Philanthropy

In This Chapter

▶ Marshalling your resources

▶ Tackling the legal niceties

▶ Taking precautions before dishing out the dosh

▶ Understanding what happens after your donation

*L*ike all important endeavours, charitable giving and philanthropy are most effective when planned properly. Therefore, you need a strategy that covers your plan for what you want to give and how to give it and helps you to analyse how effective your donating is and avoid pitfalls along the way.

The tools we describe in this chapter allow you to be more strategic, focused, and conscientious in your giving, as well as help to protect you from the nasty surprises that often sneak up on all philanthropists – whether you're experienced or a novice, or investing a lot or a little.

All philanthropists benefit from strategic planning but need to be aware of tax and legal issues related to their gifts, and are best served by monitoring the effectiveness of their gifts. In addition, the whole idea of strategic giving presumes a long-term commitment (giving a portion of your income regularly, for instance) or one that may be more complex (donating a portion of the returns on investment securities, for example). Although you can devise such a plan yourself, you may want to consult financial, legal, or tax advice to ensure that you're aware of any significant issues.

Preparing to Give: Financial Planning

Putting in place a good financial strategy is essential to carrying out effective, satisfying, and stress-free philanthropy. We guide you through the basic planning and tax advantages, and show you how to hand over the routine work to organisations that are only too glad to help out.

Financial planning helps you to think about how to balance the following three goals:

✔ To help as much as possible

✔ To help the causes you care about, now *and* in the future

✔ To make a difference in every cause you help

To achieve these aims your plan needs to include the following key components:

✔ Methods of identifying how much to give, so that you achieve your philanthropic goals without overly depleting your resources, and how you can continue your giving for the long term. (For specific strategies on donating time, talent, treasure, and transactions, refer to Chapters 12 to 15).

✔ Legal concerns and best practices that let you save time and avoid problems, legal and otherwise.

✔ Ways to recognise and address issues that arise after you write that cheque or give your credit-card information to a website.

You can just as easily find yourself in a bad financial situation from over-giving as from over-spending. At some point, your means are sure to limit what you can give financially: if you give away all your money today, you can't give in the future. Plus, giving to too many causes may mean that you have insufficient invested in each one to make the difference you desire.

Thankfully, your finances are an aspect of your life over which you can exercise great control. With careful planning, you can enthusiastically support your favourite causes without cracking your nest egg or digging into your rainy-day fund. This section has all the details.

Understanding the tax implications of charitable giving

Every country has its own rules regarding taxes and charitable giving. When deciding what and how much to give, you have to be familiar with these rules to get the most from your donation, whether it's monetary or a physical asset. You may even qualify for tax relief. Here are the general rules regarding charitable donations in the UK:

✔ **Donating through Gift Aid:** When you do so, you've already paid tax on the donated amount. The charity can then reclaim the basic rate income tax amount from Her Majesty's Revenue and Customs (HMRC). So, for example, if the basic tax rate is 25 per cent, your £100 donation through Gift Aid actually provides the charity with £125 (£100 + the reclaimed £25 of tax). If you pay a higher tax rate, you may be able to reclaim the difference between what you paid and the amount the charity reclaims.

✔ **Giving through the Payroll Giving scheme:** When you make donations directly through your pension or pay, the donation is taken out before income tax is calculated, meaning that you pay less in taxes. In order to use Payroll Giving, your employer must run a Payroll Giving scheme.

✔ **Giving assets to charity:** Can reduce your capital gains tax obligations. *Capital gains* refers to the profits you make when you sell something that you own. You can lower your tax bill when you do the following:

- Give land, buildings, or qualifying shares (shares listed on any stock exchange) to a charity.

- Sell these items to a charity for less than the market value.

✔ **Leaving gifts in your will:** The value of the gifts is deducted from your estate before the inheritance tax obligation is calculated, benefitting your heirs as well as the charity.

To benefit from tax relief, the receiving organisation must be recognised as a charity by HMRC and have a charity reference number, which you need to supply when making your claims. Other rules also apply. Be sure to consult the HMRC website, a tax expert, or a financial advisor for details.

Donating from retirement plans: A word of warning

Certain accounts, such as individual retirement accounts (IRAs) in the US, let you invest tax-free (taxes are paid when the assets are put into the account, because the contributions to an IRA account are post-tax). As a result, donating assets from these retirement plans isn't generally advantageous if other funds are available in taxable accounts. Be aware that early withdrawal of funds from IRA accounts can mean stiff penalties. If you have an IRA, check with your advisor before considering premature withdrawals from any retirement account. Although no direct equivalent of IRA accounts exists in other countries, some employers (especially financial institutions) may provide similar accounts. If you possess such a plan, obtain financial advice.

Determining which accounts to give from

Not all financial assets are created equal. If you have multiple assets – regular income, investment holdings, savings accounts, and so on – one of your first tasks when planning your philanthropic giving is to identify from which source to take your monetary gifts: some offer tax advantages (see the preceding section), which may persuade (or dissuade) you from donating from these accounts. If you're questioning or confused concerning which accounts are best suited to charitable giving, consult with a financial advisor.

To determine which accounts to use for your philanthropic giving, follow these steps:

1. **Mark up two columns on a sheet of paper.** Label the left one 'Tax advantage' and the right 'No tax advantage'.

2. **List your financial accounts and their balances in the appropriate column.** Your financial accounts include retirement accounts, savings accounts, investment (brokerage) accounts, and so on.

   - If the account offers a tax advantage for charitable gifts, list it on the left side (for instance, a current account).

   - If the account offers no tax advantage for charitable gifts, list it on the right side (for example, a company pension or retirement account in the UK).

   If you're not sure whether your account offers a tax advantage, head to the preceding section for information to help you decide.

3. **Calculate a rough total of the amount in your tax advantage accounts.** The result shows you quickly how much you have available and whether the accounts with the available funds offer any tax advantages for giving.

Think about giving from these accounts first: doing so reduces your tax burden and so increases your rate of return on the remaining assets in these accounts, allowing you to give more in the future.

For further tax information in the UK, check out the general website at www. hmrc.gov.uk and more specifically www.hmrc.gov.uk/ charities-donors. In the US, look at www.irs.gov and www.irs.gov/ Charities-&-Non-Profits/Contributors.

Giving assets that have appreciated in value from these types of accounts can make a lot of sense. Compare *giving away* shares of a stock that has appreciated 20 per cent in six months to *selling* the same stock. In the first case, you avoid the capital gains tax; in the second case, you pay capital gains taxes. Check out the preceding section for details.

Pounds and pence: Working the numbers to keep your donations flowing

In this section, we get all financially strategic and take a look at some numbers. Here are three scenarios to demonstrate how, by allotting a certain percentage of your investment income, you can make donations to your favourite charities while retaining the base amount necessary to keep the donations going, almost into perpetuity (the tax rates in these examples are only for the purposes of illustration):

- ✔ **Example 1:** You start with £10,000 and a (currently impressive) 8 per cent annual return on your investments subject to an 18 per cent tax rate. Each year you donate 5 per cent of your returns (after taxes) and 5 per cent of your principal of £10,000. Over 15 years, the £10,000 grows to about £12,000 and you donate precisely £9,359.65.

- ✔ **Example 2:** You start with £50,000, a 6 per cent annual return and an 18 per cent tax rate. You decide to donate 2 per cent of your post-tax return and 2 per cent of your principal each year. At the end of 15 years, your £50,000 has grown to more than £75,000 and you've donated over £20,000!

- ✔ **Example 3:** Consider again the £10,000 investment of Example 1, but this time you earn a 5 per cent annual return with an 18 per cent tax rate. Even if you donate just 1 per cent of your post-tax return and 1 per cent of your assets each year, you give more than £2,100 over 15 years and your £10,000 becomes nearly £16,000 over the same period.

These examples show that when you think strategically about what you give, you can avoid the traps that would-be philanthropists tend to fall into:

- ✔ Giving away too much, thereby depleting your store and undermining your ability to continue to give.

- ✔ Not giving at all for fear of depleting your gains and substantially hurting your ability to meet your financial needs – or believing that a seemingly small donation won't make much of a difference anyway.

Admittedly, financial planning around philanthropy adds another layer of complexity to your financial situation – particularly when considering large or multi-year commitments. Thankfully, however, low-cost planning tools are available that allow you to plan for the future while you're also planning to give. In the following two sections, we offer some guidance on how to determine how much of your investment income to commit to charity and how much to leave in the account, for your own financial needs or as the foundation that makes continued giving possible.

Using a spreadsheet to calculate how much to give

One simple method is to use bookkeeping software or a spreadsheet such as Excel, Gnumeric, or Calc. Copy the formula (or the 'calculation' in older, Lotus-based versions of bookkeeping software) for tax rate and re-label it 'financial giving' – this amount is how much you plan to give. If, for example, you're using Excel for this task, dozens of monthly budget templates are available through Microsoft.

Take a monthly household budget template (download one from Office Online – just choose File→New – or find one on your computer if you installed the optional extras with Office), fill in your monthly budget items and make a line item for 'Charity'. Figure out how much, in terms of financial contributions, makes sense in the context of your budget. Remember that you're likely also to contribute nonmonetary amounts (volunteering, for instance), but don't include those here. You can even make separate lines for each charity you support to build an index of where your resources are going. The end result is a budget showing how much money you commit to giving to charities on a monthly basis.

If you're giving from tax-exempt accounts or tax-advantaged accounts, include any penalties (but remove any taxes) from that calculation. Consult an accountancy firm or expert in this area with any questions you may have.

Budgeting your giving – use a spreadsheet to make it easy!

Another method of calculating how much to give is to invent a simple *coefficient* (which is an amount against which to multiply your income, for example, 0.03) that you put in your monthly budget before your weekly pay. So, if you earn £1,000 per week, you'd have £30 (with a coefficient of 0.03 or 3 per cent) to give away every week.

Advanced financial organising

If you already use a spreadsheet to keep track of your weekly or monthly expenses, you can also build ratios within the sheet that can be helpful and give you a new perspective on your giving, such as how much you give for every pound you spend eating out at restaurants. You can set this calculation up in a spreadsheet by dividing your restaurant/entertaining expenditure by your donations and then dividing that amount by 100 to yield a percentage.

This approach can help you to see how much is going where at a glance, and let you understand which pieces of your philanthropy are providing the most impact per amount spent. You can also evaluate which causes you want to give to on a recurring basis and which donations are really more closely related to a specific project or initiative. This can allow you to budget more carefully for future giving to make sure you maximise your impact.

You can even build a budget mechanism into a simple spreadsheet that shows your performance against this figure as an average from month to month, which may be helpful if you're a barrister or a consultant and your income varies substantially from month to month. An average that includes prior months' calculations may be useful to you.

Of course, you want to provide as much help and create as big a difference as possible to make life measurably better. When you make a budget for your giving, however, you can feel as though you're calculating or quantifying your generosity – and when you look at all you have, you may think that the amount you allocate for charity is paltry indeed. But the amount of money you give isn't a measure of how generous or good you are. When you draw up a budget, allocate your resources and associate a figure with your philanthropy, keep these points in mind:

- ✔ Financial donations are just one of the many ways you can reach out to help others. If you want to do more but are limited by financial constraints, donate your time or skills.

- ✔ Don't think that seemingly small donations aren't worth making. They are, even when they're one-time gifts. But when they're part of an ongoing commitment, they matter a lot (consider, if you can't give a certain amount once, giving one tenth of that amount for the next ten months).

Discovering donor-advised funds

Don't worry if you're not a whizz with spreadsheets or you don't want to push a pencil for even more hours per month. You can delegate your giving, gain a tax advantage (in many cases), and synchronise the rest of your financial life with your charitable giving with minimal effort through donor-advised funds (DAFs).

For comparison's sake, here's the traditional system of giving from investment accounts: you invest; wait while your investment grows; sell to turn your investment into cash; and make your donation. But this approach isn't very tax-efficient, because you pay taxes on the money when you make it and again (capital gains tax or, if short term in some jurisdictions including the US, tax at your ordinary income tax rate) when you sell or cash in the investment. Then you donate the money and receive a tax deduction.

Many people, however, become philanthropic while they're high earners and have a window of only ten years when their earnings are at their peak. As a result, waiting three or four years to receive a tax deduction is a substantial inconvenience. But with a DAF you receive a tax deduction as soon as you contribute, even if the money doesn't immediately go to a charity. In addition, the DAF keeps track of the basis (what you paid for something is called the basis) of the assets invested in the fund scheme, takes care of paperwork that you normally need to handle yourself, and contacts the charity to arrange the donation itself.

Here's how these funds work, courtesy of Sarah C. Libbey, President of Fidelity Charitable, the first national donor-advised programme in the USA (www.fidelitycharitable.org):

- **Give:** Make a contribution to a DAF scheme administered by a public charity and take an immediate tax deduction for that calendar year. Initial contribution minimums for some programmes are as low as £3,000 ($5,000). Though donating cash is always an option, DAFs are an especially convenient way to take advantage of the tax benefits of donating appreciated securities and/or privately held assets such as private company stock, real estate, and other personal assets to public charities.

- **Grow:** When you've made the initial contribution, advise how you want those funds to be invested. Most DAF programmes offer a choice of investment pools, enabling donors to select an investment mix that helps them meet their charitable goals.

- **Grant:** After you determine the causes, you recommend grants – on your own timetable – to specific charities, with the option of being recognised or remaining anonymous. The DAF reviews each grant to ensure that it meets IRS guidelines and that the recipient is a qualified 501(c)(3) public charity. UK DAFs operate similarly, entering into agreements only with vetted and government-approved charities. When approved, the DAF sponsor sends a cheque to the recipient charity on your behalf.

Sarah writes:

> *Donor advised funds help make people's lives easier by providing consolidated recordkeeping for each year's contributions, eliminating paperwork and simplifying tax reporting requirements. By providing a ready reserve of funds and the flexibility, ease, and convenience to support their favourite causes at any time, DAFs provide donors with many of the same advantages of private foundations – as well as many that private foundations don't offer – typically at a lower cost and without the considerable administrative burdens.*

Take a look at www.philanthropyuk.org/publications/ guide-giving/how-give/donor-advised-funds for more details.

Many people – of all levels of income and financial awareness – are able to manage their own financial affairs, including philanthropy. But we include donor-advised funds here because we think they're a smart, interesting, and low-cost way to delegate a chunk of your financial giving.

Getting Up to Speed on Legal Stuff

Legal pitfalls lie in wait for the unwary philanthropist, particularly when donating overseas, and so in this section we cover a few issues you need to know. We provide basic information about the legal and tax issues related to philanthropic giving and alert you to potential problems so that you can discuss your specific needs with your accountant or tax advisor in more detail. Taking this information on board helps to reduce your concerns and frees you up to give with more confidence.

A full discussion of the legal aspects of philanthropy would require several books. As you read this section, remember that this information isn't legal advice specific to any one person's situation and you need to consult experts you trust before making any large financial decisions.

Following the rules when claiming tax relief for charitable giving

To take advantage of tax relief on your charitable contributions, you need to follow certain rules, designed to reduce fraud and to ensure that the correct amount of relief is given to the charity and the donor:

- To qualify for tax relief, the donation must be made to an HMRC-recognised charity (with a charity reference number).

- You must fill out and submit the proper paperwork for your donations. If you complete an annual tax return, use its appropriate section; if not, contact your local tax office for details of another form to use. Find your tax office at `search2.hmrc.gov.uk/kbroker/hmrc/locator/locator.jsp`.

- You must keep the appropriate records of your donations, including the following:

  - **Gift Aid:** The amount and date of the donation and the charities involved (see the earlier 'Understanding the tax implications of charitable giving' section for more on Gift Aid).

  - **Gifts of assets (land, buildings, or shares):** Records of the donation or sale (transfer documents, paperwork showing payments, and so on).

Keep these records for at least 22 months following the year in which the donation was claimed.

Donating physical items

You can give items to charities as well as money. For example, you may donate a painting or a car or boat for a charity to auction at a fundraiser.

Although giving items to charity can be tempting, try to donate an item that the charity can use. A blanket given to a homeless shelter is more likely to be an efficient donation strategy than giving a speedboat to a hospital! The charity has to devote resources, time, and staff to finding a buyer for the item. If you have time, sell that old item yourself and donate the proceeds. This approach also avoids any controversy over what the item was worth.

Auditors from the tax authorities on both sides of the Atlantic are paying increasing attention to the value of such donated items. For example, if you donate a painting to a charity and it sells for £10,000 at a well-publicised and competitive auction, its value is probably close to £10,000. But erroneous (or even fraudulent) estimates of how much the family car is worth have brought headaches to many taxpayers. When in doubt, have a competent person appraise the item you're considering donating, and seek legal advice.

Sending donations overseas

Many people read about or visit a foreign country and want to send money or support to that place. Now, foreign giving is a complex and difficult legal area, and we don't have the space to deal adequately with it. However, we provide some general information so that you can seek out the details if foreign giving interests you.

Donating to foreign charities presents two challenges, one big and one small. The big problem is that if you live in the US, the UK, or many countries in the West, your government may have designated a charity as problematic, perhaps due to past fraud or something more ominous (such as accusations that a charity funds terrorist activity).

The UK Foreign Office and the US State Department list such charities (the 'terrorist exclusion list' in the US; the Home Office Watch List in the UK, though HMRC also keeps a watch list that sometimes varies from the Home Office's one). Other countries maintain similar lists or pursue investigations of suspicious charities (for instance, the German government's investigations and subsequent outlawing of Internationale Humanitäre Hilfsorganisation).

The small problem, which is less scary and more easily surmountable, is that an overseas charity may not have a way to give you a tax-deductible receipt in your country of tax residence. You can solve this issue through a domestically-domiciled counterpart to the foreign organisation or a fiscal sponsorship arrangement:

- **Domestically-domiciled counterpart:** A small office is usually set up in the US and files the correct paperwork and maintains its good standing with the revenue authorities, even though it's not the main office of the charity. In the UK, these offices are often in London at counterpart charities – for instance, the French charity Médecins Sans Frontières has a sister charity, Doctors Without Borders, in London that accepts donations from UK donors.

- **Fiscal sponsorship arrangement:** An authorised charity keeps the required records and issues the tax-deductible receipts on behalf of an organisation still to obtain its status. Fiscal sponsorship arrangements have been considered but not yet approved by HM Treasury.

Don't be afraid to donate to an organisation that's going through the fiscal sponsorship process, but do remember that the tax service often has a backlog of applications and the process may progress slowly. Ensure that the organisation is pursuing the status in earnest, because long delays can result from improper filings.

Using overseas bank accounts

International accounts are another issue that periodically presents itself when discussing international giving. For example, if you plan to give cash to a home charity from a foreign bank account, the best approach is to use a wire transfer.

Ask about EFT (electronic fund transfer)-to-charity policies at your bank because some waive the (sometimes substantial) fees if the destination account belongs to a charity. Currently, only a few banks do so as a matter of policy, but try asking. Ensure that the international bank account is associated with your passport number or your social security number if you plan to claim an itemised deduction (US) or tax benefit (UK).

Helping overseas charities directly

Occasionally, legal issues arise where a charity asks for a donor to pay for something directly instead of making a donation. This may be an innocent request, but should always be viewed with caution.

In one case, a charity asked an American donor to take a foreign diplomat to dinner and give him gifts in New York in the hope of greasing the wheels for the charity's operations in the diplomat's home country. Depending upon the context and other factors, however, such hospitality can run foul of the Foreign Corrupt Practices Act: Americans bribing or financially coercing foreign public officials is illegal, even if not for personal gain. The Foreign Corrupt Practices Act applies to Americans living abroad (though no equivalent law exists for UK citizens).

If you're in this situation and dealing with a recognised charity, seek legal advice. You may be better making a donation than trying to act on the charity's behalf in these situations, no matter how good your intentions.

Watching out for scams

Probably the largest legal issue in recent years, particularly with retired people, is scams, which generally fall into three categories:

- ✔ **A person or group of people posing falsely as a charity.** You can avoid falling victim to these scams by spending some time investigating the alleged charity, making sure that you write a cheque to the charity rather than an individual, and checking whether the official registered charity number (or EIN or employer identification number in the US) exists and corresponds to a charitable organisation of the same name.

- ✔ **Problematic use of money after it's donated.** Some charities misrepresent the portion of donations used for work that furthers their stated mission; sometimes the cause is an innocent mistake or the result of optimistic accounting, but occasionally it's intentional fraud. Avoid this type of scam by investigating the facts around the nature of the charity's operations and the 'market price' for them. The charity you're considering supporting isn't the only charity of its size looking for, say, a new CFO or shipping things to Kenya. See what other people pay for these things and question why your charity pays vastly more (or less) for these things. The Internet can be invaluable for such research.

- ✔ **Donor and organisation being misled by local agents, local officials, or intermediaries.** Combating this scam involves dealing only with charities who know what's happening on the ground. If a charity doesn't perform site visits to a region where it's sending help, ask why. If one doesn't maintain a staff presence in the region, ask who is present and how she's held accountable.

Tackling solicitation

An area that often draws scrutiny from the philanthropic community and regulators is overly zealous or illegal solicitation. Legal rules, including the US's 'do not call list' (part of a broader framework of consumer protection and harassment prevention legislation) and the UK's non-solicitation provisions intend to protect consumers from ongoing, aggressive solicitation.

If an organisation often runs television advertisements or sends things through the mail (direct mail campaigns generally have a success rate of less than 1 per cent), ask why they're spending money on these (often fruitless) methods of outreach. If an organisation continues to harass you after you

Lawyers doing good

Not all things legal involve worry, compliance, and taxes; legal philanthropy exists, too. The International Senior Lawyers Project (ISLP) (http://www.islp.org) recruits highly experienced lawyers and law firms to provide, completely free, urgently needed legal services to NGOs and developing country governments with scarce resources and little access to experienced legal counsel. Over the last ten years, the ISLP has sent volunteers onsite to 42 countries and delivered an estimated $70 million worth of free legal assistance. Linda D. McGill, ISLP Legal Advocate writes:

'"Experienced attorney wanted to travel to developing country and work for free to expand economic justice and human rights." This could be the job advert for a volunteer with the ISLP.

As one of ISLP's first recruits, I took a five-month sabbatical from my comfortable law practice in Portland, Maine, to volunteer with the Human Rights Law Network (HRLN) in New Delhi, India.

HRLN challenges the justice system and power structure that all too often deprive India's poorest people of basic legal, economic, and social rights. Soon I was immersed in preparing an appeal of a high-profile death penalty case that had national political significance. We drew on US and European law to argue for the exclusion of the defendant's forced confession, his right to a fair trial, and other fundamental rights that may well have been ignored in the rush to the gallows.

ISLP's theory – that experienced lawyers can effectively assist efforts in developing countries to advance economic justice and the rule of law – became a deeply satisfying reality for me. I also learned that the power of shared belief in the right to justice for all people in the world can't be underestimated. Lawyers everywhere need to work together to harness that power. ISLP provides the opportunity for action.'

make clear that you're not interested, consider using the power of social media to deduce whether it's an isolated case or common practice at this charity (searching online for the number that called you or looking up the soliciting charity on review sites is a good approach).

In the UK, concerns have arisen over the practice of chugging – 'charity mugging', which refers to charity collectors seeking donations in cash or, more likely, direct debits from people on the street. Estimates indicate that chuggers raise tens of millions of pounds for charities annually. Chugging is regulated and the chuggers must follow a variety of regulations that include handling information securely and identifying the charities on whose behalf they're working. In addition, the charities that use chuggers must fill out an application form if they want to deploy fundraisers in order to avoid having too many in any one location.

Nevertheless, critics claim that the tactics are too aggressive and some fake collectors do prey on unsuspecting donors. These concerns have reinvigorated opposition to street solicitation and new regulations are being debated.

Creating Checklists before Writing the Cheque

Making checklists is a good habit to get into as regards your philanthropic strategy, because they help ensure that you cover all the bases and don't miss anything important. But they can be difficult to make if you're not an experienced philanthropist. Therefore, we provide three checklists to use to make sure that you've thought of everything before making your donations.

Knowing where you stand financially

✔ I have a clear personal budget and understand my income, my debts, and my other obligations.

✔ I understand that philanthropy is part of my broader financial plan.

✔ I understand that researching philanthropic opportunities takes time, just as when researching investments or credit cards.

✔ I can execute the philanthropic plan I've made without sacrificing my own financial dreams.

✔ I have a good accountant and tax advisor I can contact if I have questions, run into problems, or need advice.

Knowing about the organisation and how it will use the donation

✔ I've discovered everything I can about the organisation, and I still want to support it and the work it does.

✔ I know what percentage of the money the organisation receives goes directly to its mission. I know how the organisation uses, treats, and manages its volunteers.

✔ I know where the organisation is located and I'm comfortable with the relationship between the organisation (and its staff and volunteers) and the community or place receiving the help.

✔ If this donation is more than 25 per cent of my giving for the year, I've researched this particular organisation for at least 25 per cent of my time that I've set aside for researching my giving this year.

Checking the value of your gifts

- ✔ When I volunteer my time, an hour of my time is worth —————— per hour.

- ✔ When I think of giving my expertise, it would cost some-one —————— per hour (or —————— per month) to hire someone with my skills.

- ✔ When I consider giving away money, I think of the amount I give away as a portion of my —————— [examples: income, wealth, monthly expenses, and so on]. I keep a budget for giving, which is about —————— per cent of my income or —————— per cent of my investment gains. It is —————— per cent of how much I spend on my —————— [examples: income, wealth, monthly expenses, and so on].

- ✔ When I enter into a transaction that helps the world, I spend —————— extra on my —————— [examples: car, shoes, and so on], but it's worthwhile because —————— [examples: 'it helps the environment', 'the manufacturer pays its workers fair wages', and so on).

Examining What Happens After You Give

So, you've given money to a charity: congratulations! You're a philanthropist. But your strategic concerns aren't over, and ideally you need to know the path that your donations take subsequently.

Following the money

If you use PayPal or an electronic transfer, the funds hit the organisation's bank account within one week. If you use a credit card, typically funds arrive within 48 to 72 hours. If you write a cheque, the funds clear according to the window set by the charity's account or your bank, whichever is longer.

If the charity is a small organisation, don't be surprised if someone reasonably senior contacts you about your gift. Organisations don't generally have extra staff around – and so you may receive an email from an organisation's Development Director or Chief Financial Officer and that person may have personally written the email!

On receipt of the money, the charity's 'back office' gets to work. In a large foundation, this may indeed be a back office of people in cubicles, but usually the work's handled by competent bookkeepers and volunteers, or outsourced to someone such as a partner of the Association of Charitable Foundations (`www.acf.org.uk`) in the UK or Foundation Source in the US (check out the nearby sidebar 'Working behind the scenes: Foundation Source' for details on the latter).

The charity next has to allocate the funds, which may not be that simple. Even though the organisation's budget may go, say, 80 per cent to hospitals or 75 per cent to programmes for children, that's not how each cheque at each point in time is split up. Your money is likely to be used immediately.

Some organisations allow you to 'earmark' a donation for a specific project, region, or initiative. Ones that do so often enjoy greater financial flexibility: perhaps someone else is already providing money for the organisation's overheads or it enjoys an endowment. Alternatively, it may be a way to focus donor pounds on an urgent matter, such as a natural disaster or a conflict zone. If you've earmarked your donation, check up on the specific aspect you funded and see what's going on.

If you give *discretionary funds* (those to be used as the charity decides), the money is put to work wherever it's needed in the organisation. Perhaps to pay the office's electric bill, provide a laptop for someone about to leave for Africa, or buy a plane ticket. Discretionary funds are the most useful way to give to an organisation, because it allows the organisation to decide where the money is needed most.

Giving *restricted funds,* the opposite of discretionary funds, limits how the organisation can use your donation. We encourage you to resist the temptation to restrict the use of your donations. Generally, organisations are in the best position to know where the money is needed.

Your donation may be allocated in a chunk or split among several things. When you find out which applies, circle back to your own benchmarks to see what your donation achieved and do a self-evaluation:

Working behind the scenes: Foundation Source

The American organisation Foundation Source (`www.foundationsource.com`) acts as a back office for foundations, taking care of things such as filings, financial reporting, and interactions with wealth advisors or legal staff. In the past several years, it has become a critical piece of the larger philanthropic infrastructure, managing foundations with assets ranging from $250,000 to $250 million.

Every organisation has books to keep, forms to file, and accounts to reconcile. If your charity doesn't have an on-staff or volunteer bookkeeper, your donation is likely to pass through the spreadsheets and computers of an organisation such as Foundation Source.

✔ **Ask yourself whether your donation has changed your view of the organisation or its cause.** Would you have done anything differently? Take notes to refer to later as you work to improve your future giving decisions.

✔ **Figure out what's going on at the organisation now.** Don't wait for the annual report – go to the organisation's website, get on its next Internet conference call, or watch its new video. You're a stakeholder and so feel free to find out about its future plans, the progress on current projects, and where you can help or volunteer further.

Monitoring your contributions

Some organisations have a thermometer on the website to show that other people are donating. But without this sort of indication, life can be quiet and lonely after you donate. To maintain your interest and enthusiasm, make sure that you note to which charity you gave, why, and when.

Keep a paper journal or, better, a spreadsheet. The latter allows you to link the file to your personal finance calculations and other budgeting (check out the earlier section 'Pounds and pence: Working the numbers to keep your donations flowing'). You can also compare, year-to-year, how well an organisation is performing.

Suppose that you give £50 each to three organisations this year. Next year, you still want to support these organisations, but in your view Organisation X has done much better than Organisations Y and Z. It finished a big project on time and under budget, whereas Organisation Y seems to have spent a fortune sending out a glossy magazine despite struggling to pay its staff.

The question of how to divide your £150 (or whatever you plan to give this year) among X, Y, Z, and other opportunities is something you need to consider before making further gifts.

Setting your own rules and then evaluating performance against those measurements is helpful when tracking what happened to your contributions. You can make decisions based on concrete benchmark achievements or goals, instead of on a subjective view of the organisation's progress.

For example, in March in your donor journal you write:

> *Charity Z has been saying for a year that it's making great progress on building this school, but apparently it's still not finished, and it has stopped posting progress photos on the website. I'm suspicious. If no kids are attending the school by the coming school year without a good explanation, I won't send a donation in reply to their next request.*

Keeping a record of your feelings, milestones, and dreams in this way allows you to perform a genuine reality check when things don't go as planned.

Evaluating the results

Deciding whether a charity's results are 'good enough' for you to continue giving requires you to evaluate its results.

Of course results are a difficult thing to measure for any business, but they're even harder to measure where the returns may be gradual, social, and long term. Statistics for reducing infant mortality or increasing the number of people using anti-mosquito bed nets may be calculable, but they rarely change due to the activities of only one organisation. How can you tell whether your organisation, or your donation, really made a difference?

Look at how the organisation measures itself – generally, for marketing reasons, organisations choose areas in which they perform well. Next, look at how its peers and competitors measure themselves. Probably, one of these other organisations uses different ways to measure its success. Focus on these differences and think about how the first organisation may stack up if it used the second's measuring tool instead.

Mission Measurement (www.missionmeasurement.com), one of the leaders in this area, is a firm that helps people figure out whether 'what we're doing is actually doing any good'. Mission Measurement has worked for everyone from the Gates Foundation to the Red Cross to corporations such as Cisco, PepsiCo, and Walmart. Its work represents a new layer of accountability, in essence a 'do-good audit' that allows an outside group to peek into organisations and see what impact is really happening (or not happening).

If Mission Measurement or an equivalent hasn't visited your charity:

✔ See whether you can find (and you often can, in PDF form) the organisation's last few annual reports.

✔ Look for media items that mention the organisation's efforts.

✔ Check out reports from other donors or funders (this may include foundations or even government entities) and gauge the experiences others have had when supporting the organisation.

Now stick the reports in an envelope and keep track of your philanthropic investment in this organisation just as you would any investment. Check on it periodically to see what's new. Peruse what's in the news and if it's relevant clip it out and put it in the folder. Try to get a sense of the organisation's direction, momentum, and challenges.

Philanthropy is a process of discovery; seeing what happens and being honest about the results are central to becoming a better donor. Stay interested, stay informed, and stay active.

Part IV
The Part of Tens

Enjoy an additional Part of Tens chapter online at www.dummies.com/extras/charityandphilanthropy

In this part...

- Discover the most common reasons people give, and, in the process, explore and expand your own charitable motivations.

- Learn how to share your own philanthropic story to increase your impact and inspire others to become active in philanthropy.

- Find out how, just by making small changes in your regular routine or taking that first step, you can make a difference today.

Chapter 18

Ten Compelling Reasons to Give

In This Chapter

▶ Making a positive difference in the lives of others

▶ Creating stronger bonds between communities and cultures

▶ Benefitting yourself by doing good

*P*eople decide to become philanthropists for all sorts of reasons. Some take great joy in the act of giving, whereas others are results-oriented and love to see the changes they help to create. Others still want to have a closer relationship with the people they're helping and view philanthropy as a way of building bridges and creating connections between communities.

This chapter gives you just ten of the many reasons that we've seen drive great philanthropists around the world. Whatever your personal ones, we're delighted that you're considering giving a part of what you have to the world.

Sharing is the Right Thing to Do

Being told to share what you have is probably one of the earliest commands you learn. Whether you were a child monopolising a favourite toy or grabbing the last sweet, someone undoubtedly reminded you not to hoard good things. Quite simply, sharing is the right thing to do.

In the wider world – beyond your childhood playpen or biscuit tin – resources are scarce. By sharing what you have – your time, your talent, your treasures – with other people, everyone benefits. Having the necessities of food, shelter, safety, and hope puts you in a better position to rethink, improve, and enjoy the global society you're part of.

Whether you've been blessed with a large fortune or simply good fortune, you can share what you have with others in many rewarding ways (check out Chapter 3 as a start).

Giving Makes You Feel Good

One of the most rewarding things you can do is give. But you deny yourself the full benefits if you simply write a cheque or put coins in a can.

The more involved you become in giving, the more you enjoy it. By understanding and witnessing the results of your charitable activities, you give *yourself* the gift of seeing how your giving makes a difference over time. This perspective allows you to become a more targeted and strategic philanthropist whose contributions grow more effective over time (something that this book helps you with).

Nothing feels better than doing something you feel good about and then proceeding to get even better at it all the time!

Empowering Yourself to Make Change

Changing the world is a tall order. But changing little bits of it is not only possible but also happening right now. Being part of that change is tremendously exciting.

If you want to influence the direction of the world, nudge the things around you in that direction, through your philanthropy, your volunteering or simply by listening to, helping, or supporting people already helping the world.

Help others discover the positive things happening in the world and how they can support, accelerate, and amplify the changes they believe in. The familiar proverb says 'A journey of a thousand miles begins with a single step'. Millions of people are already walking in the right direction now.

Building Friendships and Family

Giving is an activity that connects you with other people. Clearly it connects you with others who care about the same cause and with those you're helping, but if you do it with your friends and family, giving also lets you strengthen those bonds. Support your friends' causes and get your friends and family involved in the organisations you support.

Sharing your philanthropic passion with family and friends also has a practical benefit: if you want to help an organisation but you're having trouble explaining why or how, you can talk about it with friends and family and get their perspectives. Practise your 'pitch' with them. Explaining why you care about volunteering for or donating to a certain cause may help you understand your own motives better; it can even help you find ways to be a more effective giver.

Strengthening Your Community

Community goes beyond the boundaries of friends and family. It includes the neighbour you don't talk to, the barista you see each morning, the person in the next-door office, the people you encounter at local meetings and religious gatherings, and those with whom you share hobbies and interests.

You strengthen your interpersonal relationships and give back to others when your philanthropy aligns with the following:

- **Your interests:** For example, donating to arts organisations alongside fellow art appreciators
- **Your beliefs:** Such as volunteering at a homeless shelter or health clinic run by a faith-based organisation
- **Your community:** For instance, having a clean-up day with others who are enthusiastic about the local park

Taking On the Biggest Challenges

Many problems seem to have been around forever and appear difficult to tackle alone. For example, caring for the elderly, feeding the hungry, or comforting the sick seem impossibly large tasks, particularly when you consider them on a global scale.

But by working together, people can break these huge challenges into bite-sized pieces. You can choose to focus on your city or community, knowing that people in other cities or communities are combating the same issues in their areas. Such issues can't be addressed in isolation; you can learn lessons from what's happening in other places and other communities that can help all people develop the best solutions for everyone.

Building Bridges between Cultures

The world is huge and contains many different cultures, each of which can learn from and teach each other. When you engage in charitable endeavours beyond your own culture, you expand your experiences and your understanding of the world. Thousands of volunteer opportunities are available in the UK and US, some government-sponsored and some run through charitable organisations, which allow you to work, live, and give overseas.

The best way to discover another culture is to help it on its own soil. Some of these opportunities are elsewhere in the West and others take place in Asia, Africa, or South America. In addition, some offer a small salary or accommodation; others are purely voluntary. Often, air travel and other costs can be shared or provided. If you're interested in opportunities to help out beyond your own borders, head to Chapter 3 for some details.

Improving the Planet for the Next Generation

The biggest inheritance this generation leaves to the next is the planet, the most amazing, complex spaceship imaginable. Everyone needs to think carefully about how the human race maintains this shared vehicle as it commutes annually around the sun (with no train delays or overcrowded buses to worry about!).

By playing your part in being responsible stewards of these shared life-support systems, you can make the next generation's experience on the Earth more healthy and happy. Along with everyone else, your actions affect the environment and so you can choose to tailor your actions to have more positive and fewer negative impacts. Often, these changes merely require a moment of thoughtfulness and cost nothing at all. To find out more about environmental philanthropy, head to Chapter 9.

Unleashing Inspiration

People have limited time, money, and resources; but fortunately these limitations encourage creativity. By being creative in how you try to make a big difference with your limited resources, you force yourself to innovate, be inspired, and study opportunities that you can otherwise ignore.

The way you experience the world is partly a matter of how you allow yourself to be intrigued and fascinated by the world around you. So seek inspiration in all the little opportunities to help others and to realise how taking advantage in this way improves everyone's experience.

Creating Goodwill among Nations

The international implications of charity have been appreciated since Roman times. Today, people travel, talk, and work internationally more than ever. Transitioning your charitable activities to the same international mindset helps you to understand others better and build a global community that everyone can be part of.

Here are some examples:

- ✔ The relationship between America and Europe after World War II would have been very difficult without the Marshall Plan, which provided economic aid to help rebuild the devastated continent.

- ✔ Hundreds of thousands of people would have suffered more without international relief efforts after the Asian tsunami or the Haitian earthquake.

- ✔ The legacy of post-colonial aid forever links Anglophone Africa to Britain and Francophone Africa to France and Belgium.

The world is becoming more internationally connected every day. By understanding the challenges facing people around the world, we can better appreciate how to help, where our help will have the most impact, and why we are (or are not) in a position to make things better. Concurrently, by looking at how people solve problems internationally, we can look at our own communities and implement innovations from abroad. Questions like how to house the poor or how to educate the young are international questions with local solutions; learning from and helping our global neighbours is both valuable and important.

Chapter 19

Ten Ideas for Telling Your Philanthropic Story

In This Chapter

▶ Tapping into friends and family for help

▶ Hiring professionals

▶ Being creative in big and little ways

*W*hen you do something that affects you deeply, the natural response is to want to share your experience with others. One thing that most philanthropists discover is that caring about a cause isn't enough: they also want to take action. And one of the first actions you're likely to take is to share your feelings in order to educate and spur others into action as well as yourself.

A great way to do that is to inspire them with your story – your explanation of why your cause matters and why your involvement (and by implication, theirs) is needed and beneficial. In this chapter, we provide you with ten suggestions that can help you get your story out into the wider world.

Defining Your Mission

A *mission statement* is a way to describe the actions you plan to take and how you will achieve your vision for a better world. Such statements don't have to be written with fancy words – use simple language to make your values and intentions clear. Then you can look back on this statement in the future and edit it or use it to help make decisions about how to allocate your time and resources.

Think about what drives you. When you know what issue compels you to take action, you can craft a mission statement that describes your values and what actions you can take to steer the future towards the one you envision.

Here are two areas that may spark some ideas for you:

- **You seek changes in the world:** You may want everyone to have access to clean water, for example, or perhaps quality education is your priority.

- **You want the world to stay the same:** Preserving landmark buildings in the neighbourhood where you grew up, perhaps, or ensuring that future generations can see Scottish wildcats or red squirrels (two of several animals in the British Isles threatened with extinction).

Building Your Basic Storyline

No one likes listening to a mechanical or blandly clinical description of the causes you're supporting (yawn!). People want to hear your love and enthusiasm for the things you support. So lead with your passion. Here are some suggestions:

- **Write down how you became interested in the cause you support.** Was it a personal experience, a news article you read, or a volunteer opportunity?

- **Think of how you can tell the story effectively and persuasively.** What aspects of your philanthropic story are most compelling? How can you help others discover this exciting opportunity to change the world for the better?

- **Make your story entertaining and engaging.** Narratives are great ways to convey information in a compelling, entertaining way. Instead of talking about spousal abuse, for example, tell about Sally, who's living in a shelter with her children and trying to get back on her feet.

- **Keep your audience up to date on the news regarding your charity.** When an organisation you support has a success or a new project, or even a setback, think of how to integrate that information into your story. If your charity has been able to provide hundreds of mosquito nets to families in Senegal, say, share that great good news. If civil unrest has waylaid your charity's relief workers, share that, too. People tend to feel more connected to stories they're following.

Sharing Your Story through Word of Mouth

Discuss your values, charitable efforts, and philanthropic gifts with your friends. Even if you don't all share the same passions or political outlook, you can likely find common ground in discussing how to help other people. Encourage debate and discussion on which forms of charity are most effective. Tell your friends about your plans to volunteer and encourage them to come along. If you're giving to a charity, tell the friends who're likely to share your passion for that cause and encourage them to match your gift fully or partially (for more on matching gifts, see Chapter 14), or encourage them to help get the word out. Talk to your friends about their interests and join them in supporting their causes, too.

Leading by example and demonstrating reciprocity creates goodwill among your group of friends and allows you to work together on bigger and better projects in the future – doing so may even bring you closer!

Tapping into the Power of Social Media

Most people have seen friends' posts on Facebook or Twitter that alert followers to events they're planning, whether they're running a marathon for a good cause or planning to host an event for charity. But with new social media channels opening up all the time, you can use this space more creatively as a way to produce an even more compelling call-to-action from your social network. Here are some ideas:

- ✔ **Consider automating your updates:** For example, Twitter lets you build a set of tweets in advance. You can use this capability so that your friends' feeds are updated continuously as your favourite charity approaches its fundraising goals.

- ✔ **Find ways to take advantage of how content appears on Facebook:** For example, perhaps changing your profile picture to support a cause is more effective than a simple status update. Maybe building an album of fun photos from an event can lengthen the event's impact, instead of simply noting that it occurred or that you had fun.

- ✔ **Think of how you can use photos in creative ways:** For example, perhaps you can create animated images in www.tumblr.com. Animated images often create more interest than simple still images. Also, pinning clusters of related graphics on pinterest.com can increase the number of hits to each graphic as opposed to posting one photo at a time.

✔ **Combine capabilities to create even more buzz:** Using Google+, for example, you can link calendar events and important documents to provide key information and then send posts out before and after. You can also use other features, such as Google Maps, to provide directions to the event. Microsoft's Bing tools allow you to attach items such as travel or hotel deals, which are excellent for conferences or other destination events (like Google, these tools also allow you to attach maps, directions, and other essential details).

Writing Articles for Traditional Publishing Channels

Consider using your local newspaper or news channel. Most editors are eager to hear about new events and new stories; with shrinking staffing in every area of media, from writing to photography, newspapers (including online versions of traditional newspapers) increasingly depend upon user-generated content.

This tactic is particularly powerful if you support or work with a cause that has eye-catching events, large gatherings of people, or cute animals (just three examples of the many things that make for great news stories and photography).

If you're helping to plan a big event, create a good press release and work with people in your community to make sure that it gets into the right hands. After the event, announce what a success the event was and release photographs from the big day. Consider having a professional photographer on-site to make sure that you have four or five great pictures of the event, what happened, and how exciting it was. These photos are valuable not only for media stories, but also in future brochures, on your cause's website, or in recruiting speakers or volunteers for the next big event!

Writing a Book or Making a Film

An increasing number of documentary films are so-called activist documentaries. But you don't need to be an activist to make one. Simply think of a cause you want to highlight and consider how you can tell that cause's story on screen. Examples from recent years include *The Cove* (a 2009 film about dolphin hunting); *Food, Inc.* (a 2008 documentary about the agricultural industry), and *Fuel* (a 2009 documentary on energy and the oil industry). The costs of making a film can be high, but crowdfunding (which we discuss in Chapter 11) and other strategies allow more people than ever to tell stories effectively to a large audience using this medium.

If creating a film isn't for you, why not employ the arts in different ways to tell your story? You can write a book about philanthropy and share everything you know about giving, or get your friends to tell their stories (we just did!) or write a poem, a blog, or even an opera.

The point is that you can use the arts to tell your story, your cause's story, or a story that convinces everyone that your philanthropy is an amazing, worthwhile, incredible thing!

Engaging in Guerrilla Marketing

Guerrilla marketing includes using stickers, free CDs, cool graphic T-shirts, brightly-coloured bumper stickers, magnets, buttons, and temporary tattoos. Putting this sort of guerrilla marketing to use is harder than it looks but probably less expensive than you think.

Anything from a poster to a flashmob dance routine on YouTube can qualify as guerrilla marketing – the only boundaries are those of your imagination. The Internet explosion of Harlem Shake dance videos has been used to publicise everything from soft drinks to nightclubs to, yes, charitable-giving opportunities. Before that, trends from mash-up remixes to Gangnam Style dancing were used to raise awareness for various events, fundraisers, and causes.

Even a moment – or a split second – of a celebrity's endorsement can make a huge difference in your cause's visibility. This celeb doesn't have to be a film star (though if you're best buds with Brad Pitt, do let us know); it can be a well-known local personality in your community.

The trick is knowing where to start, and so take a good look around you. What stickers catch your eye in your city? What album covers do you remember, what graphics on Tumblr are memorable, what graffiti sticks in your mind? Thinking about what's memorable to you enables you to consider what other people will remember.

Hiring a Professional Publicist

If you have the financial means, you may want to consider hiring a professional publicist. Good PR people can generate much more money than they charge in fees, particularly if the publicist is interested in your cause.

A professional can help you achieve goals in four different areas:

✔ **Figuring out how to communicate your message most effectively:** Perhaps a matter of thinking of a good slogan, spokesperson, or photo/ poster/sticker/button to tell people what you're doing.

✔ **Coming up with better materials than you're able to generate in-house:** Can be valuable in mailing materials to donors, creating a nicer website, or building your image in the community.

✔ **Providing media experience to show you how to generate 'buzz' or make your organisation 'cool':** This area can be difficult for you to do without professional advice.

✔ **Helping your organisation with events planning and other tasks:** These aspects are difficult for volunteers to handle.

Although hiring someone with this expertise costs a bit, it can be less than having ill-equipped volunteers planning an event that's poorly attended or loses money. Remember that rates are always negotiable!

Throwing a Fundraiser

If you dislike the thought of fundraising, don't worry, you're not alone: many philanthropists dread it. Most people are taught as children never to talk about money and, certainly, never to request it. But asking for money is an essential part of the system that drives charities, and being able to do so in fun, innovative, and involving ways is a great skill to acquire.

Throwing a successful fundraiser starts with having a fun idea. No one wants to pay money to attend a boring party in dreadful company and so think through the following aspects:

✔ What's the purpose or theme of the event going to be?

✔ What's a realistic donation associated with an event like this one?

✔ Who's likely to attend and who do you want to attend?

✔ What's necessary for the event to be a success?

✔ How can you ensure that the event's energy isn't lost, but is harvested and kept going through the momentum of personal relationships, social media, and other points of contact?

Analysing a fundraiser through this lens increases the likelihood of you throwing a more enjoyable, successful event.

Ask yourself this question to judge your event: would you pay this amount to attend the event? Keep things light, fun, and approachable to create an event you'd love to attend!

Vetting Your Story with Family and Friends

Your friends and family are your closest allies. Enlist and encourage them to help you tell your philanthropic story, because such honest feedback can be extremely valuable. Test your story out on them and ask for their honest advice along the following lines:

✔ How can you do a better job explaining why you're so interested in this particular cause?

✔ How can you be a better storyteller, a better communicator, or a better listener?

✔ How can you show your listeners that your cause addresses their concerns?

Being honest about your strengths and weaknesses as an advocate for your cause is one of the hardest, but most valuable, parts of the philanthropic process. Getting honest, loving, and sometimes humorous feedback from people with whom you have strong connections can make your story even stronger.

Chapter 20

Ten Great Ways to Start Giving... Today

In This Chapter

▶ Getting motivated

▶ Creating your own opportunities

▶ Helping out existing programmes

Millions of people and billions of dollars are being put to work right now towards solving the world's problems – and now is an exciting time for you to join this push to a better future. In everything you do, you can make an improvement. This chapter is a real get-up-and-go, practical, rallying call that outlines ten ways you can take action today.

March forward and create the kinds of changes, shifts, and evolutions you want to see happen. Give, listen, volunteer, create, and – most importantly of all – show that you care about other people, and the future, through your actions.

Making the Commitment to Give

Saying that you're going to give is easy, but far, far better is to say it in a way that ensures that it happens:

✔ Sign a giving pledge or commit to give a monthly amount.

✔ Talk with your family, friends, or significant other, and reinforce each other's generous intentions.

✔ Remind yourself with your smartphone, a sticky note on your computer monitor, or a message stuck to the next tube of toothpaste that says 'today's the day to give or to consider how to be generous'.

✔ Work with your exercise group, faith-based group, or friends from university, supporting one another in creating, and enforcing, commitments to give.

Donating Online

Thousands of charities are doing amazing work in your community and around the world. Go online and find a recognised and established one to support today. The Charity Navigator (www.charitynavigator.org) and the Charity Commission (www.charitycommission.gov.uk/find-charities) websites are excellent, informative places to start.

Think about how much you'll give and where that amount can make the biggest difference. Often, short-term fundraising helps charities push over the next barrier, such as paying back a loan, meeting an important goal, or securing a lease on that 'just right' space. Look online for opportunities to help out with crucial financial donations and try to be the invaluable donor who's 'in the right place at the right time'.

Supporting a Local Shelter or Food Bank

Local organisations helping the less fortunate in your community can be the most rewarding places to focus your charity. These people may have suffered bad luck, made bad choices, or experienced bad events in the past, but they're trying to piece their lives together. The people who benefit from your help are on your street, in your postcode, and in your physical space. Their children play in the same parks as your children, they see the same streetscapes, and share the same neighbours.

Finding a way to help others nearby can be immensely satisfying and hugely valuable, and this type of philanthropy makes your community stronger.

Volunteering to Help Feed the Poor

As an old proverb states, 'how we spend our days is how we spend our lives'. Procrastinating is easy. We've all at one time or another put something off by saying we'll do it next week.

Instead, commit to do something this weekend that's truly meaningful – to others and to you. Nearly every area has a kitchen, food, or child lunch service that serves the poor. These activities are highly rewarding and require no special skills. Why not donate your Saturday this week?

Signing up for a Charity Walk, Run, or Cycle

Many fights are long, difficult, and expensive, such as the searches for cures to chronic diseases. Though often enormously expensive, such medical research has a value beyond money. A vaccine can help millions of people avoid the perils of disease through effective inoculation. Cures can reverse the devastating effects of chronic disease, dramatically improving the quality of life of patients and their loved ones, colleagues, and community members. Treatments can allow people to return to their lives more quickly and with fewer disabilities, and the more effective the treatment, the higher the patient's post-treatment quality of life.

Fortunately, you can help in loads of ways. One of the most popular is signing up for a charity walk, run, or cycle. In some cases, these events raise money by taking entrance fees from the participants; in others, the participants get donations from other people – a certain amount for each mile run, for instance. Regardless of how they're structured, such charity events raise money and awareness.

Reducing, Reusing, and Recycling Right Now

Changing behaviours takes effort, but it can be done. One strategy that's often successful is making small changes. For example, in the area of the environment, a small change that benefits everyone is carrying a reusable water bottle rather than buying bottled water, or packing groceries into reusable fabric shopping bags.

Small changes lead to other small changes and, before you know it, you're making a substantial difference. Here are some more ideas of things you can do today:

- ✔ Consider whether you really need to throw away all the things you currently put in a landfill. Can you perhaps compost your biological kitchen waste, use paper bags rather than plastic ones for most things, or use resealable airtight glass jars rather than plastic sandwich bags?

- ✔ Save money and the environment by switching to low-consumption lighting in your home and more fuel-efficient vehicles. You may say you don't have time to bicycle to work, but what if it offers exercise you'd otherwise not get during the day? If you have the space, growing vegetables and fruit in your garden is enjoyable and environmentally friendly.

✔ Consider whether you can shop more carefully, purchasing small quantities of perishable items to avoid waste, and buying non-perishable items in bulk to minimise packaging and transportation costs.

Think through what aspects of your lifestyle are realistic to alter and make a change today!

Supporting a Friend's Social Venture

If you have a friend with a startup, invest in it. And by that we don't mean writing a cheque (for the millions of pounds you no doubt have squirreled away!). You can help your friend's new venture become an awesome new business in dozens of ways:

✔ Donate your skills, advice, or even your emotional support. Starting a new venture is difficult and every bit of support helps, even if it's an occasional phone call to see how things are going.

✔ Introduce your friend to someone who may be able to help.

✔ Host a get-together to help your entrepreneurial friend network with people in your industry.

✔ Raise interest in your friend's prototype or new website through social media.

Lots of tiny contributions create huge success!

Joining Your Employer's Volunteer Programme

Almost all major companies (and many small, local businesses as well) have volunteer programmes. These schemes let you work on charitable projects, ranging from building houses to disaster relief to creating a new website for a charity that can't afford web-design services.

Some volunteer programmes use your professional skills (donating talent) while others only ask you to show up (giving time). Best of all, they provide a way to do good while working with people you already know.

Ask whether your company's matching programme applies to volunteer hours – many companies donate cash equal to the value of the time you donate by volunteering! Check out Chapter 14 for more details.

Initiating Your Own Social Venture

Watching from the sidelines is no fun. If you have a business idea that can make money while doing good, the world needs entrepreneurs like you!

The Social Innovation Review (Stanford University; www.ssireview.org) is a great place to discover what's generating buzz in the growing field of social ventures globally. For social responsibility in the UK, the Skoll Centre for Social Entreprenurship at Oxford's Said Business school is constantly publishing reports and hosting events related to social business. Finally, the Social Entrepreneurship Initiative (University of Chicago; research.chicagobooth.edu/sei) is a great source for more in-depth research on these types of businesses. No matter where you are in the world, there are resources for social entrepreneurship. For a detailed discussion on social ventures, flip to Chapter 10.

Stopping Making Excuses and Taking Action

Anyone can say 'I'll help tomorrow' or 'maybe next time', but that's just procrastination. Eventually you have to put your abilities and tools to work solving the world's problems. You can start small (in fact, we encourage it), but start *now!*

Appendix

Where We're Donating Our Resources and Why

One of the messages we hope you take away from this book is that there are myriad ways to give, and our goal was to provide numerous examples that would both inspire you and help you get started. Here, we each identify the charitable organisations that will receive our proceeds from this book and outline the ways in which we apply our treasure, time, talent, and transactions to the causes that are near and dear to our hearts.

Karl T. Muth

Having lived in a low-income village in the north of Uganda for over a year, and having travelled to more than fifty countries, Karl's philanthropy is divided between the developed and developing worlds.

His share of proceeds from this book will be donated to Médecins Sans Frontières (Doctors Without Borders) to help support that organisation's efforts in Uganda and South Sudan and, specifically, initiatives that improve the physical and mental health of internally-displaced people in both countries.

✔ **Time:** Karl gives over fifty hours each academic year to offer advice and introductions to students at top universities who want to make a difference. This creates unique opportunities for dozens of students each year. Currently, he is supervising Northwestern University's first economics student to undertake an independent study project in North Korea. He also sits on a variety of boards, including the advisory board of the Social Enterprise Initiative at the University of Chicago's Booth School of Business, the leading research-driven initiative of its type.

✔ **Talent:** Over the past three years, Karl has given over 2,000 consulting hours to Grameen Foundation's work in East Africa, where Grameen seeks to help the poorest of the poor. Karl, his friend Jenn Helgeson, and many others donated their professional talents and skills to ensure the largest-scale study of its type communicated an accurate picture of what day-to-day life is like for the very poor in northern Uganda. He also offers his consultancy services to other organisations and to the governments of developing countries, particularly those in Anglophone East Africa and the Caribbean.

✔ **Treasure:** For the last ten years, he has donated more than 100% of his salaried income to charitable causes in every year. In each case, he encourages the organisations he supports to use his donation strategically by soliciting 'matching' donations of equal size from other donors or by using the money to implement changes that make the organisation more efficient or effective. In addition to this substantial donation, which has been twenty to fifty times his income in some years, he has donated thousands of frequent flier miles and other types of treasure to ensure the work of organisations he supports is possible.

✔ **Transactions:** When travelling in the developing world, Karl tries to weigh – and educate others about – the benefits of doing business with local people and building meaningful relationships. He believes that even on a week-long holiday or a three-night business trip it is possible to have an influence on the local economy. He encourages other travellers to be mindful of these factors and to ask questions of local people. Going beyond 'tourism' and recognising that we have an impact as consumers wherever we step, spend, or speak is an important transformation into respect, consciousness, and presence.

John W. Kluge

Growing up the son of two successful, self-made immigrant parents, John's philanthropy stems from a deep belief in human potential, provided that basic human rights are guaranteed and barriers to opportunity are eliminated. To that end, his efforts are focused on the essential needs of sanitation, hygiene, and clean water, and to continuing his family's commitment to education.

His share of proceeds from this book will be donated to joint programmes of Toilet Hackers and Pencils of Promise, providing sanitation, hygiene, and clean water facilities in Pencils of Promise's schools and helping to protect education opportunities for young girls and boys.

✔ **Time:** John's interest in social change was first sparked while volunteering as a legislative liaison for anti-poverty organisation Rock and Wrap It Up!, spearheading the lobbying efforts of the 2008 Federal Food Donation Act, which continues to improve the food security of millions of Americans today. John now serves on a variety of boards, including UNICEF's Next Generation, Fonderie 47, Pencils of Promise, and the Advisory Board of the Stan Lee Foundation.

✔ **Talent:** For John, service is a full-time commitment. As the Co-Founder and Chief Disruption Officer of Toilet Hackers, John spends every day campaigning on behalf of the 2.5 billion people without access to basic sanitation and hygiene. He is using his expertise in policy, technology, and marketing to build a movement for sanitation for all. His first Toilet Hackers project, the First Worldwide Sanitation Hackathon, led by the World Bank's ICT and Water and Sanitation Programs, convened over 1,250 technologies, activists, and sector specialists in ten countries to build over 180 mobile or ICT prototypes to accelerate or improve access to sanitation and hygiene in developing communities.

✔ **Treasure:** Before the Gates Foundation's Giving Pledge was created, John's father committed 99 percent of his wealth to philanthropy in education and global health, specifically toward research in cancer, sepsis, and diabetes. As all of John's family's resources have been committed to search for cures, John is now marshalling resources to *deploy* cures, collaborating with other philanthropists, foundations, corporations, and even governments to grow the available treasure for the sanitation sector.

✔ **Transactions:** John believes wholeheartedly in the idea of doing good and doing well. When and where possible he supports social entrepreneurs developing products or providing services that have double or triple bottom lines, often, as in the case of Fonderie 47, becoming an investor as well as a customer. John's bespoke signet ring from Fonderie enabled the destruction of 75 assault rifles in Africa. His hope is that Fonderie's products will contribute to an Africa free from the fear of assault rifles, which are responsible for countless deaths every year and which enable and exacerbate violence against women and children, cause misallocation of resources, and prevent economic growth.

Michael Lindenmayer

Michael is deeply passionate about sanitation, education, and caregivers. He was an early adopter of Room to Read, where he designed and implemented the volunteer platform which grew from 12 volunteers to over 10,000 across 56 cities worldwide. He was also an early adopter of the Grameen Bank and co-founder of Eirene, a social venture that focuses on addressing issues that impact at least 1 billion people, and co-founder of Toilet Hackers. An associate fellow at the University of Chicago Booth Business School's New Paths to Purpose Project, Michael is Forbes contributor, focusing on purpose and philanthropy, and a frequent speaker and academic lecturer on the topic of philanthropy and purpose. He has given TED talks in both Japan and Costa Rica.

His share of the proceeds from this book will go to Toilet Hackers (`www.toilethackers.org`), which is committed to building a network of 10 million toilets and educating girls on menstrual and basic hygiene so that they can stay in school.

- ✔ **Time:** Michael dedicates 100 per cent of his time to endeavours in the areas of sanitation, caregiving, and design-led innovation. He uses his time to advocate awareness, advance field projects, and advance breakthrough innovations.

- ✔ **Talent:** Michael is well versed in building volunteer-driven organisations. He has coached, advised, and helped implement volunteer programmes at young and growing social ventures as well as at large companies seeking to build corporate social responsibility into their growth strategies. He also works with family offices that are seeking to improve the results of their philanthropic efforts.

- ✔ **Treasure:** For the past 10 years, Michael has invested his resources into building social ventures. He has seeded ventures, created challenge grants, and nurtured the scaling of high-impact endeavours.

- ✔ **Transactions:** Michael is a relentless advocate for the design of smarter, better, and more sustainable products and services. He seeks to improve the choices in the marketplace by engaging in thought leadership dialogues with the heads of innovation at firms. He advocates for people to make choices that generate a net positive impact. He sees constantly improved daily choices as the most powerful way to make the world a better place.

Index

Notes

Notes

Notes

Notes

About the Author

Karl T. Muth is a consultant, economist, finance expert, legal scholar and philanthropist who divides his time between the United Kingdom, the United States, and the Republic of Uganda.

Karl studied law in the Netherlands (Ant.) and the United States and holds graduate degrees in law (J.D.) and business (M.B.A.), the latter with a concentration in economics from the University of Chicago. He is currently a postgraduate researcher in his final year of the M.Phil./Ph.D. at the London School of Economics and Political Science. He is a Lecturer in Economics and Public Policy at Northwestern University and has served as an Executive-in-Residence at the University of Chicago's Booth School of Business. Karl's commentary and scholarship in economics, finance and law have appeared in numerous academic journals and in mainstream magazines, newspapers, television and documentary film.

Karl serves as an advisor to his family's charitable trust and works actively with other wealthy families and individuals to help them amplify, focus and understand the impact of their charitable efforts. He has traveled to more than fifty countries and has participated in philanthropic initiatives on five continents. For more than a year, he lived and worked primarily in the post-conflict zone near the Uganda – South Sudan border, studying the day-to-day lives of some of Africa's poorest communities.

For the last ten years, he has donated more than 100% of his salaried income to charitable causes in every year.

Michael T.S. Lindenmayer is an entrepreneur, designer, consultant and philanthropist who divides his time between the United States, the United Kingdom and Latin America.

Michael studied International Relations in the United States and Germany and holds a B.A. from Kalamazoo College. He is currently an associate fellow at the University of Chicago's Booth Business School. He is teamed up with the New Paths to Purpose Project, which studies the role of purpose and choice architecture.

Michael is the co-founder of Eirene a do good do well venture. Michael was an early adopter of Room to Read and the Grameen Bank. He is the co-founder of Toilet Hackers and is the Chairman of the Caregiver Relief Fund.

Michael serves as an advisor to companies, family offices and individuals to help them strengthen, scale and optimise their charitable impact. As an entrepreneur he focuses on design-led innovations and ventures that solve problems that impact at least 1 billion people.

He is a regular contributor to *Forbes* and is a frequent speaker on innovation, philanthropy and entrepreneurship.

John Kluge is the Co-Founder and Chief Disruption Officer of Toilet Hackers (www.toilethackers.org), a U.S. based non-governmental organisation accelerating access of improved sanitation and hygiene to the 2.5 billion people without a toilet.

Before launching Toilet Hackers, John founded the Digital Citizenship and Safety program as part of the Worldwide Cybersecurity Initiative at the EastWest Institute (www.ewi.info), an international, non-partisan, non-profit policy organisation, who's mission is to devise innovative solutions to pressing global security concerns.

Prior to joining EWI, John was the Projects Coordinator and Legislative Liaison for Rock and Wrap It Up!, an anti-poverty think tank, where he piloted a federal food recovery program at the Library of Congress, and spearheaded the drafting and lobbying efforts of the Federal Food Donation Act of 2008, improving the food security of 36 million underserved people in the United States.

John holds a B.A. from Columbia University.

He serves on a number of non-profit and for profit boards, including UNICEF's NextGeneration, Pencils of Promise and Fonderie 47.

He is the author of the book *John Kluge: Stories,* published by Columbia University Press (2005). John lives in New York City and is a contributor to *Forbes.*

Author's Acknowledgements

Thanks to all of our friends, family, loved ones and to our contributors, who trusted us with their thoughts, words and passions. This book was a collaborative effort and we thank our collaborators.

Special thanks to Melanie Schnoll Begun and Kevin Lynch at Morgan Stanley Private Wealth Management for helping bring us together during these past few years as friends and coauthors. Our gratitude to our friends at our publisher, Wiley and our editorial team including Tracy Barr, Andy Finch, Jo Jones, Daniel Mersey, Erica Peters and Claire Ruston.

Thanks to all the people who have hosted us in our travels, helped us understand the world's challenges and taught us what it means to be generous; each of these people contributed something to this book.

Finally, thank you to you, the reader, for your interest in giving and giving back. Together, we can make our world kinder, better and more complete.

Publisher's Acknowledgments

We're proud of this book; please send us your comments at `http://dummies.custhelp.com`. For other comments, please contact our Customer Care Department within the U.S. at 877-762-2974, outside the U.S. at (001) 317-572-3993, or fax 317-572-4002.

Some of the people who helped bring this book to market include the following:

Acquisitions, Editorial, and Vertical Websites

Project Editor: Jo Jones

Commissioning Editor: Claire Ruston

Assistant Editor: Ben Kemble

Development Editors: Tracy Barr and Andy Finch

Proofreader: Kerry Laundon

Production Manager: Daniel Mersey

Publisher: Miles Kendall

Cover Photo: ©iStockphoto.com/Simon Oxley

Take Dummies with you everywhere you go!

Whether you're excited about e-books, want more from the web, must have your mobile apps, or swept up in social media, Dummies makes everything easier .

FOR DUMMIES

A Wiley Brand

BUSINESS

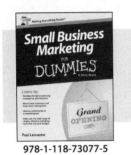  

978-1-118-73077-5   978-1-118-44349-1   978-1-119-97527-4

MUSIC

978-1-119-94276-4   978-0-470-97799-6   978-0-470-49644-2

DIGITAL PHOTOGRAPHY

978-1-118-09203-3   978-0-470-76878-5   978-1-118-00472-2

Algebra I For Dummies
978-0-470-55964-2

Anatomy & Physiology For Dummies, 2nd Edition
978-0-470-92326-9

Asperger's Syndrome For Dummies
978-0-470-66087-4

Basic Maths For Dummies
978-1-119-97452-9

Body Language For Dummies, 2nd Edition
978-1-119-95351-7

Bookkeeping For Dummies, 3rd Edition
978-1-118-34689-1

British Sign Language For Dummies
978-0-470-69477-0

Cricket for Dummies, 2nd Edition
978-1-118-48032-8

Currency Trading For Dummies, 2nd Edition
978-1-118-01851-4

Cycling For Dummies
978-1-118-36435-2

Diabetes For Dummies, 3rd Edition
978-0-470-97711-8

eBay For Dummies, 3rd Edition
978-1-119-94122-4

Electronics For Dummies All-in-One For Dummies
978-1-118-58973-1

English Grammar For Dummies
978-0-470-05752-0

French For Dummies, 2nd Edition
978-1-118-00464-7

Guitar For Dummies, 3rd Edition
978-1-118-11554-1

IBS For Dummies
978-0-470-51737-6

Keeping Chickens For Dummies
978-1-119-99417-6

Knitting For Dummies, 3rd Edition
978-1-118-66151-2

FOR DUMMIES®

A Wiley Brand

SELF-HELP

Cognitive Behavioural Therapy For Dummies
978-0-470-66541-1

Creative Visualization For Dummies
978-1-119-99264-6

Mindfulness For Dummies
978-0-470-66086-7

LANGUAGES

Spanish For Dummies
978-0-470-68815-1

Polish For Dummies
978-1-119-97959-3

British Sign Language For Dummies
978-0-470-69477-0

HISTORY

The Tudors For Dummies
978-0-470-68792-5

Medieval History For Dummies
978-0-470-74783-4

British History For Dummies
978-0-470-97819-1

Laptops For Dummies 5th Edition
978-1-118-11533-6

Management For Dummies, 2nd Edition
978-0-470-97769-9

Nutrition For Dummies, 2nd Edition
978-0-470-97276-2

Office 2013 For Dummies
978-1-118-49715-9

Organic Gardening For Dummies
978-1-119-97706-3

Origami Kit For Dummies
978-0-470-75857-1

Overcoming Depression For Dummies
978-0-470-69430-5

Physics I For Dummies
978-0-470-90324-7

Project Management For Dummies
978-0-470-71119-4

Psychology Statistics For Dummies
978-1-119-95287-9

Renting Out Your Property For Dummies, 3rd Edition
978-1-119-97640-0

Rugby Union For Dummies, 3rd Edition
978-1-119-99092-5

Stargazing For Dummies
978-1-118-41156-8

Teaching English as a Foreign Language For Dummies
978-0-470-74576-2

Time Management For Dummies
978-0-470-77765-7

Training Your Brain For Dummies
978-0-470-97449-0

Voice and Speaking Skills For Dummies
978-1-119-94512-3

Wedding Planning For Dummies
978-1-118-69951-5

WordPress For Dummies, 5th Edition
978-1-118-38318-6

Think you can't learn it in a day? Think again!

The **In a Day** e-book series from **For Dummies** gives you quick and easy access to learn a new skill, brush up on a hobby, or enhance your personal or professional life — all in a day. Easy!